How to Measure Anything

Anything

Finding the Value of "Intangibles" in Business

Third Edition

DOUGLAS W. HUBBARD

WILEY

Published by John Wiley & Sons, Inc., Hoboken, New Jersey.
First edition published by John Wiley & Sons, Inc., in 2007.
Second edition published by John Wiley & Sons, Inc., in 2010.
Published simultaneously in Canada.

For general information on our other products and services or for technical support,
please contact our Customer Care Department within the United States at (800)
762-2974, outside the United States at (317) 572-3993, or fax (317) 572-4002.

Wiley publishes in a variety of print and electronic formats and by print-on-demand.
Some material included with standard print versions of this book may not be
included in e-books or in print-on-demand. If this book refers to media such as a
CD or DVD that is not included in the version you purchased, you may download
this material at http://booksupport.wiley.com. For more information about Wiley
products, visit www.wiley.com.

Library of Congress Cataloging-in-Publication Data
Hubbard, Douglas W., 1962–
  How to measure anything : finding the value of intangibles in business /
Douglas W. Hubbard.—Third edition.
     pages cm
  Includes bibliographical references and index.
  ISBN 978-1-118-53927-9 (cloth); ISBN 978-1-118-83644-6 (ebk);
ISBN 978-1-118-83649-1 (ebk)
  1. Intangible property—Valuation.   I. Title.
  HF5681.I55H83 2014
  657'.7—dc23
                                                        2013044540
Printed in the United States of America

10 9 8 7 6 5 4 3

I dedicate this book to the people who are my inspirations for so many things: to my wife, Janet, and to our children, Evan, Madeleine, and Steven, who show every potential for being Renaissance people.

I also would like to dedicate this book to the military men and women of the United States, so many of whom I know personally. I've been out of the Army National Guard for many years, but I hope my efforts at improving battlefield logistics for the U.S. Marines by using better measurements have improved their effectiveness and safety.

Contents

Preface to the Third Edition

I can't speak for all authors, but I feel that a book—especially one based largely on ongoing research—is never really finished. This is precisely what editions are for. In the time since the publication of the second edition of this book, I continue to come across fascinating published research about the power and oddities of human decision making. And as my small firm continues to apply the methods in this book to real-world problems, I have even more examples I can use to illustrate the concepts. Feedback from readers and my experience explaining these concepts to many audiences have also helped me refine the message.

Of course, if the demand for the book wasn't still strong six years after the first edition was published, Wiley and I wouldn't be quite as incentivized to publish another edition. We also found this book, written explicitly for business managers, was catching on in universities. Professors from all over the world were contacting me to say they were using this book in a course they were teaching. In some cases it was the primary text—even though *How to Measure Anything* (*HTMA*) was never written as a textbook. Now that we see this growing area of interest, Wiley and I decided we should also create an accompanying workbook and instructor materials with this edition. Instructor materials are available at www.wiley.com.

In the time since I wrote the first edition of *HTMA*, I've written a second edition (2010) and two other titles—*The Failure of Risk Management: Why It's Broken and How to Fix It* and *Pulse: The New Science of Harnessing Internet Buzz to Track Threats and Opportunities*. I wrote these books to expand on ideas I mention in earlier editions of *How to Measure Anything* and I also combine some of the key points I make in these books into this new edition.

For example, I started writing *The Failure of Risk Management* because I felt that the topic of risk, on which I could spend only one chapter and a few other references in this book, merited much more space. I argued that a lot of the most popular methods used in risk assessments and risk management don't stand up to the bright light of scientific scrutiny. And I wasn't just talking about the financial industry. I started writing the book well before the financial crisis started. I wanted to make it just as relevant to another Hurricane Katrina, tsunami, or 9/11 as to a financial crisis. My third book, *Pulse*, deals with what I believe to be one of the most powerful new measurement instruments of the twenty-first century. It describes how the Internet and, in particular, social media can be used as a vast data source for measuring all sorts of macroscopic trends. I've also written several more articles, and the combined research from them, my other books, and comments from readers on the book's website to create new material to add to this edition.

This edition also adds more philosophy about different approaches to probabilities, including what are known as the "Bayesian" versus "frequentist" interpretations of probability. These issues may not always seem relevant to a practical "how-to" business book, but I believe it is important as a foundation for better understanding of measurement methods in general. For readers not interested in these issues, I've relegated some of the discussion to a series of "Purely Philosophical Interludes" found between some chapters, which the reader is free to study as their interests lead them. For readers who choose to delve into the Purely Philosophical Interludes, they will discover that I argue strongly for what is known as the subjective Bayesian approach to probability. While not as explicit until this edition, the philosophical position I argue for was always underlying everything I've written about measurement. Some readers who have dug in their heels on the other side of the issue may take exception to some of my characterizations, but I believe I make the case that, for the purposes of decision analysis, Bayesian methods are the most appropriate. And I still discuss non-Bayesian methods both because they are useful by themselves and because they are so widely used that lacking some literacy in these methods would limit the reader's understanding of the larger issue of measurement.

In total, each of these new topics adds a significant amount of content to this edition. Having said that, the basic message of *HTMA* is still the same as it has been in the earlier two editions. I wrote this book to correct a costly myth that permeates many organizations today: that certain things can't be measured. This widely held belief is a significant drain on the economy, public welfare, the environment, and even national security. "Intangibles" such as the value of quality, employee morale, or even the economic impact of cleaner water are frequently part of some critical business or government policy decision. Often an important decision requires better knowledge of the alleged intangible, but when an executive believes something to be immeasurable, attempts to measure it will not even be considered.

As a result, decisions are less informed than they could be. The chance of error increases. Resources are misallocated, good ideas are rejected, and bad ideas are accepted. Money is wasted. In some cases, life and health are put in jeopardy. The belief that some things—even very important things—might be impossible to measure is sand in the gears of the entire economy and the welfare of the population.

All important decision makers could benefit from learning that anything they really need to know is measurable. However, in a democracy and a free-enterprise economy, voters and consumers count among these "important decision makers." Chances are that your decisions in some part of your life or your professional responsibilities would be improved by better measurement. And it's virtually certain that your life has already been affected—negatively—by the lack of measurement in someone else's decisions in business or government.

I've made a career out of measuring the sorts of things many thought were immeasurable. I first started to notice the need for better measurement in 1988, shortly after I started working for Coopers & Lybrand as a brand-new MBA in the management consulting practice. I was surprised at how often clients dismissed a critical quantity—something that would affect a major new investment or policy decision—as completely beyond measurement. Statistics and quantitative methods courses were still fresh in my mind. In some cases, when someone called something "immeasurable," I would remember a specific example where it was actually measured. I began to suspect any claim of immeasurability as possibly premature, and I would do research to confirm or refute the claim. Time after time, I kept finding that the allegedly immeasurable thing was already measured by an academic or perhaps professionals in another industry.

At the same time, I was noticing that books about quantitative methods didn't focus on making the case that everything is measurable. They also did not focus on making the material accessible to the people who really needed it. They start with the assumption that the reader already believes something to be measurable, and it is just a matter of executing the appropriate algorithm. And these books tended to assume that the reader's objective was a level of rigor that would suffice for publication in a scientific journal—not merely a decrease in uncertainty about some critical decision with a method a non-statistician could understand.

In 1995, after years of these observations, I decided that a market existed for better measurements for managers. I pulled together methods from several fields to create a solution. The wide variety of measurement-related projects I had since 1995 allowed me to fine-tune this method. Not only was every alleged immeasurable turning out not to be so, the most intractable "intangibles" were often being measured by surprisingly simple methods. It was time to challenge the persistent belief that important quantities were beyond measurement.

In the course of writing this book, I felt as if I were exposing a big secret and that once the secret was out, perhaps a lot of apparently intractable problems would be solved. I even imagined it would be a small "scientific revolution" of sorts for managers—a distant cousin of the methods of "scientific management" introduced a century ago by Frederick Taylor. This material should be even more relevant than Taylor's methods turned out to be for twenty-first-century managers. Whereas scientific management originally focused on optimizing labor processes, we now need to optimize measurements for management decisions. Formal methods for measuring those things management usually ignores have often barely reached the level of alchemy. We need to move from alchemy to the equivalent of chemistry and physics.

The publisher and I considered several titles. All the titles considered started with "How to Measure Anything" but weren't always followed by "Finding the Value of 'Intangibles' in Business." I could have used the title of a seminar I give called "How to Measure Anything, But Only What You Need To." Since the methods in this book include computing the economic value of measurement (so that we know where to spend our measurement efforts), it seemed particularly appropriate. We also considered "How to Measure Anything: Valuing Intangibles in Business, Government, and Technology" since there are so many technology and government examples in this book alongside the general business examples. But the title chosen, *How to Measure Anything: Finding the Value of "Intangibles" in Business*, seemed to grab the right audience and convey the point of the book without necessarily excluding much of what the book is about.

As Chapter 1 explains further, the book is organized into four parts. The chapters and sections should be read in order because each part tends to rely on instructions from the earlier parts. Part One makes the case that everything is measurable and offers some examples that should inspire readers to attempt measurements even when it seems impossible. It contains the basic philosophy of the entire book, so, if you don't read anything else, read this section. In particular, the specific definition of measurement discussed in this section is critical to correctly understand the rest of the book.

In Chapter 1, I suggest a challenge for readers, and I will reinforce that challenge by mentioning it here. Write down one or more measurement challenges you have in home life or work, then read this book with the specific objective of finding a way to measure them. If those measurements influence a decision of any significance, then the cost of the book and the time to study it will be paid back many-fold.

ABOUT THE COMPANION WEBSITE

How to Measure Anything has an accompanying website at www
.howtomeasureanything.com. This site includes practical examples
worked out in detailed spreadsheets. We refer to these spreadsheets as
"power tools" for managers who need practical solutions to measurement problems which sometimes require a bit more math. Of course,
understanding the principles behind these spreadsheets is still important
so that they aren't misapplied, but the reader doesn't need to worry
about memorizing equations. The spreadsheets are already worked out
so that the manager can simply input data and get an answer.

The website also includes additional "calibration" tests used for training the reader how to subjectively assign probabilities. There are some
tests already in the appendix of the book but the online tests are there
for those who need more practice or those who simply prefer to work
with electronic files.

For instructors, there is also a set of instructor materials at www
.wiley.com. These include additional test bank questions to support the
accompanying workbook and selected presentation slides.

Acknowledgments

So many contributed to the content of this book through their suggestions, reviews, and as sources of information about interesting measurement solutions. In no particular order, I would like to thank these people:

Freeman Dyson	Pat Plunkett	Robyn Dawes
Peter Tippett	Art Koines	Jay Edward Russo
Barry Nussbaum	Terry Kunneman	Reed Augliere
Skip Bailey	Luis Torres	Linda Rosa
James Randi	Mark Day	Mike McShea
Chuck McKay	Ray Epich	Robin Hanson
Ray Gilbert	Dominic Schilt	Mary Lunz
Henry Schaffer	Jeff Bryan	Andrew Oswald
Leo Champion	Peter Schay	George Eberstadt
Tom Bakewell	Betty Koleson	David Grether
Bill Beaver	Arkalgud Ramaprasad	David Todd Wilson
Julianna Hale	Harry Epstein	Emile Servan-Schreiber
James Hammitt	Rick Melberth	Bruce Law
Rob Donat	Sam Savage	Bob Clemen
Michael Brown	Gunther Eysenbach	Michael Hodgson
Sebastian Gheorghiu	Johan Braet	Moshe Kravitz
Jim Flyzik	Jack Stenner	Michael Gordon-Smith
Eric Hills	Tom Verdier	Greg Maciag
Barrett Thompson	Richard Seiersen	Keith Shepherd
Eike Luedeling	Doug Samuelson	Chris Maddy
		Jolene Manning

Special thanks to Dominic Schilt at RiverPoint Group LLC, who saw the opportunities with this approach back in 1995 and has given so much support since then. And thanks to all of my blog readers who have contributed ideas for every edition of this book.

I would also like to thank my staff at Hubbard Decision Research, who pitched in when it really counted.

About the Author

Doug Hubbard is the president and founder of Hubbard Decision Research and the inventor of the powerful Applied Information Economics (AIE) method. His first book, *How to Measure Anything: Finding the Value of Intangibles in Business* (John Wiley & Sons, 2007, 2nd ed., 2010, 3rd ed., 2014), has been one of the most successful business statistics books ever written. He also wrote *The Failure of Risk Management: Why It's Broken and How to Fix It* (John Wiley & Sons, 2009), and *Pulse: The New Science of Harnessing Internet Buzz to Track Threats and Opportunities* (John Wiley & Sons, 2011). Over 75,000 copies of his books have been sold in five different languages.

Doug Hubbard's career has focused on the application of AIE to solve current business issues facing today's corporations. Mr. Hubbard has completed over 80 risk/return analyses of large critical projects, investments, and other management decisions in the past 19 years. AIE is the practical application of several fields of quantitative analysis including Bayesian analysis, Monte Carlo simulations, and many others. Mr. Hubbard's consulting experience totals more than 25 years and spans many industries including insurance, banking, utilities, federal and state government, entertainment media, military logistics, pharmaceuticals, cybersecurity, and manufacturing.

In addition to his books, Mr. Hubbard has been published in *CIO Magazine, Information Week, DBMS Magazine, Architecture Boston, OR/MS Today*, and *Analytics Magazine*. His AIE methodology has received critical praise from The Gartner Group, The Giga Information Group, and Forrester Research. He is a popular speaker at IT metrics and economics conferences all over the world. Prior to specializing in Applied Information Economics, his experience includes data and process modeling at all levels as well as strategic planning and technical design of systems.

## PART I

The Measurement Solution Exists

CHAPTER 1

The Challenge of Intangibles

When you can measure what you are speaking about, and express it in numbers, you know something about it; but when you cannot express it in numbers, your knowledge is of a meager and unsatisfactory kind; it may be the beginning of knowledge, but you have scarcely in your thoughts advanced to the state of science.
                              —Lord Kelvin (1824–1907), British physicist
                              and member of the House of Lords

Anything can be measured. If something can be observed in any way at all, it lends itself to some type of measurement method. No matter how "fuzzy" the measurement is, it's still a measurement if it tells you more than you knew before. And those very things most likely to be seen as immeasurable are, virtually always, solved by relatively simple measurement methods. As the title of this book indicates, we will discuss how to find the value of those things often called "intangibles" in business. The reader will also find that the same methods apply outside of business. In fact, my analysts and I have had the opportunity to apply quantitative measurements to problems as diverse as military logistics, government policy, and interventions in Africa for reducing poverty and hunger.

Like many hard problems in business or life in general, seemingly impossible measurements start with asking the right questions. Then, even once questions are framed the right way, managers and analysts may need a practical way to use tools to solve problems that might be perceived as complex. So, in this first chapter, I will propose a way to frame the measurement question and describe a strategy for solving measurement problems with some powerful tools. The end of this chapter will be an outline of the rest of the book—building further on these initial concepts. But first, let's discuss a few examples of these so-called intangibles.

THE ALLEGED INTANGIBLES

There are two common understandings of the word "intangible." It is routinely applied to things that are literally not tangible (i.e., not touchable, physical objects) yet are widely considered to be measurable. Things like time, budget, patent ownership, and so on are good examples of things that you cannot literally touch though they are observable in other ways. In fact, there is a well-established industry around measuring so-called intangibles such as copyright and trademark valuation. But the word "intangible" has also come to mean utterly immeasurable in any way at all, directly or indirectly. It is in this context that I argue that intangibles do not exist—or, at the very least, could have no bearing on practical decisions.

If you are an experienced manager, you've heard of the latter type of "intangibles" in your own organization—things that presumably defy measurement of any type. The presumption of immeasurability is, in fact, so strong that no attempt is even made to make any observation that might tell you something about the alleged immeasurable that you might be surprised to learn. Here are a few examples:

- The "flexibility" to create new products
- The value of information
- The risk of bankruptcy
- Management effectiveness
- The forecasted revenues of a new product
- The public health impact of a new government environmental policy
- The productivity of research
- The chance of a given political party winning the White House
- The risk of failure of an information technology (IT) project
- Quality of customer interactions
- Public image
- The risk of famine in developing countries

Each of these examples can very well be relevant to some major decision an organization must make. The intangible could even be the single most important determinant of success or failure of an expensive new initiative in either business or government. Yet, in many organizations, because intangibles like these were assumed to be immeasurable, the decision was not nearly as informed as it could have been. For many decision makers, it is simply a habit to default to labeling something as intangible when the measurement method isn't immediately apparent. This habit can sometimes be seen in the "steering committees" of many organizations. These committees may review proposed investments and decide which to accept or reject. The proposed investments could be related to IT, new product research and development, major real estate development, or advertising campaigns. In some cases I've observed, the committees were categorically rejecting any investment where the benefits were "soft." Important factors with names like "improved word-of-mouth advertising," "reduced strategic risk," or "premium brand positioning" were being ignored in the evaluation process because they were considered immeasurable.

It's not as if the proposed initiative was being rejected simply because the person proposing it hadn't measured the benefit (which would be a valid objection to a proposal); rather, it was believed that the benefit couldn't possibly *be* measured. Consequently, some of the most important strategic proposals were being overlooked in favor of minor cost-saving ideas simply because everyone knew how to measure some things and didn't know how to measure others. In addition, many major investments were approved with no plans for measuring their effectiveness after they were implemented. There would be no way to know whether they ever worked at all.

In an equally irrational way, an immeasurable would be treated as a key strategic principle or "core value" of the organization. In some cases decision makers effectively treat this alleged intangible as a "must have" so that the question of the degree to which the intangible matters is never considered in a rational, quantitative way. If "improving customer relationships" is considered a core value, and one could make the case that a proposed investment supported it, then the investment was justified—no matter the *degree* to which customer relationships improved at a given cost.

In some cases, a decision maker might concede that something could be measured in principle, but for various reasons is not feasible. This also renders the thing, for all practical purposes, as another "intangible" in their eyes. For example, perhaps there is a belief that "management productivity" is measurable but that sufficient data is lacking or that getting the data is not economically feasible. This belief—not usually based on any specific calculation—is as big an obstacle to measurement as any other.

The fact of the matter is that all of the previously listed intangibles are not only measurable but have already been measured by someone (sometimes my own team of analysts), using methods that are probably less complicated and more economically feasible than you might think.

YES, I MEAN *ANYTHING*

The reader should try this exercise: Before going on to the next chapter, write down those things you believe are immeasurable or, at least, you are not sure how to measure. After reading this book, my goal is that you will be able to identify methods for measuring each and every one of them. Don't hold back. We will be talking about measuring such seemingly immeasurable things as the number of fish in the ocean, the value of a happy marriage, and even the value of a human life. Whether you want to measure phenomena related to business, government, education, art, or anything else, the methods herein apply.

With a title like *How to Measure Anything*, anything less than an enormous multivolume text would be sure to leave out something. My objective does not explicitly include every area of physical science or economics, especially where measurements are already well developed. Those disciplines have measurement methods for a variety of interesting problems, and the professionals in those disciplines are already much less inclined to apply the label "intangible" to something they are curious about. The focus here is on measurements that are relevant—even critical—to major organizational decisions, and yet don't seem to lend themselves to an obvious and practical measurement solution.

So, regardless of your area of interest, if I do not mention your specific measurement problem by name, don't conclude that methods relevant to that issue aren't being covered. The approach I will talk about applies to *any* uncertainty that has some relevance to your firm, your community, or even your personal life. This extrapolation is not difficult. For example, when you studied arithmetic in elementary school, you may not have covered the solution to 347 times 79 in particular, but you knew that the same procedures applied to any combination of numbers and operations.

I mention this because I periodically receive emails from someone looking for a specific measurement problem mentioned by name in earlier editions of this book. They may write, "Aha, you didn't mention X, and X is uniquely immeasurable." The actual examples I've been given by earlier readers included the quality of education and the competency of medical staff. Yet, just as the same procedure in arithmetic applies to multiplying any two numbers, the methods we will discuss are fundamental to any measurement problem regardless of whether it is mentioned by name.

So, if your problem happens to be something that isn't specifically analyzed in this book—such as measuring the value of better product labeling laws, the quality of a movie script, or the effectiveness of motivational seminars—don't be dismayed. Just read the entire book and apply the steps described. Your immeasurable will turn out to be entirely measurable.

No matter what field you specialize in and no matter what the measurement problem may be, we start with the idea that if you care about this alleged intangible at all, it must be because it has observable consequences, and usually you care about it because you think knowing more about it would inform some decision. Everything else is a matter of clearly defining what you observe, why you care about it, and some (often surprisingly trivial) math.

THE PROPOSAL: IT'S ABOUT DECISIONS

Why do we care about measurements at all? There are just three reasons. The first reason—and the focus of this book—is that we should care about a measurement because it informs key decisions. Second, a measurement might also be taken because it has its own market value (e.g., results of a consumer survey) and could be sold to other parties for a profit. Third, perhaps a measurement is simply meant to entertain or satisfy a curiosity (e.g., academic research about the evolution of clay pottery). But the methods we discuss in this decision-focused approach to measurement should be useful on those occasions, too. If a measurement is not informing your decisions, it could still be informing the decisions of others who are willing to pay for the information. If you are an academic curious about what really happened to the woolly mammoth, then, again, I believe this book will have some bearing on how you define the problem and the methods you might use.

Upon reading the first edition of this book, a business school professor remarked that he thought I had written a book about the somewhat esoteric field called "decision analysis" and disguised it under a title about measurement so that people from business and government would read it. I think he hit the nail on the head. Measurement is about supporting decisions, and there are even "micro-decisions" to be made within measurements themselves. Consider the following points.

1. Decision makers usually have imperfect information (i.e., uncertainty) about the best choice for a decision.
2. These decisions should be modeled quantitatively because (as we will see) quantitative models have a favorable track record compared to unaided expert judgment.
3. Measurements inform uncertain decisions.
4. For any decision or set of decisions, there is a large combination of things to measure and ways to measure them—but perfect certainty is rarely a realistic option.

In other words, management needs a method to analyze options for reducing uncertainty about decisions. Now, it should be obvious that important decisions are usually made under some level of uncertainty. Still, all management consultants, performance metrics experts, or even statisticians approach measurements with the explicit purpose of supporting defined decisions.

Even when a measurement is framed in terms of some decision, that decision might not be modeled in a way that makes good use of measurements. Although subjective judgment informed by real data may be better than intuition alone, choices made entirely intuitively dilute the value of measurement. Instead, measurements can be fed directly into quantitative models so that optimal strategies are computed rather than guessed. Just think of a cost-benefit analysis in a spreadsheet. A manager may calculate benefits based on some estimates and check to see if they exceed the cost. If some input to one of the benefit calculations is measured, there is a place for that information to go and the net value of a choice can be immediately updated. You don't try to run a spreadsheet in your head.

The benefits of modeling decisions quantitatively may not be obvious and may even be controversial to some. I have known managers who simply presume the superiority of their intuition over any quantitative model (this claim, of course, is never itself based on systematically measured outcomes of their decisions). Some have even blamed the 2008 global financial crisis, not on inadequate regulation or shortcomings of specific mathematical models, but on the use of mathematical models *in general* in business decisions. The overconfidence some bankers, hedge fund managers, and consumers had in their unaided intuition was likely a significant factor as well.

The fact is that the superiority of even simple quantitative models for decision making has been established for many areas normally thought to be the preserve of expert intuition, a point this book will spend some time supporting with citations of several published studies. I'm not promoting the disposal of expert intuition for such purposes—on the contrary, it is a key element of some of the methods described in this book. In some ways expert intuition is irreplaceable but it has its limits and decision makers at all levels must know when they are better off just "doing the math."

When quantitatively modeled decisions are the focus of measurement, then we can address the last item in the list. We have many options for reducing uncertainty and some are economically preferable. It is unusual for most analysis in business or government to handle the economic questions of measurement explicitly, even when the decision is big and risky, and even in cultures that are proponents of quantitative analysis otherwise. Computing and using the economic value of measurements to guide the measurement process is, at a minimum, where a lot of business measurement methods fall short.

However, thinking about measurement as another type of choice among multiple strategies for reducing uncertainty is very powerful. If the decision to be analyzed is whether to invest in some new product development, then many intermediate micro-decisions about what to measure (e.g., emergence of competition, market size, project risks, etc.) can make a significant difference in the decision about whether to commit to the new product. Fortunately, in principle, the basis for assessing the value of information for decisions is simple. If the outcome of a decision in question is highly uncertain and has significant consequences, then measurements that reduce uncertainty about it have a high value.

Unless someone is planning on selling the information or using it for their own entertainment, they shouldn't care about measuring something if it doesn't inform a significant bet of some kind. So don't confuse the proposition that *anything can be measured* with *everything should be measured*. This book supports the first proposition while the second proposition directly contradicts the economics of measurements made to support decisions. Likewise, if measurements were free, obvious, and instantaneous, we would have no dilemma about what, how, or even whether to measure. As simple as this seems, the specific calculations tend to be surprising to those who have tended to rely on intuition for deciding whether and what to measure.

So what does a decision-oriented, information-value-driven measurement process look like? This framework happens to be the basis of the method I call Applied Information Economics (AIE). I summarize this approach in the following steps.

Applied Information Economics: A Universal Approach to Measurement
1. Define the decision.
2. Determine what you know now.
3. Compute the value of additional information. (If none, go to step 5.)
4. Measure where information value is high. (Return to steps 2 and 3 until further measurement is not needed.)
5. Make a decision and act on it. (Return to step 1 and repeat as each action creates new decisions.)

Each of these steps will be explained in more detail in chapters to come. But, in short: *measure what matters, make better decisions.* My hope is that as we raise the curtain on each of these steps in the upcoming chapters, the reader may have a series of small revelations about measurement.

A "POWER TOOLS" APPROACH TO MEASUREMENT

I think it is fair to say that most people have the impression that statistics or scientific methods are not accessible tools for practical use in real decisions. Managers may have been exposed to basic concepts behind scientific measurement in, say, a chemistry lab in high school, but that may have just left the impression that measurements are fairly exact and apply only to obvious and directly observable quantities like temperature and mass. They've probably had some exposure to statistics in college, but that experience seems to confuse as many people as it helps. After that, perhaps they've dealt with measurement within the exact world of accounting or other areas where there are huge databases of exact numbers to query. What they seem to take away from these experiences is that to use the methods from statistics one needs a lot of data, that the precise equations don't deal with messy real-world decisions where we don't have all of the data, or that one needs a PhD in statistics to use any statistics at all.

We need to change these misconceptions. Regardless of your background in statistics or scientific measurement methods, the goal of this book is to help you conduct measurements *just like a bona fide real-world scientist usually would*. Some might be surprised to learn that most scientists—after college—are not actually required to commit to memory hundreds of complex theorems and master deep, abstract mathematical concepts in order to perform their research. Many of my clients over the years have been PhD scientists in many fields and none of them have relied on their memory to apply the equations they regularly use— honest. Instead, they simply learn to identify the right methods to use and then they usually depend on software tools to convert the data they enter into the results they need.

Yes, real-world scientists effectively "copy/paste" the results of their statistical analyses of data even when producing research to be published in the most elite journals in the life and physical sciences. So, just like a scientist, we will use a "power tools" approach to measurements. Like many of the power tools you use already (I'm including your car and computer along with your power drill) these will make you more productive and allow you to do what would otherwise be difficult or impossible.

Power tools like ready-made spreadsheets, tables, charts, and procedures will allow you to use useful statistical methods without knowing how to derive them all from fundamental axioms of probability theory or even without memorizing equations. To be clear, I'm not saying you can just start entering data without knowing what is going on. It is critical that you understand some basic principles about how these methods work so that you don't misuse them. However, memorizing the equations of statistics (much less deriving their mathematical proofs) will not be required any more than you are required to build your own computer or car to use them.

So, without compromising substance, we will attempt to make some of the more seemingly esoteric statistics around measurement as simple as they can be. Whenever possible, math will be relegated to Excel spreadsheets or even simpler charts, tables, and procedures. Some simple equations will be shown but, even then, I will usually show them in the form of Excel functions that you can type directly into a spreadsheet. My hope is that some of the methods are so much simpler than what is taught in the typical introductory statistics courses that we might be able to overcome many phobias about the use of quantitative measurement methods. Readers do not need any advanced training in any mathematical methods at all. They just need some aptitude for clearly defining problems.

Some of the power tools referred to in this book are in the form of spreadsheets available for download on this book's website at www.howtomeasureanything.com. This free online library includes many of the more detailed calculations shown in this book. There are also examples, learning aids, and a discussion board for questions about the book or measurement challenges in general. And, since technologies and measurement topics evolve faster than publishing cycles of books, the site provides a way for me to discuss new issues as they arise.

A GUIDE TO THE REST OF THE BOOK

As mentioned, the chapters are not organized by type of measurement whereby, for example, you could see the entire process for measuring improved efficiency or quality in one chapter. To measure any single thing, you need to understand the sequence of steps in a process which is described sequentially in various chapters. For this reason, I do not recommend skipping around from chapter to chapter. But I think a quick review of the entire book will help the reader see when they should expect certain topics to be covered. I've grouped the 14 chapters of this book into four major parts as follows.

Synopsis of the Four Parts of This Book

Part I: The Measurement Solution Exists. The three chapters of the first section (including this chapter) address broadly the claims of immeasurability. In the next chapter we explore some interesting examples of measurements by focusing on three interesting individuals and the approaches they took to solve interesting problems (Chapter 2). These examples come from both ancient and recent history and were chosen primarily for what they teach us about measurement in general. Building on this, we then directly address common objections to measurement (Chapter 3). This is an attempt to preempt many of the objections managers or analysts have when considering measurement methods. I never see this treatment in standard college textbooks but it is important to directly confront the misconceptions that keep powerful methods from being attempted in the first place.

Part II: Before You Measure. Chapters 4 through 7 discuss important "set up" questions that are prerequisites to good measurement and that coincide with steps 1 through 3 in the previously described "universal" approach to measurement. These steps include defining the decision problem well (Chapter 4). Then we estimate the current level of uncertainty about a problem. This is where we learn how to provide "calibrated probability assessments" to represent our uncertainties quantitatively (Chapter 5). Next, we put those initial estimates of uncertainty together in a model of decision risk (Chapter 6) and compute the value of additional information (Chapter 7). Before we discuss how to measure something, these sequential steps are critical to help us determine what to measure and how much of an effort a measurement is worth.

Part III: Measurement Methods. Once we have determined what to measure, we explain some basic methods about how to conduct the required measurements in Chapters 8 through 10. This coincides with part of what is needed for step 4 in the universal approach. We talk about the general issue of how to decompose a measurement further, consider prior research done by others, and select and outline measurement instruments (Chapter 8). Then we discuss some basic traditional statistical sampling methods and how to *think* about sampling in a way that reduces misconceptions about it (Chapter 9). The last chapter of the section describes another powerful approach to sampling based on what are called "Bayesian methods," contrasts it with other methods, and applies it to some interesting and common measurement problems (Chapter 10).

Part IV: Beyond the Basics. The final section adds some additional tools and brings it all together with case examples. First, we build on the sampling methods by describing measurement instruments when the object of measurement is human attitudes and preferences (Chapter 11). Then we discuss methods in which refining human judgment can itself be a powerful type of a measurement instrument (Chapter 12). Next, we will explore some recent and developing trends in technology that will provide management with entirely new sources of data, such as using social media and advances in personal health and activity monitoring as measurement devices (Chapter 13). These three chapters also round out the remainder of step 4 and the issues of step 5 in the universal approach. Finally, we explain some case examples from beginning to end of the entire process and help the reader get started on some other common measurement problems (Chapter 14).

Again, each chapter builds on earlier chapters, especially once we get to Part 2 of the book. The reader might decide to skim later chapters, say, after Chapter 9, or to read them in different orders, but skipping earlier chapters would cause some problems. This applies even to the next two chapters (2 and 3) because, even though they may wax somewhat more philosophical, they are important foundations for the rest of the material.

The details might sometimes get complicated, but it is much less complicated than many other initiatives organizations routinely commit to. I know because I've helped many organizations apply these methods to the *really* complicated problems; allocating venture capital, reducing poverty and hunger, prioritizing technology projects, measuring training effectiveness, improving homeland security, and more. In fact, humans possess a basic instinct to measure, yet this instinct is suppressed in an environment that emphasizes committees and consensus over making basic observations. It simply won't *occur* to many managers that an "intangible" can be measured with simple, cleverly designed observations.

Again, measurements that are useful are often much simpler than people first suspect. I make this point in the next chapter by showing how three clever individuals measured things that were previously thought to be difficult or impossible to measure. Viewing the world as these individuals do—through "calibrated" eyes that see things in a quantitative light—has been a historical force propelling both science and economic productivity. If you are prepared to rethink some assumptions and can put in the effort to work through this material, you will see through calibrated eyes as well.

CHAPTER **2**

An Intuitive Measurement Habit: Eratosthenes, Enrico, and Emily

Success is a function of persistence and doggedness and the willingness to work hard for twenty-two minutes to make sense of something that most people would give up on after thirty seconds.
— Malcolm Gladwell, *Outliers: The Story of Success*

Setting out to become a master of measuring anything seems pretty ambitious, and a journey like that needs some motivational examples. What we need are some "measurement mentors"—individuals who saw measurement solutions intuitively and often solved difficult problems with surprisingly simple methods. Fortunately, we have many people—at the same time inspired and inspirational—to show us what such a skill would look like. It's revealing, however, to find out that so many of the best examples seem to be from outside of business. In fact, this book will borrow heavily from outside of business to reveal measurement methods that can be applied to business.

Here are just a few people who, while they weren't working on measurement within business, can teach business people quite a lot about what an intuitive feel for quantitative investigation should look like.

- In ancient Greece, a man estimated the circumference of Earth by looking at the lengths of shadows in different cities at noon and by applying some simple geometry.
- A Nobel Prize–winning physicist taught his students how to estimate values initially unknown to them like the number of piano tuners in Chicago.
- A nine-year-old girl set up an experiment that debunked the growing medical practice of "therapeutic touch" and, two years later, became the youngest person ever to be published in the *Journal of the American Medical Association* (*JAMA*).

None of these people ever met each other personally (none lived at the same time), but each showed an ability to size up a measurement problem and identify quick and simple observations that have revealing results. It is important to contrast their approach with what you might typically see in a business setting. The characters in these examples are or were real people named Eratosthenes, Enrico, and Emily.

HOW AN ANCIENT GREEK MEASURED THE SIZE OF EARTH

Our first mentor of measurement did something that was probably thought by many in his day to be impossible. An ancient Greek named Eratosthenes (ca. 276–194 B.C.) made the first recorded measurement of the circumference of Earth. If he sounds familiar, it might be because he is mentioned in many high school trigonometry and geometry textbooks.

Eratosthenes didn't use accurate survey equipment and he certainly didn't have lasers and satellites. He didn't even embark on a risky and potentially lifelong attempt at circumnavigating the Earth. Instead, while in the Library of Alexandria, he read that a certain deep well in Syene (a city in southern Egypt) would have its bottom entirely lit by the noon sun one day a year. This meant the sun must be directly overhead at that point in time. He also observed that at the same time, vertical objects in Alexandria (almost directly north of Syene) cast a shadow. This meant Alexandria received sunlight at a slightly different angle at the same time. Eratosthenes recognized that he could use this information to assess the curvature of Earth.

He observed that the shadows in Alexandria at noon at that time of year made an angle that was equal to one-fiftieth of an arc of a full circle—what we would call an angle of 7.2 degrees. Using geometry, he could then prove that this meant that the circumference of Earth must be 50 times the distance between Alexandria and Syene. Modern attempts to replicate Eratosthenes's calculations vary in terms of the exact size of the angles, conversion rates between ancient and modern units of measurement, and the precise distance between the ancient cities, but typical estimates put his answer within 3% of the actual value.[1] Eratosthenes's calculation was a huge improvement on previous knowledge, and his error was much less than the error modern scientists had just a few decades ago for the size and age of the universe. Even 1,700 years later, Columbus was apparently unaware of or ignored Eratosthenes's result; his estimate was fully 25% short. (This is one of the reasons Columbus thought he might be in India, not another large, intervening landmass where I reside.) In fact, a more accurate measurement than

Eratosthenes's would not be available for another 300 years after Columbus. By then, two Frenchmen, armed with the finest survey equipment available in late-eighteenth-century France, numerous staff, and a significant grant, finally were able to do better than Eratosthenes.[2]

Here is the lesson for business: Eratosthenes made what might seem an impossible measurement by making a clever calculation on some simple observations. When I ask participants in my measurement and risk analysis seminars how they would make this estimate without modern tools, they usually identify one of the "hard ways" to do it (e.g., circumnavigation). But Eratosthenes, in fact, *may not have even left the vicinity of the library* to make this calculation. One set of observations that would have answered this question would have been very difficult to make, so his measurement was based on other, simpler observations. He wrung more information out of the few facts he could confirm instead of assuming the hard way was the only way.

ESTIMATING: BE LIKE FERMI

Another person from outside business who might inspire measurements within business is Enrico Fermi (1901–1954), a physicist who won the Nobel Prize in Physics in 1938. He had a well-developed knack for intuitive, even casual-sounding measurements.

One renowned example of his measurement skills was demonstrated at the first detonation of the atom bomb, the Trinity Test site, on July 16, 1945, where he was one of the atomic scientists observing the blast from base camp. While other scientists were making final adjustments to instruments used to measure the yield of the blast, Fermi was making confetti out of a page of notebook paper. As the wind from the initial blast wave began to blow through the camp, he slowly dribbled the confetti into the air, observing how far back it was scattered by the blast (taking the farthest scattered pieces as being the peak of the pressure wave). Simply put, Fermi knew that how far the confetti scattered in the time it would flutter down from a known height (his outstretched arm) gave him a rough approximation of wind speed which, together with knowing the distance from the point of detonation, provided an approximation of the energy of the blast.

Fermi concluded that the yield must be greater than 10 kilotons. This would have been news, since other initial observers of the blast did not know that lower limit. Could the observed blast be less than 5 kilotons? Less than 2? These answers were not obvious at first. (As it was the first atomic blast on the planet, nobody had much of an eye for these things.) After much analysis of the instrument readings, the final yield estimate was determined to be 18.6 kilotons. Like Eratosthenes, Fermi was aware of a rule relating one simple observation—the scattering of confetti in the wind—to a quantity he wanted to measure. The point of this story is not to teach you enough physics to estimate like Fermi (or enough geometry to be like Eratosthenes, either), but that, rather, you should start thinking about measurements as a multistep chain of thought. Inferences can be made from highly indirect observations.

The value of quick estimates was something Fermi was known for throughout his career. He was famous for teaching his students skills to approximate fanciful-sounding quantities that, at first glance, they might presume they knew nothing about. The best-known example of such a "Fermi question" was Fermi asking his students to estimate the number of piano tuners in Chicago. His students—science and engineering majors—would begin by saying that they could not possibly know anything about such a quantity. Of course, some solutions would be to simply do a count of every piano tuner perhaps by looking up advertisements, checking with a licensing agency of some sort, and so on. But Fermi was trying to teach his students how to solve problems where the ability to confirm the results would not be so easy. He wanted them to figure out that they knew *something* about the quantity in question.

Fermi would start by asking them to estimate other things about pianos and piano tuners that, while still uncertain, might seem easier to estimate. These included the current population of Chicago (a little over 3 million in the 1930s to 1950s), the average number of people per household (two or three), the share of households with regularly tuned pianos (not more than 1 in 10 but not less than 1 in 30), the required frequency of tuning (perhaps once a year, on average), how many pianos a tuner could tune in a day (four or five, including travel time), and how many days a year the tuner works (say, 250 or so). The result would be computed:

Tuners in Chicago = Population/people per household
  × percentage of households with tuned pianos
  × tunings per year per piano/
    (tunings per tuner per day × workdays per year)

Depending on which specific values you chose, you would probably get answers in the range of 30 to 150, with something around 50 being fairly common. When this number was compared to the actual number (which Fermi would already have acquired from the phone directory or a guild list), it was always closer to the true value than the students would have guessed. This may seem like a very wide range, but consider the improvement this was from the "How could we possibly even guess?" attitude his students often started with.

This approach to solving a Fermi question is known as a Fermi decomposition or Fermi solution. This method helped to estimate the uncertain quantity but also gave the estimator a basis for seeing where uncertainty about the quantity came from. Was the big uncertainty about the share of households that had tuned pianos, how often a piano needed to be tuned, how many pianos a tuner can tune in a day, or something else? The biggest source of uncertainty would point toward a measurement that would reduce the uncertainty the most.

Technically, a Fermi decomposition is not quite a measurement. It is not based on new observations. (As we will see later, this is central to the meaning of the word "measurement.") It is really more of an assessment of what you already know about a problem in such a way that it can get you in the ballpark. The lesson for business is to avoid the quagmire that uncertainty is impenetrable and beyond analysis. Instead of being overwhelmed by the apparent uncertainty in such a problem, start to ask what things about it you *do* know. As we will see later, assessing what you currently know about a quantity is a very important step for measurement of those things that do not seem as if you can measure them at all.

A Fermi Decomposition for a New Business

Chuck McKay, with the firm Wizard of Ads, encourages companies to use Fermi questions to estimate the market size for a product in a given area. An insurance agent once asked Chuck to evaluate an opportunity to open a new office in Wichita Falls, Texas, for an insurance carrier that currently had no local presence there. Is there room for another carrier in this market? To test the feasibility of this business proposition, McKay answered a few Fermi questions with some Internet searches. Like Fermi, McKay started with the big population questions and proceeded from there.

According to City-Data.com in 2006, there were 62,172 cars in Wichita Falls. According to the Insurance Information Institute, the average automobile insurance annual premium in the state of Texas was $837.40. McKay assumed that almost all cars have insurance, since it is mandatory, so the gross insurance revenue in town was $52,062,833 each year. The agent knew the average commission rate was 12%, so the total commission pool was $6,247,540 per year. According to Switchboard.com, there were 38 insurance agencies in town, a number that is very close to what was reported in Yellowbook. com. When the commission pool is divided by those 38 agencies, the average agency commissions are $164,409 per year.

(*continued*)

This market was probably getting tight since City-Data.com also showed the population of Wichita Falls fell from 104,197 in 2000 to 99,846 in 2005. Furthermore, a few of the bigger firms probably wrote the majority of the business, so the revenue would be even less than that—and all this before taking out office overhead.

McKay's conclusion: A new insurance agency with a new brand in town didn't have a good chance of being very profitable, and the agent should pass on the opportunity.

(Note: These are all exact numbers. But soon we will discuss how to do the same kind of analysis when all you have are inexact ranges.)

EXPERIMENTS: NOT JUST FOR ADULTS

Another person who seemed to have a knack for measuring the world was Emily Rosa. Although Emily published one of her measurements in the *Journal of the American Medical Association*, or simply *JAMA*, she did not have a PhD or even a high school diploma. At the time she conducted the measurement, Emily was a 9-year-old working on an idea for her fourth-grade science fair project. She was just 11 years old when her research was published, making her the youngest person ever to have research published in the prestigious medical journal and perhaps the youngest in any major, peer-reviewed scientific journal.

In 1996, Emily saw her mother, Linda, watching a videotape on a growing industry called "therapeutic touch," a controversial method of treating ailments by manipulating the patients' "energy fields." While the patient lay still, a therapist would move his or her hands just inches away from the patient's body to detect and remove "undesirable energies," which presumably caused various illnesses. Linda was a nurse and a long-standing member of the National Council Against Health Fraud (NCAHF). But it was Emily who first suggested to her mother that she might be able to conduct an experiment on such a claim.

With the advice of her mother, Emily initially recruited 21 therapists for her science fair experiment. The test involved Emily and the therapist sitting on opposite sides of a table. A cardboard screen separated them, blocking each from the view of the other. The screen had holes cut out at the bottom through which the therapist would place her hands, palms up, and out of sight. Emily would flip a coin and, based on the result, place her hand four to five inches over the therapist's left or right hand. (This distance was marked on the screen so that Emily's hand would be a consistent distance from the therapist's hand.) The therapists, unable to see Emily, would have to determine whether she was holding her hand over their left or right hand by feeling for her energy field. Emily reported her results at the science fair and got a blue ribbon—just as everyone else did.

Linda mentioned Emily's experiment to Dr. Stephen Barrett, whom she knew from the NCAHF. Barrett, intrigued by both the simplicity of the method and the initial findings, then mentioned it to the producers of the TV show *Scientific American Frontiers* shown on the Public Broadcasting Service. In 1997, the producers shot an episode on Emily's experimental method. Emily managed to convince 7 of the original 21 therapists to take the experiment again for the taping of the show. She now had a total of 28 separate tests, each with 10 opportunities for the therapist to guess the correct hand.

This made a total of 280 individual attempts by 21 separate therapists (14 had 10 attempts each while another 7 had 20 attempts each) to feel Emily's energy field. They correctly identified the position of Emily's hand just 44% of the time. Left to chance alone, they should get about 50% right with a 95% confidence interval of +/- 6%. (If you flipped 280 coins, there is a 95% chance that between 44% and 56% would be heads.) So the therapists may have been a bit unlucky (since they ended up on the bottom end of the range), but their results are not out of bounds of what could be explained by chance alone. In other words, people "uncertified" in therapeutic touch—you or I—could have just guessed and done as well as or better than the therapists.

With these results, Linda and Emily thought the work might be worthy of publication. In April 1998, Emily, then 11 years old, had her experiment published in *JAMA*. That earned her a place in the *Guinness Book of World Records* as the youngest person ever to have research published in a major scientific journal and a $1,000 award from the James Randi Educational Foundation.

James Randi, retired magician and renowned skeptic, set up this foundation for investigating paranormal claims scientifically. (He advised Emily on some issues of experimental protocol.) Randi created the $1 million "Randi Prize" for anyone who can scientifically prove extrasensory perception (ESP), clairvoyance, dowsing, and the like. Randi dislikes labeling his efforts as "debunking" paranormal claims since he just assesses the claim with scientific objectivity. But since hundreds of applicants have been unable to claim the prize by passing simple scientific tests of their paranormal claims, debunking has been the net effect. Even before Emily's experiment was published, Randi was also interested in therapeutic touch and was trying to test it. But, unlike Emily, he managed to recruit only one therapist who would agree to an objective test—and that person failed.

After these results were published, therapeutic touch proponents stated a variety of objections to the experimental method, claiming it proved nothing. Some stated that the distance of the energy field was really one to three inches, not the four or five inches Emily used in her experiment.[3] Others stated that the energy field was fluid, not static, and Emily's unmoving hand was an unfair test (despite the fact that patients usually lie still during their "treatment").[4] None of this surprises Randi. "People always have excuses afterward," he says. "But prior to the experiment every one of the therapists were asked if they agreed with the conditions of the experiment. Not only did they agree, but they felt confident they would do well." Of course, the best refutation of Emily's results would simply be to set up a controlled, valid experiment that conclusively proves therapeutic touch *does* work. No such refutation has yet been offered.

Randi has run into retroactive excuses to explain failures to demonstrate paranormal skills so often that he has added another small demonstration to his tests. Prior to taking the test, Randi has subjects sign an affidavit stating that they agreed to the conditions of the test, that they would later offer no objections to the test, and that, in fact, they expected to do well under the stated conditions. At that point Randi hands them a sealed envelope. After the test, when they attempt to reject the outcome as poor experimental design, he asks them to open the envelope. The letter in the envelope simply states, "You have agreed that the conditions were optimum and that you would offer no excuses after the test. You have now offered those excuses." Randi observes, "They find this extremely annoying."

Emily's example provides more than one lesson for business. First, even touchy-feely-sounding things like "employee empowerment," "creativity," or "strategic alignment" must have observable consequences if they matter at all. I'm not saying that such things are "paranormal," but the same rules apply.

Second, Emily's experiment demonstrated the effectiveness of simple methods routinely used in scientific inquiry, such as a controlled experiment, sampling (even a small sample), randomization, and using a type of "blind" to avoid bias from the test subject or researcher. These simple elements can be combined in different ways to allow us to observe and measure a variety of phenomena.

Also, Emily showed that useful levels of experimentation can be understood by even a child on a small budget. Linda Rosa said she spent just $10 on the experiment. Emily could have constructed a much more elaborate clinical trial of the effects of this method using test groups and control groups to test how much therapeutic touch improves health. But she didn't have to do that because she simply asked a more basic question. If the therapists can do what they claimed, then they must, Emily reasoned, *at least be able to feel the energy field*. If they can't do that (and it is a basic assumption of the claimed benefits), then everything about therapeutic touch is in doubt.

She could have found a way to spend much more if she had, say, the budget of one of the smaller clinical studies in medical research. Over the years, many of the largest pharmaceutical firms have been clients of mine and I can tell you (without breaching any nondisclosure agreements) that they would have a hard time spending less than $30 million in a phase 3 clinical trial. But Emily determined all she needed with more than adequate accuracy. That was good enough even for *JAMA*.

Emily's example demonstrates how simple methods can produce a useful result. Her experiment was far less elaborate than most others published in the journal, but the simplicity of the experiment was actually considered a point in favor of the strength of its findings. According to George Lundberg, the editor of the journal, *JAMA*'s statisticians "were amazed by its simplicity and by the clarity of its results."[5]

Perhaps you are thinking that Emily is a rare child prodigy. Even as adults, most of us would be hard-pressed to imagine such a clever solution to a measurement problem like this. According to Emily herself, nothing could be further from the truth. At the time I was writing the second edition of this book (2009), Emily Rosa was working on her last semester for a bachelor's degree in psychology at the University of Colorado–Denver. She volunteered that she had earned a relatively modest 3.2 GPA and describes herself as average. Still, she does encounter those who expect anyone who has published research at the age of 11 to have unusual talents. "It's been hard for me," she says, "because some people think I'm a rocket scientist and they are disappointed to find out that I'm so average." Having talked to her, I suspect she is a little too modest, but her example does prove what can be done by most managers if they tried.

I have at times heard that "more advanced" measurements like controlled experiments should be avoided because upper management won't understand them. This seems to assume that all upper management really does succumb to the Dilbert Principle (cartoonist Scott Adam's tongue-in-cheek rule that states that only the least competent get promoted).[6] In my experience, if you explain it well, upper management will understand it just fine. Emily, explain it to them, please.

Example: Mitre Information Infrastructure

An interesting business example of how a business might measure an "intangible" by first testing if it exists at all is the case of the Mitre Information Infrastructure (MII). This system was developed in the late 1990s by Mitre Corporation, a not-for-profit that provides federal agencies with consulting on system engineering and information

(*continued*)

technology. MII was a corporate knowledge base that spanned insular departments to improve collaboration.

In 2000, *CIO* magazine wrote a case study about MII. The magazine's method for this sort of thing is to have a staff writer do all the heavy lifting for the case study itself and then to ask an outside expert to write an accompanying opinion column called "Critical Analysis." The magazine often asked me to write the opinion column when the case was anything about value, measurement, risk, and so on, and I was asked to do so for the MII case.

The "Critical Analysis" column is meant to offer some balance in the case study since companies talking about some new initiative are likely to paint a pretty rosy picture. The article quotes Al Grasso, the chief information officer (CIO) at the time: "Our most important gain can't be as easily measured—the quality and innovation in our solutions that become realizable when you have all this information at your fingertips." However, in the opinion column, I suggested one fairly easy measure of "quality and innovation":

> *If MII really improves the quality of deliverables, then it should affect customer perceptions and ultimately revenue.[7] Simply ask a random sample of customers to rank the quality of some pre-MII and post-MII deliverables (make sure they don't know which is which) and if improved quality has recently caused them to purchase more services from Mitre.[8]*

Like Emily, I proposed that Mitre not ask quite the same question the CIO might have started with but a simpler, related question. If quality and innovation really did get better, shouldn't someone at least be able to tell that there is any difference? If the relevant judges (i.e., the customers) can't tell, in a blind test, that post-MII research is "higher quality" or "more innovative" than pre-MII research, then MII shouldn't have any bearing on customer satisfaction or, for that matter, revenue. If, however, they can tell the difference, then you can worry about the next question: whether the revenue improved enough to be worth the investment of over $7 million by 2000. Like everything else, if Mitre's quality and innovation benefits could not be detected, then they don't matter. I'm told by current and former Mitre employees that my column created a lot of debate. However, they were not aware of any such attempt to actually measure quality and innovation. Remember, the CIO said this would be the most important gain of MII, and it went unmeasured.

NOTES ON WHAT TO LEARN FROM ERATOSTHENES, ENRICO, AND EMILY

Taken together, Eratosthenes, Enrico, and Emily show us something very different from what we are typically exposed to in business. Executives often say, "We can't even begin to guess at something like that." They dwell *ad infinitum* on the overwhelming uncertainties. Instead of making any attempt at measurement, they sometimes prefer to be stunned into inactivity by the apparent difficulty in dealing with these uncertainties. Fermi might say, "Yes, there are a lot of things you don't know, but what *do* you know?"

Other managers might object: "There is no way to measure that thing without spending millions of dollars." As a result, they opt not to engage in a smaller study—even though the costs might be very reasonable—because such a study would have more error than a larger one. Yet perhaps even this uncertainty reduction might be worth millions, depending on the size, uncertainty, and frequency of the decision it is meant to support. Eratosthenes and Emily might point out that useful observations can tell you something you didn't know before—even on a budget—if you approach the topic with just a little more creativity and less defeatism.

Eratosthenes, Enrico, and Emily each inspire us in different ways. Eratosthenes had no way of computing the error on his estimate, since statistical methods for assessing uncertainty would not be around for over two more millennia. However, if he would have had a way to compute uncertainty, the uncertainties in measuring distances between cities and exact angles of shadows might have easily accounted for his relatively small error. Fortunately, we do have those tools available to us. The concept of measurement as "uncertainty reduction" and not necessarily the elimination of uncertainty is a central theme of this book.

We learn a related but different lesson from Enrico Fermi. Since he won a Nobel Prize, it's safe to assume that Fermi was an especially proficient experimental and theoretical physicist. But the example of his Fermi question showed, even for the rest of us non–Nobel Prize winners, how we can estimate things that, at first, seem too difficult even to attempt to estimate. Although his insight on advanced experimental methods of all sorts would be enlightening, I find that the reason intangibles seem intangible is almost never for lack of the most sophisticated measurement methods. Usually things that seem immeasurable in business reveal themselves to much simpler methods of observation, once we learn to see through the illusion of immeasurability. In this context, Fermi's value to us is in how we determine our current state of knowledge about a thing as a precursor to further measurement.

Unlike Fermi's example, Emily's example is not so much about initial estimation since her experiment made no prior assumptions about how probable the therapeutic touch claims were. Nor was her experiment about using a clever calculation instead of infeasible observations, like Eratosthenes's. Her calculation was merely based on standard sampling methods and did not itself require a leap of insight like Eratosthenes's simple geometry calculation.

Emily demonstrated that useful observations are not necessarily complex, expensive, or even, as is sometimes claimed, beyond the comprehension of upper management, even for ephemeral concepts like touch therapy (or strategic alignment, employee empowerment, improved communication, etc.).

We will build even further on the lessons of Eratosthenes, Enrico, and Emily in the rest of this book. We will learn ways to assess your current uncertainty about a quantity that improve on Fermi's methods, some sampling methods that are in some ways even simpler than what Emily used, and simple methods that would have allowed even Eratosthenes to improve on his estimate of the size of a world that nobody had yet circumnavigated.

Alliteration was not the only reason I limited this list of measurement mentors to Eratosthenes, Enrico, and Emily. These three examples were chosen because of the different lessons they can teach us about measurement at this early point in the book. But later I will be giving due credit to a few more individuals who, for me, inspired specific measurement solutions.

We will discuss the research of psychologists like Paul Meehl who showed that simple statistical models outperformed human judgment in a wide range of tasks. Other psychologists, like Amos Tversky and Daniel Kahneman showed how we can measure and improve our skill at assigning subjective probabilities. This is an important consideration when assessing our initial uncertainty about a problem (as mentioned previously, this is a critical step in our decision-oriented framework for measurement).

Given only the examples discussed so far, we can see that some of the things that might initially seem immeasurable were measurable with a little more resourcefulness. These examples alone don't necessarily address *all* of the reasons someone might use to argue that something is truly immeasurable. Still, all of the reasons for perceived immeasurability ultimately boil down to a very short list. So, in the next chapter, we will consider each of these arguments and why each of them is flawed.

Notes

1. M. Lial and C. Miller, *Trigonometry*, 3rd ed. (Chicago: Scott, Foresman, 1988).
2. Two Frenchmen, Pierre-François-André Méchain and Jean-Baptiste-Joseph Delambre, calculated Earth's circumference over a seven-year period during the French Revolution on a commission to define a standard for the meter. (The meter was originally defined to be one 10-millionth of the distance from the equator to the pole.)
3. Letter to the Editor, *New York Times*, April 7, 1998.
4. "Therapeutic Touch: Fact or Fiction?" *Nurse Week*, June 7, 1998.
5. "A Child's Paper Poses a Medical Challenge," *New York Times,* April 1, 1998.
6. Scott Adams, *The Dilbert Principle* (New York: Harper Business, 1996).
7. Although a not-for-profit, Mitre still has to keep operations running by generating revenue through consulting billed to federal agencies.
8. Douglas Hubbard, "Critical Analysis" column accompanying "An Audit Trail," *CIO*, May 1, 2000.

## CHAPTER 3

The Illusion of Intangibles: Why Immeasurables Aren't

There are just three reasons why people think that something can't be measured. Each of these three reasons is actually based on misconceptions about different aspects of measurement. I will call them *concept*, *object*, and *method*.

1. *Concept of measurement.* The definition of measurement itself is widely misunderstood. If one understands what "measurement" actually means, a lot more things become measurable.
2. *Object of measurement.* The thing being measured is not well defined. Sloppy and ambiguous language gets in the way of measurement.
3. *Methods of measurement.* Many procedures of empirical observation are not well known. If people were familiar with some of these basic methods, it would become apparent that many things thought to be immeasurable are not only measurable but may already have been measured.

A good way to remember these three common misconceptions is by using a mnemonic like "howtomeasureanything.com," where the *c*, *o*, and *m* in ".com" stand for concept, object, and method. Once we learn that these three objections are misunderstandings of one sort or another, it becomes apparent that everything really is measurable.

In addition to these reasons why something can't be measured, there are also three common reasons why something *shouldn't* be measured. The reasons often given for this are:

1. The economic objection to measurement (i.e., any measurement would be too expensive).

2. The general objection to the usefulness and meaningfulness of statistics (i.e., "You can prove anything with statistics").
3. The ethical objection (i.e., we shouldn't measure it because it would be immoral to measure it).

Unlike the concept, object, and method list, these three objections don't really argue that a measurement is impossible but they are still arguments against attempting a measurement. I will show that of these three arguments, only the economic objection has any potential merit, but even that one is overused.

THE CONCEPT OF MEASUREMENT

As far as the propositions of mathematics refer to reality, they are not certain; and as far as they are certain, they do not refer to reality.
—Albert Einstein (1879–1955)

Although this may seem a paradox, all exact science is based on the idea of approximation. If a man tells you he knows a thing exactly, then you can be safe in inferring that you are speaking to an inexact man.
—Bertrand Russell (1873–1970), British mathematician and philosopher

For those who believe something to be immeasurable, the concept of measurement, or rather the *mis*conception of it, is probably the most important obstacle to overcome. If we incorrectly think that measurement means meeting some nearly unachievable standard of certainty, then few things will be measurable even in the physical sciences.

I routinely ask those who attend my seminars or conference lectures what they think "measurement" means. (It's interesting to see how much thought this provokes among people who are actually in charge of some measurement initiative in their organization.) I usually get answers like "to quantify something," "to compute an exact value," "to reduce to a single number," or "to choose a representative amount," and so on. Implicit or explicit in all of these answers is that measurement is certainty—an exact quantity with no room for error. If that was really what the term means, then, indeed, very few things would be measurable.

But when scientists, actuaries, or statisticians perform a measurement, they are using a different *de facto* definition. In their respective fields, each of these professions has learned the need for a precise use of certain words, sometimes very different from how the general public uses them. Consequently, members of these professions usually are much less confused about the meaning of the word "measurement." The key to this precision is that their specialized terminology goes beyond a one-sentence definition and is part of a larger theoretical framework. In physics, for example, gravity is not merely a dictionary term, but a component of specific equations that relate gravity to such concepts as mass, distance, and its effect on space and time. Likewise, if we want to understand measurement with that same level of precision, we have to know something about the theoretical framework behind it—or we really don't understand it at all.

A Definition of Measurement: An "Information Theory" Version

Definition of Measurement

Measurement: A quantitatively expressed reduction of uncertainty based on one or more observations.

For all practical decision-making purposes, we need to treat measurement as *observations that quantitatively reduce uncertainty*. A mere reduction, not necessarily elimination, of uncertainty will suffice for a measurement. Even if scientists don't articulate this definition exactly, the methods they use make it clear that, to them, measurement is only a probabilistic exercise. Certainty about real-world quantities is usually beyond their reach. The fact that some amount of error is unavoidable but can still be an improvement on prior knowledge is central to how experiments, surveys, and other scientific measurements are performed.

The practical differences between this definition and the most popular definitions of measurement are enormous. Not only does a true measurement not need to be infinitely precise to be considered a measurement, but the lack of reported error—implying the number is exact—can be an indication that empirical methods, such as sampling and experiments, were not used (i.e., it's not really a measurement at all). Real scientific methods report numbers in ranges, such as "the average yield of corn farms using this new seed increased between 10% and 18% (95% confidence interval)." Exact numbers reported without error might be calculated "according to accepted procedure," but, unless they represent a complete count of an entire population (e.g., the change in my pocket), there is a good chance they do not represent the real limits of our knowledge about the thing being measured. Enron, Lehman Brothers, or Fannie Mae's asset valuations, for example, surely followed *some* accounting standards and yet were not necessarily related to reality.

This conception of measurement might be new to many readers, but there are strong mathematical foundations—as well as practical reasons—for looking at measurement this way. Measurement is, at least, a type of information, and there is a rigorous theoretical construct for information. A field called "information theory" was developed in the 1940s by Claude Shannon. Shannon was an American electrical engineer, mathematician, and all-around savant who dabbled in robotics and computer chess programs.

In 1948, he published a paper titled "A Mathematical Theory of Communication,"[1] which laid the foundation for information theory and, I would say, measurement in general. Current generations don't entirely appreciate this, but his contribution can't be overstated. Information theory has since become the basis of all modern signal processing theory. It is the foundation for the engineering of every electronic communications system, including every microprocessor ever built. It is the theoretical ancestor that eventually enabled me to write this book on my laptop, and you to buy it on Amazon or read it on a Kindle.

Shannon proposed a mathematical definition of information as the amount of uncertainty reduction in a signal, which he discussed in terms of the "entropy" removed by a signal. To Shannon, the receiver of information could be described as having some prior state of uncertainty. That is, the receiver already knew something, and the new information merely removed some, not necessarily all, of the receiver's uncertainty. The receiver's prior state of knowledge or uncertainty can be used to compute such things as the limits to how much information can be transmitted in a signal, the minimal amount of signal to correct for noise, and the maximum data compression possible.

This "uncertainty reduction" point of view is what is critical to business. Major decisions made under a state of uncertainty—such as whether to approve large information technology (IT) projects or new product development—can be made better, even if just slightly, by reducing uncertainty. Such an uncertainty reduction can be worth millions.

A Variety of Measurement Scales

So, a measurement doesn't have to eliminate uncertainty after all. A mere *reduction* in uncertainty counts as a measurement and can potentially be worth much more than the cost of the measurement. But there is another key concept of measurement that would surprise most people: A measurement doesn't have to be about a quantity in the way that we normally think of it. Note that the definition I offer for measurement says a measurement is "quantitatively expressed." The uncertainty, at least, has to be quantified, but the subject of observation might not be a quantity itself—it could be entirely qualitative, such as a membership in a set. For example, we could "measure" something where the answer is yes or no—like whether a patent will be awarded or whether a merger will happen—while still satisfying our precise definition of measurement. But our uncertainty about those observations must still be expressed quantitatively (e.g., there is an 85% chance we will win the patent dispute; we are 93% certain our public image will improve after the merger, etc.).

The view that measurement applies to questions with a yes/no answer or other qualitative distinctions is consistent with another accepted school of thought on measurement. In 1946, the psychologist Stanley Smith Stevens wrote an article called "On the Theory of Scales and Measurement."[2] In it he describes different scales of measurement, including "nominal," "ordinal," "interval," and "ratio" scales. Nominal measurements are simply "set membership" statements, such as whether a fetus is male or female, or whether you have a particular medical condition. In nominal scales, there is no implicit order or sense of relative size. A thing is simply in one of the possible sets.

Ordinal scales, however, allow us to say one value is "more" than another, but not by how much. Examples of these are the four-star rating system for movies or Mohs hardness scale for minerals. A "4" on either of these scales is "more" than a "2" but not necessarily twice as much. In ordinal scales, there are no defined units of measure so that adding "1" always means adding the same amount.

In contrast, homogeneous units such as dollars, kilometers, liters, volts, and the like tell us not just that one thing is more than another, but by how much. These "ratio" scales can also be added, subtracted, multiplied, and divided in a way that makes sense. Whereas seeing four one-star movies is not necessarily as good as seeing one four-star movie, a four-ton rock weighs exactly as much as four one-ton rocks. Interval scales are almost like ratio scales in that they have defined units but the "zero" is an arbitrary point, like the Celsius scale for temperature. A zero on the Celsius scale doesn't mean "no temperature." As such, we can compute a difference between two Celsius temperatures, but we can't say 20 Celsius is twice the temperature of 10 Celsius. Temperature measured on the Kelvin scale, however, is a ratio scale and all the ratio scale operations can apply.

Nominal and ordinal scales in particular might challenge our preconceptions about what "scale" really means, but they can still be useful for observations. To a geologist, it is useful to know that one rock is harder than another, without necessarily having to know by how much—which is all that the Mohs hardness scale really does.

Stevens and Shannon each challenge different aspects of the popular definition of measurement. Stevens was more concerned about a taxonomy of different types of measurement but was silent on the all-important concept of uncertainty reduction. Shannon, working in a different field altogether, was probably unaware of and unconcerned with how Stevens, a psychologist, mapped out the field of measurements just two years earlier. However, I don't think a practical definition of measurement that accounts for all the sorts of things a business might need to measure is possible without incorporating both of these concepts.

There is a field of study called "measurement theory" that attempts to deal with both of these issues and more. In measurement theory, a measurement is a type of "mapping" between the thing being measured and numbers. The theory gets very esoteric, but if we focus on the contributions of Shannon and Stevens, there are many lessons for managers. The commonplace notion that presumes measurements are exact quantities ignores the usefulness of simply reducing uncertainty, especially if eliminating uncertainty is not feasible (as is usually the case). And not all measurements even need to be about a conventional quantity. Measurement applies to discrete, nominal points of interest like "Will we win the lawsuit?" or "Will this research and development project succeed?" as well as continuous quantities like "How much did our revenue increase because of this new product feature?" In business, decision makers make decisions under uncertainty. When that uncertainty is about big, risky decisions, then uncertainty reduction has a lot of value—and that is why we will use this definition of measurement.

Bayesian Measurement: A Pragmatic Concept for Decisions

When I talk about measurement as "uncertainty reduction" I imply that there is some prior state of uncertainty to be reduced. And since this uncertainty can change as a result of observations, we treat uncertainty as a feature of the observer, not *necessarily* the thing being observed. When I observe the average weight of salmon in a river by sampling them, I'm not changing their weight, but I am changing my uncertainty about their weights. I say "necessarily" because there are some notable cases where observation does change the object of observation (see *A Purely Philosophical Interlude #1* after this chapter) but, even when it does, we can still use uncertainty to describe the state of the observer.

We quantify this initial uncertainty and the change in uncertainty from observations by using probabilities. This means that we are using the term "probability" to refer to the personal state of uncertainty of an observer or what some have called a "degree of belief." If you are almost certain that the majority of your customers will buy a new model of your product, you may say there is a 97% probability of it. If you are unsure you may say there is a 50% probability (as we will see later, this is actually a skill you can learn). Likewise, if you are very uncertain about the average daily commute time of workers in the Greater Chicago Metropolitan Area, you may say there is a 90% probability that the true value falls within 10 minutes and 90 minutes per day. If you had more information, you might give a much narrower range and still assign a 90% probability that the true value falls within that range.

This view of probabilities is called the "Bayesian" interpretation. The original inspiration for this interpretation, Thomas Bayes, was an eighteenth-century British mathematician and Presbyterian minister whose most famous contribution to statistics would not be published until after he died. His simple formula, known as Bayes' theorem, describes how new information can update prior probabilities. "Prior" could refer to a state of uncertainty informed mostly by previously recorded data but it can also refer to a point before any objective and recorded observations. At least for the latter case, the prior probability often needs to be subjective.

For decision making, this is the most relevant use of the word "probability." Later, we will see why we need to know the economic value of measurements—and in order to know that we need to explicitly quantify our prior state of uncertainty and change in uncertainty. The Bayesian approach does this while also greatly simplifying some problems and allowing us to get more use out of limited information.

Many scientists and statisticians, but not all of them, interpret probability differently. This alternative view is known as the "frequentist" interpretation of probability. In this view, probability is not a state of an observer, but an objective feature of some system. Further discussion comparing Bayesian and frequentist views are provided in the *Purely Philosophical Interlude* sections between some of the chapters, starting with the first one at the end of this chapter. I've relegated this discussion to the interludes because, while the topics are interesting and even important for a broader understanding, the details of these debates are not always directly related to our practical needs. In fact, in practice, these interpretations may often approach the same answers. There are also philosophical variations on the Bayesian view but we will keep the taxonomy simple for our purposes. (Note that Bayesian is capitalized only because it is derived from a proper name while frequentism is not. This is simply convention and not itself some petty demotion of frequentism compared to Bayesianism.)

Even for those scientists not declaring they use the Bayesian interpretation, the uncertainty reduction is at least implied by virtue of the fact that they *believe they are learning something* through a measurement.

The difference between them and their colleagues who use Bayesian methods is not that they didn't have a change in a prior state of uncertainty. The difference was that the Bayesians were just explicitly quantifying the initial state of uncertainty and the change in uncertainty. And in both cases—Bayesian or not—they are at least quantifying the uncertainty about the final state of uncertainty post-measurement. In other words, they must still quantify their postmeasurement error even if they didn't explicitly quantify the change in error due to the measurement.

Keep in mind that, while subjective, the uncertainty we refer to is not just irrational and capricious. We need subjective uncertainties to at least be mathematically coherent as well as consistent with repeated, subsequent observations. A rational person can't simply say, for instance, that there is a 75% chance of winning a bid for a government contract *and* an 82% chance of losing it (these two possibilities should have a total probability of 100%). Also, if someone keeps saying they are 100% certain of their predictions and they are consistently wrong, then we can reject their subjective uncertainties on objective grounds just as we would with the readings of a broken digital scale or ampmeter.

There are also cases where the uncertainty of a rational person should match an "objective frequency" interpretation of probability—consistent with the frequentists' view of probability—when they have sufficient knowledge of a system. For example, the frequency of occurrence of a "2" on a roll of two six-sided dice is 1 in 36 and this probability would also represent my uncertainty about getting a 2 on the next roll since I know the rules of this simple system. Unfortunately, we rarely have that kind of knowledge of a simple, well-defined system in real-world decisions. So, regardless of whether we have objective frequencies as a guide, we can still describe the uncertainty of a person using probabilities. In Chapter 5, you will learn more about how probabilities can be subjective and yet a rational, realistic representation of a person's uncertainty.

Finally, we need to remember that there is another edge to the "uncertainty reduction" sword. Total elimination of uncertainty is not necessary for a measurement but there *must be some* expected uncertainty reduction. If a decision maker or analyst engages in what they believe to be measurement activities, but their estimates and decisions actually get worse on average, then they are not actually reducing their error and they are not conducting a measurement according to our definition. Unfortunately, many such activities occupy businesses and governments.

For example, we discussed how ordinal scales can be a valid form of a measurement. But they can be misused. It is common for organizations to use ordinal scales in some sort of "weighted score" to evaluate alternatives in a decision. This often involves operations that are technically invalid for ordinal scales (multiplication and addition) and the evidence about the performance of these methods (i.e., whether they measurably improve decisions) is either non-existent or negative. Using numbers alone doesn't make a weighted score a measurement. It must reduce uncertainty and for that uncertainty reduction to be valuable it must improve some decision.

These finer points will be developed further in chapters to come. But, until then, the key lesson is that measurements are more than you knew before about something that matters.

THE OBJECT OF MEASUREMENT

A problem well stated is a problem half solved.
> —Charles Kettering (1876–1958), American inventor, holder of 300 patents, including electrical ignition for automobiles

There is no greater impediment to the advancement of knowledge than the ambiguity of words.
> —Thomas Reid (1710–1769), Scottish philosopher

Even when the more useful concept of measurement (as uncertainty-reducing observations) is adopted, some things seem immeasurable because we simply don't know what we mean when we first pose the question. In this case, we haven't unambiguously defined the *object* of measurement. If someone asks how to measure "strategic alignment" or "flexibility" or "customer satisfaction," I simply ask: "What do you mean, exactly?" It is interesting how often people further refine their use of the term in a way that almost answers the measurement question by itself.

In my seminars, I often ask the audience to challenge me with difficult or seemingly impossible measurements. In one case, a participant offered "mentorship" as something difficult to measure. I said, "That sounds like something one would like to measure. I might say that more mentorship is better than less mentorship. I can see people investing in ways to improve it, so I can understand why someone might want to measure it. So, what do *you* mean by 'mentorship'?" The person almost immediately responded, "I don't think I know," to which I said, "Well, then maybe that's why you believe it is hard to measure. You haven't figured out what it is."

Once managers figure out what they mean and why it matters, the issue in question starts to look a lot more measurable. This is usually my first level of analysis when I conduct what I've called "clarification workshops." It's simply a matter of clients stating a particular, but initially ambiguous, item they want to measure. I then follow up by asking "What do you mean by <fill in the blank>?" and "Why do you care?"

This applies to a wide variety of measurement problems, but I've had many occasions to apply this to IT in particular. In 2000, when the Department of Veterans Affairs asked me to help define performance metrics for IT security, I asked: "What do you mean by 'IT security'?" and over the course of two or three workshops, the department staff defined it for me with increasingly specific language. They eventually revealed that what they meant by "IT security" were things like a reduction in unauthorized intrusions and virus attacks. They proceeded to explain that these things impact the organization through fraud losses, lost productivity, or even potential legal liabilities (which they may have narrowly averted when they recovered a stolen notebook computer in 2006 that contained the Social Security numbers of 26.5 million veterans). All of the identified impacts were, in almost every case, obviously measurable. "Security" was a vague concept until they decomposed it into what they actually expected to observe. Even with examples from very different problems I used a similar method to help define the problem. Whether the measurement challenge is about security, the environment, or public image, there are two methods that seem to help with the particularly hard-to-define problems. I use what I call a "clarification chain" or, if that doesn't work, perhaps a type of thought experiment.

The clarification chain is just a short series of connections that should bring us from thinking of something as an intangible to thinking of it as tangible. First, we recognize that if X is something that we care about, then X, by definition, must be detectable in some way. How could we care about things like "quality," "risk," "security," or "public image" if these things were totally undetectable, in any way, directly or indirectly? If we have reason to care about some unknown quantity, it is because we think it corresponds to desirable or undesirable results in some way. Second, if this thing is detectable, then it must be detectable in some amount. If you can observe a thing at all, you can observe more of it or less of it. Once we accept that much, the final step is perhaps the easiest. If we can observe it in some amount, then it must be measurable.

For example, once we figure out that we care about an "intangible" like public image because it impacts specific things like advertising by customer referral, which affects sales, then we have begun to identify how to measure it. Customer referrals are not only detectable, but detectable in some amount; this means they are measurable. I may not specifically take workshop participants through every part of the clarification chain on every problem, but if we can keep these three components in mind, the method is fairly successful.

The clarification chain is a variation on an idea described by the early twentieth-century psychologist Edward Lee Thorndike: "[I]f a thing exists, it exists in some amount, if it exists in some amount, it can be measured" (as quoted by the psychologist Paul Meehl[3]). Thorndike (1874–1949) was part of the "behaviorist" movement in psychology which tried to focus psychology on what could be observed—in contrast to the unverifiable abstractions of Freud. I merely modified it to focus not on whether something exists, but whether it also matters and that if it matters the "amount" we concern ourselves with must be observable.

Clarification Chain

1. If it matters at all, it is detectable/observable.
2. If it is detectable, it can be detected as an amount (or range of possible amounts).
3. If it can be detected as a range of possible amounts, it can be measured.

I may also try a type of "thought experiment." Imagine you are an alien scientist who can clone not just sheep or even people but entire organizations. Let's say you were investigating a particular fast food chain and studying the effect of a particular intangible, say, "employee empowerment." You create a pair of the same organization calling one the "test" group and one the "control" group. Now imagine that you give the test group a little bit more "employee empowerment" while holding the amount in the control group constant. What do you imagine you would actually observe—in any way, directly or indirectly—that would change for the first organization? Would you expect decisions to be made at a lower level in the organization? Would this mean those decisions are better or faster? Does it mean that employees require less supervision? Does that mean you can have a "flatter" organization with less management overhead? If you can identify even a single observation that would be different between the two cloned organizations, then you are well on the way to identifying how you would measure it.

These same clarifications are required for something as seemingly different, abstract—and yet important—as "ecological sustainability." This was a measurement challenge I worked on recently for the Consultative Group on International Agricultural Research (CGIAR) through the World Agroforestry Centre headquartered in Nairobi, Kenya. As usual, we have to define our terms. The current literature in the field proposed lots of methods for measuring this.[4,5,6] But it seemed to me that none of the work dealt with the more fundamental questions first: What does "sustainability" even mean, independent of whether it is related to ecological issues or not? What do we see when we see examples of increased sustainability?

I proposed that if X were "more sustainable" than an alternative, then X must have some effect on future undesirable outcomes. To be more sustainable, X must reduce the magnitude of the event, reduce the probability of it, or defer it. For example, if the outcome we wish to avoid is the collapse of an agricultural system resulting in famine and poverty, then we are reducing the severity of it (i.e., the number of people and duration), reducing the probability of it happening at all, or delaying it. None of these needs to be or even could be reduced to zero, yet a reduction in these quantities does indicate more sustainability.

It also helps to state *why* we want to measure something in order to understand *what* is really being measured. The purpose of the measurement is often the key to defining what the measurement is really supposed to be. In the first chapter, I argued that all measurements of any interest to a manager must support at least one specific decision. For example, I might be asked to help someone measure the value of crime reduction. But when I ask why they care about measuring that, I might find that what they really are interested in is building a business case for a specific biometric identification system for criminals. Or I might be asked how to measure collaboration only to find that the purpose of such a measurement is to resolve whether a new document management system is required. In each case, the purpose of the measurement gives us clues about what the measure really means and how to measure it. In addition, we find several other potential items that may need to be measured to support the relevant decision. In Chapter 4, we will examine in more detail how decisions were defined in real-world examples involving IT security and ecological sustainability (which, when clarified, turn out to have a lot in common).

Identifying the object of measurement really is the beginning of almost any scientific inquiry, including the truly revolutionary ones. Business managers need to realize that some things seem intangible only because they just haven't defined what they are talking about. Figure out what you mean and you are halfway to measuring it.

THE METHODS OF MEASUREMENT

When thinking about measurement methods, someone may imagine a fairly direct case of measurement. If you measure the length of a table to see how it would fit in a dining room or if you measure the time spent to resolve a particular client problem at a call center, there is no larger "unseen" population you are trying to assess. You have direct access to the entire object of measurement. If this is the limit of what one understands about measurement methods then, no doubt, many things will seem immeasurable.

Most of the apparently difficult measurements, however, involve indirect deductions and inferences. We need to infer something "unseen" from something "seen." Eratosthenes couldn't directly see the curvature of Earth, but he could deduce it from shadows and the knowledge that Earth was roughly spherical. Emily Rosa could not directly measure how therapeutic touch allegedly heals, but she could conduct an experiment to test a prerequisite claim (the therapist would at least have to detect an energy field to support the claim that this healing method worked). And she didn't lament not having access to "all the data" about detection of energy fields—she simply sampled some of them.

Studying populations too large or dynamic to see all at once is what statistics is really all about. The term "statistics" was introduced by the philosopher, economist, and legal expert Gottfried Achenwall in 1749. He derived the word from the Latin *statisticum*, meaning "pertaining to the state." Statistics was literally *the quantitative study of the state*. At first, the only technique for measuring something about a population was to attempt to conduct a complete count of the entire population—a census. In those days in particular, a census was extremely expensive and was sometimes such a long process that the population might change quite a bit during the census. So, for practical reasons, this evolved into a set of methods that can be used to make inferences about a larger population based on some samples and indirect observations. Obviously, one can't see the entire population of a state at once, but one can sample it economically.

Perhaps someone understands that measurement can be based on a sample of a larger population, but what they vaguely remember about college statistics is getting in the way. They may barely recall, but misunderstand, concepts like "statistical significance." What they seem to learn more than anything else in their college courses is that there are a lot of reasons why a measurement might be flawed—such as possible errors one could make in the data selection, calculations, and interpretation of results. After the first exposure to an initial stats course, a proper measurement may seem like a lofty goal. What students apparently don't usually learn is that sometimes even small samples can tell you something that improves the odds of making a better bet in real decisions.

We need to learn—or relearn—that several proven measurement methods can be used for a variety of issues to help measure something we may have at first considered immeasurable. Here are a few examples involving inferences about something unseen from something seen:

- *Measuring with very small random samples of a very large population:* You can learn something about the distribution of a population from a small sample of potential customers, employees, and so on—especially when there is currently a great deal of uncertainty.
- *Measuring the size of a mostly unseen population:* Even when the size of the population itself is unknown, something about the size can be inferred. There are clever and simple methods for measuring the number of a certain type of fish in the ocean, the average amount per year people spend online, the percentage of staff following a new procedure correctly, the number of production errors in a new product, or the number of unauthorized access attempts in your system that go undetected.
- *Measuring when many other, even unknown, variables are involved:* We can determine whether the new "quality program" is the reason for the increase in sales as opposed to the economy, competitor mistakes, or a new pricing policy.
- *Measuring the risk of rare events:* The chance of a launch failure of a rocket that has never flown before, another September 11th–type attack, another levee failure in New Orleans, or another major financial crisis can all be informed in valuable ways through observation and reason.
- *Measuring subjective preferences and values:* We can measure the value of art, free time, or reducing risk to your life by assessing how much people actually pay for these things both in terms of their money and their time.

Most of these approaches to measurements are just variations on basic methods involving different types of sampling and experimental controls and, sometimes, choosing to focus on different types of questions that are indirect indicators of what we are trying to measure. Basic methods of observation like these are often absent from certain decision-making processes in business, perhaps because such quantitative procedures are considered to be some elaborate, overly complicated process. Such methods are not usually considered to be something you might do, if necessary, on a moment's notice with little cost or preparation—and yet, as Emily Rosa showed us, they can be.

The Power of Small Samples: The Rule of Five

Here is a very simple example of a quick measurement of a large population anyone can do with an easily computed statistical uncertainty.

Suppose you want to consider more telecommuting for the employees of your business. One relevant factor when considering this type of initiative is how much time the employees spend commuting every day. You could engage in a formal office-wide census of this question, but let's suppose there are 10,000 employees in your firm. A census would give you the exact answer but it would also be time-consuming and expensive.

Suppose, instead, you just randomly pick five people. There are some other issues we'll get into later about what constitutes "random," but, for now, let's just say you cover your eyes and pick names from the employee directory. Contact these people and arrange to record their actual commute times on some randomly selected day for each person. Let's suppose the values you get are 30, 60, 45, 80, and 60 minutes. Can you use this sample of only five to estimate the *median* of the entire population (the point at which half the population is lower and half is higher)? Note that in this case the "population" is not just the number of employees but the number of individual commute times (for which there are many varying values even for the same employee).

I've been presenting sampling problems with just five samples to attendees of my seminars and conference sessions for years. I ask who thinks the sample is "statistically significant." Those who remember something about that idea seem only to remember that it creates some kind of difficult threshold that makes meager amounts of data useless (more on that to come). In some conferences, almost every attendee would say the sample is not statistically significant. I suspect that a large proportion of those who abstained from answering were just questioning whether they understood what statistically significant means. As it turns out, this latter group was the more self-aware of the two. Unlike the first group, they at least knew they didn't know what it really meant.

I then ask what the chance is that the median of the population is between the highest and lowest values in the sample of five (30 and 80). Most answers I've gotten were around 50%, and some were as low as 10%. After all, out of a population of 10,000 people (and perhaps millions of individual commute times per year), what could a mere sample of five tell us?

But, when we do the math, we see there is a 93.75% chance that the median of the entire population of employees is between those two numbers. I call this the "Rule of Five." The Rule of Five is simple, it works, and it can be proven to be statistically valid for a wide variety of problems. With a sample this small, the range might be very wide, but if it is significantly narrower than your previous range, then it counts as a measurement.

It might seem impossible to be 93.75% certain about anything based on a random sample of just five, but it works. To understand why this method works, it is important to note that the Rule of Five estimates

Rule of Five

There is a 93.75% chance that the median of a population is between the smallest and largest values in any random sample of five from that population.

only the median of a population. Remember, the median is the point where half the population is above it and half is below it. If we randomly picked five values that were all above the median or all below it, then the median would be outside our range. But what is the chance of that, really?

The chance of randomly picking a value above the median is, by definition, 50%—the same as a coin flip resulting in "heads." The chance of randomly selecting five values that happen to be all above the median is like flipping a coin and getting heads five times in a row. The chance of getting heads five times in a row in a random coin flip is 1 in 32, or 3.125%; the same is true with getting five tails in a row. The chance of *not* getting all heads or all tails is then 100% − 3.125% × 2, or 93.75%. Therefore, the chance of at least one out of a sample of five being above the median *and* at least one being below is 93.75% (round it down to 93% or even 90% if you want to be conservative). Some readers might remember a statistics class that discussed statistics for very small samples. Those methods were more complicated than the Rule of Five, but, for reasons I'll discuss in more detail later, the answer is really not much better. (Both methods make some simplifying assumptions that work very well in practice.)

We can improve on a rule of thumb like this by using simple methods to account for certain types of bias. Perhaps recent, but temporary, construction increased everyone's "average commute time" estimate. Or perhaps people with the longest commutes are more likely to call in sick or otherwise not be available for your sample. Still, even with acknowledged shortcomings, the Rule of Five is something that the person who wants to develop an intuition for measurement keeps handy.

Even Smaller Samples: The Urn of Mystery

A sample of five doesn't seem like much, but, if you are starting out with a *lot* of uncertainty, it might be possible to make a useful inference on even less data. Suppose you wanted to estimate a percentage of some population that has some characteristic. We call this a "population proportion" problem. A population proportion could refer to the percentage of employees who take public transportation to work, the percentage of farmers in Kenya who use a particular farming technique, the percent-age of people with a particular gene, or the percentage of trucks on the road that are overweight. In each of these cases, how many employees, farmers, or trucks would I have to sample to estimate the stated popula-tion proportions? Obviously, if I conducted a complete census, I would know the population proportion exactly. But what can be inferred from a smaller sample?

In my seminars I ask participants to consider an example I call the "Urn of Mystery." Suppose I have a warehouse full of large urns. Each urn is filled with marbles and each marble is either green or red. The percent-age of marbles that are green in a single urn can be anything between 0% and 100%, and all percentages are equally likely. (We call this a "uni-form" distribution.) The remaining portion of the urn is red marbles. In other words, one urn could be 15% green and 85% red, another urn 43% green and 57% red, and so on. Assume the marbles are thoroughly and randomly mixed in each urn.

Suppose then we were to engage in a betting game. I draw one urn at random from the entire warehouse and then I bet on the majority color of marbles for that urn. I can choose either green or red for each urn and I should be right 50% of the time over repeated games. If I gave you 2 to 1 odds and you bet $10 each time (you pay $10 if I win, I pay you $20 if I lose) and agreed to play through 100 urns, you should be eager to play me. You should expect to net about $500, plus or minus $100 or so, by the end of the game.

But let's say you decide that, to be fair, I can draw a single marble from each urn at random before I place my bet on which color is the majority. I would do it in a way that would not allow me to view the rest of the marbles, such as a spigot like a gumball machine at the bottom of the urn. Now should you play the betting game with me? How often would I win?

Like the five sample problem, I've been posing this question to my audiences in seminars and conferences. Note that these are managers and executives but also analysts and scientists—many of whom have advanced degrees in life sciences, engineering, math, and physical sciences. Most will answer that this single sample either tells them nothing (i.e., the probability of a given vote being the majority is still 50%) or that it provides a very small marginal indication in favor of the majority being the same as the selected sample—perhaps 51%. A few give answers with higher probabilities—perhaps 60% or 70%.

Only a handful has ever given the right answer: 75%. Of those, only three have been able to explain the calculation. That's right: If you ran-domly select one sample out of a large population, even a population that numbers thousands or millions, where you initially believed the population proportion can be anything between 0% and 100%, there is a 75% chance that the characteristic you observe in that sample is the same as the majority. Let's call this the "Single Sample Majority Rule" or, if you prefer something more fanciful, "The Urn of Mystery Rule."

Anyone who gave their opponent in this game this advantage should no longer expect to come out ahead. Even if you paid me $10 whenever I was right and I paid you $20 when I was wrong, my average win is $2.50 per bet. Over 100 bets I have a 95% chance of winning at least some money and a 50% chance I'll win more than $250.

The Single Sample Majority Rule (i.e., The Urn of Mystery Rule)

Given maximum uncertainty about a population proportion—such that you believe the proportion could be anything between 0% and 100% with all values being equally likely—there is a 75% chance that a single randomly selected sample is from the majority of the population.

The math for the Urn of Mystery is just a bit more involved than the Rule of Five but it is covered in more detail in Chapter 10. Also, I'm providing one of the "power tools" I spoke of to explain this further. If you go to "Downloads" on the www.howtomeasureanything.com website, you will see a spreadsheet that shows both the calculation for this and a simulation (so you won't need to have an actual warehouse of urns to test this claim). If you are inclined to take a notebook computer or tablet to a bar, you can use this simulation to win bar bets (bar bet instructions are included in the spreadsheet). But if you do find a skeptic of the Urn of Mystery Rule, please act responsibly with your newfound power-tool and try not to rob them blind.

Our Small-Sample Intuition versus Math

The Rule of Five and the Single Sample Majority Inference are clearly counterintuitive to most people. But the math is right about these methods, so it is our intuition that is wrong. Why is our intuition wrong? Often people object that the sample is too small compared to the population size. There is sometimes a misconception that an informative sample should be a significant percentage of the entire population. (If this were the requirement, no measurement in biology or physics would be remotely possible, since population sizes are often—and literally—astronomical.) But mathematically we can prove that the Rule of Five and the Single Sample Majority Inference work even with *infinite* population sizes.

In order to appreciate the effect of these small samples, it's important to remember how little we knew before the sample. The information from a very small sample is underestimated when a decision maker starts with a high degree of uncertainty, which is the case with the Single Sample Majority Inference. Indeed, the initial state of uncertainty couldn't possibly be any higher for a population proportion than to say it's somewhere between 0% to 100% with a uniform distribution. This is essentially the same as knowing nothing other than the logical limits of a population proportion.

Misconceptions about probabilities are behind this misinterpretation of samples. If you believe that a sample could randomly err by a much larger margin than is likely, you might think that even proper random samples without any bias still tell you virtually nothing. In one study, psychologists Daniel Kahneman and Amos Tversky showed that people will routinely overestimate the probability of extreme sample results.[7] Subjects in their study were told that 10 babies were born per day in a given region and then the subjects were asked to estimate the probability that, of those 10, none would be boys, one would be a boy, and so on up to 10. Kahneman and Tversky discovered that, on average, subjects thought that the chance of 0 out of 10 boys was 2.5%. The correct answer is less than one tenth of 1%. In other words, the estimate was over 25 times too high. Subjects also estimated that there was a 14% chance of getting less than 3 boys out of 10 whereas the correct answer is about 5.3%.

Curiously, the subjects' estimates for the probabilities of various outcomes didn't change even as the sample size increased dramatically. They estimated the chance of getting 400 or fewer boys out of 1000 births was about the same as getting 4 or fewer out of 10. The actual chance of four or fewer births out of 10 being boys is 39%, while getting 400 or fewer out of 1000 is actually less than 1 in 7 billion.

Another study conducted by Kahneman and Tversky seems to contradict this finding, at least at first glance. They surveyed fellow psychologists who were familiar with statistical testing methods common in their published research (the study is not clear how the researchers determined familiarity—a concern given criticisms of the profession mentioned later this chapter). Subjects were asked for the probability that a 10-sample study would confirm a theory given that a previous 20-sample study confirmed it. The estimates of the probability that the second study would confirm the results were consistently too high. Kahneman and Tversky referred to this as "belief in the law of small numbers."[8]

It appears that even a person's misconceptions about probabilities may contradict each other—they underestimate probabilities in some cases and overestimate in others. It is also important to note that "confirmed" in the latter experiment means according to a very specific set of statistical criteria we will discuss in later chapters. The reader will see that these criteria are not without controversy and, as such, the survey may be as much about the frequently misinterpreted meaning of this testing method as it is about inference errors of psychologists. Still, one thing is clear: Our subjective interpretations of the reliability of samples must depend on the accuracy of our ideas about probability. In this last study, Kahneman and Tversky stated:

> *Our thesis is that people have strong intuitions about random sampling; that these intuitions are wrong in fundamental respects; that these intuitions are shared by naive subjects and by trained scientists; and that they are applied with unfortunate consequences in the course of scientific inquiry.*
>
> —Kahneman, Tversky

Whether over- or underestimating the effects of samples, we find that we should not rely on our intuition about what a sample may tell us or not. The problem is that when managers make choices about whether to bother to do a random sample in the first place, they are making this judgment intuitively. So presumptions about how a sample might affect our uncertainty are likely to be wrong.

An important lesson comes from the origin of the word *experiment*. "Experiment" comes from the Latin *ex-*, meaning "of/from," and *periri*, meaning "try/attempt." It means, in other words, to get something by trying. The statistician David Moore, the 1998 president of the American Statistical Association, goes so far as to say: "If you don't know what to measure, measure anyway. You'll learn what to measure."[9] We might call Moore's approach the Nike method: the "Just do it" school of thought. This sounds like a "Measure first, ask questions later" philosophy of measurement, and I can think of a few shortcomings to this approach if taken to extremes. But it has some significant advantages over much of the current measurement-stalemate thinking of some managers.

Chapters 9 and 10 will delve into these sampling issues even more. For now, just know that the objection "A method doesn't exist to measure this thing" is never valid.

ECONOMIC OBJECTIONS TO MEASUREMENT

At the beginning of this chapter, we reviewed that the three reasons why it may appear that something can't be measured—the concept, object, and method objections—are all simply illusions. But there are also objections to measurement based not on the belief that a thing can't be measured but that it *shouldn't* be measured.

The only valid reason to say that a measurement shouldn't be made is that the cost of the measurement exceeds its benefits. This situation certainly happens in the real world. In 1995, I developed the method I called Applied Information Economics—a method for assessing uncertainty, risks, and intangibles in any type of big, risky decision you can imagine. A key step in the process (in fact, the reason for the name) is the calculation of the economic value of information. I'll say more about this later, but a proven formula from the field of decision theory allows us to compute a monetary value for a given amount of uncertainty reduction. I put this formula in an Excel macro and, for years, I've been computing the economic value of measurements on every variable in scores of various large business decisions. I found some fascinating patterns through this calculation but, for now, I'll mention this: Most of the variables in a business case had an information value of zero. Still, something like one to four variables were both uncertain enough and had enough bearing on the outcome of the decision to merit deliberate measurement efforts.

Usually, Only a Few Things Matter—But They Usually Matter a Lot

In most business cases, most of the variables have an "information value" at or near zero. But usually at least some variables have an information value that is so high that some deliberate measurement effort is easily justified.

So, while there are certainly variables that do not justify measurement, a persistent misconception is that unless a measurement meets an arbitrary standard (e.g., adequate for publication in an academic journal or meets generally accepted accounting standards), it has no value. This is a slight oversimplification, but what makes a measurement of high value is a lot of uncertainty combined with a high cost of being wrong. Whether it meets some other standard is irrelevant for our decision-making purposes. If you are betting a lot of money on the outcome of a variable that has a lot of uncertainty, then even a marginal reduction in your uncertainty has a computable monetary value. For example, suppose you think developing an expensive new product feature will increase sales in one particular demographic by up to 12%, but it could be a lot less. Furthermore, you believe the initiative is not cost-justified unless sales are improved by at least 9%. If you make the investment and the increase in sales turns out to be less than 9%, then your effort will not reap a positive return. If the increase in sales is very low, or even possibly negative, then the new feature will be a disaster and a lot of money will have been lost. Measuring this would have a very high value.

When someone says a variable is "too expensive" or "too difficult" to measure, we have to ask "Compared to what?" If the information value of the measurement is literally or virtually zero, of course, no measurement is justified. But if the measurement has any significant value, we must ask: "Is there any measurement method at all that can reduce uncertainty enough to justify the cost of the measurement?" Once we recognize the value of even partial uncertainty reduction, the answer is usually "Yes."

Consider the Urn of Mystery. The information value of sampling a single marble is the difference between what your average payoff would be with the marble and what the average payoff would be without the marble. Suppose now we had equal wins (you win $10 if I guess the wrong majority color and I win $10 if I'm right) but you charged me $2 on each urn to take a single marble sample. Should I pay the $2? In this case, my average payoff now without the sample is $0 (I win $10 half the time and lose $10 half the time). But if I took one sample from the urn before each bet, that information increased my average net win to 75% × $10 + 25% × (–$10) = $5. So the value of the information is $5 and the cost is $2 for a net gain of $3 per bet. So, yes, I should pay for the sample—and play the game as much as my opponents will agree to play (or until they run out of money).

A variation on the economic objection to measurement is how it influences not management decisions but the behaviors of others in ways that may or may not be the intended outcome. For example, performance metrics for a help desk based on how many calls it handles may encourage help desk workers to take a call and conclude it without solving the client's problem. A well-known example of this is the so-called Houston Miracle of the Texas school system in the 1990s. Public schools were under a new set of performance metrics to hold educators accountable for results. It is now known that the net effect of this "miracle" was that schools were incentivized to find ways to drop low-achieving students from the rolls. This is hardly the outcome most taxpayers thought they were funding.

I call this an economic objection because the claim is that the real outcomes are not the benefits originally aimed for and, in fact, can have significantly negative effects. But this confuses the issues of measurements and incentives. For any given set of measurements, there are a large number of possible incentive structures. This kind of objection presumes that since one set of measurements was part of an unproductive incentive program, then *any* measurements must incentivize unproductive behavior. Nothing could be further from the truth. If you can define the outcome you really want, give examples of it, and identify how those consequences are observable, then you can design measurements that will measure the outcomes that matter. If anything, the problem in Texas was that managers again were simply measuring what seemed simplest to measure (i.e., just what they currently knew how to measure), not what mattered most.

Another variation of the economic objection is based on the idea that quantitative models simply don't improve estimates and decisions. Therefore, no cost of measurement is justified and we should simply rely on the alternative: unaided expert judgment. This is not only a testable claim but, in fact, *has been tested* with studies that rival the size of the largest clinical drug trials.

One pioneer in testing the claims about the performance of experts was the famed psychologist Paul Meehl (1920–2003). Starting with research he conducted as early as the 1950s, he gained notoriety among psychologists by measuring their performance and comparing it to quantitative models. Meehl's extensive research soon reached outside of psychology and showed that simple statistical models were outperforming subjective expert judgments in almost every area of judgment he investigated including predictions of business failures and the outcomes of sporting events. As you might guess, the psychologists had a hard time swallowing these incendiary findings. No doubt, it would have perturbed bankers and other professionals he evaluated if his research had as much impact outside of psychology as it did inside. After gathering a large number of similar findings in many fields he stated:

> *There is no controversy in social science which shows such a large body of qualitatively diverse studies coming out so uniformly in the same direction as this one. When you're pushing 90 investigations [now closer to 150], predicting everything from the outcome of football games to the diagnosis of liver disease and when you can hardly come up with a half dozen studies showing even a weak tendency in favor of the [human expert], it is time to draw a practical conclusion.*[10]

Others would continue to find similar results. Meehl and his colleagues went on to apply a more rigorous standard of comparison to a set of 136 individual studies comparing expert judgment to what the researcher called "mechanical" models. They concluded that he found more "ties" between experts and statistical models than Meehl did (about half), but in terms of results that were clear wins, they were much more likely to be in favor of the statistical model (about 40% were clear wins for statistics, about 10% were clear wins for the expert judges).[11,12]

Another researcher conducted one of the largest and longest running studies of the performance of experts at predictions. Philip Tetlock tracked the forecasts of 284 experts in many topics over a 20-year period. In total, he had gathered more than 82,000 individual forecasts covering elections, wars, economics, and more. Tetlock summarized these findings in his book *Expert Political Judgment: How Good Is It? How Can We Know?*[13] His conclusion was perhaps even more strongly worded than Meehl's:

> *It is impossible to find any domain in which humans clearly outperformed crude extrapolation algorithms, less still sophisticated statistical ones.*

In the face of overwhelming evidence, one might think the presumed superiority of expert opinion should at least be in doubt in those cases where it is not debunked entirely. But this is not the case. Where the objections to statistics are countered with empirical evidence, the argument merely mutates into a different strategy of denouncing the *meaningfulness or even ethics* of probabilities and other numbers especially when applied to people.

THE BROADER OBJECTION TO THE USEFULNESS OF "STATISTICS"

> *After all, facts are facts, and although we may quote one to another with a chuckle the words of the Wise Statesman, "Lies—damned lies—and statistics," still there are some easy figures the simplest must understand, and the astutest cannot wriggle out of.*
> —Leonard Courtney, First Baron Courtney, Royal Statistical Society president (1897–1899)

Another objection is based on the idea that, even though a measurement is possible, it would be meaningless because statistics and probability itself are meaningless ("Lies, Damned Lies, and Statistics," as it were[14]). As we saw, even among educated professionals, there are often profound misconceptions about simple probabilities, statistics, and decisions under uncertainty. Unfortunately, the two Kahneman and Tversky studies mentioned so far are just the tip of the iceberg. Some misconceptions are so stunning that it's hard to know where to begin to address them. Here are a few examples I've run into:

> "Everything is equally likely, because we don't know what will happen."
> —*Mentioned by someone who attended one of my seminars*

"I don't have any tolerance for risk at all because I never take risks."
—*The words of a midlevel manager at an insurance company client of mine*
"How can I know the range if I don't even know the mean?"
—*Said by a client of Sam Savage, PhD, colleague and promoter of statistical analysis methods*
"How can we know the probability of a coin landing on heads is 50% if we don't know what is going to happen?"
—*A graduate student (no kidding) who attended a lecture I gave at the London School of Economics*
"You can prove anything with statistics."
—*A very widely used phrase about statistics*

Let's address the last comment first. I will offer a $10,000 prize, right now, to anyone who can use statistics to prove the statement "You can prove anything with statistics." By "prove" I mean in the sense that it can be published in any major math or science journal. The test for this will be that it *is* published in any major math or science journal (such a monumental discovery certainly will be). By "anything" I mean, literally, anything, including every statement in math or science that has already been conclusively disproved. I will use the term "statistics," however, as broadly as possible. The recipient of this award can resort to any accepted field of mathematics and science that even partially addresses probability theory, sampling methods, decision theory, and so on. I originally announced this prize in the first edition of this book in 2007 and, like the Randi Prize for proof of the paranormal (mentioned in Chapter 2), it still goes unclaimed. But unlike the Randi Prize, not a single person has even attempted to claim it (at the time of this edition in 2014). Perhaps the claim "You can prove anything with statistics" is even more obviously absurd than paranormal claims like "I can read your mind."

The point is that when people say, "You can prove anything with statistics," they probably don't really mean "statistics," they just mean broadly the use of numbers (especially, for some reason, percentages). And they really don't mean "anything" or even "prove." What they really mean is that "numbers can be used to confuse people, especially the gullible ones lacking basic skills with numbers." With this, I completely agree, but it is an entirely different claim.

The other statements I just listed tend to be misunderstandings about more fundamental concepts behind probabilities, risk, and measurements in general. Clearly, the reason we use probabilities is specifically because we can't be certain of outcomes. Obviously, we all take some risks just driving to work, and we all, therefore, have some level of tolerance for risk.

As with the "You can prove anything with statistics" claim, I usually find that the people making these other irrational claims don't even quite mean what they say, and their own choices will betray their stated beliefs. If you ask someone to enter a betting pool to guess the outcome of the number of heads in 12 coin tosses, even the person who claims odds can't be assigned will prefer the numbers around or near six heads. The person who claims to accept no risk at all will still fly to Moscow using Aeroflot (an airline with a safety record worse than any U.S. carrier) to pick up a $1 million prize.

In response to the skeptics of statistical models he met in his own profession, Paul Meehl proposed a variation on the game of Russian roulette.[15] In his modified version there are two revolvers: one with one bullet and five empty chambers and one with five bullets and one empty chamber. Meehl then asks us to imagine that he is a "sadistic decision-theorist" running experiments in a detention camp. Meehl asks, "Which revolver would you choose under these circumstances? Whatever may be the detailed, rigorous, logical reconstruction of your reasoning processes, can you honestly say that you would let me pick the gun or that you would flip a coin to decide between them?"

Meehl summarized the responses: "I have asked quite a few persons this question, and I have not yet encountered anybody who alleged that he would just as soon play his single game of Russian roulette with the five-shell weapon." Clearly, those who answered Meehl's question didn't really think probabilities were meaningless. As we shall see before the end of this chapter, Meehl's hypothetical game is less "hypothetical" than you might think.

Meehl often noted that, sometimes, the objection to using stats boils down to nothing more than an irrational fear of numbers causing some to believe math somehow detracts from understanding or appreciation. On the one hand, the most mathematically competent can experience an overwhelming sense of awe from a revelation provided by an equation. The famed mathematician and logician Bertrand Russell once said, "*Mathematics*, rightly viewed, possesses not only truth, but supreme *beauty*. . . ." And even for many baseball fans there is particular delight in understanding the game through statistics. (This was throughout the history of the game, even before management found out how to make better teams with it.)

On the other hand, some believe that the mere use of stats somehow actually reduces enjoyment not only of the people using the math but others not using it. *New York Times* writer Murray Chase once complained about the new "stats mongers" in baseball saying that the introduction of what he called "new age stats" actually "threatens to undermine most fans' enjoyment of baseball and the human factor therein."[16] Really? What remarkable malevolent powers math has indeed if it can be used to deny—at some unspecified distance—enjoyment even to those not using it. He concluded, "People play baseball. Numbers don't." True. Numbers don't actually *play* baseball. But numbers are used to determine outcomes of games. Furthermore, words don't actually play baseball, either. I don't count myself as a big baseball fan but, apparently, for many fans, numbers can paint a much more enjoyable picture of the game than the words of a math-phobic sports writer.

ETHICAL OBJECTIONS TO MEASUREMENT

Let's discuss one final reason why someone might argue that a measurement shouldn't be made. This objection comes in the form of some sort of *ethical* objection to measurement. The potential accountability and perceived finality of numbers combine with a previously learned distrust of "statistics" to create resistance to measurement. Beyond the mere claim of a reduction of appreciation mentioned previously, measurements can even be perceived as "dehumanizing" an issue. There is often a sense of righteous indignation when someone attempts to measure touchy topics, such as the value of an endangered species or even a human life, yet it is done routinely and for good reason.

The Environmental Protection Agency (EPA) and other government agencies have to allocate limited resources to protect our environment, our health, and even our lives. One of the many IT investments I helped the EPA assess was a Geographic Information System (GIS) for better tracking of methyl mercury, a substance suspected of actually lowering the IQ of children who are exposed to high concentrations. To assess whether this system is justified, we must ask an important, albeit uncomfortable, question: Is the potentially avoided IQ loss worth the investment of more than $3 million over a five-year period? Someone might choose to be morally indignant at the very idea of even asking such a question, much less answering it. You might think that any IQ point for any number of children is worth the investment.

But wait. The EPA also had to consider investments in other systems that track effects of new pollutants that sometimes result in premature death. The EPA has limited resources, and there are a large number of initiatives it could invest in that might improve public health, save endangered species, and improve the overall environment. It has to compare initiatives by asking "How many children and how many IQ points?" as well as "How many premature deaths?"

Sometimes we even have to ask, "How premature is the death?" Should the death of a very old person be considered equal to that of a younger person, when limited resources force us to make choices? At one point, the EPA considered using what it called a "senior death discount." A death of a person over 70 was valued about 38% less than a person under 70. Some people were indignant with this and, in 2003, the controversy caused then EPA administrator Christine Todd Whitman to announce that this discount was used for "guidance," not policy making, and that it was discontinued.[17] Of course, even saying they are the same is itself a measurement of how we express our values quantitatively. But if they are the same, I wonder how far we can take that equivalency. Should a 99-year-old with several health problems be worth the same effort to save as a 5-year-old? Whatever your answer is, it is a measurement of the relative value you hold for each.

If we insist on being ignorant of the relative values of various public welfare programs (which is the necessary result of a refusal to measure their value), then we will almost certainly allocate limited resources in a way that solves less valuable problems for more money. This is because there is a large combination of possible investments to address these issues and the best answer, in such cases, is never obvious without some understanding of magnitudes.

In other cases, it seems the very existence of any error at all (which, we know, is almost always the case in empirical measurements) makes an attempted measure morally outrageous to some. Stephen J. Gould, author of *The Mismeasure of Man*, had vehemently argued against the usefulness, or even morality, of measurements of the intellect using IQ or "g" (the general factor or intelligence that is supposed to underlie IQ scores). He said: "'g' is nothing more than an artifact of the mathematical procedure used to calculate it."[18] Although IQ scores and "g" surely have various errors and biases, they are, of course, not just mathematical procedures but are also based on observations (scores on tests). And since we now understand that measurement does not mean "total lack of error," the objection that intelligence can't be measured because tests have error is toothless.

Other researchers point out that the view that measures of intelligence are not measures of any real phenomenon is inconsistent with the fact that these different "mathematical procedures" are highly correlated with each other[19] and even correlated with social phenomena like criminal behavior or income.[20] Even presuming substantial errors in testing methods, how can IQ be a purely arbitrary figure if it correlates so well with other observations in reality? I won't attempt to resolve that dispute here, but I am curious about how Gould, if he were alive today, would have addressed issues like the environmental effects of a toxic substance that affects mental development. Return to the EPA project where we considered the uncertain but potentially significant effects of exposure to methyl mercury. Since one of the most ghastly effects of methyl mercury on children is potential IQ points lost, is Gould saying no such effect can be real, or is he saying that even if it were real, we dare not measure it because of errors among the subjects? Either way, we would have to end up ignoring the potential health costs of this toxic substance and we might be forced—lacking information to the contrary—to reserve funds for another program. Too bad for the kids.

Of course, the real cost of ignoring statistics because of misguided ethics is not limited to environmental policy. Meehl's Russian roulette question was tragically similar to a real-world case of a psychotically depressed patient. In the very same paper, Meehl states that, based on historical data, the chance of a psychotically depressed patient committing suicide is one in six.[15] Meehl explains:

"If the responsible clinician does not recognize a psychotically depressed patient as such, and (therefore) fails to treat him as having a suicide risk of this magnitude, what he is in effect doing is handing the patient a revolver with one live shell and five empty chambers."

In an actual case Meehl recounts, a young but well-meaning clinician gave such a patient a weekend pass from the hospital. During the pass, the patient got access to a gun and killed himself. The patient exhibited behaviors that were convincing evidence of this level of depression—namely, being utterly mute. The clinician was just not aware of the risks implied by the data. It seemed to Meehl that the clinician (who Meehl points out had a 3.8 GPA) was not even trained to appreciate how such statistical information could have saved a life. In the same paper, he goes on to say:

Some of those who are "teaching" and "supervising" him either don't know these things themselves or don't think it is important for him to know them. This hapless student is at the educational mercy of a crew that is so unscholarly, antiscientific, "groupy-groupy," and "touchy-feely" that they have almost no concern for facts, statistics, diagnostic assessment, or the work of the intellect generally.

Meehl's statement is not kind, but, more importantly, not wrong. Meehl had often lamented that many in the clinical psychology profession have developed a kind of "anti-statistics" attitude. In his writings he has spent much time refuting objections he encounters—like the alleged "ethical" concerns of "treating a patient like a number" or that statistics aren't "holistic" enough or the belief that their years of experience are preferable to simple statistical abstractions.[10]

What strikes me the most about the objections Meehl encounters is how very familiar they are to me in my experience outside of psychology.

I've heard the same objections—sometimes word-for-word—from some managers and policy makers. The real tragedy of Meehl's example is that such thinking is so common. In these cases, protecting decision makers' sensitivities about statistics is, apparently, considered more important than protecting shareholders or even public health and safety.

The fact is that the preference for ignorance over even marginal reductions in ignorance is never the moral high ground. If decisions are made under a self-imposed state of higher uncertainty, policy makers (or even businesses like, say, airplane manufacturers) are betting on our lives with a higher chance of erroneous allocation of limited resources. In measurement, as in many other human endeavors, ignorance is not only wasteful but can also be dangerous.

> *Ignorance is never better than knowledge.*
> —Enrico Fermi, winner of the 1938 Nobel Prize for Physics

REVERSING OLD ASSUMPTIONS

Many decision makers avoid even trying to make an observation by thinking of a variety of obstacles to measurements. If you want to measure how much time people spend in a particular activity by using a survey, they might say: "Yes, but people won't remember exactly how much time they spend." Or if you were getting customer preferences by a survey, they might say: "There is so much variance among our customers that you would need a huge sample." If you were attempting to show whether a particular initiative increased sales, they respond: "But lots of factors affect sales. You'll never know how much that initiative affected it." Objections like this are statements that are not themselves based on calculations. The fact is, these people have no idea whether such issues will make measurement futile. They simply presume it.

Such critics are working with a set of vague preconceptions about the difficulty of measurement. They might even claim to have a background in measurement that provides some authority (e.g., they took two semesters of statistics 10 or 20 years ago). I won't say those presumptions actually turn out to be true or untrue in every particular case. However, I will say they are unproductive if they are simply presumptions. What can be inferred from the data already possessed or the likelihood that new data would reduce uncertainty are conclusions that can be made after some specific calculations, though these are virtually never attempted prior to making claims about the impossibility of measurement.

Let's make some deliberate and productive assumptions instead of ill-considered presumptions. I propose a contrarian set of assumptions

---

Four Useful Measurement Assumptions

1. It's been measured before.
2. You have far more data than you think.
3. You need far less data than you think.
4. Useful, new observations are more accessible than you think.

---

that—because they are assumptions—may not always be true in every single case but in practice turn out to be much more effective.

It's Been Measured Before

No matter how difficult or "unique" your measurement problem seems to you, assume it has been done already by someone else, perhaps in another field if not your own. If this assumption turns out not to be true, then take comfort in knowing that you might have a shot at a Nobel Prize for the discovery. Seriously, I've noticed that there is a tendency among professionals in every field to perceive their field as unique in terms of the burden of uncertainty. The conversation generally goes something like this: "Unlike other industries, in our industry every problem is unique and unpredictable," or "Problems in my field have too many factors to allow for quantification," and so on. I've done work in lots of different fields, and some individuals in most of these fields make these same claims. So far, each one of them has turned out to have fairly standard measurement problems not unlike those in other fields.

In the next chapter we talk about conducting initial research for a measurement problem. While it is common for academics to dig up prior research, this practice seems to be vastly underutilized by management. When managers think about measuring productivity, performance, quality, risk, or customer satisfaction, it strikes me as surprisingly rare that the first place they start is looking for existing research on the topic. Even with tools like Google and Google Scholar that make this simpler than ever before, there is a tendency with many managers to start each problem from scratch. Fortunately, this is easy to fix.

It is also helpful to have some diversity in one's knowledge of measurement methods across different fields—or at least have just enough breadth to know that there may be similar methods worth exploring. If you realize that problems in very different industries or professions will be mathematically similar to something you may be working with, you are more likely to at least consider looking outside of your comfort zone for a solution. Starting in Chapter 9, for example, we will start to talk about methods for what might seem to some to be impossible measurements.

You Have Far More Data than You Think

The information you need to answer the question is somewhere within your reach and, if you just took the time to think about it, you might find it. Few executives are even remotely aware of all the data that are routinely tracked and recorded in their organization. The things you care about measuring are also things that tend to leave tracks, if you are resourceful enough to find them.

One way to underestimate the amount of available data is to assume that only direct answers to our questions are useful. Eratosthenes saw data about the curvature of the Earth in the angles that shadows made. Enrico Fermi showed his students that they had more data than they thought regarding the number of piano tuners in Chicago (since they knew something about the population, ownership of pianos, how many pianos could be tuned in a day, etc.). If they thought that the only data they could use was cartography data that circumnavigated the globe or a detailed jobs survey of piano tuners, Eratosthenes and Enrico could easily have thrown up their hands in despair. Like many managers confronting a measurement that appears to be difficult, they would not have gotten past the perceived obstacle of having little or no data. Most scientific discoveries are far from direct observations. Nature often leaves the scientist only a trail of tiny crumbs and faint clues.

It may be hard to see related information, however, if we think of each situation as so unique that data from other situations is irrelevant. I could say that each project is unique, therefore data about previous projects tells me nothing about what I'm trying to measure. This would be similar to your life insurance company being unable to compute your insurance premium stymied by the lack of data on *your death*. The only data they have on your death rate is the fact that you have not yet died. In this hypothetical example of the stumped actuaries, they might insist that since you are a unique individual with unique habits, DNA, and environment, they could not compare you to other people.

This is actually a type of fallacy. I've called it the Fallacy of Close Analogy but something similar was called The Uniqueness Fallacy. This fallacy is based on that idea that if a situation is unique, there is nothing in general we can learn by examining other situations. Examining different situations may not be perfect, but it is an improvement. As Paul Meehl showed, interpolating from statistical data outperformed experts even when each situation was "unique" in some way (e.g., judging the risk of parole violations or the potential of an applicant for medical school). Indeed, if we can't learn anything from somewhat dissimilar situations, then what is the basis for *experience*? I have heard managers say that since each new product is unique, they cannot extrapolate from historical data . . . therefore, they have to rely on their experience. Note that this is said *with no hint of irony.*

Real-life insurance companies encounter no such obstacle. They realize that, even though we are each unique, they can interpolate the risk of paying out life insurance claims by examining the mortality rates of people of different ages, genders, health, habits, and so on. The fallacy of close analogy causes one to define an unnecessarily small group as the population of interest. In the same way, each new information system implemented in a company is unique, but they have a long history of implementing new information systems.

In my book, *The Failure of Risk Management,* I recounted an example from NASA where mission scientists and engineers believed each mission was so unique that one simply could not extrapolate from past mission experience—and, therefore, they were better off relying on their experienced judgment. But this is a testable claim. For over 100 space mission projects, the judgments of the scientists and engineers regarding the risk of cost overruns, schedule overruns, and chance of mission failure was assessed.[21]

Even though each mission *really was arguably unique* for one or many reasons, the model based on historical data was consistently better than the mission scientists and engineers at predicting overruns of cost and schedule and even mission failures. Again, it is important to remember that experience of the NASA scientists and engineers, like the statistical models, must be based on historical data. If there is no basis to apply statistical models and scientific evidence, then there can be no basis for experience, either. The uniqueness fallacy seems like the basis for many of the objections Paul Meehl encountered within his profession. Each patient is unique, and therefore nothing can be generalized from past experience—at least quantitatively. For some reason, many psychologists seem to believe that qualitative opinions of experts always evade the same uniqueness fallacy objections.

Furthermore, with the massive amount of data publicly available today, any claim about a shortage of data should not be taken on faith. New tools and data sources are continuously created and, if we are resourceful, they can be leveraged. For example, if I want to know how my book sales are going from week to week, but my publisher only reports total sales each month, I can still infer an approximate number based on the continuously updated Amazon book ranks. Research shows how presidential approval ratings can be inferred from tracking Twitter traffic. Other research shows how changes in unemployment and retail sales can be estimated by tracking data from tools like Google Trends.

The amount of publicly available data added every day to the Internet—particularly social media—exceeds the data collected in the Census of the United States in a decade. What we can analyze from that is limited more by our imagination than the amount of data available. This was the topic of my book *Pulse: The New Science of Harnessing Internet Buzz to Track Threats and Opportunities*. This and other new tools, like the revolution in personal measurement devices with socially shared data (for measuring weight, activity, sleep, and much more) will be covered more in Chapter 13 of this book, "New Measurement Instruments for Management." As we advance further into the twenty-first century, we should find a shortage of data to be rarer and rarer. If Eratosthenes could estimate the size of the planet from data about a few shadows, I wonder what he could have done now.

You Need Far Less Data than You Think

As we showed with the Rule of Five and the Single Sample Majority Inference, small samples can be informative, especially when you start from a position of minimal information. In fact, mathematically speaking, *when you know almost nothing, almost anything will tell you something*. Kahneman and Tversky showed that the error of a sample is often overestimated, which results in an underestimation of the value of a sample. Granted, they also showed other situations where the value of a sample can be overestimated, but only in the interpretation of a very specific kind of hypothesis testing problem which is not really representative of most sample interpretations for decision makers.

When we work out how much "uncertainty reduction" we get from a given set of data in more practical examples, managers are often surprised by how much they learned from a little bit of data. I've met statistically sophisticated scientists who didn't believe in the Rule of Five or the Single Sample Majority Inference until they worked out the math for themselves. But, as Eratosthenes shows us, there are clever ways to squeeze interesting findings from minute amounts of data. Enrico showed us that we can get useful information by simply decomposing a problem and estimating its components. Emily showed us that we don't need a giant clinical trial to debunk a popular healthcare method.

Having More and Needing Less than You Think: An Example from Measuring Teaching Effectiveness

Here is one extreme case of the "You have more data than you think" and the "You need less data than you think" assumptions from the world of measuring teaching methods in public school systems. Dr. Bruce Law is the Head of School for Chicago Virtual Charter School (CVCS). CVCS is an innovative public school that teaches primarily through online, remote-learning methods that emphasize individualized curricula. Dr. Law asked me to help define some useful metrics and measurement methods to evaluate the performance of teachers and the school. As is always the case, the first big part of the issue was defining what "performance" meant in these situations and how this information was expected to affect real decisions.

Dr. Law's primary concern was, at first, not having enough data to measure quantities like "student engagement" and "differentiation" as outcomes of effective teaching. But as we talked, I found that the majority of the classes are taught online with an interactive web-conferencing tool that records every teaching session. This online tool allows students to "raise hands," ask questions by either voice or text chat, and interact with the teacher in the instructional session. Everything the teachers or students say or do online is recorded. *The problem was not a lack of data but the existence of so much data* that wasn't in a structured, easily analyzed database. Like most managers confronted with a similar situation, CVCS imagined it could not measure anything meaningful without reviewing all the data (i.e., listening to every minute of every session). So we defined a couple of sampling methods that allowed the managers to select recordings of sessions and particular slices of time, each a minute or two long, throughout a recorded session. For those randomly chosen time slices, they could sample what the teacher was saying and what the students were doing.

As Dr. Law put it, they went from thinking they had no relevant data, to "Yes, we have lots of data, but who has to the time to go through all of that?" to "We can get a good sense of what is going on instructionally without looking at all of it."

We will find in later chapters that the first few observations are usually the highest payback in uncertainty reduction for a given amount of effort. In fact, it is a common misconception that the higher your uncertainty, the more data you need to significantly reduce it. Again, when you know next to nothing, you don't need much additional data to tell you something you didn't know before.

Useful, New Observations Are More Accessible than You Think

Scientific method isn't just about *having* data. It's also about *getting* data. Emily Rosa didn't already have the data she needed to test the ability of touch therapists to detect auras. So she just set up a simple and economical experiment to get the data. Even if you really do lack the data currently to make a useful measurement, there are informative new observations that can be gathered if we are resourceful.

When it comes to methods to gather new data, try working with the assumption that the first approach you think of is the "hard way" to measure. Assume that, with a little more ingenuity, you can identify an easier way. The Cleveland Orchestra, for example, wanted to measure whether its performances were improving. Many business analysts might propose some sort of randomized patron survey repeated over time. Perhaps they might think of questions that rate a particular performance (if the patron remembers) from "poor" to "excellent," and maybe they would evaluate the performance on several parameters and combine all these parameters into a "satisfaction index."

The Cleveland Orchestra was just a bit more resourceful with the data available: It started counting the number of standing ovations. While there is no obvious difference among performances that differ by a couple of standing ovations, if we see a significant increase over several performances with a new conductor, then we can draw some useful conclusions about that new conductor. It was a measurement in every sense, a lot less effort than a survey, and—some would say—more meaningful. (I can't disagree.)

So, don't assume that the only way to reduce your uncertainty is to use an impractically sophisticated method. Are you trying to get published in a peer-reviewed journal, or are you just trying to reduce your uncertainty about a real-life business decision? Build on the "You need less data than you think" assumption and you may find that you don't have to gather as much data as you thought.

Above all else, the intuitive experimenter, as we showed the origin of the word "experiment" denotes, *makes an attempt*. It's a habit. Unless you believe you already know in advance the precise outcome of an attempted observation—of any kind—then that observation tells you something you didn't already know. Make a few more observations, and you know even more. Think of measurement as iterative. Start measuring it. You can always adjust the method based on initial findings.

There might be the rare case where, only for lack of the most sophisticated measurement methods, something seems immeasurable. But for those things labeled "intangible," more advanced, sophisticated methods are almost never what are lacking. Things that are thought to be intangible tend to be so uncertain that even the most basic measurement methods are likely to reduce some uncertainty.

Notes

1. C. Shannon, "A Mathematical Theory of Communication," *The Bell System Technical Journal* 27 (July/October, 1948): 379–423, 623–656.
2. S. S. Stevens, "On the Theory of Scales and Measurement," *Science* 103 (1946): 677–680.
3. Paul E. Meehl, "The Power of Quantitative Thinking". Speech delivered at the meeting of the American Psychological Society, Washington, DC, May 23, 1998.
4. Dariush Hayati, Zahra Ranjbar, and Ezatollah Karami, "Measuring Agricultural Sustainability," *Sustainable Agriculture Reviews* 5 (2011): 73–100.
5. Thomas M. Parris and Robert W. Kates, "Characterizing and Measuring Sustainable Development," *Annual Review of Environment and Resources* 28 (2003): 559–586.
6. Lin Zhen and Jayant K. Routray, "Operational Indicators for Measuring Agricultural Sustainability in Developing Countries," *Environmental Management* 32, no. 1 (2003): 34–46.
7. Daniel Kahneman and Amos Tversky, "Subjective Probability: A Judgment of Representativeness," *Cognitive Psychology*, 3 (1972): 430–454.
8. Amos Tversky and Daniel Kahneman, "Belief in the Law of Small Numbers," *Psychological Bulletin* 76, no. 2 (1971): 105–110, doi:10.1037/h0031322.
9. George W. Cobb, "Reconsidering Statistics Education: A National Science Foundation Conference," *Journal of Statistics Education* 1 (1993): 63–83.
10. Paul Meehl, "Causes and Effects of My Disturbing Little Book," *Journal of Personality Assessment* 50 (1986): 370–375.
11. William M. Grove and Paul E. Meehl, "Comparative Efficiency of Informal (Subjective, Impressionistic) and Formal (Mechanical, Algorithmic) Prediction Procedures: The Clinical-Statistical Controversy," *Psychology, Public Policy, and Law* 2 (1996): 293–323. doi:10.1037//1076-8971.2.2.293.
12. William M. Grove, David H. Zald, Boyd S. Lebow, Beth E. Snitz, and Chad Nelson, "Clinical versus Mechanical Prediction: A Meta-Analysis," *Psychological Assessment* 12, no. 1 (2000): 19–30.
13. Philip E. Tetlock, *Expert Political Judgment: How Good Is It? How Can We Know?* (Princeton, NJ: Princeton University Press, 2006).
14. This statement is often incorrectly attributed to Mark Twain, although he surely helped to popularize it. Twain got it from either one of two nineteenth-century British politicians, Benjamin Disraeli or Henry Labouchere.
15. Paul E. Meehl, "Why I Do Not Attend Case Conferences," *Psychodiagnosis: Selected Papers* (Minneapolis: University of Minnesota Press, 1973).

16. Murray Chass, "As Season Approaches, Some Topics Should Be Off Limits," *New York Times*, February 2, 2007.
17. Katharine Q. Seelye and John Tierney, "'Senior Death Discount' Assailed: Critics Decry Making Regulations Based on Devaluing Elderly Lives," *New York Times*, May 8, 2003.
18. Stephen Jay Gould, *The Mismeasure of Man* (New York: W. W. Norton, 1981).
19. Reflections on Stephen Jay Gould's *The Mismeasure of Man*: John B. Carroll, "A Retrospective Review," *Intelligence* 21 (1995): 121–134.
20. K. Tambs, J. M. Sundet, P. Magnus, and K. Berg, "Genetic and Environmental Contributions to the Covariance between Occupational Status, Educational Attainment, and IQ: A Study of Twins," *Behavior Genetics* 19, no. 2 (March 1989): 209–222.
21. C. W. Freaner, R. E. Bitten, D. A. Bearden, and D. L. Emmons, "An Assessment of the Inherent Optimism in Early Conceptual Designs and Its Effect on Cost and Schedule Growth." Paper presented at the Space Systems Cost Analysis Group/Cost Analysis and Forecasting/European Aerospace Cost Engineering Working Group 2008 Joint International Conference, European Space Research and Technology Centre, Noordwijk, The Netherlands, May 15–16, European Space Agency, Paris, France.

A Purely Philosophical Interlude #1

The Great Schism (in statistics): Bayesians versus Frequentists

It is unanimously agreed that statistics depends somehow on probability. But, as to what probability is and how it is connected with statistics, there has seldom been such complete disagreement and breakdown of communication since the Tower of Babel.
— L. J. Savage (1917–1971), American mathematician[1]

One might think that statisticians would have by now agreed upon a definition for probability. In fact, there is a long-running debate on this topic between two camps: the Bayesians and the frequentists. Both camps are mathematically sound and defended by great thinkers. Throughout the early- to mid-twentieth century, nothing put a spotlight on this divide as much as a series of debates between the frequentist biologist Ronald A. Fisher and the Bayesian geophysicst and astronomer Harold Jeffreys. In fact, it was Fisher who coined the term "Bayesian" as a derogatory reference to proponents of the contrary view. These British citizens were both knighted for their scientific contributions and both are known perhaps more for their work in statistics than in their original fields.

As previously mentioned, I will be using the Bayesian interpretation for entirely practical reasons. That is, we use probability as the state of uncertainty of an observer, not a physical property of what is being observed. To the frequentists, on the other hand, probability is an objective aspect of reality independent of personal knowledge. To them, a probability is a feature of reality like mass or distance which is independent of whether there is even anyone to observe it. It is their position that only this view of probability can be considered to be "objective."

In an attempt to define probability in an objective way, frequentists have to define it as a type of idealized frequency limit—the proportion of times something would occur only in a strictly repeatable process in a purely random fashion and over an infinite number of trials. Bayesians would argue that none of these conditions apply in the real world. This definition becomes a purely mathematical abstraction that relies on inadequately defined concepts like "random" and still fails to avoid subjectivity. More on this in other *Purely Philosophical Interludes* throughout the book.

I need to add in this first Purely Philosophical Interlude that, while we will treat uncertainty as the state of a person, not a state of a thing, it is possible that a change in uncertainty of the observer, through observation, also changes the state of the thing observed. Some readers will note that this occurs in quantum physics. In this field it is conventional to speak of uncertainty as an actual feature of the particle itself, not just a state of the observer. However, there is debate even on this in physics. A small and growing group of physicists hold a view called "quantum Bayesianism" or simply Qbism. Respected physicists like Edwin T. Jaynes (b. 1922, d. 1998) and his contemporaries make a rigorous case for the idea that even uncertainty in quantum mechanics is ultimately still only observer uncertainty and that this greatly simplifies certain problems in the field.

This may seem entirely tangential to our understanding of uncertainty from the point of view of decision making, but it illustrates a point. If a person believes that the subjective view of probability—the view that probability really only describes the state of an observer—seems unscientific or less rigorous in any way than the frequentists' position, that would be a mistake. Jaynes, who specialized in the undeniably scientific field of quantum mechanics, explains why.

> *We are now in possession of proven theorems and masses of worked out numerical examples. As a result, the superiority of Bayesian methods is now a thoroughly demonstrated fact in a hundred different areas. One can argue with a philosophy; it is not so easy to argue with a computer printout, which says to us: 'Independently of all your philosophy, here are the facts of actual performance'. . . . Thus we continue to argue vigorously for the Bayesian methods; but we ask the reader to note that our arguments now proceed by citing facts rather than proclaiming a philosophical or ideological position.*
> —Edwin T. Jaynes, *Probability Theory: The Logic of Science*, 1995

Note

1. Leonard J. Savage, *The Foundations of Statistics* (New York: John Wiley & Sons, 1954).

## PART II

Before You Measure

## CHAPTER 4

Clarifying the Measurement Problem

Confronted with apparently difficult measurements, it helps to put the proposed measurement in context. Prior to making a measurement, we need to answer the following:

- What is the decision this measurement is supposed to support?
- What is the definition of the thing being measured in terms of observable consequences and how, exactly, does this thing matter to the decision being asked (i.e., how do we compute outcomes based on the value of this variable)?
- How much do you know about it now (i.e., what is your current level of uncertainty)?
- How does uncertainty about this variable create risk for the decision (e.g., is there a "threshold" value above which one action is preferred and below which another is preferred)?
- What is the value of additional information?

In this chapter, we will focus on the first two questions. Once we have answered them, we can determine what we know now about the uncertain quantity, the amount of risk due to that uncertainty, and the value of reducing that uncertainty further. That covers the next three chapters. In the Applied Information Economics (AIE) method I have been using, these are the first questions I ask with respect to anything I am asked to measure. The answers to these questions often completely change not just *how* organizations should measure something but *what* they should measure.

The first two questions define what this measurement means within the framework of the decisions which depend on it. In the context of management, if a measurement matters at all, it is because it must have some conceivable effect on decisions and behavior. If managers can't identify a decision that could be affected by a proposed measurement and how it could change those decisions, then the measurement simply has no value.

For example, if you wanted to measure "product quality," it becomes relevant to ask what actions could be affected by having less uncertainty about it and to ask the more general question of what "product quality" means. Are you using the information to decide on whether to change an ongoing manufacturing process? If so, how bad does quality have to be before you make changes to the process? Are you measuring product quality to compute management bonuses in a quality program? If so, what's the formula? All this, of course, depends on you knowing exactly what you mean by "quality" in the first place.

When I was with Management Consulting Services in what was then the "Big 8" firm of Coopers & Lybrand in the late 1980s, I was on a consulting engagement with a small regional bank that was wondering how to streamline its reporting processes. The bank had been using a microfilm-based system to store the 60-plus reports it got from branches every week, most of which were elective and not required for regulatory purposes. These reports were generated because someone in management—at some point in time—thought they needed to know the information. These days, a good Oracle programmer might argue that it would be fairly easy to create and manage these queries; at the time, however, keeping up with these requests for reports was beginning to be a major burden. When I asked bank managers what decisions these reports supported, they could identify only a few cases where the elective reports had, or *ever could*, change a decision. Perhaps not surprisingly, the same reports that could not be tied to real management decisions were rarely even read. Even though someone initially had requested each of these reports, the original need was apparently forgotten. Once the managers realized that many reports simply had no bearing on decisions, they understood that those reports must, therefore, have no value.

Years later, a similar question was posed to me by staff of the Office of the Secretary of Defense. They wondered what the value was of a large number of weekly and monthly reports. When I asked if they could identify a single decision that each report could conceivably affect, they found quite a few that had no effect on any decision. Likewise, the information value of those reports was zero.

Once we have defined our terms and how decisions are impacted, we still have two more questions: How much do you know about this now and what is it worth to measure? You have to know what it is worth to measure because you would probably come up with a very different measurement for quality if measuring it is worth $10 million per year than if it is worth $10,000 per year. And we can't compute the value until we know how much we know now. So, next, we describe this approach as a series of specific steps that will guide us through much of the rest of the book.

TOWARD A UNIVERSAL APPROACH TO MEASUREMENT

In Chapter 1, I proposed a five-step outline for a decision-oriented framework, which applies universally to any measurement problem. Even with all the measurements there are to make, any measurements that inform real decisions could benefit from that particular procedure. Every component of this procedure is well known to some particular field of research or industry, but few routinely put them together into a coherent method.

Now, let's add a bit more detail to each of these five steps—starting, of course, with defining the decision. These steps, the basis of Applied Information Economics, also outline the remaining chapters of the book:

1. *Define a decision problem and the relevant uncertainties.* If people ask "How do we measure X?" they may already be putting the cart before the horse. The first question is "What is your dilemma?" Then we can define all of the variables relevant to the dilemma and determine what we really mean by ambiguous ideas like "training quality" or "economic opportunity." (This step is the focus of this chapter.)
2. *Determine what you know now.* We need to quantify your uncertainty about unknown quantities in the identified decision. This is done by learning how to describe your uncertainty in terms of ranges and probabilities. This is a teachable skill. Defining the relevant decision and how much uncertainty we have about it helps us determine the risk involved (covered in Chapters 5 and 6).
3. *Compute the value of additional information.* Information has value because it reduces risk in decisions. Knowing the "information value" of a measurement allows us to both identify what to measure as well as informing us about how to measure it (covered in Chapter 7).

   If there are no variables with information values that justify the cost of any measurement approaches, skip to step 5.

4. *Apply the relevant measurement instrument(s) to high-value measurements.* We cover some of the basic measurement instruments, such as random sampling, controlled experiments, and some more obscure variations on these. We also talk about methods that allow us to squeeze more out of limited data, how to isolate the effects of one variable, how to quantify "soft" preferences, how new technologies

can be exploited for measurement, and how to make better use of human experts (covered in Chapters 8 to 13).

Repeat step 3.

5. *Make a decision and act on it.* When the economically justifiable amount of uncertainty has been removed, decision makers face a risk versus return decision. Any remaining uncertainty is part of this choice. To optimize this decision, the risk aversion of the decision maker can be quantified. An optimum choice can be calculated even in situations where there are enormous combinations of possible choices. We will build on these methods further with a discussion about quantifying risk aversion and other preferences and attitudes of decision makers. This and all of the previous steps are combined into practical project steps (covered in Chapters 11, 12, and 14).

Repeat step 1. (Even the subsequent tracking of results about a decision just made is always in the context of future decisions.)

THE UNEXPECTED CHALLENGE OF DEFINING A DECISION

As our five-step approach indicates, measurements start with defining a decision. However, defining the real decision may not be as obvious as it first looks. Many managers believe they need to measure something but, when pressed, have a hard time articulating a specific action the measurement would inform. Here are a few examples:

- I've heard managers say that they need to measure, say, project performance in order to track project progress. Of course, this is a circular statement. The question they need to ask is what might they change about the project if they knew more about its progress? Could they cancel it? Would they accelerate its implementation? Would they reallocate funds within the project?
- Managers may say they need to measure their carbon footprint or corporate image simply because these things are important. They are. But they are only important to *measure* if knowledge of the value could cause us to take different actions.
- Managers may simply say that some measurement helps make better decisions—but without specifying any particular decision. An unidentified decision is no better than having no decision in mind at all. If someone says they need to measure ecological impacts of residential development projects in order to make better development decisions, we don't let them off the hook just yet. We ask, "Okay, which specific decisions?"

- Sometimes the stated measurement implies a decision that is non-sensical. I've had IT clients who asked how they could measure the value of IT and I've had government agencies ask about the value of clean drinking water. What decision is implied by this proposed measurement? Are they measuring benefits for a cost-benefit justification of the item in question? In other words, are they seriously considering doing without IT or clean water? The problem is incorrectly presented as a yes/no choice among extremes—a false dichotomy. The real question may be whether some particular IT project is justified or whether some specific water policy is required. If those are the choices, the required measurements are not simply the total value of IT or clean water.
- In some cases the participants are impatient and want to skip the decision definition. Instead, they might simply want to "start measuring" or "start modeling." I tell my clients that this is sort of like being impatient with an architect designing a new building. Before knowing even the location of the building and even before determining that the building is a warehouse, residential home, or office building, some want to start pouring concrete and nailing boards together. The failure of getting the purpose identified correctly first has already lead to years of debate based on ambiguities. In some cases, the issues we were measuring were previously long-running disagreements which were only solved once they got the problem well-defined.

Dashboards and Decisions: Do They Go Together?

The difficulty of connecting measurements to decisions seems to start at the highest levels in an organization. Consider the popular set of tools known as corporate "dashboards." Dashboards are meant to be "at-a-glance" summaries, accessible through some secure website, of the organization's performance. The display often consists of dials and gauges in an attempt to emulate actual dashboards in planes or cars, but it also usually displays charts and graphs. The data consists of a dozen or more variables that could be financial, revenue, project status, or anything else the manager feels they need to know on a regular basis. A dashboard can definitely be a very powerful tool.

It is also routinely a wasted resource. The data on the dashboard was usually not selected with specific decisions in mind based on specific conditions for action. It was often merely hoped that when

(continued)

the right conditions arose in the data, the manager would recognize a need to act and already know what action is required in sufficient detail that they could react without any delay. It is usually not, for example, worked out in advance that when revenue at a particular store or region drops by 10% compared to seasonally and economically adjusted sales targets, that a predefined project will be executed to correct it. Nor was it worked out in advance that the 10% change was the point that justified that particular action.

Consequently, there is a risk that the need to act will be too subtle to be immediately and consistently detected among the combination of variables on the dashboard. It will be acted upon later than necessary or could be missed entirely. Another risk is that once the need to act is correctly identified, the manager will waste time deciding what to do and designing a specific response when the contingency could have been worked out in advance. These unnecessary delays in action can cost far more than the bother of simply articulating decisions in advance.

Decision-Oriented Measurements: For Scientists, Too

Dr. Keith Shepherd is a scientist who recognized the need to tie measurements of ecological impact to specific decisions. He is the principal soil scientist and science domain leader in land health in the World Agroforestry Centre (ICRAF) based in Nairobi—a part of the Consultative Group on International Agricultural Research (CGIAR) first mentioned in Chapter 3. In 2013, my team was helping CGIAR determine the key ecological, agricultural, and economic metrics to track for a proposed metrics database.

CGIAR realized that the reason for their measurements was to support decisions about agricultural and environmental interventions funded by the Bill & Melinda Gates Foundation, the World Bank, national governments, and other donors. Dr. Shepherd and his colleagues identified not one decision but a portfolio of different types of decisions about such topics as providing financial incentives for water management, building small dams versus large dams, and funding irrigation programs. In each area, we identified a specific pilot decision. In all, we had created seven different decision models.

Each decision model was in an Excel spreadsheet and included what the scientists refer to as an "impact pathway." The impact pathway simply shows how one thing affects another—fundamentally no different than models we would make for decisions related to the major technology investments or government policies. These different decision models would then be aggregated into an Intervention Decision Model (IDM) that could be reused on future decisions. This was a significant effort for HDR that involved everyone on my small team for several months and dozens of scientists from many fields. But the effort was appropriate given the number and significance of decision models we were creating. We were, after all, creating models so that donor resources could have a maximum return on reducing ecological impacts, famine, clean water shortages, and poverty throughout the developing world. Measuring such things as biodiversity, food security, and drought resistance provided my team the opportunity to see within one initiative virtually every kind of challenge I've seen in 20 years of solving complex measurement problems.

Identifying the decisions and building the decision models were just as challenging for CGIAR as they were for any other client in industry or government. Indeed, some of the decision models took several workshops just to identify a single specific decision to model. As Dr. Shepherd observed:

> *We discovered that it was difficult for researchers to think about measurements in terms of specific decisions their research would support and the specifics of alternative interventions that they might recommend. Previously, research managers would urge researchers to identify which variables they should be measuring to track progress towards achieving development goals, but without reference to any specific decision. They are used to thinking about how to measure quantities of interest, but not why.*

As ingrained as measurements-for-the-sake-of-measurements seemed to be with many of the scientists, they did understand the need for measurements to support specific decisions. Dr. Shepherd added, "We realized that forecasting intervention impacts with AIE not only implicitly laid out the impact pathway, but also pointed us to which metrics had highest value."

How to Get to a Real Decision

Working through these decision definitions usually requires some significant face-time with clients. When I work with clients on large measurement and decision analysis projects, the way we implement the first couple of steps in the five-step process is to conduct a series of workshops involving key decision makers and selected subject matter experts (SMEs). The SMEs represent the most knowledgeable individuals in the organization on the topic being considered. If the project is about some major mining engineering initiative, the SMEs could be key mining engineers and geologists. If the decision involves whether to develop a new medical device, the SMEs would be the firm's medical and device engineering experts.

We've conducted many of these workshops and the pattern is clear. By the time this edition goes to print, we will have been conducting these types of projects for about 20 years and we will have completed over 80 of these major decision analysis and measurement projects. Of these projects, the majority required at least one half-day-long workshop simply to define the decision or set of decisions. This is required even in some cases where the client initially believed they knew exactly what the decision was before the project began.

In one case, a federal government client in 2002 had written a 65-page report describing in detail a particular high-density data storage technology and a potential implementation of it—all in advance of our analysis project. It was presumed that we would probably be able to eliminate one workshop simply because the decision was so well defined. But when they got down to the reality of modeling a specific decision, they realized that they never actually agreed on specific alternative strategies for implementing the technology. Was the decision about whether they were going to implement this technology at all or was it simply a question of how it would be implemented? Was the decision about whether to roll it out across the enterprise or simply to replace an older technology in one area? So, in order to make sure you are talking about a real decision, make sure it has the following properties.

Requirements for a Decision

- A decision has two or more realistic alternatives. It could be to fund a new product-development project or not. It could be to build a dam or not. It could be to expend resources to reduce exposure to some risk. But it cannot be a false-dichotomy—as we saw is sometimes the case when managers want to know the value of IT or the value of clean drinking water. If the alternative is not a serious consideration (i.e., doing without IT or clean water altogether) then there are not two viable alternatives.
- A decision has uncertainty. If there is no uncertainty about a decision, then it's not really much of a dilemma. Perhaps this is a bit redundant with the first rule (there need to be at least two realistic alternatives) since if there is no uncertainty, that's probably not much different than saying only one alternative is realistic. Even so, it's worth restating. There have to be two or more choices *and the best choice is not certain.*

- A decision has potentially negative consequences if it turns out you took the wrong position. Just as a lack of uncertainty makes for no real dilemma in a decision, the lack of any consequence also means there is no dilemma. If you funded a project that turned out to be a flop, or if you failed to approve a new product that turned out to be a major success for a competitor, those are negative consequences of a decision. There is a type of loss even if both choices have positive outcomes, but when one is more positive than the other. In this case, the loss is an "opportunity loss." You gave up something even better.
- Finally, a decision has a decision maker. Difficulty defining a decision sometimes comes down to simply identifying whose decision it is.

If someone is having a hard time getting their measurement problem to fit a specific decision according to these rules, they may be making some unnecessary presumptions about what constitutes a decision. A measurement must still influence an uncertain decision with potential consequences, but decisions have a variety of forms that fit this standard. At least one of the following decision forms fits any given problem if that problem constitutes a real decision.

Potential Forms of a Decision
- A decision can be one big thing or many little things. Decisions do not have to be limited to one-time choices set before us—like developing a new product or approving a merger. They could be a large number of small, recurring decisions like whether to hire a person or implement an IT security control. In the former case, the analysis of the decision may be unique and not used again. In the latter case the model we create for the decision is not made just for some immediate choice, but will be reused many times over. Or they could be a portfolio of several different kinds of one-time decisions like a set of different types of environmental policy decisions.
- A decision can be about a discrete or continuous choice. We don't have to think of decisions as binary "either-or" propositions. They can be choosing an optimal value along some wide continuum. Whether or not to build a new factory is a discrete decision, but the capacity for that factory is not. You can choose to build a factory with a particular production capacity and that capacity can be a million units per year, 10 million, or any other value. As always, there is a cost of making the wrong decision but, in the case of making choices about continuous values, there is a cost of overshooting and undershooting

some ideal answer and the larger the error the larger the cost of the error.

- Decisions can be with one or many stakeholders including collaborating and/or competing parties. The SMEs and managers involved in modeling a decision may not be (and often are not) those making the actual decision. Decision makers may be entirely outside of the organization doing the analysis, the customer of a company trying to demonstrate its value, or a group of activist citizens arguing to political leaders that one policy is better than another. But there is always an agent of the decision.

IF YOU UNDERSTAND IT, YOU CAN MODEL IT

A decision has to be defined well enough to be modeled quantitatively. This is often where much of the remaining ambiguity is laid bare. Think of a quantitative decision model as just another Fermi decomposition. It could be as simple as identifying the various costs, the various benefits, and computing the difference. The simple act of attempting to calculate this forces a degree of clarity on what decision is being addressed. These estimates and calculations in a spreadsheet constitute a simple, but legitimate decision model. The outcome of the model indicates some action.

A Ridiculously Simple (But Completely Legitimate) Decision Model

- Estimated Costs of Action X.
- Estimated Benefits of Action X.
- If Benefits of Action X exceed Costs of Action X, execute Action X.

(Now just decompose costs and benefits into more detail as needed.)

A simple cost-benefit analysis could be decomposed further to show how different costs and benefits create a "cash flow" over time. This is simply a year-by-year (or quarter-by-quarter, etc.) list of net monetary benefits. These cash flows are the basis for computing a "Net Present Value" or some other financial calculation that takes into account the timing of the benefit (money later is less valuable to you than the same amount received earlier). For a simple example of these kinds of calculations, go to www.howtomeasureanything.com and download the examples spreadsheet for this chapter. We won't get into the details of those calculations here except to say that just doing this calculation forces a choice about the relevant metric for the decision and the time frame of the benefits and costs.

The monetary values for each benefit or cost by year can themselves be decomposed further into more variables. For example, we might compute a benefit about an efficiency improvement by multiplying, say, the number of people working in some activity, the cost of each person per year, the percentage of time spent on some unproductive activity, and the percentage of that unproductive activity that was eliminated. This could also be changed over time to account for growth in business volumes or labor costs. Admittedly, even this is a simplified example that ignores some issues—like the benefits of productivity improvements that might not necessarily lead to reductions in a labor force—but even those issues could be decomposed further if necessary.

A more sophisticated statistical model based purely on historical data could be a decision model if the output represents a specific recommended action. Or a model can be a slightly more elaborate computer simulation with probabilities for a range of potential outcomes. We will be resorting to both of these methods later in this book.

When we decompose a decision this way we get new insights. First, you find that there are several other important variables that pertain to the judgment. You might find that there are a lot of other things to measure besides what you first thought you needed to measure, and that one of these new variables is the most important measurement of all (more on this in Chapter 7). Second, it turns out that merely decomposing highly uncertain estimates provides a huge improvement to estimates. What Fermi knew intuitively has actually been confirmed experimentally.

From the 1970s to the 1990s, decision-science researchers Donald G. MacGregor and J. Scott Armstrong, both separately and together, conducted experiments about how much estimates can be improved by decomposition.[1] For their various experiments, they recruited hundreds of subjects to evaluate the difficulty of estimates like the circumference of a given coin or pairs of men's pants made in the United States per year. Some of the subjects were asked to directly estimate these quantities while a second group was instead asked to estimate decomposed variables, which were then used to estimate the original quantity. For example, for the pairs of men's pants made in the United States per year, the second group would estimate the U.S. population of men, the number of pairs of pants men buy per year, the percentage of pants made overseas, and so on. Then the first group's estimate (made without the benefit of decomposition) was compared to the group that estimated the decomposed variables and then computed the original amount.

Armstrong and MacGregor found that decomposition didn't help much if the estimates of the first group already had relatively little error—like estimating the circumference of a U.S. $.50 coin in inches. But where the error of the first group was high—as they were with estimates for men's pants manufactured in the United States or the total number of auto accidents per year—then decomposition was a huge benefit. They found that for the most uncertain variables a simple decomposition—none of which was more than five variables—*reduced error by a factor as much as 10 or even 100*. Imagine if this was a real-world decision with big uncertainties. Decomposition itself is certainly worth the time.

As Paul Meehl showed, even our intuition is a type of decision model. It's just that our intuition models have a high degree of additional inconsistencies, logical inference errors, and unstated assumptions which are not visible for others to inspect. Of course, explicit, quantitative models are also never perfect. But they can avoid some of the errors of unaided intuition. As the great statistician George Box put it, "Essentially, all models are wrong, but some are useful."[2] And Meehl's research would cause us to add the corollary ". . . and some models are measurably more useful than others."

So the question is never whether a decision can be modeled or even whether it can be modeled quantitatively. We are modeling it even if we rely on intuition and anything that can be modeled intuitively can be represented in a quantitative model that at least avoids some of the errors of intuition. The question is whether we are clear-headed enough about the issue to do so.

Shortly, we will review the beginning pieces of a "decision model" for an IT security investment. I chose to elaborate on this particular example not because this is a book about IT security, but because IT security seems to capture several important features of the kinds of decision models we need to develop. Namely, it has a lot of apparent "intangibles" and it has a lot of uncertainty and risk.

If security is better, then some risks should decrease. If that is the case, then we need to know what we mean by "risk." There are some who think of uncertainty and risk as immeasurable themselves. Not only are they measurable, they are key to understanding measurement in general. Uncertainty and risk are going to be so critical to all of our decision models that I'll take a little time now to clarify these two variables.

GETTING THE LANGUAGE RIGHT: WHAT "UNCERTAINTY" AND "RISK" REALLY MEAN

We find no sense in talking about something unless we specify how we measure it; a definition by the method of measuring a quantity is the one sure way of avoiding talking nonsense. . . .
— Sir Hermann Bondi, mathematician and cosmologist[3]

Even though "risk" and "uncertainty" frequently are dismissed as immeasurable, they are aspects of almost any conceivable decision model one could make, especially for the "big" decisions in life and business. Fortunately, a thriving industry depends on measuring both and does so routinely. One of the industries I've consulted for the most, insurance, is one example. Yet even in a business that routinely quantifies risk, the measurability of risk is still often doubted. I remember once conducting a business-case analysis for a director of IT in a Chicago-based insurance company. He said, "Doug, the problem with IT is that it is risky, and there's no way to measure risk." I replied, "But you work for an insurance company. You have an entire floor in this building for actuaries. What do you think they do all day?" His expression indicated that he was having an epiphany at that moment. He had suddenly realized the incongruity of declaring risk to be immeasurable while working for a company that measures risks of insured events on a daily basis.

Quantitative clarity is a strong foundation for the advancement of any field. Consider how the word "force" was used in the English language for centuries before Sir Isaac Newton defined it mathematically. Today it is sometimes used interchangeably with terms like "energy" or "power"— but not by physicists and engineers. When aircraft designers use the term, they know precisely what they mean in a quantitative sense (and those of us who fly frequently appreciate their effort at clarity). Likewise, the decision maker requires unambiguous and quantitatively sound definitions for uncertainty and risk regardless of how others may use them.

There are actually multiple definitions of risk and uncertainty in use and most are both confused and confusing. Many contradict definitions that are both quantitatively sound and already widely used. (See *A Purely Philosophical Interlude #2.*) Fortunately, decision makers who have to make real world decisions with limited information and significant consequences do not have to be distracted by the semantics. We just need to define what works best for the purpose of making practical decisions. So, let me propose definitions for uncertainty, risk, and their respective measurements. (See inset "Definitions for Uncertainty, Risk, and Their Measurements.")

> ## Definitions for Uncertainty, Risk, and Their Measurements
>
> **Uncertainty:** The lack of complete certainty, that is, the existence of more than one possibility. The "true" outcome/state/result/value is not known.
>
> **Measurement of Uncertainty:** A set of probabilities assigned to a set of possibilities. For example: "There is a 60% chance this market will more than double in five years, a 30% chance it will grow at a slower rate, and a 10% chance the market will shrink in the same period."
>
> **Risk:** A state of uncertainty where some of the possibilities involve a loss, catastrophe, or other undesirable outcome.
>
> **Measurement of Risk:** A set of possibilities each with quantified probabilities and quantified losses. For example: "We believe there is a 40% chance the proposed oil well will be dry with a loss of $12 million in exploratory drilling costs."

So, according to the definitions I just provided, measuring uncertainty and risk involves assigning probabilities. We will get to how we assign these probabilities a little later, but at least we have defined what we mean—which is always a prerequisite to measurement. These definitions are not only relevant to how we measure the example we are using here: security and the value of security. They are also, as we will see, the most useful among the many contradicting definitions when discussing *any* other type of measurement problem we have.

Now that we have defined "uncertainty" and "risk," we have a better toolbox for defining terms like "security" (or "safety," "reliability," and "quality," but more on that later). When we say that security has improved, we generally mean that particular risks have decreased. If I apply the definition of risk given earlier, a reduction in risk must mean that the probability and/or severity (loss) decreases for a particular list of events. That is the approach I briefly mentioned earlier to help measure one very large IT security investment—the $100 million overhaul of IT security for the Department of Veterans Affairs.

AN EXAMPLE OF A CLARIFIED DECISION

Believe it or not, when it comes to clarifying decisions, many businesses could learn something from looking at some government agencies. This defies some stereotypes about each. Many government employees imagine the commercial world as an almost mythical place of incentive-driven efficiency and motivation where fear of going out of business keeps everyone on their toes (but perhaps not so much after the 2008 financial crisis). I often hear government workers lament that they are not as efficient as a business. To those in the business world, however, the government (federal, state, or other) is a synonym for bureaucratic inefficiency and unmotivated workers counting the days to retirement.

I've done a lot of consulting in both worlds, and I would say that neither generalization is entirely true. The fact is that large businesses with vast internal structures still have workers so far removed from the economic realities of business that their jobs are as bureaucratic as any job in government. And I'm here to bear witness to the fact that the U.S. federal government, while certainly the largest bureaucracy in history, has many motivated and passionately dedicated workers. In that light, I will use an example from my government clients as a great example for business to follow.

Here is a little more background on the IT security measurement project for Veterans Affairs, which I briefly mentioned in the last chapter. In 2000, an organization called the Federal CIO Council wanted to conduct some sort of test to compare different performance measurement methods. As the name implies, the Federal CIO Council is an organization consisting of the chief information officers of federal agencies and many of their direct reports. The council has its own budget and sometimes sponsors research that can benefit all federal CIOs. After reviewing several approaches, the CIO Council decided it should test Applied Information Economics.

The CIO Council decided it would test AIE on the massive, newly proposed IT security portfolio at the Department of Veterans Affairs (VA). My task was to identify performance metrics for each of the security-related systems being proposed and to evaluate the portfolio, under the close supervision of the council. Whenever I had a workshop or presentation of findings, several council observers from a variety of agencies, such as the Department of Treasury, the FBI, or Housing and Urban Development, were often in attendance. At the end of each workshop, they compiled their notes and wrote a detailed comparison of AIE to another popular method currently used in other agencies.

The VA's previous approach to measuring security focused on activities like counting the number of people who completed certain security training courses and the number of desktops that had certain systems installed. In other words, the VA wasn't measuring *results* at all. All previous measurement efforts focused on what was considered easy to measure. Prior to my work with the CIO Council, some people considered the ultimate impact of security to be immeasurable, so no attempt was made to achieve even marginally less uncertainty.

The first question I asked the VA is similar to the first questions I ask on most measurement problems: "What decision is this measurement for?" Then, shortly thereafter, I ask: "What do you mean by 'IT security'? What does improved IT security look like? What would we see or detect that would be different if security were better or worse? Furthermore, what do we mean by the value of security?"

As usual, the challenge was not initially defined as a decision-making problem. At first, they knew they simply needed to measure IT security, but didn't at first identify why. After some probing, it turned out that they were considering some major improvements in IT security and measurements in IT security must at least inform these upcoming decisions if nothing else. The VA had an upcoming investment decision involving seven proposed IT security projects that total about $130 million over five years. (Exhibit 4.1 lists the seven proposed investments.) The reason for these measurements was to determine which if any of the proposed investments were justified and, after they were implemented, whether improvements in security justified further investment or some other intervention (e.g., changes to the systems or an addition of new systems).

The next question became a bit more difficult for my client. IT security might not seem like the most ephemeral or vague concept we need

Exhibit 4.1 IT Security for the Department of Veterans Affairs

Security Systems	Events Averted or Reduced	Costs Averted
Public Key Infrastructure (key encryption/ decryption, etc.)	Pandemic virus attacks	Productivity losses
Biometric/single sign-on (fingerprint readers, security card readers, etc.)	Unauthorized system access: external (hackers) or internal (employees)	Fraud losses Legal liability/ improper disclosure
Intrusion-detection systems		Interference with mission (for the VA, this mission is the care of veterans)
Security-compliance certification program for new systems	Unauthorized physical access to facilities or property	
New antivirus software		
Security incident reporting system	Other disasters: fire, flood, tornado, etc.	
Additional security training		

to measure, but project participants soon found that they didn't *quite* know what they meant by that term. It was only through being forced to model these specific decisions and decomposing the relevant variables that they realized how much they had to clarify what security really meant.

It was clear, for example, that reduced frequency and impact of "pandemic" virus attacks is an improvement in security, but what is "pandemic" or, for that matter, "impact"? Also, it might be clear that an unauthorized access to a system by a hacker is an example of a breach of IT security, but is a theft of a laptop? How about a data center being hit by a fire, flood, or tornado? At the first meeting, participants found that while they all thought IT security could be better, they didn't have a common understanding of exactly what IT security was.

It wasn't that different parties had already developed detailed mental pictures of IT security and that each person had a different picture in mind. Up to that point, *nobody* had thought about those details in the definition of IT security. Once group members were confronted with specific, concrete examples of IT security problems and IT security decisions, they came to agreement on a very unambiguous and comprehensive model of what it is.

They resolved that improved IT security means a reduction in the frequency and severity of a specific list of undesirable events. In the case of the VA, they decided these events should specifically include virus attacks, unauthorized access (logical and physical), and certain types of other disasters (e.g., losing a data center to a fire or hurricane). Each of these types of events entails certain types of cost. Exhibit 4.1 presents the proposed systems, the events they meant to avert, and the costs of those events.

Therefore, each of the proposed systems improved security by some amount by virtue of reducing the frequency or impact of specific events. Each of those events would have impacts represented as a specific combination of costs. A virus attack, for example, tends to have an impact on productivity, while unauthorized access might result in productivity loss, fraud, and perhaps even legal liability resulting from improper disclosure of private medical data and the like.

With these definitions, we have a much more specific understanding of what "improved IT security" really means and, therefore, of *how to measure it*. When I ask the question, "What are you observing when you observe improved IT security?" VA management can now answer specifically. The VA participants realized that when they observe "better security," they are observing a reduction in the frequency and impact of these detailed events. They achieved the first milestone to measurement.

You might take issue with some aspects of the definition. You may (justifiably) argue that a fire is not, strictly speaking, an IT security risk. Yet the VA participants determined that, within their organization, they did mean to include the risk of fire. Aside from some minor differences about what to include on the periphery, I think what we developed is the basic model for any IT security measurements.

With the parameters we developed, we were set to measure some very specific things. We built a spreadsheet model that included all of these effects. This was really just another example of asking a few "Fermi decomposition" questions. For virus attacks, we asked:

- How often does the average pandemic (agency-wide) virus attack occur?
- When such an attack occurs, how many people are affected?
- For the affected population, how much did their productivity decrease relative to normal levels?
- What is the duration of the downtime?
- What is the cost of labor lost during the productivity loss?

If we knew the answer to each of these questions, we could compute the cost of agency-wide virus attacks as:

Average Annual Cost
of Virus Attacks   = Number of attacks
                          × Average number of people affected
                          × Average productivity loss
                          × Average duration of downtime (hours)
                          × Annual cost of labor
                          ÷ 2,080 hours per year (The number of
                          hours is a government standard.[4])

Of course, this calculation considers only the cost of the equivalent labor that would have been available if the virus attack had not occurred. It does not tell us how the virus attack affected the care of veterans or other losses. Nevertheless, even if this calculation excludes some losses, at least it gives us a conservative lower bound of losses. Exhibit 4.2 shows the answers for each of these questions.

These ranges reflect the uncertainty of security experts who have had previous experience with virus attacks at the VA. With these ranges, the experts are saying that there is a 90% chance that the true values will fall between the upper and lower bounds given. I trained these experts so that they were very good at assessing uncertainty quantitatively. In effect, they were "calibrated" like any scientific instrument to be able to do this.

Exhibit 4.2 Department of Veterans Affairs Estimates for the Effects of Virus Attacks

Uncertain Variable	The value is 90% likely to fall between or be equal to these points:	
Agency-wide virus attacks per year (for the next five years)	2	4
Average number of people affected	25,000	65,000
Percentage productivity loss	15%	60%
Average duration of productivity loss	4 hours	12 hours
Loaded annual cost per person (most affected staff would be in the lower pay scales)	$50,000	$100,000

These ranges may seem merely subjective, but the subjective estimates of some persons are demonstrably—measurably—better than those of others. We were able to treat these ranges as valid because we knew the experts had demonstrated, in a series of tests, that when they said they were 90% certain, they would be right 90% of the time.

So far, you have seen how to take an ambiguous term like "security" and break it down into some relevant, observable components. By defining what "security" means, the VA made a big step toward measuring it. By this point, the VA had not yet made any observations to reduce its uncertainty. All it did was quantify its uncertainty by using probabilities and ranges.

There are many other measurements that go under different names than "security" but are actually closely related or identical. In the work we did with CGIAR in Nairobi, we needed to measure parameters like "ecological sustainability," "drought resilience," and "food security" of agricultural practices. As always, we got the client to describe why they need to measure this in terms of the decisions they would need to support. Like security, measurements dealing with sustainability, resilience, food security, dependability, reliability, and so on are ultimately measures of risk reduction. Once this leap is made, one can leverage many mathematical tools for quantitatively assessing risk. (This realization clarifies discussions that might otherwise have gone on for years.)

So, how did the security and ecology experts determine ranges in which they could be "90% certain?" It turns out that the ability of a person to assess odds can be calibrated—just like any scientific instrument is calibrated to ensure it gives proper readings. Calibrated probability assessments are the key to measuring your current state of uncertainty about anything. Learning how to quantify your current uncertainty about any unknown quantity is an important step in determining how to measure something in a way that is relevant to your needs. Developing this skill is the focus of the next chapter.

Notes

1. Donald G. MacGregor and J. S. Armstrong, "Judgmental Decomposition: When Does It Work?" *International Journal of Forecasting* 10, no. 4 (1994): 495–506.
2. George E. P. Box and Norman R. Draper, *Empirical Model-Building and Response Surfaces* (New York: John Wiley & Sons, 1987).
3. Hermann Bondi, *Relativity and Common Sense: A New Approach to Einstein* (Garden City, NY: Anchor Books, 1964).
4. Two thousand and eighty hours per year is an Office of Management and Budget and Government Accountability Office standard for converting loaded annual salaries to equivalent hourly rates.

A Purely Philosophical Interlude #2

Defining Risk and Uncertainty

The meaning of "uncertainty" and "risk" and the distinction between them seems ambiguous even for some experts in the field and there are multiple definitions of each in use. In 1921 the University of Chicago economist Frank Knight wrote *Risk, Uncertainty and Profit*, which some consider to be a seminal work on the topic. In it he states, "The essential fact is that 'risk' means in some cases a quantity susceptible of measurement, while at other times it is something distinctly not of this character. . . . It will appear that a measurable uncertainty, or 'risk' proper, as we shall use the term, is so far different from an unmeasurable one that it is not in effect an uncertainty at all."[1]

To clear up what Knight saw as some ongoing confusion about these terms, he offered his definitions. To Knight, if we can't put a probability on some event, then the event is considered uncertain. If you can put a probability on an event, then it is considered a risk—without regard to whether the probability is for a potential loss.

Many economists and other academics will cite Knight's definition as the "proper" use of the terms even today. But Knight's definitions of risk and uncertainty didn't clear up anything and the definitions were never universally accepted. In fact, it contradicted other quantitatively sound definitions in wide use before and after Knight's proposed definition. Knight's definition of uncertainty rested on it being immeasurable and, as you will gather from the title of this book, I argue that nothing is truly immeasurable.

Indeed, the decision sciences routinely write about "decisions under uncertainty" where uncertainty is defined with quantified probabilities. Physicists routinely talk about measuring uncertainty—again with probabilities. And, to any actuary, one cannot be measuring risk unless the magnitude of loss is identified as well. Even among economists there was and still is no universal agreement with Knight. An article in the *Quarterly Journal of Economics*—published 26 years before Knight's definition—defined risk as a "chance of damage or loss."[2] A year after Knight's definition, an article in *Economica* explains how uncertain judgments are quantified with probabilities.[3]

To add further confusion, different professions continue to add their own unique definitions of risk. In project management, some have decided that risk should include the *positive* outcomes (i.e., you have a "risk" that the project will succeed). This contradicts the use of the term by actuaries and the term "uncertainty" already encompasses outcomes that aren't necessarily losses. There are a few other variations I refute in my book, *The Failure of Risk Management*.[4] But here, I will simply propose the definitions we will use (see inset "Definitions for Uncertainty, Risk, and Their Measurements"). These definitions are consistent with the common use of the terms in physics, insurance, decision science, and English dictionaries.

Notes

1. Frank Knight, *Risk, Uncertainty and Profit* (New York: Houghton Mifflin, 1921), 19–20.
2. John Haynes, "Risk as an Economic Factor," *The Quarterly Journal of Economics* (1895): 409–449.
3. A. Wolf, "Studies in Probability I: Probability," in *John Maynard Keynes: Critical Responses, Volume 1,* ed. Charles R. McCann (London: Taylor & Francis, 1922), 339–349.
4. Douglas W. Hubbard, *The Failure of Risk Management: Why It's Broken and How to Fix It* (Hoboken, NJ: John Wiley & Sons, 2009).

## CHAPTER 5

Calibrated Estimates: How Much Do You Know *Now*?

The most important questions of life are indeed, for the most part, really only problems of probability.
—Pierre Simon Laplace, Théorie Analytique des Probabilités, 1812

How many hours per week do employees spend addressing customer complaints? How much would sales increase with a new advertising campaign? Even if you don't know the exact values to questions like these, you still know *something*. You know that some values would be impossible or at least highly unlikely. Knowing what you know now about something actually has an important and often surprising impact on how you should measure it or even whether you should measure it. In fact, quantifying our current level of uncertainty is a key part of the statistical methods we are using and the second step in the universal measurement approach—just after defining the decision and just before computing the value of additional information. What we need is a way to express how much we know now, however little that may be. To do that, we need a way to know if we are any good at expressing uncertainty.

One method to express our uncertainty about a number is to think of it as a range of probable values. In statistics, a range that has a particular chance of containing the correct answer is called a *confidence interval* (CI). A 90% CI is a range that has a 90% chance of containing the correct answer. For example, you can't know for certain exactly how many of your current prospects will turn into customers in the next quarter, but you think that probably no less than three prospects and probably no more than seven prospects will sign contracts. If you are 90% sure the actual number will fall between three and seven, then we can say you have a 90% CI of three to seven. You may have computed these values with all sorts of sophisticated statistical inference methods, but you might just have picked them out based on your experience. Either way, the values should be a reflection of your uncertainty about this quantity. (See "A Purely Philosophical Interlude #3" for a caveat on this use of the meaning of the CI.)

You can also use probabilities to describe your uncertainty about specific discrete "either/or" conditions or events, such as whether a given prospect will sign a contract in the next month. You can say that there is a 70% chance that this will occur, but is that "right"? One way we can determine if a person is good at quantifying uncertainty is to look at all the prospects the person assessed and ask, "Of the large number of prospects she was 70% certain about closing, did about 70% actually close? Where she said she was 80% confident in closing a deal, did about 80% of them close?" And so on. This is how we know how good we are at subjective probability assessment. We compare our expected outcomes to actual outcomes.

Unfortunately, extensive studies have shown that very few people are naturally calibrated estimators.[1-7] Calibrated probability assessments were an area of research in decision psychology in the 1970s and 1980s and up to today. Leading researchers in this area included Daniel Kahneman, winner of the 2002 Nobel Prize in Economics, and his colleague Amos Tversky, first mentioned in Chapter 3. Decision psychology concerns itself with how people actually make decisions, however irrational, in contrast to many of the management science or quantitative analysis methods taught in business schools, which focus on how to work out optimal decisions in specific, well-defined problems. Decision psychology shows that almost everyone tends to be biased either toward "overconfidence" or "underconfidence" about our estimates and the vast majority of those are overconfident (see inset, "Two Extremes of Subjective Confidence"). Putting odds on uncertain events or ranges on uncertain quantities is not a skill that arises automatically from experience and intuition.

Two Extremes of Subjective Confidence

Overconfidence: When an individual routinely overstates knowledge and is correct less often than he or she expects. For example, when asked to make estimates with a 90% confidence interval, far fewer than 90% of the true answers fall within the estimated ranges.

Underconfidence: When an individual routinely understates knowledge and is correct much more often than he or she expects. For example, when asked to make estimates with a 90% confidence interval, far more than 90% of the true answers fall within the estimated ranges.

Fortunately, some of the work by other researchers shows that better estimates are attainable when estimators have been trained to remove their personal estimating biases.[8-15] Researchers discovered that odds makers and bookies were generally better at assessing the odds of events than, say, executives. They also made some disturbing discoveries about how bad physicians are at putting odds on unknowns like the chance of a malignant tumor or the chance a chest pain is a heart attack. They reasoned that this variance among different professions shows that putting odds on uncertain things must be a learned skill.

Researchers learned how experts can measure whether they are systematically underconfident, overconfident, or have other biases about their estimates. Once people conduct this self-assessment, they can learn several techniques for improving estimates and measuring the improvement. In short, researchers discovered that *assessing uncertainty is a general skill that can be taught with a measurable improvement.*

CALIBRATION EXERCISE

Let's benchmark how good you are currently at quantifying your own uncertainty by taking a short quiz. Exhibit 5.1 contains 10 90% CI questions and 10 binary (i.e., true/false) questions. Unless you are a *Jeopardy* grand champion, you probably will not know all of these general knowledge questions with certainty (although some are very simple). But they are all questions you probably have some idea about. These are similar to the exercises I give attendees in my workshops and seminars. The only difference is that the tests I give have more questions of each type, and I present several tests with feedback after each test. This calibration training generally takes about half a day. Yet even with this small sample, we will be able to detect some important aspects of your skills. More importantly, the exercise should get you to think about the fact that your current state of uncertainty is itself something you can quantify.

Instructions: Exhibit 5.1 contains 10 of each of these two types of questions.

1. **90% Confidence Interval (CI).** For each of the 90% CI questions, provide both an upper bound and a lower bound. Remember that the range should be wide enough that you believe there is a 90% chance that the answer will be between your bounds.
2. **Binary Questions.** Answer whether each of the statements is "true" or "false," then circle the probability that reflects how confident you are in your answer. For example, if you are absolutely certain in your answer, you should say you have a 100% chance of getting the answer right. If you have no idea whatsoever, then your chance should be

Exhibit 5.1 Sample Calibration Test

Question	90% Confidence Interval	
	Lower Bound	Upper Bound
1. In 1938, a British steam locomotive set a new speed record by going how fast (mph)?		
2. In what year did Sir Isaac Newton publish the Universal Laws of Gravitation?		
3. How many inches long is a typical business card?		
4. The Internet (then called "Arpanet") was established as a military communications system in what year?		
5. In what year was William Shakespeare born?		
6. What is the air distance between New York and Los Angeles (miles)?		
7. What percentage of a square could be covered by a circle of the same width?		
8. How old was Charlie Chaplin when he died?		
9. How many pounds did the first edition of this book weigh?		
10. The TV show *Gilligan's Island* first aired on what date?		

Statement	Answer (True/False)	Confidence that you are correct (circle one)
1. The ancient Romans were conquered by the ancient Greeks.		50% 60% 70% 80% 90% 100%
2. There is no species of three-humped camels.		50% 60% 70% 80% 90% 100%
3. A gallon of oil weighs less than a gallon of water.		50% 60% 70% 80% 90% 100%
4. Mars is always farther away from Earth than Venus.		50% 60% 70% 80% 90% 100%
5. The Boston Red Sox won the first World Series.		50% 60% 70% 80% 90% 100%
6. Napoleon was born on the island of Corsica.		50% 60% 70% 80% 90% 100%
7. "M" is one of the three most commonly used letters.		50% 60% 70% 80% 90% 100%
8. In 2002 the price of the average new desktop computer purchased was under $1,500.		50% 60% 70% 80% 90% 100%
9. Lyndon B. Johnson was a governor before becoming vice president.		50% 60% 70% 80% 90% 100%
10. A kilogram is more than a pound.		50% 60% 70% 80% 90% 100%

the same as a coin flip (50%). Otherwise (probably usually), it is one of the values between 50% and 100%.

Of course, you could just look up the answers to any of these questions, but we are using this as an exercise to see how well you estimate things you can't just look up (e.g., next month's sales or the actual productivity improvement from some new technology).

Important hint: The questions vary in difficulty. Some will seem easy while others may seem too difficult to answer. But no matter how difficult the question seems, you still know something about it. Focus on what you *do* know. For the range questions, you know of some bounds beyond which the answer would seem absurd (e.g., you probably know Newton wasn't alive in ancient Greece or in the twentieth century). Similarly, for the binary questions, even though you aren't certain, you have some opinion, at least, about which answer is more likely.

Once you have finished, we can gauge how calibrated you are. This is useful for improving your calibration but it is also an opportunity to introduce a measurement problem using a very small number of samples. As with all measurement problems, measuring your calibration can start with a question of the form "What would I expect to see if . . . ?" In this case, we could ask "What would we expect to see if you were calibrated?"

Regarding the 90% CI questions, if you were calibrated and if you had taken not 10 but tens of thousands of questions, then you should have gotten just about exactly 90% within your 90% CIs. With just 10 questions, however, there will be a lot more chance involved. Just as we don't expect that *every* time we flip 10 coins, we will see exactly 5 heads, we wouldn't literally expect everyone in a group of perfectly calibrated people to get exactly 9 out of 10 answers within their intervals.

Therefore, a person who would only get half of the answers within their 90% CIs in a test of thousands of questions could have gotten lucky and got 9 within their CI on a 10-question test. Or a person who actually got 90% of the answers within their 90% CIs could have been unlucky and gotten only 6 out of 10 in this small sample. What we need to do is to determine *how lucky or how unlucky* these results would be. To compute the chance of various outcomes we can use what is known as a "binomial" distribution calculation, which we will cover in Chapters 9 and 10. We will describe the details later but for now, I will just say that we are asking what the chance is that we would get a given number of "hits" (in this case, answers within our stated intervals) out of ten "trials" (the number of questions on the test) with a given probability of a hit per trial (in this case, 90%).

This calculation would show that the chance that a calibrated person would get 6 or less answers out of 10 questions within their intervals is only about 1.3%. We can also see that the chance a calibrated person would get 3 or less out of 10 within their intervals is less than 1 in 100,000. Even though this is a small test, a score this low would be extraordinarily unlikely for a calibrated person. Therefore, it is reasonable to infer that a person who does this poorly is overconfident.

By comparing this to actual results from not just you, but a large group of people, we can see that most people will do poorly enough that this simple test is sufficient to demonstrate most people are very overconfident. Between 1996 and the time of this writing, 927 individuals have taken our current form of calibration training. This totals to more than 100,000 individual test items, and more calibration sessions are being recorded nearly every month. Note that the tests are not all identical to the test you see printed in this chapter. Several entirely separate sets of trivia questions in 10-question tests were used during this period and we noticed very little difference among tests.

Exhibit 5.2 compares the idealized expected results of a set of perfectly calibrated individuals to the actual results of our 927 test subjects. This shows that while only 1.3% (about 12 out of 927) should have gotten 6 or less out of 10, in fact, about 71% did that poorly. Again, it is possible for a person to be that unlucky but it's not feasible for 660 out of 927 to be that unlucky. We also see that even out of all the tests, it is highly unlikely that *anybody* should have gotten 3 or less out of 10 and yet we see that this was the case 224 times (24% of the total).

The same chart tells us that if these subjects were well calibrated, we should expect to see that about 99% of people taking a 10-question 90% CI test should get at least 7 of the 10 of the answers within their stated

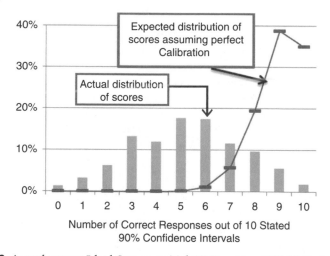

Exhibit 5.2 Actual versus Ideal Scores: Initial 10 Question 90% CI Test

ranges. In reality, only 29% did that well. And even if you did do that well, it doesn't necessarily mean you are calibrated. A further analysis of our data can show that calibration on the first test is rare enough that if you did that well it is actually still more likely that you are overconfident but lucky. On average, people are getting about 53% of the answers within their intervals. A person as overconfident as the average person actually has about a 23% chance of getting at least 7 within their stated intervals. In other words, most people who scored that high can be accounted for as the expected outcome of that many people with average overconfidence getting a bit lucky.

Knowing the odds that a calibrated person would get a given result is not the same as the chance that a person is calibrated. Glossing over certain details for the moment, your test performance can be interpreted like this: If you got 7 to 10 within your range, you *might* be calibrated; if you got 6 or less right, you are very likely to be overconfident; if you got 5 or less right, you are almost certainly overconfident and by a large margin. In the same manner, we need to compare expected to actual outcomes in the true/false questions. The expected outcome for your answers to these questions, however, is not a fixed number since your confidence could be different for each answer and different from others who take the test. Unlike the 90% CI test, your confidence for each answer on this test could range from 50% to 100%. If you said you were 100% confident on all 10 questions, you are expecting to get all 10 correct. If you were only 50% confident on each question (i.e., you thought your odds were no better than a coin flip), you expected to get about half of them right. To compute the expected outcome, convert each of the percentages you circled to a decimal (i.e., .5, .6 . . . 1.0) and add them up. Let's say your confidence in your answers was 1, .5, .9, .6, .7, .8, .8, 1, .9, and .7, totaling to 7.9. This means your "expected" number correct was 7.9.

People generally fare slightly better on the true/false tests, but, on average, they still tend to be overconfident—and overconfident by enough that even a small sample of 10 can usually detect it. On average, individuals expected to get 72% of true/false questions like these correct but, in reality, answered just 65% of them correctly. And those with higher confidence did not match it with proportionally higher performance. For example, of those who expected to get *at least* 9 out of 10 correct, the average percentage that was actually correct was just 72% (up from the 65% average for all participants).

If you did perform better on the true/false test, it may simply be because, statistically, this test is less precise. That is, it is easier for a calibrated person to be unlucky and for an uncalibrated person to appear calibrated in this small sample of questions. With this size of test, what we can tell is that if you were confident you would get at least eight correct, you should get more than half right. For the purposes of our calibration training, I generally use only the average score of the group I'm training as evidence of overconfidence for the entire group and I pay little attention to individual scores. Later in the training we double the number of questions in a test and this provides a better picture of individual performance. For tests with 20 questions, most participants should get the expected score to within +/–2.5 of the actual score.

And here is another simple check on overconfidence with true/false questions that happens to be independent of test size: If you said you were 100% confident on any answer, you *must* get it right. Getting even one 100% confident answer wrong is sufficient evidence that you are overconfident. Remarkably, just over 15% of responses where the stated confidence was 100% turned out to be wrong and some individuals (we will see shortly) would get a third or more of their "certain" answers wrong. Apparently, even a 100% confidence, on average, indicates something less than an 85% chance of being right.

At this point, I need to warn the readers about a common confusion in statistics which also turns out to be essential in understanding our calibration training results and to understanding measurement in general. It is easy to confuse the following two very different questions:

- "What is the chance a hypothesis is true given this observation?"
- "What is the chance of this observation assuming an idealized random situation?"

The previous calculations interpreting calibration results answer the second question—in this case, "What is the chance of a given result assuming the subject was perfectly calibrated?" In other words, if we assumed there really was a 90% chance of each 90% CI containing the estimated value, what is the chance that they would get the result we see? If the outcome was extremely unlikely in the idealized situation of perfect calibration, we have grounds to doubt the person is calibrated. If this is all we did, we would actually have completed what is considered the "frequentist" approach to the problem (as discussed in several of the Purely Philisophical Interludes throughout the book).

Determining the chance of seeing a given result in some idealized situation is relatively simple and it is useful but it is not the same as the probability that a person is calibrated. Computing the chance that you are calibrated based on this small sample requires using this information *and* the prior probabilities we assign to you being calibrated and getting these results. We talk about how we can compute this later in this chapter and again in more detail in Chapter 10.

CALIBRATION TRICK: BET MONEY (OR EVEN JUST PRETEND TO)

If you did about as well as most people on the calibration test, you found plenty of room for improvement. Simply practicing with multiple tests may improve calibration scores but, for most people, becoming well calibrated also requires learning some specific techniques. One particularly powerful tactic for becoming more calibrated is to *pretend to bet money*.

Consider another 90% CI question: What is the average weight in tons of an adult male African elephant? As you did before, provide an upper and lower bound that are far apart enough that you think there is a 90% chance the true answer is between them. Now consider the two following games:

> **Game A.** You win $1,000 if the true answer turns out to be between your upper and lower bounds. If not, you win nothing.
>
> **Game B.** You spin a dial divided into two unequal "pie slices," one comprising 90% of the dial and the other just 10%. If the dial lands on the large slice, you win $1,000. If it lands on the small slice, you win nothing (i.e., there is a 90% chance you win $1,000). (See Exhibit 5.3.)

Which do you prefer? The dial has a stated chance of 90% that you win $1,000 and a 10% chance you win nothing. If you are like most people (about 80% of the people to whom we pose this question), you prefer to spin the dial. But why would that be? The only explanation is that you think the dial has a higher chance of a payoff. The conclusion we have to draw is that the 90% CI you first estimated is really not your 90% CI. It might be your 50%, 65%, or 80% CI, but it can't be your 90% CI. We say, then, that your initial estimate was probably overconfident. You express your uncertainty in a way that indicates you have less uncertainty than you really have.

An equally undesirable outcome is to prefer option A, where you win $1,000 if the correct answer is within your range. This means that

Exhibit 5.3 Spin to Win!

you think there is *more* than a 90% chance your range contains the answer, even though you are representing yourself as being merely 90% confident in the range. In other words, this is usually the choice of the underconfident person.

The only desirable answer you can give is if you set your range just right so that you would be indifferent between options A and B. This means that you believe you have a 90% chance—not more and not less—that the answer is within your range. For an overconfident person (i.e., most people), making these two choices equivalent means increasing the width of the range until options A and B are considered equally valuable. For the underconfident person—as rare as that may be—the range should be narrower than first estimated.

You can apply the same test, of course, to the binary questions. Let's say you were 80% confident about your answer to the question about Napoleon's birthplace. Again, you give yourself a choice between betting on your answer being correct or spinning the dial. In this case, however, the dial pays off 80% of the time. If you prefer to spin the dial, you are probably less than 80% confident in your answer. Now let's suppose we change the payoff odds on the dial to 70%. If you then consider spinning the dial just as good (no better or worse) as betting on your answer, then you should say that you are really about 70% confident that your answer to the question is correct.

In my calibration training classes, I've been calling this the "equivalent bet test." Some examples in the decision psychology literature refer to this as an "equivalent urn" involving drawing random lots from an urn, but they are essentially the same. The equivalent bet tests whether you are really 90% confident in a range by comparing it to a bet which you should consider to be equivalent. Research indicates that even just pretending to bet money significantly improves a person's ability to assess odds.[7] In fact, *actually* betting money turns out to be only slightly better than pretending to bet. (More on this in the Chapter 13 discussion about prediction markets.)

Equivalent bets might sound too subjective and qualitative for the basis of quantitative probabilities. But in fact, starting in the early twentieth century a type of equivalent bet was offered by prominent mathematicians and statisticians as the very *definition* of probability itself. One promoter of the definition was Italian statistician and actuary, Bruno de Finetti (1906–1985). As an actuary at the giant Italian insurance company Assicurazioni Generali, de Finetti was more concerned with practical financial decisions than philosophical debates about purist definitions of probability. In 1937, de Finetti proposed that, like an insurance company, the probability you place on an event is reflected by the price you would put on a type of contract that paid some amount on a given event. For example, the contract could pay X if a particular politician is convicted of a crime for which he was indicted.

Then you set a price for that contract—perhaps you set a price of $60 for a contract that pays $100 if the conviction is successful. He would show this as a price of .6 relative to the payoff.

Then de Finetti proposed that you have another party decide which side of that bet they want to take. If they think you set the price too high, they would sell you such a contract at that price. If they think you set the price too low, they would buy one from you instead. De Finetti pointed out that the best strategy for you would be one where you would be indifferent as to which position you had to take once you set the price. In other words, you would have to set the price where you saw no arbitrage opportunity. He referred to this as *coherence* in your price.

In statistics and mathematics, we might often see the notation "P(X)" to mean the probability of X. De Finetti actually used the notation of Pr(X) instead to mean both probability of X and price of X. He meant to *equate* price and probability. He referred to this as the *operational subjective* definition of probability and he went about showing how this is a perfectly mathematically valid conception. He later stated that he might have approached this a little differently given more recent developments in the relative utilities of different outcomes and how losses are considered differently than gains especially if they are large compared to your existing wealth (more on this in the last section of this book). But, having said that, de Finetti's operational subjective is right on target for what real decision makers need. He was reiterating the subjective view of probability held by so many great mathematicians and scientists of his day and later.

It's worth noting that simply using the equivalent bet may be the single most effective tactic for becoming calibrated. When I give calibration training, I routinely ask who is applying the equivalent bet. Those who admit they were not using it consistently seem to be much more likely to be those struggling to get calibrated.

Getting Equivalent Bets Right

To illustrate the equivalent bet and to test understanding of it, I sometimes ask participants in calibration training to test another person's stated probability or confidence interval with an equivalent bet. If they are testing another participant's 90% CI for some quantity, I expect them to ask, "What would you prefer: (1) to win $1,000 if the correct answer is within your bounds *or* (2) to spin a dial that gives a 90% chance of paying off $1,000?" But for some reason this seems to confuse most people who first attempt this. I've heard the following variations and many more.

(continued)

These are *not* the Equivalent Bet Test
- "Would you prefer to be 90% confident or spin a dial that pays $1,000?"
- "Would you prefer to be right 90% of the time or to have $1,000?"

Keep in mind that in the two options the first option should make no reference to a probability—you simply win money on the condition that the answer is within your bounds. The second option makes no reference to your answer at all, it is simply the outcome of a random dial spin. People are not preferring to "be 90% confident" or not and they are not making a statement about whether they prefer cash. Both options pay the same amount of cash but on different conditions— one based on your answer and one on a random dial spin. In the case of a 90% CI question, the random dial spin should always pay off with a 90% chance. For testing a true/false confidence, change the payoff of the dial spin to the stated confidence.

FURTHER IMPROVEMENTS ON CALIBRATION

The academic research so far indicates that training has a significant effect on calibration. We already mentioned the equivalent bet test, which allows us to pretend we are tying personal consequences to the outcomes. Research (and my experience) proves that another key method in calibrating a person's ability to assess uncertainty is repetition and feedback. To test this, we ask participants a series of trivia questions similar to the quiz you just took. They give me their answers, then I show them the true values, and they test again. However, it doesn't appear that any single method completely corrects for the natural overconfidence most people have. To remedy this, I combined several methods for improving calibration and found that most people could be nearly perfectly calibrated.

Another calibration training method involves asking people to identify potential problems for each of their estimates. Just assume your answer is wrong and then explain to yourself why you were wrong. For example, your estimate of sales for a new product may be in line with sales for other start-up products with similar advertising expenditures. But when you think about your uncertainty regarding catastrophic failures or runaway successes in other companies as well as your uncertainty about the overall growth in the market, you may reassess the initial range. Academic researchers found that this method by itself significantly improves calibration.[16] It appears that we are simply not wired to doubt our own proclamations once we make them. We have to make a deliberate effort to challenge what could be wrong with our own estimates.

I also asked experts who are providing range estimates to look at each bound on the range as a separate "binary" question. A 90% CI means there is a 5% chance the true value could be greater than the upper bound and a 5% chance it could be less than the lower bound. This means that estimators must be 95% sure that the true value is less than the upper bound. If they are not that certain, they should increase the upper bound until they are 95% certain. A similar test is applied to the lower bound. Performing this test seems to avoid the problem of "anchoring" by estimators. Researchers discovered that once we have a number stuck in our head, our other estimates tend to gravitate toward it. (More on this to come in Chapter 12.) Some estimators say that when they provide ranges, they think of a single number and then add or subtract an "error" to generate their range. This might seem reasonable but, because of anchoring, it actually tends to cause estimators to produce overconfident ranges (i.e., ranges that are too narrow). Looking at each bound alone as a separate binary question of "Are you 95% sure it is over/under this amount?" cures our tendency to anchor.

You can also force your natural anchoring tendency to work the other way. Instead of starting with a point estimate and then making it into a range, start with an absurdly wide range and then start eliminating the values you know to be extremely unlikely. If you have no idea how much a new plastic injection molding factory will cost, start with a range of $1,000 to $10 billion and start making it narrower. The new equipment alone will cost $12 million, so you raise the lower bound. A figure of $1 billion is more than all of the other factories you have combined, so you can lower the upper bound. And keep narrowing it from there as you eliminate absurd values.

I sometimes call this the "absurdity test." It reframes the question from "What do I think this value could be?" to "What values do I know to be ridiculous?" We look for answers that are obviously absurd and then eliminate them until we get to answers that are still unlikely but not entirely implausible. This is the edge of our knowledge about that quantity.

After a few calibration tests and practice with methods like listing potential problems, using the equivalent bet, and anti-anchoring, estimators learn to fine-tune their "probability senses." Most people get nearly perfectly calibrated after just a half-day of training. Most important, even though subjects may have been training on general trivia, the calibration skill transfers to any area of estimation.

I've provided two additional calibration tests of each type—ranges and binary—in the appendix. Try applying the methods summarized in Exhibit 5.4 to improve your calibration.

Exhibit 5.4 Methods to Improve Your Probability Calibration

Repetition and feedback. Take several tests in succession, assessing how well you did after each one and attempting to improve your performance in the next one.

Equivalent bets. For each estimate, use the equivalent bet to test if that range or probability really reflects your uncertainty.

Consider potential problems. Think of at least two reasons why you should doubt your assessment.

Avoid anchoring. Think of range questions as two separate binary questions of the form "Are you 95% certain that the true value is over/under (pick one) the lower/upper (pick one) bound?"

Reverse the anchoring effect. Start with extremely wide ranges and narrow them with the "absurdity test" as you eliminate highly unlikely values.

CONCEPTUAL OBSTACLES TO CALIBRATION

The methods just mentioned don't help if someone has irrational ideas about calibration or probabilities in general. While I find that most people in decision-making positions seem to have or are able to learn useful ideas about probabilities, some have surprising misconceptions about these issues. Here are some comments I've received while taking groups of people through calibration training or eliciting calibrated estimates after training:

- "My 90% confidence can't have a 90% chance of being right because a subjective 90% confidence will never have the same chance as an objective 90%."
- "This is my 90% confidence interval but I have absolutely no idea if that is right."
- "We couldn't possibly estimate this. We have no idea."
- "If we don't know the exact answer, we can never know the odds."
- "Why not just put a ridiculously wide range on everything, then every range will be right?"
- "But my ranges are so wide they will be useless. What good is that?"
- "How can I know what the true probability is?"
- "This is just a test of trivia knowledge, not a test of how well we assign probabilities."
- "Only calibration questions within our own field should be used. Being calibrated with general trivia does not improve calibration with specialized topics."

The first statement was made by a chemical engineer and is indicative of the problem he was initially having with calibration. As long as he sees his subjective probability as inferior to objective probability, he won't get calibrated. However, after a few calibration exercises, he did find that he could subjectively apply odds that were correct as often as the odds implied; in other words, his 90% confidence intervals contained the correct answers 90% of the time. In other words, he found that we can objectively measure his performance at a subjective task.

The next three objections in the previous list are fairly similar to each other. They are all based in part on the idea that not knowing exact quantities is the same as knowing nothing of any value. The woman who said she had "absolutely no idea" if her 90% confidence interval was right was talking about her answer to one specific question on the calibration exam. The trivia question was "What is the wingspan of a 747, in feet?" Her answer was 100 to 120 feet. Here is an approximate re-creation of the discussion:

Me: Are you 90% sure that the value is between 100 and 120 feet?

Calibration Student: I have no idea. It was a pure guess.

Me: But when you give me a range of 100 to 120 feet, that indicates you at least believe you have a pretty good idea. That's a very narrow range for someone who says they have no idea.

Calibration Student: Okay. But I'm not very confident in my range.

Me: That just means your real 90% confidence interval is probably much wider. Do you think the wingspan could be, say, 20 feet?

Calibration Student: No, it couldn't be that short.

Me: Great. Could it be less than 50 feet?

Calibration Student: Not very likely. That would be my lower bound.

Me: We're making progress. Could the wingspan be greater than 500 feet?

Calibration Student: [pause] . . . No, it couldn't be that long.

Me: Okay, could it be more than a football field, 300 feet?

Calibration Student: [seeing where I was going]. . . . Okay, I think my upper bound would be 250 feet.

Me: So then you are 90% certain that the wingspan of a 747 is between 50 feet and 250 feet?

Calibration Student: Yes.

Me: So your real 90% confidence interval is 50 to 250 feet, not 100 to 120 feet.

During our discussion, the woman progressed from what I would call an unrealistically narrow range to a range she really felt 90% confident contained the correct answer. She no longer said she had "no idea" that the range contained the answer because the new range represented what she actually knew.

This example is one reason I like to be careful about how I use the word "assumption" in my analysis. An assumption is a statement we treat as true for the sake of argument, regardless of whether it is true. Assumptions about quantities are necessary if you have to use deterministic accounting methods with exact points as values. You could never know an exact point with certainty so any such value must be an assumption. But if you are allowed to model your uncertainty with ranges and probabilities, you do not have to state something you don't know for a fact. If you are uncertain, your ranges and assigned probabilities should reflect that. If you have "no idea" that a narrow range is correct, you simply widen it until it reflects what you do know—with 90% confidence.

It is easy to get lost in how much you don't know about a problem and forget that there are still some things you *do* know. Enrico Fermi showed his skeptical students that even when the question first sounded like something they couldn't possibly estimate, there were ways to come to reasonable ranges. There is nothing we will likely ever need to measure where our only bounds are negative infinity to positive infinity.

Here is an example of a (paraphrased) discussion I've had with a client after calibration training while trying to elicit some estimate for a real-world problem. This example is a little different from the last dialog, where the woman gave an unrealistically narrow range during calibration training. The next conversation comes from the security example we were working on with the Department of Veterans Affairs (VA). The expert initially gave no range at all and simply insisted that it could never be estimated. He went from saying he knew "nothing" about a variable to later conceding that he actually is very certain about some bounds.

Me: If your systems are being brought down by a computer virus, how long does the downtime last, on average? As always, all I need is a 90% confidence interval.

Security Expert: We would have no way of knowing that. Sometimes we were down for a short period, sometimes a long one. We don't really track it in detail because the priority is always getting the system back up, not documenting the event.

Me: Of course you can't know it exactly. That's why we only put a range on it, not an exact number. But what would be the longest downtime you ever had?

Security Expert: I don't know, it varied so much. . . .

Me: Were you ever down for more than two entire workdays?

Security Expert: No, never two whole days.

Me:	Ever more than a day?
Security Expert:	I'm not sure . . . probably.
Me:	We are looking for your 90% confidence interval of the average downtime. If you consider all the downtimes you've had due to a virus, could the average of all of them have been more than a day?
Security Expert:	I see what you mean. I would say the average is probably less than a day.
Me:	So your upper bound for the average would be . . . ?
Security Expert:	Okay, I think it's highly unlikely that the average downtime could be greater than 10 hours.
Me:	Great. Now let's consider the lower bound. How small could it be?
Security Expert:	Some events are corrected in a couple of hours. Some take longer.
Me:	Okay, but do you really think the average of all downtimes could be 2 hours?
Security Expert:	No, I don't think the average could be that low. I think the average is at least 6 hours.
Me:	Good. So is your 90% confidence interval for the average duration of downtime due to a virus attack 6 hours to 10 hours?
Security Expert:	I took your calibration tests. Let me think. I think there would be a 90% chance if the range was, say, 4 to 12 hours.

This is a typical conversation for a number of highly uncertain quantities. Initially the experts may resist giving any range at all, perhaps because they have been taught that in business, the lack of an exact number is the same as knowing nothing or perhaps because they will be "held accountable for a number." But, again, *the lack of having an exact number is not the same as knowing nothing.* The security expert knew that an average virus attack duration of 24 working hours (three work-days), for example, would have been absurd. Likewise, it was equally absurd that it could be only an hour. But in both cases this is knowing something, and it quantifies the expert's uncertainty. A range of 6 to 10 hours is much less uncertainty than a range of 2 to 20 hours. Either way, the amount of uncertainty itself is of interest to us.

The last two dialogs are examples of absurdity tests in the reverse-anchoring approach I mentioned earlier. I apply it whenever I get the "There is no way I could know that" response or the "Here's my range, but it's a guess" response. No matter how little experts think they know about a quantity, it always turns out that there are still values they know are absurd. Again, the point at which a value ceases to be absurd and starts to become unlikely but somewhat plausible is the edge of their uncertainty about the quantity. As a final test, I give them an equivalent bet to see if the resulting range is really a 90% confidence interval.

The Greek poet and philosopher Horace seemed to intuitively understand over 2,000 years ago that even when there is a lot of uncertainty, you still have some basis for a range. He said "There is a measure in everything. There are fixed limits beyond which and short of which right cannot find a resting place." All he needed to do was to express that range with a probability on it and he would have a confidence interval.

The conceptual obstacle "Why don't I just put ridiculously wide ranges on everything, then everything will be right?" is a misunderstanding of the objective. Your objective is to state a range that represents your 90% CI. This means that you set your range such that you think there is a 5% chance the value is below your lower bound and a 5% chance it is above your upper bound. Making the ranges wide enough so that every range contains the answer is effectively a 100% confidence interval and it likely contains values you know to be highly unlikely or even impossible. It is not, in other words, a representation of your uncertainty. When it comes to communicating your uncertainty, you would have just committed the equally undesirable error of underconfidence as opposed to overconfidence. Of course, such a strategy will fail the equivalent bet test we described.

One could also apply a trick to make either the CI score or the true/false score appear calibrated without actually being calibrated. You could just not even read the true/false questions, pick an answer at random, and say you were 50% confident on each. Likewise, on a 10-question range test you could choose a ridiculous range on 9 questions and then deliberately get one wrong. Again, both of these strategies fail the equivalent bet, neither is a representation of your uncertainty, and neither helps in training for real world estimation problems.

The concern that ranges are too wide to be useful is not uncommon. Many people will find that for some CI questions their ranges were so wide that the upper bound was 10 or 100 times as much as the lower bound. But if that was their uncertainty, then that was the answer we wanted. The objection seems to assume either that the estimate will not be measured further or that there is some other valid reason to use a less honest representation of one's uncertainty. First, keep in mind the universal measurement approach described earlier and that modeling your initial uncertainty is an interim step, not the end goal. Our next step is to compute the value of additional information based on your current uncertainty. If your ranges and probabilities do not reflect your honest uncertainty, then the computed information values will be wrong and, therefore, the measurement priorities will be wrong. Second, there is sometimes a belief that an honest range would be embarrassing and that "I could never present that range to management." But we need to know the uncertainty you actually have, not the uncertainty you *wish* you had. And, again, don't assume that this range is what you end up with. Our information value calculations may indicate it needs to be measured further.

The third from the last of the conceptual obstacles I mentioned is based on a lack of understanding of the definition of probability we are using. If someone asks "But how do I know what the true probability is?" they are implicitly presuming that the probability is an objective thing that exists independent of their own knowledge about it—like the mass of a particular rock or the temperature of the sea at a particular location and time. Instead, we are using the version of probability that applies to decisions. The probability you assign is only a description of *your* uncertainty. Someone who has more or less information than you will assign different probabilities. As Bruno de Finetti wrote:

> *[I]n the conception we follow and sustain here, only subjective probabilities exist—i.e., the degree of belief in the occurrence of an event attributed by a given person at a given instant and with a given set of information.*[18]

The probability you assign using tools like the equivalent bet or de Finetti's no-arbitrage strategy is simply your current state of uncertainty. Here is a fortunate fact: When it comes to assessing your own uncertainty, *you* are the world's leading expert.

THE EFFECTS OF CALIBRATION TRAINING

Of the list of examples of conceptual obstacles to calibration, the last two were particular empirical claims. Those two claims—whether calibration tests merely test someone's skill at trivia or whether the topic of the trivia mattered—are actually both testable hypotheses. Testing these claims about calibration starts with the same kinds of questions that we would have for any measurement problem—namely, what are the observable consequences of those claims? In other words, what should we see if those claims were true and what do we actually see?

Since I started calibrating people in 1995, I've been tracking how well people do throughout a series of trivia tests and even how well-calibrated people do in estimating real-life uncertainties after those events have come to pass. My calibration methods and tests have evolved a lot but have been fairly consistent since 2001. The 927 individuals I mentioned earlier have also gone all the way through this half-day of training. They each took two to four more rounds of tests for ranges and true/false questions. While the initial tests were always 10 questions, the last two to four rounds of tests would contain 20 questions to improve the measurements of individual calibration. They either kept taking tests until they were calibrated or until we ran out of the allotted time of 3.5 hours. (The 927 already excludes individuals who had some unplanned interruption which kept them from completing the training.)

Prior to starting this calibration training in 1995, I researched the previous academic literature on calibration and calibration training. By that time, there were several studies but the number of participants in academic experiments ranged only from a few to 80 at most and the majority of these studies did not attempt to measure the effects of training methods to improve calibration.[19] Based on those few small studies that did attempt to measure calibration training, I knew to expect significant, but imperfect, improvements toward calibration. What I was less certain of was the variance I might see in the performance from one individual to the next. The academic research usually shows aggregated results for all the participants in the research, so we can see only an average for a group. When I aggregate the performance of those in my workshops, I get a result very similar to the prior research.

Exhibit 5.5 shows the aggregated results of the range questions for all participants who have taken the current version of the training (as of the fall of 2013) for each of the tests given in the workshop.[20] The horizontal axis is the number of the test and the vertical axis shows what percentage of answers fell within their stated 90% CI. Those who showed significant evidence of good calibration early were excused from subsequent tests. (This turned out to be a strong motivator for performance.) These results seem to indicate significant improvement in the first two or three tests but then a leveling off short of ideal calibration. Since most academic research shows only aggregate results, not results by individuals, most report that ideal calibration is very difficult to reach.

Exhibit 5.5 Aggregate Group Performance

But because I could break down my data by specific persons, I saw another interesting phenomenon. Exhibit 5.6 compares the distribution of the actual number of correct responses on the final 20-question test to the expected distribution of correct responses for a calibrated group. Clearly, the responses in the final 20-question test are much closer to ideally calibrated than the first test shown earlier in Exhibit 5.2. We also know that lucky uncalibrated responses of a large number of tests will be distributed differently than the calibrated responses. We can use this data to estimate how many were uncalibrated even if they got lucky and happened to do well on the last test. We can't always tell who exactly is calibrated or not but we can tell, as a whole, how likely it was that someone was calibrated instead of just lucky.

The distribution we see in Exhibit 5.6 looks very close to the distribution we would expect in a group where about 80% reach ideal calibration with the remainder falling short of average. Most of the remaining 20% who did not reach calibration (15% of the total) showed significant improvement from their first test. Approximately 5% of all who took the calibration training appear to show no improvement at all in

Exhibit 5.6 90% Confidence Interval Test Score Distribution after Training (Final 20-Question Test)[21]

the course of the training. In short, most students perform superbly by the end of the training; it is a few poor performers who bring down the average.

Why is it that about 5% of people are apparently unable to improve at all in calibration training? Whatever the reason, it often turns out not to be that relevant. Virtually every single person we ever relied on for actual estimates was in the first two groups and almost all were in the first ideally calibrated group. Those who seemed to resist any attempt at calibration were, even before the testing, almost never considered to be the relevant expert or decision maker for a particular problem. It may be that they were less motivated, knowing their opinion would not have much bearing. Or it could be that those who lacked aptitude for such problems just don't tend to advance to the level of the people we need for the estimates. Either way, it's academic.

So now let's consider the two objections stated at the beginning of this subchapter. Are these tests merely a measure of trivia knowledge and is it true that they would not be relevant for real-world estimation tasks? First, if calibration training was merely a test of trivia knowledge why would we see that, on average, performance improved so much on each test? Could it be that the last tests simply used easier questions than the first tests in the exercise? No. The tests were randomly ordered with each training session. A test may be the first test with one group and the last test with another. Also, questions were completely and randomly redistributed among different tests three times in the last decade. So some accidental arrangement of the questions from harder to easier cannot be the reason calibration scores improve. Second, if this were merely a test of skill at trivia, why would we see improvement at all? Is this concern based on the idea that the person's general trivia knowledge—in topics ranging from world history, sports, entertainment, science, and geography— actually improved during the series of four or five tests? That hardly seems remotely reasonable, either.

Finally, is there reason to believe that calibration training with general trivia questions does not actually improve performance in real-world estimation relevant to some special profession or topic? The way to test that would be to compare some people who took calibration training to those who did not and then track their performance on their actual estimation tasks.

Fortunately, I've done this. One of the first such experiments I performed was run in 1997. I was asked to train the analysts of the IT advisory firm Giga Information Group (since acquired by Forrester Research, Inc.) in assigning odds to uncertain future events. Giga was an IT research firm that sold its research to other companies on a subscription basis. Giga had adopted the method of assigning odds to events it was predicting for clients, and it wanted to be sure it was performing well.

I trained 16 Giga analysts using the methods I described earlier. At the end of the training, I gave them 20 specific IT industry predictions they would answer as true or false and to which they would assign a confidence. The test was given in January 1997, and all the questions were stated as events occurring or not occurring by June 1, 1997 (e.g., "True or False: Intel will release its 300 MHz Pentium by June 1," etc.). As a control, I also gave the same list of predictions to 16 of their chief information officer (CIO) clients at various organizations. After June 1 we could determine what actually occurred. I presented the results at Giga World 1997, their major IT industry symposium for the year. Exhibit 5.7 shows the results. Note that some participants opted not to answer all of the questions, so the response counts on the chart don't add up to 320 (16 subjects times 20 questions each) in each of the two groups.

The horizontal axis is the chance the participants gave to their prediction on a particular issue being correct. The vertical axis shows how many of those predictions turned out to be correct. An ideally calibrated person should be plotted right along the dotted line. This means the person was right 70% of the time he or she was 70% confident in the predictions, 80% right when he or she was 80% confident, and so on. You see that the analysts' results (where the points are indicated by small squares) were very close to the ideal confidence, easily within allowable error. The results appear to deviate the most from perfect calibration at the low end of the scale, but this part is

Exhibit 5.7 Calibration Experiment Results for 20 IT Industry Predictions in 1997

still within acceptable limits of error. (The acceptable error range is wider on the left of the chart and narrows to zero at the right.) Of all the times participants said they were 50% confident, they turned out to be right about 65% of the time. This means they might have known more than they let on and—only on this end of the scale—were a little underconfident. It's close; these results might be due to chance. There is a 1% chance that 44 or more out of 68 would be right just by flipping a coin.

The deviation is a bit more significant—at least statistically if not visually—at the other end of the scale. Where the analysts indicated a high degree of confidence, chance alone only would have allowed for slightly less deviation from the expected result, so they are a little overconfident on that end of the scale. But, overall, they are very well calibrated.

In comparison, the results of clients who did not receive any calibration training (indicated by the small triangles) were very overconfident. The numbers next to their calibration results show that there were 58 instances when a particular client said he or she was 90% confident in a particular prediction. Of those times, the clients got less than 60% of those predictions correct. Clients who said they were 100% confident in a prediction in 21 specific responses got only 67% of those correct. This group of CIOs may have been unusually overconfident when they said they were 100% certain but, otherwise, all of these results are consistent with what has typically been observed in several other calibration studies over the past several decades.

Equally interesting is the fact that the Giga analysts didn't actually get more answers correct. (The questions were general IT industry, not focusing on analyst specialties.) They were simply more conservative—but not obviously overly conservative—about when they would put high confidence on a prediction. Prior to the training, however, the calibration of the analysts on general trivia questions was just as bad as the clients were on predictions of actual events. The results are clear: The difference in accuracy is due entirely to calibration training, and the calibration training—even though it uses trivia questions—works for real-world predictions needed for their actual jobs.

Many of my previous readers and clients have run their own calibration workshops and saw varying results depending on how closely they followed these procedures. In every case where they could not get as many people calibrated as I observed in my workshops, I find they did not actually try to teach all of the calibration strategies mentioned in Exhibit 5.4. In particular, they did not cover the equivalent bet, which seems to be one of the most important calibration strategies. Those who followed these strategies and practiced with them on every exercise invariably saw results similar to mine.

Motivation and experience in estimating may also be a factor. I usually give my training to experienced managers and analysts, most of whom knew they would be called on to make real-world estimates with their new skills. Dale Roenigk of the University of North Carolina–Chapel Hill gave this same training to his students and noticed a much lower rate of calibration (although still a significant improvement). Unlike managers, students are rarely asked for estimates; this may have been a factor in their performance. And they had no real motivation to perform well. As I observed in my own workshops, those who did not expect their answers to be used in the subsequent real-world estimation tasks were almost always those who showed little or no improvement.

Even though a few individuals have had some initial difficulties with calibration, most are entirely willing to accept calibration and see it as a key skill in estimation. One such individual is Pat Plunkett—the program manager for Information Technology Performance Measurement at the Department of Housing and Urban Development (HUD) and a thought leader in the U.S. government for the use of performance metrics. He has seen people from various agencies get calibrated since 2000. In 2000, Plunkett was still with the General Services Administration and was the driver behind the CIO Council experiment that brought these methods into the VA. Plunkett sees calibration as a profound shift in thinking about uncertainty. He says: "Calibration was an eye-opening experience. Many people, including myself, discovered how optimistic we tend to be when it comes to estimating. Once calibrated, you are a changed person. You have a keen sense of your level of uncertainty."

Perhaps the only U.S. government employee who has seen more people get calibrated than Plunkett was Art Koines, at the time a senior policy advisor at the Environmental Protection Agency, where dozens of people have been calibrated. Like Plunkett, he was also surprised at the level of acceptance. "People sat through the process and saw the value of it. The big surprise for me was that they were so willing to provide calibrated estimates when I expected them to resist giving any answer at all for such uncertain things."

The calibration skill was a big help to the VA team in the IT security case. The VA team needed to show how much it knew and how much it didn't know in order to quantify its uncertainty about security. The initial set of estimates (all ranges and probabilities) represent the current level of uncertainty about the quantities involved. As we will soon see, knowing one's current level of uncertainty provides an important basis for the rest of the measurement process.

There is one other extremely important effect of calibration. *In addition to improving one's ability to subjectively assess odds, calibration seems to eliminate many objections to probabilistic analysis in decision making.* Prior to calibration training, people might feel any subjective estimate was useless. They might believe that the only way to know a CI is to do the math they vaguely remember from first-semester statistics. They may distrust probabilistic analysis in general because all probabilities seem arbitrary to them. But after a person has been calibrated, I have almost never heard them offer such challenges. In fact, it seems the only ones who persist with such objections are those that never reached calibration at the end of the training. It may be because conceptual obstacles are what keep them from reaching calibration or it may be that their own failure to reach calibration is interpreted by some as evidence that the calibration approach is conceptually flawed. The latter would be a hard position to maintain when the person is surrounded by colleagues who managed to get calibrated (which is usually the case).

Apparently, the hands-on experience of being forced to assign probabilities, and then seeing that this was a measurable skill in which they could see real improvements, addresses these objections. Although this was not an objective I envisioned when I first started calibrating people, I came to learn how critical this process was in getting them to accept the entire concept of probabilistic analysis in decision making.

You now understand how to quantify your current uncertainty by learning how to provide calibrated probabilities. Knowing how to provide calibrated probabilities is critical to the next steps in measurement. Chapters 6 and 7 will teach you how to use calibrated probabilities to compute risk and the value of information.

Notes

1. B. Fischhoff, L. D. Phillips, and S. Lichtenstein, "Calibration of Probabilities: The State of the Art to 1980," in *Judgment under Uncertainty: Heuristics and Biases,* eds. D. Kahneman and A. Tversky (New York: Cambridge University Press, 1982).
2. D. Lawrence and C. Wright, "Cultural Differences in Viewing Uncertainty and Assessing Probabilities," *Theory and Decision Library* 16 (1977): 507–519.
3. Gerd Gigerenzer, Ulrich Hoffrage, and Heinz Kleinbölting, "Probabilistic Mental Models: A Brunswikian Theory of Confidence," *Psychological Review* 98 (1991): 254–267. doi:10.1037//0033-295X.98.4.506.
4. Gordon F. Pitz, "Subjective Probability Distributions for Imperfectly Known Quantities," In *Knowledge and Cognition* (Oxford: Lawrence Erlbaum, 1974).
5. Peter Juslin, "The Overconfidence Phenomenon as a Consequence of Informal Experimenter-Guided Selection of Almanac Items," *Organizational Behavior and Human Decision Processes* 57, no. 2 (1994): 226–246. doi:10.1006/obhd .1994.1013.

6. T. Hazard and C. Peterson, "Odds versus Probabilities for Categorical Events," *Decisions and Designs, Inc. Technical Report* 73–2, McLean, VA, 1973.

7. D. Kahneman and A. Tversky, "Subjective Probability: A Judgment of Representativeness," *Cognitive Psychology* 4 (1972): 430–454; and D. Kahneman and A. Tversky, "On the Psychology of Prediction," *Psychological Review* 80 (1973): 237–251.

8. Fischoff, Phillips, and Lichtenstein, "Calibration of Probabilities."

9. G. T. G. Choo, "Training and Generalization in Assessing Probabilities for Discrete Events," *Technical Report* 76, no. 5 (1976): 12–13.

10. Joe K. Adams and Pauline Austin Adams, "Realism of Confidence Judgments," *Psychological Review* 68 (1961): 33–45.

11. Pauline Adams and Joe Adams, "Training in Confidence-Judgments," *American Journal of Psychology* 71 (1958): 747–751.

12. S. Lichtenstein and B. Fischhoff, "Do Those Who Know More Also Know More about How Much They Know?" *Organizational Behavior and Human Performance* 20, no. 2 (1977): 159–183. doi:10.1016/0030-5073(77)90001-0.

13. S. Lichtenstein and B. Fischoff, "How Well Do Probability Experts Assess Probability?" *Decision Research Report* 80–5, Eugene, OR, 1980.

14. S. Lichtenstein and B. Fischhoff, "Training for Calibration," *Organizational Behavior and Human Performance* 26, no. 2 (1980): 149–171. doi:10.1016/0030-5073(80)90052-5.

15. Robert C. Pickhardt and John B. Wallace, "A Study of the Performance of Subjective Probability Assessors," *Decision Sciences* 5, no. 3 (1974): 347–363.

16. Asher Koriat, Sarah Lichtenstein, and Baruch Fischhoff, "Reasons for Confidence," *Journal of Experimental Psychology: Human Learning & Memory* 6, no. 2 (1980): 107–118. doi:10.1037//0278-7393.6.2.107.

17. William Feller, *An Introduction to Probability Theory and Its Applications* (New York: John Wiley & Sons, 1957), 19.

18. Bruno de Finetti, A. Machi, and A. Smith, *Theory of Probability. A Critical Introductory Treatment, Volume 1* (New York: John Wiley & Sons, 1974), xi.

19. Philip Tetlock's much larger study of 284 participants over a 20-year period, totaling over 82,000 individual estimates, was not published until 2006 and did not attempt to measure effects of training.

20. Note that these calibration figures are slightly different from the figures in the first and second editions of this book because of a large number of new samples (i.e., participants in calibration training).

21. This chart shows results for 808 subjects. Of the 927 subjects who took the initial 10-question test, 119 did not actually participate in all of the calibration training. Most of these 119 were situations where we intended to only conduct a sample test for illustration purposes (for a conference audience or other short meeting). The remainder of these 119 could not complete planned half-day of training due to unanticipated interruptions.

A Purely Philosophical Interlude #3

Confidence in Confidence Intervals: Does 90% Confidence Mean 90% Probability?

All possible definitions of probability fall short of the actual practice.
—William Feller (1906–1970),
American mathematician[1]

Throughout this book, I will refer to a 90% CI as a range of values (indicated by an upper and lower bound) that has a 90% probability of containing the true value. I will use this definition regardless of whether the CI was determined subjectively or—as Chapters 9 and 10 will show—with additional sample data. By doing so, I'm using the previously-mentioned Bayesian interpretation of probability which treats probability as an expression of the uncertainty or "degree of belief" of the person providing the estimate.

But, as we already saw, the frequentists' interpretation contradicts this view of probability. Consequently, they also have a different view of a CI. If I computed the 90% CI of, say, the estimate of the mean weight of a new breed of chickens to be 2.45 to 2.78 pounds after three months, they would argue that it is incorrect to say there is a 90% probability that the true population mean is within the interval. They would say the true population mean is either in the range or not.

But that particular interpretation is not as useful when our decision is whether to, say, buy the new breed of chicken. The subjective Bayesian interpretation is more useful in making risky decisions. According to de Finetti's definition, if you set a price of $90 for a chance to win $100 if the true mean of chicken weights turns out to be within the interval, and if you were indifferent as to which side of the bet you were on, then you think there is a 90% probability that the true mean is within the interval. In our "equivalent bet" variation, you would be indifferent between a game where you win $100 if the true mean weight of the chickens were within the stated interval and a game where you win $100 based on a spin of a dial that gives you a 90% chance of winning. Someone with less knowledge would put a wider range on it and someone with more knowledge would use a narrower range.

In an attempt to reconcile potential ambiguity about confidence intervals, some have developed alternative intervals, referring to them as "credibility intervals," "fiducial intervals," "prediction intervals," and more. But there really is no relevant ambiguity if we simply accept the subjective interpretation of probability to begin with. Whether we are assessing a current state (like the current weight of all such chickens that are three months old) or making a prediction (what this breed will weigh in three months), the de Finetti approach applies. And this use of a CI applies even when the estimate is made without data or informed with new data. As I said before, this interpretation, like the frequentists' interpretation, is entirely mathematically sound. After all, if either position could be proven as the "one true" position, then they would be called "theorems" or "laws" not merely "interpretations." I am willing to bet, however, that if real money was on the line, an experiment involving frequentist statisticians betting on various confidence intervals and dial-spins would show they would also act like Bayesians.

In many published works in the empirical sciences, physicists,[2] epidemiologists,[3] and paleobiologists[4] explicitly and routinely describe a confidence interval as having a *probability* of containing the estimated value. Yet it appears that nobody has ever had to retract an article because of it—nor should anyone. Likewise neither should decision makers be dissuaded from using information that improves decisions.

So, like most decision scientists, we will act as if a 90% confidence interval has a 90% probability of containing the true value (and we never run into a mathematical paradox because of it).

Notes

1. William Feller, *An Introduction to Probability Theory and Its Applications* (New York: John Wiley & Sons, 1957), 19.
2. Frederick James, *Statistical Methods in Experimental Physics,* 2nd ed. (Hackensack, NJ: World Scientific Publishing, 2006), 215; and Byron P. Roe, *Probability and Statistics in Experimental Physics,* 2nd ed. (New York: Springer Verlag, 2001), 128.
3. C. C. Brown, "The Validity of Approximation Methods for the Interval Estimation of the Odds Ratio," *American Journal of Epidemiology* 113 (1981): 474–480.
4. Steve C. Wang and Charles R. Marshal, "Improved Confidence Intervals for Estimating the Position of a Mass Extinction Boundary," *Paleobiology* 30 (January 2004): 5–18.

## CHAPTER 6

Quantifying Risk through Modeling

It is better to be approximately right than to be precisely wrong.
—Warren Buffett

We've defined the difference between uncertainty and risk. Initially, quantifying uncertainty is just a matter of putting our calibrated ranges or probabilities on unknown variables. Subsequent measurements reduce uncertainty about the quantity and, in addition, quantify the new state of uncertainty. As discussed in Chapter 4, risk is simply a state of uncertainty where some possible outcomes involve a loss of some kind. Generally, the implication is that the loss is something dramatic, not minor. But for our purposes, any loss will do.

Risk is itself a quantity that has a lot of relevance on its own. But it is also a foundation of further measurement for decision making. As we will see in Chapter 7, risk reduction is the basis of computing the value of a measurement, which is in turn the basis of selecting what to measure and how to measure it. Remember, if a measurement matters to you at all, it is because it must inform some decision that is uncertain and has negative consequences if it turns out wrong.

This chapter discusses a basic tool for almost any kind of risk analysis and some surprising observations you might make when you start using this tool. But first, we need to separate from this some popular schemes that are often used to measure risk but really offer no insight.

HOW *NOT* TO QUANTIFY RISK

What many organizations do to assess risk is not very enlightening. The methods I propose for assessing risk would be familiar to an actuary, statistician, or financial analyst. But some of the most popular methods for measuring risk look nothing like what an actuary might be familiar with. Many organizations simply say a risk is "high," "medium," or "low." Or perhaps they rate it on a scale of 1 to 5. When I find situations like this, I sometimes ask how much "medium" risk really is. Is a 5% chance of losing more than $5 million a low, medium, or high risk? Nobody knows. Is a medium-risk investment with a 15% return on investment better or worse than a high-risk investment with a 50% return? Again, nobody knows because the statements themselves are ambiguous.

Researchers have shown, in fact, that such ambiguous labels don't help the decision maker at all and actually add an error of their own. They add imprecision by forcing a kind of rounding error that, in practice, gives the same score to hugely different risks.[1] Worse yet, in my 2009 book, *The Failure of Risk Management,* I show that users of these methods tend to cluster responses in a way that magnifies this effect[2] (more on this in Chapter 12).

In addition to these problems, the softer risk "scoring" methods management might use make no attempt to address the typical human biases discussed in Chapter 5. Most of us are systematically overconfident and will tend to underestimate uncertainty and risks unless we avail ourselves of the training that can offset such effects.

To illustrate why these sorts of classifications are not as useful as they could be, I ask attendees in seminars to consider the next time they have to write a check (or pay over the web) for their next auto or homeowner's insurance premium. Where you would usually see the "amount" field on the check, instead of writing a dollar amount, write the word "medium" and see what happens. You are telling your insurer you want a "medium" amount of risk mitigation. Would that make sense to the insurer in any meaningful way? It probably doesn't to you, either.

It is true that many of the users of these methods will report that they feel much more confident in their decisions as a result. But, as we will see in Chapter 12, this feeling should not be confused with evidence of effectiveness. We will learn that studies have shown that it is quite possible to experience an increase in confidence about decisions and forecasts without actually improving things—or even by making them worse.

For now, just know that there is apparently a strong placebo effect in many decision analysis and risk analysis methods. Managers need to start to be able to tell the difference between feeling better about decisions and actually having better track records over time. There must be measured evidence that decisions and forecasts actually improved. Unfortunately, risk analysis or risk management—or decision analysis in general—rarely has a performance metric of its own.[3] The good news is that some methods have been measured, and they show a real improvement.

REAL RISK ANALYSIS: THE MONTE CARLO

Using ranges to represent your uncertainty instead of unrealistically precise point values clearly has advantages. When you allow yourself to use ranges and probabilities, you don't really have to assume anything you don't know for a fact. But precise values have the advantage of being simple to add, subtract, multiply, and divide in a spreadsheet. So how do we add, subtract, multiply, and divide in a spreadsheet when we have no exact values, only ranges? Fortunately, there is a practical, proven solution, and it can be performed on any modern personal computer.

One of our measurement mentors, Enrico Fermi, was an early user of what was later called a "Monte Carlo simulation." A Monte Carlo simulation uses a computer to generate a large number of scenarios based on probabilities for inputs. For each scenario, a specific value would be randomly generated for each of the unknown variables. Then these specific values would go into a formula to compute an output for that single scenario. This process usually goes on for thousands of scenarios.

Fermi used Monte Carlo simulations to work out the behavior of large numbers of neutrons. In the 1930s, he knew that he was working on a problem that could not be solved with conventional integral calculus. But he could work out the odds of specific results in specific conditions. He realized that he could, in effect, randomly sample several of these situations and work out how neutrons would behave in a system. In the 1940s, several mathematicians—most famously Stanislaw Ulam, John von Neumann, and Nicholas Metropolis—continued to work on similar problems in nuclear physics and started using computers to generate the random scenarios. At this time they were working on the atomic bomb for the Manhattan Project and, later, the hydrogen bomb at Los Alamos. At the suggestion of Metropolis, Ulam named this computer-based method of generating random scenarios after Monte Carlo, a famous gambling hotspot, in honor of Ulam's uncle, a gambler.[4] What Fermi begat, and what was later reared by Ulam, von Neumann, and Metropolis, is today widely used in business, government, and research. A simple application of this method is working out the return on an investment when you don't know exactly what the costs and benefits will be.

Apparently, it is not obvious to some that uncertainty about the costs and benefits of some new investment is really the basis of that investment's risk. I once met with the chief information officer (CIO) of an investment firm in Chicago to talk about how the company can measure the value of information technology (IT). She said that they had a "pretty good handle on how to measure risk" but "I can't begin to imagine how to measure benefits." On closer look, this is a very curious combination of positions. She explained that most of the benefits the company attempts to achieve in IT investments are improvements in basis points (1 basis point = 0.01% yield on an investment)—the return the company gets on the investments it manages for clients. The firm hopes that the right IT investments can facilitate a competitive advantage in collecting and analyzing information that affects investment decisions. But when I asked her how the company came up with a value for the effect on basis points, she said staffers "just pick a number."

In other words, as long as enough people are willing to agree on (or at least not too many object to) a particular number for increased basis points, that's what the business case is based on. While it's possible this number is based on some experience, it was also clear that she was more uncertain about this benefit than any other. But if this was true, how was the company measuring risk? Clearly, it was a strong possibility that the firm's largest risk in new IT, if it was measured, would be the possibility that this benefit is too low to justify an investment. She was not using ranges to express her uncertainty about the basis point improvement, so she had no way to incorporate this uncertainty into her risk calculation. Even though she felt confident the firm was doing a good job on risk analysis, she wasn't really doing any risk analysis at all. She was, in fact, merely experiencing the previously mentioned placebo effect from one of the ineffectual risk "scoring" methods.

I've noticed that once someone who was using scoring methods sees how their problems can be solved with a probabilistic model, they are converts. Long after the cybersecurity risk analysis I did for the VA, I was asked to create a risk analysis for cybersecurity for a large, integrated healthcare delivery system. The director in charge of cybersecurity engaged Hubbard Decision Research to develop a probabilistic model to replace their previous score-based model. The previous method required his security experts to rate several risk factors on a one to nine scale and then add these up to produce a low, medium, high or extreme likelihood and severity. In its place, we built an easy-to-use Excel-based tool which would run just 5,000 simulations for a series of risk events based on a few risk indicators his security experts would provide.

Since we were doing the actual math, we could answer questions like "What is the chance that this set of risks will have total losses of over $10 million over the next five years?" There was no way, of course, that the previous method, limited to using ambiguous labels like "Low, Medium, High, Extreme," could possibly answer questions about the probability of different total losses. The director doesn't see how he could ever return to the previous way of doing business.

In fact, *all* risk in any project investment ultimately can be expressed by one method: the ranges of uncertainty on the costs and benefits and probabilities on events that might affect them. If you know precisely the amount and timing of every cost and benefit (as is implied by traditional business cases based on fixed point values), you literally have no risk. There is no chance that any benefit would be lower or cost would be higher than you expect. But all we really know about these things is the range, not exact points. And because we only have broad ranges, there is a chance we will have a negative return. That is the basis for computing risk, and that is what the Monte Carlo simulation is for.

AN EXAMPLE OF THE MONTE CARLO METHOD AND RISK

This is an extremely basic example of a Monte Carlo simulation for people who have never worked with it before but have some familiarity with the Excel spreadsheet. If you have worked with a Monte Carlo tool before, you probably can skip these next few pages.

Let's say you are considering leasing a new machine for one step in a manufacturing process. The one-year lease is $400,000 with no option for early cancellation. So if you aren't breaking even, you are still stuck with it for the rest of the year. You are considering signing the contract because you think the more advanced device could save some labor and raw materials and because you think the maintenance cost will be lower than the existing process.

Your calibrated estimators gave the following ranges for savings in maintenance, labor, and raw materials. They also estimated the annual production levels for this process.

- Maintenance savings (MS): $10 to $20 per unit
- Labor savings (LS): –$2 to $8 per unit (note the negative lower bound)
- Raw materials savings (RMS): $3 to $9 per unit
- Production level (PL): 15,000 to 35,000 units per year
- Annual lease (breakeven): $400,000

Now you compute your annual savings very simply as:

$$\text{Annual Savings} = (MS + LS + RMS) \times PL$$

Admittedly, this is an unrealistically simple example. The production levels could be different every year, perhaps some costs would improve further as experience with the new machine improved, and so on. But we've deliberately opted for simplicity over realism in this example.

If we just take the midpoint of each of these ranges, we get:

$$\text{Annual savings} = (\$15 + \$3 + \$6) \times 25,000 = \$600,000$$

It looks like we do better than the required breakeven, but there are uncertainties. So how do we measure the risk of this lease? First, let's define risk for this context. Remember, to have a risk, we have to have uncertain future results with some of them being a quantified loss. One way of looking at risk would be the chance that we don't break even—that is, we don't save enough to make up for the $400,000 lease. The farther the savings undershoot the lease, the more we have lost. The $600,000 is the amount we save if we just choose the midpoints of each uncertain variable. How do we compute what that range of savings really is and, thereby, compute the chance that we don't break even?

Since these aren't exact numbers, usually we can't just do a single calculation to determine whether we met the required savings. Some methods allow us to compute the range of the result given the ranges of inputs under some limited conditions, but in most real-life problems, those conditions don't exist. As soon as we begin adding and multiplying different types of distributions, the problem usually becomes what a mathematician would call "unsolvable" or "having no solution." This is exactly the problem the physicists working on atomic fission ran into. To resolve this problem, Monte Carlo simulations use a *brute-force approach* made possible with computers. We randomly pick a bunch of exact values—thousands—according to the ranges we prescribed and compute a large number of exact values. Then we use those randomly chosen values to compute a single result in each of thousands of scenarios. After the thousands of possible results are calculated, the probabilities of different results can be estimated.

In this example, each scenario is a set of randomly generated values for labor savings, maintenance savings, and so on. After each set is generated, those values are used in the annual savings calculation. Some of the annual savings results will be higher than $600,000 and some will be lower. Some will even be lower than the $400,000 required to break even. After thousands of scenarios are generated, we can determine how likely it is that the lease will be a net gain.

You can run a Monte Carlo simulation easily with Excel on a PC, but we need a bit more information than just the 90% confidence interval (CI) for each of the variables. We also need the *shape* of the distribution. Some shapes are more appropriate for certain values than other shapes. One that is often used with the 90% CI is the well-known "normal" distribution. The normal distribution is the familiar-looking bell curve where the probable outcomes are bunched near the middle but trail off to ever less likely values in both directions. (See Exhibit 6.1.)

With the normal distribution, I will briefly mention a related concept called the *standard deviation*. People don't seem to have an intuitive understanding of a standard deviation, and because it can be replaced by a calculation based on the 90% CI (which people do understand intuitively), I won't focus on it here. Exhibit 6.1 shows that there are 3.29 standard deviations in one 90% CI, so we just need to make the conversion.

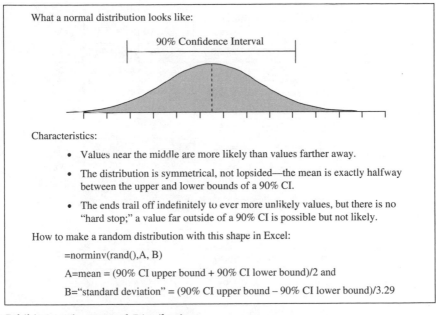

What a normal distribution looks like:

90% Confidence Interval

Characteristics:

- Values near the middle are more likely than values farther away.

- The distribution is symmetrical, not lopsided—the mean is exactly halfway between the upper and lower bounds of a 90% CI.

- The ends trail off indefinitely to ever more unlikely values, but there is no "hard stop;" a value far outside of a 90% CI is possible but not likely.

How to make a random distribution with this shape in Excel:

=norminv(rand(),A, B)

A=mean = (90% CI upper bound + 90% CI lower bound)/2 and

B="standard deviation" = (90% CI upper bound – 90% CI lower bound)/3.29

Exhibit 6.1 The Normal Distribution

For our problem, we can just make a random number generator in a spreadsheet for each of our ranges. Following the instructions in Exhibit 6.1, we can generate random numbers for maintenance savings with the Excel formula:

$$=norminv(rand(\ ),15,(20–10)/3.29)$$

Likewise, we follow the instructions in Exhibit 6.1 for the rest of the ranges. Some people might prefer using the random number generator in the Excel Analysis Toolpack, and you should feel free to experiment with it. I'm showing this formula in Exhibit 6.2 for a bit more of a hands-on approach. (Download this spreadsheet from www.howtomeasureanything .com.)

We arrange the variables in columns as shown in Exhibit 6.2. The last two columns are just the calculations based on all the previous columns. The Total Savings column is the formula for annual savings (shown earlier) based on the numbers in each particular row. For example, scenario 1 in Exhibit 6.2 shows its Total Savings as ($9.27 + $4.30 + $7.79) × 23,955 = $511,716 (inputs are shown rounded to nearest cent, but actual values produce the output as shown). You don't really need the "Breakeven Met?" column; I'm just showing it for reference. Now let's copy it down and make 10,000 rows.

Scenario #	Maintenance Savings	Labor Savings	Materials Savings	Units Produced	Total Savings	Breakeven Met?
1	$ 9.27	$4.30	$7.79	23,955	$511,716	Yes
2	$15.92	$2.64	$9.02	26,263	$724,127	Yes
3	$17.70	$4.63	$8.10	20,142	$612,739	Yes
4	$15.08	$6.75	$5.19	20,644	$557,860	Yes
5	$19.42	$9.28	$9.68	25,795	$990,167	Yes
6	$11.86	$3.17	$5.86	17,121	$358,166	**No**
7	$15.21	$0.46	$4.14	29,283	$580,167	Yes
⇩	⇩	⇩	⇩	⇩	⇩	⇩
9,999	$14.68	$(0.22)	$5.32	33,175	$655,879	Yes
10,000	$ 7.49	$(0.01)	$8.97	24,237	$398,658	**No**

Exhibit 6.2 Simple Monte Carlo Layout in Excel

We can use a couple of other simple tools in Excel to get a sense of how this turns out. The "=countif()" function allows you to count the number of values that meet a certain condition—in this case, those that are less than $400,000. Or, for a more complete picture, you can use the histogram tool in the Excel Analysis Toolpack. That will count the number of scenarios in each of several "buckets," or incremental groups. Then you can make a chart to display the output, as shown in Exhibit 6.3. This chart shows how many of the 10,000 scenarios came up in each $100,000 increment. For example, just over 1,000 scenarios had values between $300,000 and $400,000.

You will find that about 14% of the results were less than the $400,000 breakeven. This means there is about a 14% chance of losing money, which is a meaningful measure of risk. But risk doesn't have to mean just the chance of a negative return on investment. In the same way we can measure the "size" of a thing by its height, weight, girth, and so on, there are a lot of useful measures of risk. Further examination shows that there is a 3.5% chance that the factory will lose more than $100,000 per year instead of saving money. However, generating no benefit at all is virtually impossible. This is what we mean by "risk analysis." We have to be able to compute the odds of various levels of losses. If you are truly measuring risk, this is what you can do. Again, for a spreadsheet example of this Monte Carlo problem, see the website at www.howtomeasureanything.com.

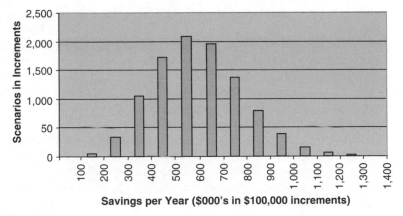

Exhibit 6.3 Histogram

A shortcut can apply in some situations. If we had all normal distributions and we simply wanted to add or subtract ranges—such as a simple list of costs and benefits—we might not have to run a Monte Carlo simulation. If we just wanted to add up the three types of savings in our example, we can use a simple calculation. Use these six steps to produce a range:

1. Subtract the midpoint from the upper bound for each of the three cost savings ranges: in this example, $20 − $15 = $5 for maintenance savings; we also get $5 for labor savings and $3 for materials savings.
2. Square each of the values from the last step: $5 squared is $25, and so on.
3. Add up the results: $25 + $25 + $9 = $59.
4. Take the square root of the total: SQRT($59) = $7.68.
5. Total up the means: $15 + $3 + $6= $24.
6. Add and subtract the result from step 4 from the sum of the means to get the upper and lower bounds of the total, or $24 + $7.68 = $31.68 for the upper bound, $24 − $7.68 = $16.32 for the lower bound.

So the 90% CI for the sum of all three 90% CIs for maintenance, labor, and materials is $16.32 to $31.68. In summary, the range interval of the total is equal to the square root of the sum of the squares of the range intervals. (Note: If you are already familiar with the 90% CI from a basic stats text or have already read ahead to Chapter 9, keep in mind that $7.68 is not the standard deviation. $7.68 is the difference between the midpoint of the range and either of the bounds of a 90% CI, which is 1.645 standard deviations.)

You might see someone attempting to do something similar by adding up all the "optimistic" values for an upper bound and "pessimistic" values for the lower bound. This would result in a range of $11 to $37 for these three CIs, which slightly exaggerates the 90% CI. When this calculation is done with a business case of dozens of variables, the exaggeration of the range becomes too significant to ignore. It is like thinking that rolling a bucket of six-sided dice will produce all 1s or all 6s. Most of the time, we get a combination of all the values, some high, some low. Using all optimistic values for the optimistic case and all pessimistic values for the pessimistic case is a common error and no doubt has resulted in a large number of misinformed decisions. The simple method I just showed works perfectly well when you have a set of 90% CIs you would like to add up.

But we don't just want to add these up; we want to multiply them by the production level, which is also a range. The simple range addition method doesn't work with anything other than subtraction or addition so we would need to use a Monte Carlo simulation. A Monte Carlo simulation is also required if these were not all normal distributions. Although a wide variety of shapes of distributions for all sorts of problems is beyond the scope of this book, it is worth mentioning two others besides the normal distribution: the uniform distribution and the binary distribution. There are many more types of distributions than this and some will be briefly mentioned later in this chapter. For now, we will focus on some simple distributions to get you started. You will learn to add more as you master them.

One realism-enhancing improvement to our simple machine leasing model can illustrate how the uniform and binary distributions could be used. What if there was a 10% chance of a loss of a major account that would, by itself, drop the demand (and therefore the production levels) by 1,000 units per month (i.e., 12,000 units per year)? We could model this as a discrete either/or event that could happen at any time of the year. This would be a major, sudden drop in demand that the previous normal distribution doesn't adequately model.

We would just add a couple of columns to our table. For each scenario, we would have to determine if this event occurred. If it did, we would have to determine when during the year it occurred so the production levels for the year could be determined. For those scenarios where the contract loss does not occur, we don't need to change the production level. The next formula could adjust the production level we generated previously with the normal distribution:

Production level considering possibility of a major contract loss:

$PL_{w/contract\ loss} = PL_{normal} - 1,000$ units × (Contract Loss × Month Remaining)

As a binary event, the "Contract Loss" has a value of one 10% of the time and zero 90% of the time. This would be modeled using the equation in Exhibit 6.4 (where P is set to 0.1). This is also called a "Bernoulli distribution," after the seventeenth-century mathematician Jacob Bernoulli, who developed several early concepts about the theory of probability.

The "Months Remaining" (in the year), however, might be a uniform distribution, as shown in Exhibit 6.5 (where "upper bound" is set to 12 months and "lower bound" is 0). If we choose a uniform distribution, we are effectively saying that any date during the year for this loss of a contract is just as likely as any other date.

If the contract is not lost, "Contract Loss" is zero and no change is made to the previous, normally distributed production level. If the contract is lost early in the year (where months remaining in the year is high), we lose more orders than if we had lost the contract later in the year. The spreadsheet at www.howtomeasureanything.com for the Monte Carlo example also shows this alternative contract loss example. Each of these distributions will come up later when we discuss the value of information.

Our Monte Carlo simulation can be made as elaborate and realistic as we like. We can compute the benefits over several years, with uncertain growth rates in demand, losing or gaining individual customers, and the possibility of new technology destroying demand. We can even model

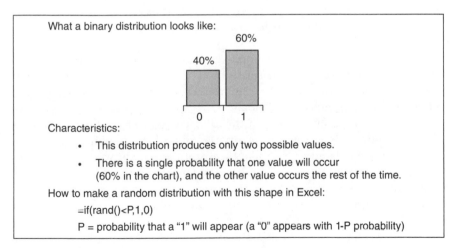

Exhibit 6.4 The Binary (a.k.a. Bernoulli) Distribution

What a uniform distribution looks like:

100% Confidence Interval

Characteristics:
- All values between the bounds are equally likely.
- The distribution is symmetrical, not lopsided—the mean is exactly halfway between the upper and lower bounds.
- The bounds are "hard stops" and are, in effect, a "100% CI"—nothing above the upper bound nor below the lower bound is possible.

How to make a random distribution with this shape in Excel:

=rand()*(UB-LB)+LB

UB = Upper bound

LB = Lower bound

Exhibit 6.5 The Uniform Distribution

the entire factory floor, simulating orders coming in and jobs being assigned to machines. We can have inventory levels going up and down and model work stoppages if we run out of something and have to wait for the next delivery. We can model how the flow would change or stop if one machine broke down and jobs had to be reassigned or delayed.

All of this might be relevant to a decision to lease or buy new equipment or even a new factory. If the risk is high enough (i.e., a big investment with lots of uncertainty), such an elaborate simulation could easily be justified to support our decision. And every uncertain variable in the model is a candidate for a measurement that could reduce our uncertainty.

It might seem easy to get carried away with the detail of a model. Remember, *all* models are abstractions. There is always detail you leave out, no matter how elaborate the model becomes. <u>So we don't ask whether a model lacks some detail. Of course it does. What we ask is whether our model improved on the alternative model</u> (which may simply be intuition) by enough to justify the cost of the new model. Even a relatively simple Monte Carlo like the example we showed here can be enlightening. We have only scratched the surface of Monte Carlo simulations but, like anything else, start simple and improve your skills over time. Exhibit 6.6 is a list of concepts you might want to pick up once you've mastered the basics.

What we haven't discussed about the previous example is whether you would find it an acceptable risk. In the example, the average over a

Exhibit 6.6 Optional: Additional Monte Carlo Concepts for the More Ambitious Student

Concept and Its Complexity	Description (All additional examples are on the book's website at www.howtomeasureanything.com along with a suggested reading list.)
More Distributions (No more complicated than anything else discussed so far)	It's worth having a few more distributions in your tool box to handle a variety of situations because sometimes the wrong distribution can be wrong by a lot. It can be shown that a normal distribution is a very bad approximation for a variety of phenomena including fluctuations of the stock market, the cost of software projects, or the size of an earthquake, plague, or storm. I show more examples of each of these distributions on the book's website.
Correlations (Still not too much more complicated)	Some of the variables in a model might not be independent of each other. For example, if a union contract affects the hourly rates of both maintenance workers and production workers, they are probably correlated. We can address that by generating correlated random numbers for them or, preferably, by modeling what they have in common explicitly. I show both solutions on the website.
Markov Simulations (Getting more complicated)	These are simulations where a single scenario is itself separated into a large number of time intervals, each of which affects the following time interval. This can apply to complex manufacturing systems, stock prices, the weather, computer networks, and construction projects. Again, see a very simple example on the website.
Agent-Based Models (Getting very complicated)	Just as Markov simulations split up the problem into time intervals, we can also have separate simulations for a large number of individuals acting independently or somewhat in concert. The term *agent* often implies that each actor follows a set of decision rules. Traffic simulations are an example of models made up of a multitude of agents (vehicles) for a large number of time intervals. A very, *very* simple example of this is illustrated on the book's website.

large number of runs is about $600,000 in net benefits with a 14% chance the machine lease would be a net loss. Would you take this bet? If not, how much would the average benefits have to increase to justify the 14% chance of a loss? How much would the chance of loss have to decrease to make it acceptable? If you would have accepted the bet, how much would chance of loss have to increase or average net benefits decrease before you would have to reject it? What if the chance of loss was not changed but the *magnitude* of a loss was?

A common simplifying approach to quantifying a risk is simply to multiply the likelihood of some loss by the amount of the loss. This is simple but can be misleading. This assumes the decision maker is "risk neutral." That is, if I offered you a 10% chance to win $100,000, you would actually be willing to pay as much as $10,000 for it. And you would consider it equivalent to a 50% chance of winning $20,000 or an 80% chance of winning $12,500. But the fact is that most people are not really risk neutral.

Determining how much risk is acceptable for a given return is a critical part of an organization's risk analysis. To make consistent choices, it is important to quantify these various trade-offs in order to clearly state how risk averse or risk tolerant an organization really is. As we will find out later, all sorts of random, arbitrary, and irrelevant factors affect our decisions more than we would like to think. They even affect our *preferences* more than we would like to think. Documenting what your risk preferences really are is like measuring all risks by the same standard ruler instead of by a ruler that changes every day. When we get to Chapter 11, we will see how preferences like these can be nailed down.

TOOLS AND OTHER RESOURCES FOR MONTE CARLO SIMULATIONS

Fortunately, we don't have to build Monte Carlo simulations from scratch these days. Many tools can be very helpful and improve the productivity of an analyst trained in the basics. They range from simple sets of Excel macros—what I use—combined with a practical consulting approach to very sophisticated packages.

A fellow evangelist in the use of Monte Carlo simulations in business is Sam Savage, a Stanford University professor who developed a tool he calls Insight.xla. Savage focuses on trying to sell an intuitive philosophy about using probabilistic analysis. He also has some ideas about how to institutionalize the entire process of creating Monte Carlo simulations. If different parts of the same organization are using simulations, Savage believes organizations should use a common pool of shared distributions instead of inventing their own distributions for common values. Furthermore, he believes the definition of the distribution itself sometimes can be a technical challenge that requires certain proficiency with the mathematics.

Savage has an interesting approach that he calls Probability Management: "Suppose we just took [the problem of generating probability distributions] out of your hands. Now what's your excuse for not using probability distributions? Some people don't know how to generate a probability distribution—they don't know how to generate electricity either, but they still use it."

His idea is to appoint a chief probability officer (CPO) for the firm. The CPO would be in charge of managing a common library of probability distributions for use by anyone running Monte Carlo simulations. Savage invokes concepts like the Stochastic Information Packet (SIP), a pre-generated set of 100,000 random numbers for a particular value. Sometimes different SIPs would be related. For example, the company's revenue might be related to national economic growth. A set of SIPs that are generated so they have these correlations are called "SLURPS" (Stochastic Library Units with Relationships Preserved). The CPO would manage SIPs and SLURPs so that users of probability distributions don't have to reinvent the wheel every time they need to simulate inflation or healthcare costs.

I would add a few other things to make Monte Carlo simulations as formally defined and accepted as accounting processes in organizations:

- *Certification of analysts.* Right now, there is not a lot of quality control for decision analysis experts. Only actuaries, in their particular specialty of decision analysis, have extensive certification requirements. As it is now for actuaries, certification in decision analysis should eventually be an independent not-for-profit program run by a professional association. Some other professional certifications now partly cover these topics but fall far short in substance in this particular area. For this reason, I began certifying individuals in Applied Information Economics because there was an immediate need for people to be able to prove their skills to potential employers.
- *Certification of calibrated estimators.* As we discussed earlier, an uncalibrated estimator has a strong tendency to be overconfident. Any calculation of risk based on his or her estimates will likely be significantly understated. However, a survey I once conducted showed that calibration is almost unheard of among those who build Monte Carlo models professionally, even though a majority used at

least some subjective estimates. (About a third surveyed used mostly subjective estimates.)[5] Calibration training will be one of the simplest improvements to risk analysis in an organization.

- *Well-documented procedures and templates for how models are built from the input of various calibrated estimators.* It takes some time to smooth out the wrinkles in the process. Most organizations don't need to start from scratch for every new investment they are analyzing; they can base their work on that of others or at least reuse their own prior models. I've executed nearly the same analysis procedure following similar project plans for a wide variety of decision analysis problems from IT security, military logistics, and entertainment industry investments. But when I applied the same method in the same organization on different problems, I often found that certain parts of the model would be similar to parts of earlier models. An insurance company would have several investments that include estimating the impact on "customer retention" and "claims payout ratio." Manufacturing-related investments would have calculations related to "marginal labor costs per unit" or "average order fulfillment time." These issues don't have to be modeled anew for each new investment problem. They are reusable modules in spreadsheets.

- *Adoption of a single automated tool set.* Exhibit 6.7 shows a few of the many tool sets available. You can get as sophisticated as you like, but starting out doesn't require any more than some good spreadsheet-based tools. I recommend starting simple and adopting more extensive tool sets as the situations demand.

Exhibit 6.7 A Few Monte Carlo Tools

Tool	Made by	Description
AIE Wizard	Hubbard Decision Research, Glen Ellyn, IL	Excel-based set of macros; also computes value of information and portfolio optimization; emphasizes methodology over the tool and provides consulting for practical implementation issues.
Crystal Ball	Oracle (previously Decisioneering, Inc., purchased by Oracle), Denver, CO	Excel based; a wide variety of distributions; a fairly sophisticated tool. Broad user base and technical support. Has adopted Savage's SIPs and SLURPS and Disk utility.

Tool	Made by	Description
@Risk	Palisade Corporation, Ithaca, NY	Another Excel-based tool; main competitor to Crystal Ball. Many users and technical support.
XLSim	Stanford University Professor Sam Savage, AnalyCorp	Inexpensive package designed for ease of learning and use. Savage also provides seminars and management protocols for making Monte Carlo methods practical in organizations.
Risk Solver Engine	Frontline Systems, Incline Village, NV	Unique Excel-based development platform to perform "interactive" Monte Carlo simulations quickly. Supports SIP and SLURP formats.
Analytica	Lumina Decision Systems, Los Gatos, CA	Uses an extremely intuitive graphical interface that allows complex systems to be modeled as a kind of flowchart of interactions.
SAS	SAS Corporation, Raleigh, NC	Goes well beyond the Monte Carlo; extremely sophisticated package.
IBM SPSS Statistics	SPSS Inc., Chicago, IL	Also goes far beyond the Monte Carlo; tends to be more popular among academics.
Mathematica	Wolfram Research, Champaign, IL	Another extremely powerful tool that does much more than Monte Carlo; used primarily by scientists and mathematicians.
ModelRisk	Vose Software, Gent, Belgium	Another Monte Carlo Excel add-in; developed by the renowned risk and Excel author, David Vose.
RiskAmp	Structured Data, LLC, New York, NY and San Francisco, CA	Another full-featured Monte Carlo Simulation Engine for risk analysis within Excel.
R	Licensed by Free Software Foundation	A widely used and free statistics programming language. Like SAS, SPSS, and Mathmatica, it does a lot more than Monte Carlos.

THE RISK PARADOX AND THE NEED FOR BETTER RISK ANALYSIS

Building a Monte Carlo simulation is barely much more complicated than constructing any spreadsheet-based business case. In fact, by almost any measure of complexity, the Monte Carlo simulations I built to assess the risk of large major decisions, such as IT projects, construction projects, or research and development investments, are in every case significantly less complex than the projects I'm analyzing.

Still, by some standards, Monte Carlo simulations can seem a bit complex. But are they too complex to be practical in business? Not by a long shot. Just like any other complex business problem, management can bring in people with the skills to do the simulations.

Despite this fact, quantitative risk analysis based on Monte Carlo simulations has not been universally adopted. Many organizations employ fairly sophisticated risk analysis methods on particular problems; for example, actuaries in an insurance company define the particulars of an insurance product, statisticians analyze the ratings of a new TV show, and production managers are using Monte Carlo simulations to model changes in production methods. But those very same organizations do *not* routinely apply those same sophisticated risk analysis methods to much bigger decisions with more uncertainty and more potential for loss.

In the spring of 1999, I was teaching a seminar to a group of executives wanting to learn about risk analysis for IT. I began to explain a few basic concepts for Monte Carlo simulations and asked whether anyone was using such methods to assess risk. Usually respondents who claim to assess risk just apply subjective "high," "medium," or "low" assessments with no quantitative basis whatsoever. My objective is to help attendees to differentiate between this kind of fluff and the kind of analysis an actuary would recognize. One of my students said he routinely applied analysis just like this using a common Monte Carlo tool. Impressed, I said, "You are the first IT executive I've ever met who already does this." He said, "No, I'm not in IT. I do analysis of production methods for Boise Cascade" (the paper and wood company). I asked, "Which do you think is more risky, IT investments or paper production?" He agreed that IT was riskier but added that the company never applies Monte Carlo simulation methods to IT.

Risk Paradox

If an organization uses quantitative risk analysis at all, it is usually for routine operational decisions. The largest, most risky decisions get the least amount of proper risk analysis.

Over the years, in case after case, I have found that if organizations apply quantitative risk analysis at all, it is on relatively routine, operational-level decisions. The largest, most risky decisions are subject to almost no risk analysis—at least not any analysis that an actuary or statistician would be familiar with. I refer to this phenomenon as the "risk paradox."

Almost all of the most sophisticated risk analysis is applied to less risky operational decisions while the riskiest decisions—mergers, IT portfolios, big research and development initiatives, and the like—receive virtually none (or at least not the kind that passes as real, quantitative risk analysis). Why is this true? Perhaps it is because there is a perception that operational decisions—approving a loan or computing an insurance premium—seem simpler to quantify but the truly risky decisions are too elusive to quantify. This is a serious mistake. As I have shown, there is nothing "immeasurable" about the big decisions.

Granted, the 2008 financial crisis showed that some models were flawed. Those flaws were based in part on flawed assumptions about the distribution of price changes. (Specifically, that changes followed a normal distribution.) Nassim Taleb, a popular author and critic of methods used in the financial industry, points out many such flaws but does not include the use of Monte Carlo simulations among them.[6,7] He himself is a strong proponent of these simulations. Monte Carlo simulations are simply the way we do the math with uncertain quantities. Abandoning Monte Carlos because of the failures of the financial markets makes as much sense as giving up on addition and subtraction because of the failure of accounting at Enron or AIG's overexposure in credit default swaps.

In fact, the *lack* of a more widespread use of Monte Carlo simulations may be causing organizations to give up major benefits and expose themselves to significant avoidable risks. A modeler who works at Palisade Corporation (the makers of the @Risk Monte Carlo tool), once offered me some anecdotal evidence of the effectiveness of better quantitative modeling. He pointed out that prior to the financial crisis, Goldman Sachs, Morgan Stanley, and Deutsche Bank were all @Risk users while Merrill Lynch, Bear Stearns, and Lehman Brothers were not (the former three firms survived the crisis well). Fortunately, we also have a bit more evidence than these anecdotes. Two extensive studies on the use of Monte Carlos find that the use of these tools actually can be shown to improve forecasts and decisions and enhance the overall financial performance of the firm:

1. For over 100 unmanned space probe missions, NASA has been applying both a soft "risk score" and more sophisticated Monte Carlo simulations to assess the risks of cost and schedule overruns and

mission failures. The cost and schedule estimates from Monte Carlo simulations, on average, have less than half the error of the traditional accounting estimates.[8]

2. A study of oil exploration firms shows a strong correlation between the use of quantitative methods, including Monte Carlo simulations, to assess risks and a firm's financial performance.[9,10]

Detailed computer simulations are considered standard practice in many other areas. Modern weather forecasting has allowed us to at least foresee the possibility of a hurricane hitting a major city much earlier than used to be possible. Structural models of buildings subjected to earthquakes are used to test designs. Many of these simulations also depend on Monte Carlo methods to generate thousands or even millions of possible scenarios.

The most common objection I might hear for building Monte Carlos is, however, the *practicality* of modeling real world problems in what strikes some as an academic abstraction. This is the case even when it is pointed out that building Monte Carlo simulations is routine in many industries or that my own team has built practical models in areas as diverse as film, IT security, military R&D, military logistics, environmental policy, new medical devices, and so on. I've never heard this objection from anyone with experience actually building such models.

Critics of the practicality of probabilistic models may also be imagining some level of complexity which may not be required. It is worth noting—again—that all models leave out some realism and all models have error. What matters is that some models have measurably less error than others. As Meehl and Tetlock were able to show in Chapter 3, even relatively simple probabilistic models outperform human experts even in areas where human expertise is presumed superior.

Fortunately, this skepticism about probabilistic models seems to persist only up until they actually see one built. But doubts about the practicality of building Monte Carlo simulations are not just the anxiety of dealing with an unfamiliar method. I mentioned earlier that there is also a belief in most organizations that their problem is somehow uniquely complex compared even to the many areas where I and many others have already done this. Even when I point out that this is actually one of the most common concerns I hear, I might still sometimes hear something like "Yes, but our problem *really is* uniquely complex." To a certain extent, I agree. Problems managers deal with are all as unique as a snowflake—just like all the other snowflakes.

Once again, the reason why a measurement is important to a business or government agency is because of the existence of risk. Without risk, information would literally have no value to decision making.

Now that you understand the concepts of uncertainty and risk in specific quantitative terms, we can move on to a rarely used but very powerful tool in measurement: computing the value of information.

Notes

1. D. V. Budescu, S. Broomell, and H. Por, "Improving Communication of Uncertainty in the Reports of the Intergovernmental Panel on Climate Change," *Psychological Science* 20, no. 3 (2009): 299–308; and L. A. Cox Jr., "What's Wrong with Risk Matrices?" *Risk Analysis* 28, no. 2 (2008): 497–512.
2. Douglas W. Hubbard, *The Failure of Risk Management* (Hoboken, NJ: John Wiley & Sons, 2009), 130–135.
3. D. Hubbard and D. Samuelson, "Modeling without Measurements: How the Decision Analysis Culture's Lack of Empiricism Reduces Its Effectiveness," *OR/MS Today* 36, no. 5 (October 2009): 26–33.
4. Ulam Stanislaw, *Adventures of a Mathematician* (Berkeley: University of California Press, 1991).
5. Douglas W. Hubbard, *The Failure of Risk Management* (Hoboken, NJ: John Wiley & Sons, 2009), 172–174.
6. Nassim Taleb, *The Black Swan: The Impact of the Highly Improbable* (New York, NY: Random House, 2007).
7. Nassim Taleb, *Fooled by Randomness: The Hidden Role of Chance in Life and in the Markets* (New York, NY: Random House Trade Paperbacks, 2005).
8. Ibid., 237–238.
9. G. S. Simpson, F. E. Lamb, J. H. Finch, and N. C. Dinnie, "The Application of Probabilistic and Qualitative Methods to Asset Management Decision Making," presented at SPE Asia Pacific Conference on Integrated Modelling for Asset Management, April, 25–26, 2000, Yokohama, Japan.
10. William Bailey, Benoît Couët, Fiona Lamb, Graeme Simpson, and Peter Rose, "Taking Calculated Risks," *Oilfield Review* 12, no. 3 (Autumn 2000): 20–35.

## CHAPTER 7

Quantifying the Value of Information

If we could quantify the value of information itself, we could use that to determine the value of conducting measurements. If we knew this value, we would probably choose to measure completely different things, perhaps even fewer things, and probably much more economically. We would probably spend more effort and money measuring things we never measured before, and we would probably ignore some things we routinely measured in the past.

The McNamara Fallacy

"The first step is to measure whatever can be easily measured. This is okay as far as it goes. The second step is to disregard that which can't easily be measured or to give it an arbitrary quantitative value. This is artificial and misleading. The third step is to presume that what can't be measured easily isn't important. This is blindness. The fourth step is to say that what can't easily be measured really doesn't exist. This is suicide."

—Charles Handy, *The Empty Raincoat* (1995),
describing the Vietnam-era measurement policies
of Secretary of Defense Robert McNamara

As mentioned first in Chapter 1, there are really only three basic reasons why information ever has value to a business:

1. Information reduces uncertainty about decisions that have economic consequences.
2. Information affects the behavior of others, which has economic consequences.
3. Information sometimes has its own market value.

The solution to the first of these three has existed since the 1950s in a field of mathematics called "decision theory," an offshoot of game theory. It is also the method we focus on, mostly because it is more relevant to typical management problems and because the other two are somewhat simpler. Before I explain the value of information in the context of decisions, let's briefly discuss the value of its effects on the behavior of others and its potential market value.

The value of information regarding its effect on human behavior is, of course, exactly equal to the value of the difference in human behavior. Measuring productivity may have bearing on uncertain decisions about major investments. But it also has a value because those whose productivity is being measured may, in response, become more productive. If measuring productivity itself results in a 20% increase in productivity, the monetary value of that productivity increase is the "incentive" value of the measurement. We do need to consider the issues discussed in Chapter 3 about how incentives from measurements may have unforeseen effects. But these effects, too, are at least observable—and therefore measurable—once the incentives are in place.

If the value of information is its market value, then we have a market forecasting problem no different from estimating the sales for any other product. If we are collecting information on traffic at city intersections at various times of day to sell to firms that evaluate retail locations, then the value of that measurement is our expected proceeds from the sale of that information less the cost of gathering the data.

All of the measurement methods we discuss in this book are relevant to both the measurement of the market value and the measurement of the incentive value of information. But most of the reasons we measure something in business are at least partially related to how the measurement affects management decisions. This is what the rest of this chapter is about.

THE CHANCE OF BEING WRONG AND THE COST OF BEING WRONG: EXPECTED OPPORTUNITY LOSS

The formula for the value of information can be understood both mathematically and intuitively. We can make better "bets" (i.e., decisions) when we can reduce uncertainty (i.e., make measurements) about them. Knowing the value of the measurement affects how we might measure something or even whether we need to measure it at all.

If you are uncertain about a business decision (and a calibrated person should be realistic about the level of uncertainty), that means you have a chance of making the wrong decision. By "wrong," I mean that the consequences of some alternative would have turned out to be preferable and you would have selected that alternative, if only you had known. The cost of being wrong is the difference between the wrong choice you took and the best alternative available—that is, the one you would have chosen if you had perfect information.

For example, if you are going to invest in a bold new advertising campaign, you are hoping the investment will be justified. However, you don't know for a fact that it will be successful. Historically, you know there have been ad campaigns that, while they initially appeared to have all the look of a great idea, turned out to be a market flop. Some of the more catastrophic examples have even helped competitors. On the plus side, the right campaign sometimes can directly result in a major increase in revenue. Of course, it does no good to stand still and make no investments in your business just because there is a chance of being wrong. So, based on the best information you have so far, perhaps the default decision is to go ahead with the campaign—but there may be a value to measuring it first.

As I mentioned in Chapter 6, the existence of this decision risk and the desire to reduce it is the reason the decision maker needs a measurement. In the ad campaign example, we are dealing with a special case of measurement—the forecast—which is a measurement of likely future outcomes. To compute the value of measuring the likelihood of success of an ad campaign, you have to know both what your loss would be if the campaign turns out to be a bad investment and the chance it will turn out to be a bad investment. If there was no chance that the campaign would fail or if there were no loss if you failed, there would be no need whatsoever to reduce uncertainty about it—the decision would be risk-free and obvious.

Just to keep the example very simple, let's look at a binary situation—you either fail or succeed, period. Suppose you could make $40 million profit if the ad works and lose $5 million (the cost of the campaign) if it fails. Then suppose your calibrated experts say they would put a 40% chance of failure on the campaign. With this information, you could create a table, as shown in Exhibit 7.1.

Exhibit 7.1 Extremely Simple Expected Opportunity Loss Example

Variable	Campaign Works	Campaign Fails
Chance of outcome (success or failure)	60%	40%
Impact if campaign is approved	+$40 million	−$5 million
Impact if campaign is rejected	$0	$0

The Opportunity Loss (OL) for a particular alternative is just the cost if we chose that path and it turns out to be wrong. The Expected Opportunity Loss (EOL) for a particular strategy is the chance of being wrong times the cost of being wrong. Since this term "expected" will show up again, know that when someone is using this term in the context of decision science, what they mean is "probability-weighted average." Given the information in Exhibit 7.1, we can compute two EOLs depending on whether the ad campaign is approved or rejected:

Expected Opportunity Loss if Approved: $5m × 40% = $2m
Expected Opportunity Loss if Rejected: $40m × 60% = $24m

Remember, EOL exists because you are uncertain about the possibility of negative consequences of your decision. If you could reduce this uncertainty, the EOL would also be reduced. In regard to making business decisions, *that* is what a measurement is really for.

EOL is also an expression of risk. It is the simple "risk-neutral" solution first mentioned in Chapter 6. We simply multiply the chance of a loss times the amount of the loss, regardless of how risk averse the decision maker may be. It is a good basis for computing the value of information without getting too complex. But also it is not far off the mark even if we do consider aversion to risk. The cost of measurement is generally small compared to the cost of the decisions the measurement will support. When a risk-averse person takes a large number of very small bets, their choices will be close to risk neutral. With your own money, you may not consider a 20% chance to lose $100,000 to be exactly equal to a certain reward of $20,000, but you may consider a 20% chance of winning $10 to be very close to $2. If you could buy a thousand bets for $1.50 each, you should consider that a bargain. Likewise, your value of information for each of the potential measurements of a large investment decision would be fairly risk neutral compared to the investment itself.

All measurements that have decision-value must reduce the uncertainty of some quantity that affects some decision with economic consequences. The bigger the reduction in EOL, the higher the value of a measurement. The difference between the EOL before a measurement (perhaps based only on initial calibrated estimates) and the EOL after a measurement is called the "Expected Value of Information" (EVI). In other words, the value of information is equal to the value of the reduction in risk.

Computing the EVI of a measurement before we make the measurement requires us to estimate how much uncertainty reduction we can expect. This sometimes is complicated, depending on the variable being measured, but there is a shortcut. The easiest measurement value to compute is the Expected Value of Perfect Information (EVPI). If you could eliminate uncertainty, EOL would be reduced to zero. So the EVPI is simply the EOL of your chosen alternative. In the example, the "default" decision (what you would do if you didn't make a further measurement) was to approve the campaign, and—as explained—that EOL was $2 million. So the value of eliminating any uncertainty about whether this campaign would succeed is simply $2 million. If you could only reduce but not eliminate uncertainty, the EVI would be something less.

Value of Information

Expected Value of Information (EVI) = Reduction in expected opportunity loss (EOL) i.e., $EVI = EOL_{Before\ Info} - EOL_{After\ Info}$

Where

EOL = chance of being wrong $\times$ cost of being wrong

Expected Value of Perfect Information (EVPI) = $EOL_{Before\ Info}$ (EOL_{After} is zero if information is perfect)

A slightly more complicated, but much more common and realistic method is the EOL calculation where your uncertainty is about a continuous value, not just two extremes like "succeed" and "fail." It's more common to need to compute the value of a measurement where the uncertain variable has a range of possible values. The method for computing this information value is not fundamentally different from how we computed the value of a simple binary problem. We still need to compute an EOL.

THE VALUE OF INFORMATION FOR RANGES

In the ad example, suppose instead of expressing the results as only two possible outcomes, the results are a range of possible values—a much more realistic model. A calibrated expert in marketing was 90% certain that the sales directly resulting from this ad campaign could be anywhere from 150,000 units to 300,000 units. However, we have to sell at least a certain amount to make this ad campaign break even. The risk is that we don't sell enough to make it worthwhile.

Let's say that given our gross margin we make $25 per unit sold. We would have to sell at least 200,000 additional units to break even on a $5 million campaign. Anything less than 200,000 units sold means the campaign is a net loss, but more so as we drop farther below this point. If we sell exactly 200,000, we neither lose nor gain. If we didn't sell any, we would have lost the cost of the ad campaign, $5 million. (You might say the business would lose more than just the cost of the campaign, but let's keep it simple.) In this situation, what is the value of reducing uncertainty about the effect of the campaign?

A formula that computes how much we lose depending on the outcome is called a "loss function." In this case the loss calculation depends on whether we sold less than 200,000 units or more. For each of these conditions the loss function is:

- Less than 200,000 units sold, Loss = (200,000-units sold)*$25
- 200,000 units or more sold, Loss = 0

In MS Excel, I could write this as =if(units<200,000,(200,000-units)* 25,0), where "units" refers to some cell that contains the number of units sold.

Loss functions can come in many forms and can be much more elaborate if the situation requires. In this particular case we lose money when we are below the threshold but there are cases where we could lose money when we are over the threshold. A loss function can also be nonlinear so that losses accelerate the further away from the breakeven point. It could also level off at some maximum loss. Once we have the distribution for some range variable and the loss function for it, we can compute its EVPI by slicing up the distribution into lots of tiny parts, then work out the expected loss for each part, and then add them all up. Exhibit 7.2 illustrates this.

Exhibit 7.2 EOL "Slices" for Range Estimates

If you want to see the details of this process you can either follow these five steps or you can just download the Chapter 7 examples from www.howtomeasureanything.com:

1. Slice the distribution up into hundreds or thousands of small segments. In the case of the units sold, I might want to create a spreadsheet where I show a table with increments of 1,000 units. Each row shown is actually the middle of a small range starting at 0 units sold all the way up to 200,000 units sold. I don't need to go any higher because results greater than 200,000 units would have a loss of zero. (If you do go past 200,000 units, be sure to add an if() statement to make the loss zero if units sold is greater than 200,000.) That would make a table of 200 rows.
2. Use the loss function to compute the opportunity loss for each segment. For each row in the table, use the loss function to compute a loss. For the row with 100,000 units sold, our loss would be (200,000-100,000)*25=$2.5 million . . . and so on for all the other rows.
3. Compute the probability for each segment. For normal distributions, use the method shown in the "Computing an 'Incremental Probability'" inset. Calculations for other distributions are available in the Chapter 7 spreadsheets downloadable from www.howtomeasureanything.com.
4. Multiply the opportunity loss of each segment by its probability.
5. Total all the products from Step 4 for all segments.

Computing an "Incremental Probability"

The "Normdist()" function is one of many functions in Excel that are used to compute probabilities in a distribution. In the previous chapter, we showed how we can generate a normally distributed random number using the norminv() function. That is just the inverse of the Normdist() function. With the normdist() function we can work out the probability that a value is less than X in a normal distribution with a given mean and standard deviation. We would write it as:

=normdist(X,mean,sd, 1)

If we are starting with a 90% CI on a normal distribution, recall that the mean is just halfway between the upper and lower bounds and that the standard deviation (sd) is just (upper bound – lower bound)/3.29. The "1" is a switch that tells Excel that you want the probability of not just X but anything less than X. If you put a "0" in that position it tells you the probability that the value will be in that segment with units as wide as the units used for the mean and

(continued)

standard deviation. There are many cases where we don't want to do this (i.e., where the unit is large compared to range—such as when we state a 90% confidence interval of 0.8 to 1.5). So we will use a method that gives us more control over the segment sizes.

If we decide we want to set the increment size to 1,000, as in this example, we compute the probability of a value being within a given increment by taking the difference of two Normdist() functions as follows where we substitute "i" with 1,000:

=normdist(x+i/2, mean, sd, 1)-normdist(x-i/2,mean,sd,1)

This "incremental probability" will come up often in other calculations so it will be useful to become familiar with it. The Chapter 7 spreadsheet provided on www.howtomeasureanything.com will show examples of this. We will also show how this can be done with other distributions.

When completed, the table for computing the expected opportunity loss for the range should look something like Exhibit 7.3. All of the values in the Expected Loss column are added up to compute the total EOL (i.e., EVPI) for the object of this measurement. Again, the entire table with all of the Excel calculations worked out in advance can be downloaded from Chapter 7 examples at www.howtomeasureanything.com.

When the values in the last column of Exhibit 7.3 are added up, you get the EVPI—in this case, about $200,000 (it just worked out to this, don't confuse this with the breakeven for units-sold in this example).

Exhibit 7.3 Example EVPI Calculation for Segments in a Range (total number of rows in actual table would be 20)

Units Demanded	Loss	Incremental Probability of a Segment	Expected Loss (Loss × Incremental Probability)
0	5,000,000	0.000000045	$0.225287
1,000	4,975,000	0.000000050	$0.249724
2,000	4,950,000	0.000000056	$0.276672
....	....	....	....
200,000	0	0.007529	$0

This is a kind of computational brute-force solution called a discrete approximation. It is used in many areas of mathematics where applying lots of computing power is easier than solving the exact equation. A discrete approximation will come up a lot in our analysis and it's worth pointing out some considerations about how some increment choices affect a rounding error. This error is usually very small and easily reduced by using more and smaller increments in the analysis and adding more realistic rules. For example, using the middle value is a bit of an approximation for an increment. To address this, we could have simply had one row *per unit* so that we had 200,000 rows in the table. This would refine the EVPI a bit further but not by much.

Also note our distribution allows for some chance of a negative value. Even our first increment includes a negative value—since zero is the middle then the lower bound is slightly negative (–500 units). In fact, even though our table ignores it, our distribution could theoretically generate negative results even further below zero. We might insist that we can't really sell negative units so perhaps we would like to eliminate that possibility. We could use a different distribution that can't generate a negative number at all. However, the normdist() function would show that, with our stated 90% CI, there is less than a one in two million chance that our normal distribution would generate a negative number. So this improvement wouldn't make much difference, either. In short, discrete approximations like this will always have some rounding error. You always have the option of refining the discrete approximation further, but you will find that further resolution reaches diminishing returns quickly.

I also created a procedure you can use without a spreadsheet by using a couple of the following charts and some simple arithmetic. As a prelude to this calculation, we need to decide which of the upper and lower bounds on the 90% CI is the "best bound" (BB) and "worst bound" (WB). Clearly, sometimes a bigger number is better (e.g., revenue) and sometimes a smaller number is better (e.g., costs). In the ad campaign example, small is bad, so the WB is the 150,000 units and the BB is 300,000 units. From this, we are going to compute a value I'll call the Relative Threshold (RT). This quantity tells us where the threshold sits relative to the rest of the range. See Exhibit 7.4 for a visual explanation of RT.

We are going to use this value to compute EVPI in four steps:

1. Compute Relative Threshold: RT = (Threshold – WB)/(BB – WB). For our example, the best bound is 300,000 units, the worst bound is 150,000 units, and the threshold is 200,000 units, so RT = (200,000 – 150,000)/(300,000 – 150,000) = 0.33.
2. Locate the RT in the vertical axis of Exhibit 7.5.

Exhibit 7.4 Example of the Relative Threshold

3. Look directly to the right of the RT value and you will see two sets of curves—one for normal distributions on the left and one for uniform distributions on the right. Because our example is a normal distribution, find the point on the curve for normal distributions that is directly to the right of our RT value. I will call this value the Expected Opportunity Loss Factor (EOLF). Here our EOLF is 53.

4. Compute EVPI as: EVPI = EOLF/1,000 × OL per unit × (BB – WB). Our example has an opportunity loss per unit of $25. This gives an EVPI = 53/1,000 × 25 × (300,000 – 150,000) = $198,750.

This calculation shows that a measurement (in this case, a forecast) about the number of units that will be sold could theoretically be worth as much as $198,750. This is close enough to our answer from the spreadsheet example of about $200,000. Remember, this number is an absolute maximum and assumes a measurement that eliminates uncertainty. Although eliminating uncertainty is almost always impossible, this simple method provides an important benchmark for how much we should be willing to spend.

The procedure for a uniform distribution is the same, except, of course, we need to use the uniform distribution column of curves. In either the uniform or the normal distribution case, some important caveats should be understood. This simple method applies only to linear losses. That is, for each unit we undershoot the threshold by, we lose a fixed amount—$25 in our example. If we plotted the loss against the units sold, it would be a straight line (i.e., linear). But if the loss accelerated or decelerated in some way, the EOLF chart may not be a very close

*RT (Threshold – Worst Bound)/(Best Bound – Worst Bound);
see Exhibit 7.4 for more detail.

Exhibit 7.5 Expected Opportunity Loss Factor Chart

estimate. For example, if we are uncertain about a compounding interest rate, the loss we have below whatever threshold we define would not go up like a straight line.

It's also important to note that if the normal distribution has to be truncated in some way, or if any other distribution shape besides normal or uniform is required, the chart may, again, not be a close approximation. We could say that it's impossible to sell less than zero units. But we could also say that it is possible that a real flop in an advertising campaign would not only not sell more units but detract from existing sales—it has happened before.

If you have an important measure with a high information value, it may be worth doing the extra math I described for breaking down the distribution into a large number of slices. Using either this chart or the simple spreadsheet tool on the website will be a good approximation.

Value of Information Analysis on the Supplementary Website

On the website www.howtomeasureanything.com under "Chapter 7 examples," you can download a detailed Excel-based calculator for VIA with examples from this book.

BEYOND YES/NO: DECISIONS ON A CONTINUUM

So far, we have looked at computing the value of information for the simple success/fail situation—where you are either wrong or not—and the estimate of a continuous value where you can be wrong by a little, or wrong by a lot. But while the latter situation was for a continuous value, both situations were for binary *decisions*. The value may be continuous but it is being measured to support a decision about whether or not to make some investment—a yes or no choice.

There are types of decisions where both the quantities being estimated and the decision itself is a continuum. A decision that involves choosing an optimal amount in a range of possible amounts could be picking the capacity for a new factory. Instead of an either/or investment decision, this decision involves choosing a capacity that could be, say, one million units per year, 2 million, 10 million, or any other number of units per year. In this case the opportunity loss is zero if you happen to pick the perfect answer. Any other answer—whether too high or too low—involves some loss.

In this kind of estimation problem we have a kind of bi-directional loss function or, if you prefer to think of it this way, two loss functions: one for losses related to overestimating something and one for losses related to underestimating something. If we are trying to optimize the capacity for a new factory, we would like to make a factory that exactly meets actual demand for this product. Overestimating the demand means we would have built a factory that was too large and we wasted capital to create capacity that went unused. If we underestimate demand, we will lose sales that we otherwise would have gotten if we could keep up with the orders. Exhibit 7.6 shows this kind of bidirectional loss function.

As with the earlier loss function, the expected loss is a probability-weighted average total over all losses. The difference here is that we have to pick an estimate that minimizes the total expected loss of both over- and underestimating. If we had perfectly symmetrical loss functions such that the loss of overestimating by a given amount is the same as the loss

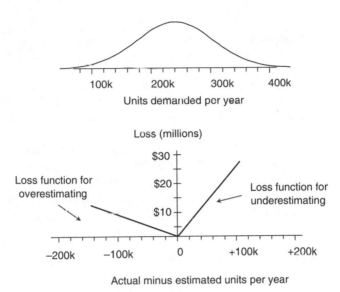

Units demanded per year

Loss (millions)

Loss function for overestimating

Loss function for underestimating

$30

$20

$10

−200k   −100k   0   +100k   +200k

Actual minus estimated units per year

Exhibit 7.6 Loss Functions for Decisions on a Continuum

of underestimating by a given amount, then our best bet is to choose the exact middle of the range.[1] Any other point will have a higher expected loss. Note that with this loss function, the cost of underestimating is higher than the cost of overestimating. In this case, if we chose the exact middle of our range (240,000 in this case) the expected loss would not be minimized.

Once we have determined the choice that minimizes expected loss, then the total EOL at that point is the EVPI. In other words, we choose the optimal strategy at our current level of uncertainty and compute the EOL from that point. The Chapter 7 examples on the www .howtomeasureanything.com website show this calculation, too.

Zilliant: A Pricing Example for Decisions on a Continuum

Setting the price for a new product is another decision that involves choosing a position among a range of values. If you set the price too high, you lose sales and if you set the price too low, you've needlessly given up revenue. The ideal price—if only you knew it— would maximize profit. The optimal price depends on a measure of "price elasticity," the ratio of a change quantity sold to a change in

(continued)

price. While mentioned in first semester microeconomics courses, actually measuring it is frequently considered too complex to be practical.

This is particularly problematic in the competitively priced world of business-to-business sales (B2B). Manufacturers and distributors often have catalogs containing tens of thousands or hundreds of thousands of items. As daunting as it might sound, many firms have relied on pricing experts to pick prices for each item in their catalog which are then further modified by the judgments of sales people making deals. Consistent errors in overpricing or underpricing as well as random variation from one deal to the next can result in the loss of significant revenue and profit.

Fortunately, there are alternatives. A leading software company specializing in pricing for the B2B market is Zilliant, a client of mine based in Austin, Texas. The company not only measures the margins and profits at a granular level, but also can detect differences in price elasticity for specific customer and product combinations, and use that to provide future price guidance.

So how does Zilliant measure the optimal price for thousands of items, given the inherent complexity and scarcity of B2B pricing and cost data? "B2B sales people will tell you that every deal, every customer is different, and there's some truth to that," said Eric Hills, Chief Evangelist and SVP at Zilliant. "Our science finds the similarities in price response patterns hidden in the heterogeneous sales transactions, and makes the most of it by applying the same core principles from *How to Measure Anything*: You have more and need less data than you think." (I couldn't have said it better.)

Zilliant's technology effectively uses the same type of EOL calculations we just discussed for overpricing and underpricing along with some additional Bayesian inference methods the company has developed. Where data are more abundant, the measurements are not only more robust, but they also lend insights into customer-product combinations where data are sparser.

Zilliant recognizes that the value is not in achieving perfection but in outperforming the alternative. Zilliant prices are consistently and measurably better than the judgments of sales people or pricing analysts. Hills adds that the effects are measurable because "At its core, price optimization is about revenue and profit improvement. Our customers can measure the benefits directly."

THE IMPERFECT WORLD: THE VALUE OF PARTIAL UNCERTAINTY REDUCTION

In the examples so far, we computed the Expected Value of Perfect Information (EVPI), showing the value of eliminating uncertainty, not just reducing it. The EVPI calculation can be useful by itself, since at least we know a cost ceiling we should never exceed to make the measurement. But often we have to live with merely reducing our uncertainty, especially when we are talking about something like sales forecasts from ad campaigns. At such times it would be helpful to know not just the maximum we might spend under ideal conditions but what a given real-life measurement (with real-life error remaining) should be worth. In other words, we need to know the Expected Value of Information, not merely the Expected Value of *Perfect* Information.

The Expected Value of Information (EVI) curve refers to all information values, whether the information is perfect or not. Other academic sources may sometimes refer to an EVI as Expected Value of Imperfect Information (EVII) or Expected Value of Sample Information (EVSI) to differentiate it from EVPI. But simply dropping the "perfect" suffices to generalize the term to include something less than the elimination of uncertainty.

We also need to consider the Expected Cost of Information (ECI). The ECI is simply how much we expect to pay for a given amount of information (i.e., uncertainty reduction). Remember, in the context of decision analysis, the word "expected" always means "probability weighted average." So to compute the ECI, we consider the range of possible outcomes of a measurement, the cost of each, the expected uncertainty reduction of each possible outcome, and then compute the weighted average of all costs and uncertainty reductions. Computing both the EVI and ECI functions would seem to be a daunting task, but Exhibit 7.7 points to some simple rules of thumb to keep in mind. This exhibit shows that as certainty increases (i.e., uncertainty is reduced), both EVI and ECI increase but at very different rates.

The general shape of the EVI curve could be called convex relative to the horizontal axis—meaning that it bows upward (the midpoint of the curve is above a straight line drawn between its highest and lowest values). This means that the value of information tends to rise more quickly with small reductions in uncertainty but levels off as we approach perfect certainty. With many measurements, perfect certainty cannot be reached but, with enough effort, we can get very close. However, no matter how much uncertainty we remove, the EVI can never exceed the EVPI.

Exhibit 7.7 The Value verses Cost of Partial Information

The amount of curvature of the EVI is determined by many factors, including the amount of the initial uncertainty, the shape of its distribution (normal, uniform, binary, etc.), and the details of the loss function. Some EVIs are "flatter" but are curved at least a little. This curvature means that a measurement that would reduce the uncertainty of the original range by half would have an EVI of *a little more* than half the EVPI, a reduction of 70% of the uncertainty would be worth a bit more than 70% of the EVPI, and so on until EVI and EVPI converge at perfect certainty. For the ad campaign example, the procedure described using Exhibit 7.5 should produce an EVPI of about $198,750. Therefore, if you think you could reduce your uncertainty by half for a study that costs only $80,000, then you are justified to do the study (but probably not justified by much). If you can do the study for $20,000, then consider it a bargain.

Another characteristic of the EVI curve to keep in mind is that it is possible to have uncertainty about the measured quantity but literally have no uncertainty about the resulting decision, especially if it is a binary (yes/no) decision. For example, if the calibrated expert wanted to give our range a *uniform* distribution of 150,000 to 300,000 units sold, the expert is saying, in effect, that there is no chance of selling more than 300,000 units or selling less than 150,000. If the threshold is 200,000 units and we can make a measurement that at least allows us to move up the lower bound to some value greater than 200,000 units sold, we will have eliminated the possibility of a loss. In examples like this, the biggest jump in EVI is up to the point where the uncertainty reduction is just enough that it becomes possible to eliminate a chance of loss. The difference in value between a measurement that could reduce uncertainty by half and one that could reduce uncertainty by three-quarters may be very small. Once we have eliminated the chance of a loss (or determined for certain that the loss will occur), any additional measurement has no value—at least for this decision.

Using either the spreadsheet method or Exhibit 7.5, you can estimate the EVI by recognizing EVPI as an absolute ceiling and keeping the general shape of an EVI curve in mind. You may think that we are making approximations upon approximations, but it often results in a "good enough" measurement. Estimating the EVPI for a proposed measurement already has some uncertainty of its own, so fine precision on the EVI is not always that useful. Also, the variables that you should measure—those that have high information values—tend to have the highest information value by an extremely large margin. Often they are 10 or 100 times as much (or more) as the value of the next most valuable measurements. In practice, the estimation error for an EVI usually won't come close to making a difference in what you select for measurement.

The ECI curve bends the other direction. If we call the direction of the EVI curve convex, this is the concave direction. A straight line drawn between its lowest and highest points will be above the midpoint on the curve. Additional uncertainty reduction becomes more and more expensive as we approach an uncertainty of zero. In the case of random sampling out of some large population, our sample size would have to approach a complete census to eliminate uncertainty. However, the uncertainty at first tends to fall away relatively quickly at the beginning of the measurement. The effects of the first few observations relative to much more observation will be discussed in more detail in Chapter 9. But for now, just know that each additional decrease in uncertainty usually takes more effort than previous decreases in uncertainty.

Knowing something about the monetary value and cost of the information in a measurement puts a new light on what is "measurable." If someone says a measurement would be too expensive, we have to ask, "Compared to what?" If a measurement that would just reduce uncertainty by half costs $50,000 but the EVPI is $5,000,000, then the measurement certainly is not "too expensive." Indeed, it would be a bargain. But if the information value is zero, then any measurement is too expensive. Some measurements might have marginal information values—say, a few thousand dollars; not enough to justify some formal effort at measurement but a bit too much just to ignore. For those measurements,

I try to think of approaches that can quickly reduce a little uncertainty—say, finding a related study or making a few phone calls to a few more experts.

With the EVI curve and the ECI curve, we learn the value of iterative measurements. While the EVI curve shows that the value of information levels off, the ECI curve takes off like a rocket as we approach the usually unattainable state of perfect certainty. This fact tells us that we should normally think of measurement as a series of small efforts. Don't try to hit it out of the ballpark in the first attempt. Each measurement iteration can tell you something about how—and whether—to conduct the next iteration.

Knowing the shape of the EVI and ECI curves also tells us that a typical assumption about measurement is wrong. It is often assumed that if you have a lot of uncertainty, you need a lot of data to reduce it. In fact, as first pointed out in Chapter 3, *just the opposite is true.*

When you have a lot of uncertainty, you don't need much new data to tell you something you didn't know before. An example from a workshop I once conducted about the measurement of the effectiveness of healthcare issue awareness campaigns illustrates this point. I asked a workshop participant for her 90% confidence interval for the percentage of teens in the Chicago region who have been made aware of the cancer risks of indoor tanning. Her estimate was 2% to 50%. I think the upper bound is very optimistic, but she had a lot of uncertainty and she needed a wide range. With a range this wide, how many teenagers would she have to survey to reduce it significantly? And if her range was only 11% to 15%, how many teenagers would she have to survey to significantly reduce *that* range? She would have to survey far more people in the second case than in the first to reduce uncertainty by half. When anyone assumes we need a lot of data to measure something that is extremely uncertain they are invariably making this error.

A Common Measurement Myth

Myth: When you have a lot of uncertainty, you need a lot of data to tell you something useful.

Fact: If you have a lot of uncertainty now, you don't need much data to reduce uncertainty significantly. When you have a lot of certainty already, *then* you need a lot of data to reduce uncertainty significantly.

In other words—**if you know almost nothing, almost anything will tell you something.**

Perishable Information Values

The relatively high return on small uncertainty reductions is magnified further when we consider time-sensitive decisions. For example, if you are considering major investments in real estate when the market is low, the opportunity may itself evaporate if you take too long to make a decision. Reducing uncertainty doesn't just take money, it takes time. This may lead to the type of decision error Howard Raiffa, one of the pioneers of decision theory, referred to as "solving the right problem too late."

Consider the situation where we can always spend more time to reduce uncertainty—either through some additional effort like a survey or simply by waiting to see how things turn out. In the case of real estate prices, commodities, stocks, or many other measurements that depend on predictions, I can eventually get perfect certainty about what happens if I just wait. For example, on July 15, 2011, I had uncertainty about where the price of gold would be in two years. By July 15, 2013, I had perfect certainty about gold prices on that date but any opportunities I had to capitalize on that certainty would, of course, have disappeared. When decisions are time sensitive and additional measurements take time, we can think of this as decreasing EVPI for the decision.

Exhibit 7.8 shows the EVI, ECI, and EVPI on a chart where the horizontal axis is now "time" instead of "certainty." The maximum EVI is still, as before, constrained by the EVPI. The difference now is that EVPI is

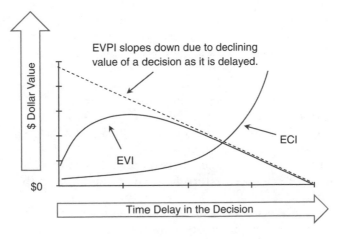

Note that the optimal measurement (the point of maximum difference between EVI and ECI) is shifted left of where it would be without a declining EVPI.

Exhibit 7.8 The Effect of Time Sensitivity on EVPI and EVI decreasing and, therefore, EVI must decrease accordingly instead of just leveling off. The net effect of this is that the optimal value of information is shifted left relative to where it would be if we assumed EVPI is constant. We don't have to consider that ECI would necessarily change with time-sensitive measurements, but if that were the case, it could be considered as well.

Measurements for most real-world decisions have some sort of time-value constraint, so this effect would almost always be present. This is yet another point in favor of preferring small, iterative observations over the typically presumed alternatives. Once again, chasing perfect certainty or surrendering to unaided expert opinion are both costly mistakes.

Information Values for Multiple Variables

Another example of incomplete information is measuring just a few variables out of a large number of variables in a decision. This is actually the most common way I find myself approaching a measurement problem. I've never had to work out the information value for a single isolated uncertain variable. The real question is always which out of a large set of uncertain variables should receive additional measurement effort.

This is a more challenging information value calculation because the information value of one variable can change depending on the values of other variables. Recall that part of the information value approach for discrete yes/no decisions involves finding a threshold. If you have a cost-benefit analysis and the costs are at the high end of the potential range, the "threshold" for benefit variables will be different than if costs were on the low end of the range. Most variables will change the thresholds of most other variables in the same decision model.

There are two methods you could use to deal with this additional complexity. The first method is a simple approximation where you hold all variables at their mean except for one. Then you find the threshold of that variable and compute its information value. Then reset that variable to its mean and go on to another. Do this for every variable in the decision model. This method is a very rough approximation because it ignores interrelationships among variables as their values change.

Another more elaborate—but more accurate—method starts by running a simulation that shows our expected loss at our current level of uncertainty. I call this the Overall EOL or the Decision EOL. This is simply the average of all outcomes given our current (default) decision assuming we don't measure any further. If, at our current level of uncertainty, our default decision was to reject an investment, but it turns out it would have been a good idea, then the amount we would have made is the opportunity loss in that scenario. In scenarios where our decision turned out to be correct, our opportunity loss was zero. All of these results averaged together—zeros and non-zero values alike—is the Overall EOL.

We then run a series of Monte Carlo simulations where we pretend we knew one selected variable in the model exactly. We apply a decision rule that tells the model what I would have done differently if I knew only that variable exactly. If knowing this variable was informative, my opportunity losses from making a bad decision (the Overall EOL) should go down.

The change in Overall EOL by eliminating uncertainty for a single variable is the "Individual EVPI" for that variable. If I consider one more variable then the EOL may go down a bit further. The difference in Overall EOL from knowing the first variables and knowing the first and second variables together is the "marginal individual EVPI" for the second variable.

For example, one of the models we developed for CGIAR was the Tana River Basin Integrated Water Management System. It is an investment ranging in the tens of millions of U.S. dollars with benefits expected over a 30-year period. It had a total of 90 uncertain variables and the Overall EOL was $24 million. The net effect of the initiative was to improve farming practices, increase incomes among poor farmers, and improve food and water security. One potential cost of introducing intensive farming practices was an increase in the amount of CO_2 produced (modern farming using high-intensity nitrogen fertilizing and machinery produces more food per acre per year but also produces more CO_2 for a given amount of food production).

For this model, no single measurement could make a difference in the decision if we simply held all other variables at their mean value. But measuring *clusters* of variables could start to make a difference in the overall EOL. This is because the investment was positive enough that the decision makers would need "bad news" on not just one, but several variables before they would make a different decision that was indicated by this model.

One of the most uncertain variables which also had a big impact on the decision was the equivalent economic costs of an additional ton of CO_2 in the atmosphere. As you can imagine, some people insist that additional CO_2 has little global impact while some imagine worst-case scenarios. The science is somewhere in the middle and there can be understandable disagreement even among scientists (who nearly all agree that more CO_2 in the atmosphere is a problem). But since we are using probabilistic methods, we don't have to choose any particular point with certainty. There is some literature that may guide us on how to put a cost on CO_2 but we still had to use a fairly wide range. Still, measuring that alone wouldn't have any chance of changing the optimal strategy. The experts also had considerable uncertainty regarding the cost of programs to pay farmers for environmentally beneficial activities and how much intensive farming methods would contribute to CO_2, only if all three of those were measured together would we see overall EOL go down at all—doing so reduced overall EOL to $16 million. Measuring variables related to rural migration patterns reduced EOL again to $12.7 million. The first cluster of measurements, therefore, gave us an information value of $8 million ($24 million minus $16 million) and the next cluster had an information value of $3.3 million ($16 million minus $12.7 million). Measuring the next four highest information value variables reduced the EOL to under $4 million. After that, most of the remaining 90 variables in the model had information values of zero or close to zero. We won't get into the details of this method in this book but readers who have some background in decision theory can easily replicate this method from the description I provided. For other readers, the simpler methods discussed earlier will handle most of the problems.

THE EPIPHANY EQUATION: HOW THE VALUE OF INFORMATION CHANGES EVERYTHING

In my consulting practice, I've been applying a slightly more sophisticated version of the process I just described. By 1999, I had completed the very quantitative Applied Information Economics analysis on about 20 major investments. At that time, all of my projects still were related only to information technology (IT) investments. Each of these business cases had 40 to 80 variables, such as initial development costs, adoption rate, productivity improvement, revenue growth, and so on. For each of these business cases, I ran a macro in Excel that computed the information value for each uncertain variable using the method similar to what I just briefly described for computing information values on multiple variables in a model. I used this value to figure out where to focus measurement efforts.

When I ran the macro that computed the value of information for each of these variables, I began to see this pattern:

- The vast majority of variables in almost all models had an information value of zero. That is, the current level of uncertainty about most variables was acceptable, and no further measurement was justified (first mentioned in Chapter 3).
- The variables that had high information values were routinely those that the client never measured. In fact, the high-value variables often were completely absent from previous business cases. (They excluded chance of project cancellation or the risk of low user adoption.)

- The variables that clients used to spend the most time measuring were usually those with a very low (even zero) information value (i.e., it was highly unlikely that additional measurements of the variable would have any effect on decisions).

After organizing and evaluating all the business cases and their information value calculations, I was able to confirm this pattern. I wrote an article about my findings that was published in *CIO* magazine.[2]

At the time of this writing, however, I've applied this same test to more than 60 additional projects and I found out that this effect is not limited to IT. I noticed the same phenomena arise in projects relating to research and development, military logistics, the environment, venture capital, facilities expansion, and the CGIAR sustainable farming model. The highest-value measurements almost always are a bit of a surprise to the client. Again and again, I found that clients used to spend a lot of time, effort, and money measuring things that just didn't have a high information value while ignoring variables that could significantly affect real decisions. I quit calling the concept the "IT Measurement Inversion" and renamed it the "Measurement Inversion." In quite a few different fields, the things that get measured just don't matter as much as what is ignored.

Furthermore, I often find that when clients measure something completely different—as a result of knowing the information value—many times they view the actual findings as a great revelation. In other words, if you want a revelation about your decision, look at a high-value measurement you were previously ignoring. Exhibit 7.9 shows measurement inversion examples from a few different types of decision problems.

| Low-Value, Typical Measurements | Examples:
Time spent in an activity
Attendance to sales training
Near-term costs of a project
Number of violations found in safety inspections |
| High-Value, Usually Ignored Measurements | Examples:
Value of an activity
Effect of sales training on sales
Long-term benefits of a project
Reduction in risk of catastrophic accidents |

Typical Attention — Economic Relevance

Exhibit 7.9 Measurement Inversion

The Measurement Inversion

In a decision model with a large number of uncertain variables, the economic value of measuring a variable is usually inversely proportional to how much measurement attention it typically gets.

Apparently, our intuition about what to measure fails us more often than not. Because most organizations lack a method for quantifying the value of conducting a measurement, they are almost guaranteed to measure all the wrong things. It is not that things like project costs and hours per week on some activity should not be measured, but an inordinate amount of attention is given to them when there are much bigger uncertainties in other areas.

Why does the Measurement Inversion happen? First people measure what they know how to measure or what they believe is easy to measure. You probably know the old joke about the drunk looking for his wallet in the well-lit street, even though he knows he lost it in the dark bar. He justifies this by saying the light is better out in the street. If the organization is used to using, say, surveys to measure things, uncertainties that are best measured with other methods probably don't get measured as often. If the organization is good at measuring things based on data-mining methods, it will tend to measure only variables that lend themselves to that approach.

Why is this such a frequently recurring error? By now, it should be clear that uncertainty is part of what makes a variable have a high information value, along with how much the variable impacts the decision. When you have a lot of past examples for something you are asked to estimate, you probably have less uncertainty about it compared to something you've never measured before. If you've never measured it before, you may lack even a fundamental sense of scale for the quantity. So, the things you measured the most in the past have less uncertainty, and therefore less information value, when you need to estimate them for future decisions.

My graduate quantitative methods professor used to quote Abraham Maslow frequently by stating, "If your only tool is a hammer, then every problem looks like a nail." This seems to apply to quite a lot of businesses and government agencies. The measurement methods they use provide a comfort level. Even though methods to measure something like the impact of, for example, customer satisfaction on revenue are well developed in some firms, other firms resist using those methods and instead focus on lower-value measurements they feel more familiar with.

Perhaps another reason for the measurement inversion is that managers might tend to measure things that are more likely to produce good news. After all, why measure the benefits if you have a suspicion there might not be any? Of course, that tends to be the thinking of people asking for money or justifying their jobs, not the person who has to sign the checks. The solution in this case is simple: Don't let the champions of an investment be the only ones responsible for measuring their own performance. Executives who approve and evaluate a manager's initiatives need their own source of measurements.

Finally, not knowing the business value of the information from a measurement means people can't put the difficulty of a measurement in context. As mentioned earlier, a measurement they feel is "too difficult" actually might be perceived as practical if they understood that the information value was many times the expected cost. A large consumer credit company once asked me for a proposal on measuring the benefits of a worldwide IT infrastructure investment that would easily exceed $100 million. After hearing more about the nature of the problem, I estimated that the study would cost $100,000 to $130,000 (a 90% CI, of course). The company responded by saying that it needed to keep costs down to $25,000. (I declined the business.) The original proposal was probably less than one-tenth of 1% of the estimated size of a highly uncertain, risky investment. In some industries, a much less risky investment would get an even more detailed analysis than what I proposed. Conservatively, the value of the information the study would have produced would likely have been in the millions of dollars.

In 2009, I published this and another curious finding in a periodical for quantitative analysts called *OR/MS Today* titled "Modeling without Measurements: How the Decision Analysis Culture's Lack of Empiricism Reduces Its Effectiveness."[3] My coauthor Douglas Samuelson and I pointed out that while most variables in large, uncertain decisions had no information value, usually there were at least some with a significant information value which easily justified further measurements.

We showed that surveys of Monte Carlo modeling experts, however, had revealed that empirical measurement was rarely part of decision analysis where Monte Carlo simulations were used. Apparently, the analysts would elicit probabilities and confidence intervals from experts (almost always without calibrating them), run thousands of scenarios, produce a distribution of the results, and then say "Done." This is not just a Measurement Inversion but rather a "Measurement Aversion" even among quantitatively sophisticated analysts.

The value of additional measurements would, in fact, never be put in proper context in these cases because the value of additional measurements would not be computed at all. At most, the modeling experts would assess a "sensitivity" for each variable in the model. A sensitivity analysis simply identifies which variables the outcomes of the model are most sensitive to. This can be useful but it says nothing more informative than an information value calculation and, since a sensitivity analysis isn't expressed in monetary terms, it doesn't give sufficient practical guidance for a decision maker who has to choose what to measure and how to measure it.

For these reasons, I call the formula for the value of information the "epiphany equation." It seems that to have a truly profound revelation, you almost always have to look at something other than what you have been looking at in the past. Being able to compute the value of information has caused organizations to look at completely different things—and doing so has frequently resulted in a surprise that changed the direction of a major decision.

Measurement Inversion Example

A stark illustration of the Measurement Inversion for IT projects can be seen in a large UK-based insurance client of mine that was an avid user of a software complexity measurement method called "function points." This method was popular in the 1980s and 1990s as a basis of estimating the effort for large software development efforts. This organization had done a very good job of tracking initial estimates, function point estimates, and actual effort expended for over 300 IT projects. The estimation required three or four full-time persons as "certified" function point counters. This was by far the most deliberate effort the company expended on measuring any aspect of proposed software development projects.

But a very interesting pattern arose when I compared the function point estimates to the initial estimates provided by project managers and the final effort calculated by the time tracking system. The costly, time-intensive function point counting did change the initial estimate but, on average, it was no closer to the actual project effort than the initial estimate. In other words, sometimes function point estimates improved the initial estimate and sometimes they gave an answer that was farther from the actual effort at the completion of the project. Not only was this the single largest measurement effort in the IT organization, it literally added *no* value, since it didn't reduce uncertainty at all. Certainly, more emphasis on measuring the benefits of the proposed projects—or almost anything else—would have been money better spent.

SUMMARIZING UNCERTAINTY, RISK, AND INFORMATION VALUE: THE PRE-MEASUREMENTS

Understanding how to measure uncertainty is key to measuring risk. Understanding risk in a quantitative sense is key to understanding how to compute the value of information. Understanding the value of information tells us what to measure and about how much effort we should put into measuring it. Putting all of this data in the context of quantifying uncertainty reduction is central to understanding what measurement is all about. They are the three "pre-measurements" we conduct prior to any measurement.

Putting everything from this chapter together, we can come away with a few new ideas. First, we know that the early part of any measurement usually is the high-value part. Don't attempt a massive study to measure something if you have a lot of uncertainty about it now. Define it, assess your current uncertainty, and determine how much it matters to the decision by computing its information value. Then, if it's a high value measurement, measure a little bit, remove some uncertainty, and evaluate what you have learned. Were you surprised? Is further measurement still necessary? Did what you learn in the beginning of the measurement give you some ideas about how to change the method? Iterative measurement gives you the most flexibility and the best bang for the buck.

We also learned that if you aren't computing the value of a measurement, you are very likely measuring some things that are of little or no value and ignoring some high-value items. In addition, you probably don't know how to measure it efficiently. You may even be spending too much or spending too little time measuring something. You might dismiss a high-value measurement as "too expensive" because you could not put the cost in context with the value.

Lessons from Computing the Value of Information

Value of Measurement Matters. If you don't compute the value of measurements, you are probably measuring the wrong things, the wrong way.

Be Iterative. The highest-value measurement is the beginning of the measurement, so do it in bits and take stock after each iteration.

Everything up to this point in the book is just "Phase 1" for measuring those things often thought to be impossible to measure. We have taken what might have been a very ambiguous concept and defined it in terms of how it matters to us and how we observe it. We have measured uncertainty, risk, and the value of information. Now we can get to the next step.

Interestingly, this is as far as the Department of Veterans Affairs IT security metrics project and the CGIAR sustainable agriculture projects, mentioned in previous chapters, needed to go. The object of these projects was just to figure out what to measure; actual measurements would be carried out over the next several years. To the VA and to CGIAR, knowing the value of measurement was useful in itself. Both organizations learned which measurements will matter most to future decisions.

The next step for us is to go beyond just stating current uncertainty and computing the value of measuring the things we need to know. Now that we know what to measure and about how much we can spend on the measurement, we can set out to design a way to measure it.

Notes

1. Assuming the estimate is also symmetrical, like a normal or uniform distribution.
2. Douglas Hubbard, "The IT Measurement Inversion," *CIO Enterprise Magazine*, April 15, 1999.
3. D. Hubbard and D. Samuelson, "Modeling without Measurements: How the Decision Analysis Culture's Lack of Empiricism Reduces Its Effectiveness," *OR/MS Today* (October 2009).

PART III

Measurement Methods

CHAPTER 8

The Transition: From What to Measure to How to Measure

If you've applied the lessons of the previous chapters to your measurement problem, you've defined the issue in terms of what decision it affects and how you observe it, you've quantified your uncertainty about it, and you've computed the value of additional information. Based on the information values, you selected what to measure from among all of the variables in the decision and you have a good idea of the level of effort that would be appropriate. All of that was really what you do before you begin measuring. Now we need to figure out how to reduce our uncertainty further—in other words, to conduct the actual measurement.

It's time to introduce some concepts behind powerful and practical empirical methods. Given the way we have defined measurement, the oft-heard phrase "empirical measurement" is redundant. Empirical refers to the use of observation as evidence for a conclusion. (You might also hear the equally redundant phrase "empirical observation.") Empirical methods are formal, systematic approaches for making observations to avoid or at least reduce certain types of errors that observations (and observers) are likely to have. And observation is not limited to sight, although this is a commonly assumed notion. Observation may not even be direct; it may be augmented by the use of measurement instruments. This is, in fact, almost always the case in the modern physical sciences as well as social sciences.

We are still focusing on those things that are often considered to be immeasurable in business. Fortunately, the approach to addressing many of these issues does not involve the most sophisticated methods. Remember, the objective for this book is to show that many of the things a manager might consider immeasurable are actually measurable. The only question is whether they are important enough to measure (e.g., had a high information value relative to the cost of measurement).

A few relatively simple methods will suffice to measure most of these issues. The real obstacles to measurement, as we are discovering, are mostly conceptual, not the lack of understanding of dozens of much more complicated methods. After all, in those areas where fairly sophisticated methods are used, there is little debate about whether the object of measurement is measurable. Such sophisticated measurement methods were developed precisely because someone understood that the object was measurable. Why write a two-volume treatise on quantitative clinical chemistry, for example, if both the author and the targeted readers didn't assume from the beginning that the topic is entirely measurable? I will leave it to others to describe specialized quantitative methods for specific scientific disciplines. You picked up this book because you are unclear how other, "softer" topics can be treated with rigor.

In this chapter, we ask a few questions so that we might be able to determine the appropriate category of measurement methods. Those questions are:

- *What are the parts of the thing we're uncertain about?* Decompose the uncertain thing so that it is computed from other uncertain things. Of course, you already decomposed the decision to model it. This step involves further decomposition of a variable in that decision model which had a high information value.
- *How has this (or its decomposed parts) been measured by others?* Chances are, you're not the first to encounter a particular measurement problem, and there may even be extensive research on the topic already. Reviewing the work of others is called "secondary research."
- *How do the "observables" identified lend themselves to measurement?* You've already answered how you observe the item in question. Follow through with that to identify how you observe the parts you identified in the first item above. And secondary research may already answer this for you.
- *How much do we really need to measure it?* Take into account the previously computed current state of uncertainty, the threshold, and value of information. These are all clues that point toward the right measurement approach. If the Expected Value of Perfect Information (EVPI) is $1,000, I'm probably limited to a couple of hours of effort at most. If the EVPI is millions of dollars and we have some time, a much more deliberate and extensive experiment, survey, or other study is justified.
- *What are the sources of error?* Think about how observations might be misleading. What sorts of biases or inconsistencies could be an issue and how might we control for them? Does the method of observation itself tend to observe some results more often? How much is the random error in sampling compared to the size of the effect I'm trying to see? Remember, don't just be paralyzed with the "exception

anxiety" we previously discussed. But if you identify the issues then you can find a way to address them.

- *What instrument do we select?* Based on your answers to the previous questions, identify and design a measurement instrument. Once again, secondary research may provide guidance.

With these questions in mind, it is time to discuss how tools are used for measurement.

TOOLS OF OBSERVATION: INTRODUCTION TO THE INSTRUMENT OF MEASUREMENT

The names we use for things and how those names change throughout history reveal a lot about how our ideas about them have changed. The scientific instrument is a good example of this. Prior to the Industrial Revolution, especially during the European Renaissance, scientific instruments were often called "philosophical engines." They were devices for answering what were the "deep" questions of the time. Galileo used a pendulum and an inclined plane down which he would roll balls to measure the acceleration due to gravity. (The story of him dropping weights from the Leaning Tower of Pisa might be fiction.) Daniel Fahrenheit's mercury thermometer quantified what was previously considered the "quality" of temperature. These devices revealed not just a number but something fundamental about the nature of the universe the observers lived in. Each one was a keyhole through which some previously secret aspect of the world could be observed.

By the time of the industrialist inventors like Thomas Edison and Alexander Graham Bell in the later nineteenth century, research and development had become a mass-production business. Prior to this time, instruments were often made to specification for an individual. By the time of Edison and Bell, devices were being produced uniformly and in large quantities. Scientific instruments started to become much more utilitarian. While the early nineteenth-century gentlemen philosophers of the natural world might have displayed their new microscopes alongside expensive art, the microscopes used by the industrialist inventors were fit for display only in laboratories that, by today's standards, would almost be considered sweatshops. Perhaps not surprisingly, it was at this time that some of the public began to perceive science and scientific observation as a bit less of a fanciful pursuit of deep knowledge and more like drudgery.

Even today, for many people, a measurement instrument generally connotes a device—perhaps a complicated-looking piece of electronic equipment—designed to quantify some obscure physical phenomenon, such as a Geiger counter measuring radiation or a scale measuring weight. Actually, the term "instrument" is used much more broadly by many people in different fields. In educational assessment, for example, researchers call a survey, a test, or even an individual question an instrument. And that is a legitimate use of the term.

The measurement instrument, like any tool, gives an advantage to the user. The simple mechanical tool gives an advantage like leverage for the human muscle by multiplying the force it can exert. Likewise, the measurement instrument enhances the human senses by detecting things we cannot detect directly. It also can aid reasoning and memory by doing quick calculations and storing the result. Even a particular experimental method arguably aids human perception and in this sense is itself a measurement instrument. If we want to know how to measure anything, it is in this broadest sense that we need to use the term.

Here is one helpful method for thinking about a measurement instrument: try to recapture the fascination Galileo and Fahrenheit had for observing the "secrets" of their environment. They didn't think of devices for measurement as complex contraptions to be used by esoteric specialists in arcane research. The devices were simple and obvious. Nor were they, like some managers today, dismissive of instruments because they had limitations and errors of their own. *Of course* they have errors. The question is "Compared to what?" Compared to the unaided human? Compared to no attempt at measurement at all? Keep the purpose of measurement in mind: uncertainty reduction, not necessarily uncertainty *elimination*.

Compared to unaided human observation and judgment, instruments generally have seven advantages. They don't need to have all the advantages to qualify as instruments; any combination will suffice. Often even one advantage is an improvement on unaided human observation.

1. *Instruments detect what you can't detect.* A voltmeter detects voltage across a circuit, a microscope magnifies, a cloud chamber shows the trails of subatomic particles. This ability is, perhaps, what is most commonly thought of in relation to an instrument.
2. *Instruments are more consistent.* Left to their own devices, humans are very inconsistent. An instrument, whether it is a scale or a customer survey, is generally more consistent than expert judgment.
3. *Instruments can be calibrated to account for error.* Calibration is the act of measuring something for which you already know the answer to test not the object of measurement but the instrument itself. We might calibrate a scale by placing on it a weight we know to be exactly one gram. In Chapter 5, we calibrated your ability to assess odds by asking questions where the answer was already known.

In this way, we can adjust for or at least know what the error is for a proper instrument.

4. *An instrument often includes a method for offsetting a particular error, which is often called a "control."* A controlled experiment, for example, compares the thing being measured to some baseline. If you want to know if a new sales force automation system improves repeat business, you need to compare it to customers and sales reps who aren't using the system. Perhaps some sales reps use it more than others or perhaps the rollout has not gone to every region or product line. Using a control group allows for comparisons between those using and those not using the new system (more on this in the next chapter).

5. *Instruments deliberately don't see some things.* Instruments are useful when they ignore factors that bias human observations. For example, removing names from essay tests graded by teachers removes the possible bias a teacher might have about some students. In clinical research studies, neither doctors nor patients know who is taking a drug and who is taking a placebo. This way, patients cannot bias their experience and doctors cannot bias their diagnosis.

6. *Instruments record.* The image of the old electrocardiograph machine spinning out long ribbons of paper displaying the activity of the heart is a good example of how the instrument is a recording tool. Of course, today the record is often entirely digital and can be accessed through collaborative tools on the Cloud. Instruments don't rely on selective and faulty human memory. Gamblers, for example, routinely overestimate their skill because they don't really keep track of their progress. The best measure of their progress is the drop in cash in their bank accounts. I could keep a diary of my daily activities or I can wear one of many personal activity monitors on the market. "Big Data" is the inevitable extrapolation from the recordings of instruments that outnumber humans—including "instruments" like websites, financial transaction tools, and so on.

7. *Instruments take a measurement faster and cheaper than a human.* It could be possible to hire enough people to physically count inventory every hour of every day in a large grocery store. But point-of-sale scanners do it more cheaply. A state trooper could compute highway speeds with a stopwatch and distance markers, but a radar gun would give the answer before the speeder got away and give it more accurately. If an instrument does nothing else, cost reduction alone could be reason enough to use it.

According to these criteria, a shepherd who counts sheep using beads on a string is using an instrument. The string is calibrated, it records, and without it the shepherd would probably make more errors. Sampling procedures and experimental approaches themselves are instruments and are often referred to in that way even if they do not use any mechanical or electronic devices. Some would question the value of broadening this definition. A customer survey, for example, doesn't necessarily detect anything humans can't. But it should at least be consistent as well as calibrated. And if it is a web-based survey, it will be cheaper to conduct and easier to analyze (more about this in Chapter 13). Those who would reject the idea of a customer survey being a measurement instrument forget the whole point of measurement. How uncertain would they be *without* the instrument?

There are so many measurement methods for so many types of measurement challenges that no one book could address them all in detail. But the abundance of available methods reassures us that no matter what the measurement issue is, a well-developed solution exists. And even though it is impractical to try to fit a complete measurement encyclopedia in this book, broad basic categories of simple methods solve quite a few problems. Furthermore, these methods can be used in combination to create a variety of approaches to specific measurement problems.

In our resolve to measure anything, the "Four Useful Measurement Assumptions" (mentioned in Chapter 3) are worth reiterating:

1. It's been done before—don't reinvent the wheel.
2. You have access to more data than you think—it might just involve some resourcefulness and original observations.
3. You need less data than you think, if you are clever about how to analyze it.
4. An adequate amount of new data is probably more accessible than you first thought.

DECOMPOSITION

Some very useful uncertainty-reducing methods are technically not actual measurements because they do not involve making new observations of the world. But they are often a very practical next step in determining how to measure something. Many times they can reveal that the estimator actually knew more than he or she let on in the initial calibrated estimate. As Enrico Fermi taught us, simply decomposing a variable into the parts that make it up can be an enlightening first step. Decomposition involves figuring out how to compute something very uncertain from other things that are a lot less uncertain or at least easier to measure.

Decompose It

Many measurements start by decomposing an uncertain variable into constituent parts to identify directly observable things that are easier to measure.

Recall that in Chapter 4, we showed how MacGregor and Armstrong empirically verified the simple decomposition of an estimate like Fermi proposed. They showed that highly uncertain estimates are the most likely to be improved by just a little decomposition. Of course, it is the highly uncertain variables in our decisions that will tend to have a high information value indicating they require further measurement.

A good decomposition will include at least some variables that are more directly observable. In fact, most measurements in the empirical sciences are done exactly like this: indirectly. For example, neither the mass of an electron nor the mass of Earth is observed directly. Other observations are made from which these values can be computed.

In Chapter 4, decomposition was used as a method for developing the components of the initial decision model. Once information values are computed, decomposition can be used again to add more detail to that part of the model. This alone is a different approach to the modeling process. When most decision models are initially created, whether it is a business case for an investment in a new technology or the value of a new public works project, assumptions are unavoidably made about where the model needs to be decomposed into further detail than in other areas.

Instead, we can let the information-value calculations drive where the model should be more detailed. We resist the temptation to make an unwieldy, detailed model before the first information values are calculated. We decompose just those variables where the uncertainty is extremely high. Once the information value is computed we can decide which parts of the model should be more detailed through additional decomposition.

For example, our initial decision model might have been for software that would improve the collaboration among engineers in different departments. The decomposition at that stage identified various initial and ongoing costs of this new technology and it identified multiple benefits. Some benefits were related to avoiding certain types of errors in designs, eliminating the costs of previous communication and documentation systems, and productivity improvements of engineers and other staff spending less time on unproductive tasks. Now suppose the productivity improvement had a significant information value while most of the other variables had an EVPI that was negligible. Suppose that your previous estimate was that the new engineering collaboration tools will improve productivity of engineers by 5% to 40%. Part of the uncertainty for estimators comes from the fact that they are trying to approximate, in their heads, some other variables they don't know firsthand. They don't know, for example, exactly how many engineers work in the area that would be affected the most.

Measuring how many engineers work in the area seems like an obvious and simple step in measurement. Yet those who insist that something cannot ever be measured resist even this. In such cases, a facilitator can be a big help. A facilitated discussion could go like this:

Facilitator: Previously you gave me a calibrated estimate of a 5% to 40% productivity improvement for your engineers with this new engineering collaboration software. Because this particular variable had the highest information value for the business case of whether to invest in the new software, we have to reduce our uncertainty further.

Engineer: That's a problem. How can we measure a soft thing like productivity? We don't even track document management as an activity, so we have no idea how much time we spend in it now.

Facilitator: Well, do you think that productivity will improve because there are certain tasks they will spend less time doing?

Engineer: I suppose so, yes.

Facilitator: What activities do engineers spend a lot of time at now that they will spend much less time at if they used this tool? Be as specific as possible.

Engineer: Okay. I guess they would probably spend less time searching for relevant documents. But that's just one item.

Facilitator: Great, it's a start. How much time do they spend at this now per week, and how much do you think that time will be reduced? Calibrated estimates will do for now.

Engineer: I'm not sure . . . I suppose I would be 90% confident the average engineer spends between one and six hours each week just looking for documents. Equipment specs, engineering drawings, procedural manuals, and so on are all kept in different places, and most are not in electronic form.

Facilitator: Good. How much of that would go away if they could sit at their desks and do queries?

Engineer: Well, even when I use automated search tools like Google, I still spend a lot of time searching through irrelevant data, so automation could not reduce time spent in searching by 100%. But I'm sure it would go down at least by half, maybe as high as 80%.

Facilitator: Does this vary for the type of engineer?

Engineer: Sure. Engineers with management roles spend less time at this. They depend on subordinates more often. However, engineers who focus on particular compliance issues have to research lots of documents. Various technicians also would use this.

Facilitator: Okay. How many engineers and technicians fall into each of these categories, and how much time do they each spend in this activity?

We go on in this way until we've identified a few different categories of staff, each spending a different amount of time in document searching and each with a different potential reduction in this time spent. The staff members may also vary by how much they adopt the new technology and other factors.

The previous dialog is actually a reconstruction of a specific conversation I had with engineers in a major U.S. nuclear power utility. During the meeting, we also identified other tasks, such as distribution, quality control, and the like, that might be reduced by document management systems. As before, the time spent in each of these tasks varied by the type of engineer or technician.

In short, part of the reason these engineers gave such a wide range for a productivity improvement is that they were imagining all of these variances among different types of engineers without explicitly breaking it down this way. Once they broke it down, they found that some numbers were fairly certain (e.g., the headcount for each engineer type, or the fact that some types spend most or little of their time in this activity) and that the uncertainty about the original number came primarily from one or two specific

> **Decomposition effect:** The phenomenon that the decomposition itself sometimes turns out to provide such a sufficient reduction in uncertainty that further uncertainty reduction through new observations are not required.

items. If we found that they were more uncertain just about time spent replicating or tracking down lost documents and then only for a certain class of engineers, we would have a big clue about where to begin a measurement.

The 80 or more major risk/return analyses I've done in the past 20 years consisted of a total of over 7,000 individual variables, or an average of almost 90 variables per model. Of those 7,000 variables, a little over 180 (about 2 per model) required further measurement according to the information value calculation. Most of these, about 150, had to be decomposed further to find a more easily measured component of the uncertain variable. Other variables offered more direct and obvious methods of measurement, for example, having to determine the gas mileage of a truck on a gravel road (by just driving a truck with a fuel-flow meter) or estimating the number of bugs in software (by inspecting samples of code).

But almost a third of the variables that were decomposed required no further measurement after decomposition. In other words, about 25% of the high-value measurements were addressed with decomposition alone.[1] Calibrated experts already knew enough about the variable; they just needed a more detailed model that more explicitly expressed the detailed knowledge they had. As the work of MacGregor and Armstrong showed, decomposition alone is a big help especially when quantities are highly uncertain. Of course, these are exactly the quantities that will tend to have higher information values in decisions.

Most of those variables that were decomposed had one or more of their components measured; for example, as part of a larger productivity improvement measurement, a survey was administered to one group of people to measure time spent on a specific activity. For these variables, decomposition was one critical step in understanding how to learn more about the thing being analyzed.

The entire process of decomposition itself is a gradual conceptual revelation for those who think that something is immeasurable. All of Fermi's students were either engineering or science majors and most were initially stumped until Fermi used some decomposition. Like any engineer who faces the initially daunting task of how to build a suspension bridge in a way that has never been done before, decomposition addresses any measurement problem systematically, identifying its component parts. And, like the bridge engineer, this analysis of parts at each step redefines and refines the nature of the problem we face. The decomposition of an "immeasurable" variable is an important step toward measurement and sometimes is a sufficient uncertainty reduction itself.

SECONDARY RESEARCH: ASSUMING YOU WEREN'T THE FIRST TO MEASURE IT

The standard approach to measurement in business, it seems, is for some smart people to start with the assumption that, being smart, they themselves will have to invent the method for a new measurement. In reality, however, such innovation is almost never required. Just *assume* someone measured the item in question, something close to it, or at least used a method that inspires a solution to the current problem.

Research of existing literature still does not seem to be an ingrained skill within management even though it is considered a basic step in scientific inquiry. But it has gotten a lot easier. All my research now starts with the Internet. No matter what measurement problem I'm attempting to resolve, I start by doing homework with Google and Bing. Then, of course, I may still end up in the library, but with more direction and purpose.

There are just a few tricks in using the Internet for secondary research. If you are looking for information that has been applied to measurement methods, you will probably find that most Internet searching is unproductive unless you are using the right search terms. It takes practice to use Internet searches effectively, but these tips should help.

- *If I'm really new to a topic, I don't start with Google.* I start—very cautiously—with Wikipedia.org, the online collaborative encyclopedia. Wikipedia contains well over 4 million articles, and a surprising number cover business and technology topics that might be considered too obscure for traditional encyclopedia sets. A good article usually includes links to other sites, and controversial topics tend to have lengthy discussions attached so you can decide for yourself what information to accept. *But let the reader beware.* Anyone can post information on Wikipedia, almost all posts are under pseudonyms, and there is "vandalism" of articles. Treat Wikipedia as a starting point, not a hard source.
- *Use search terms that tend to be associated with research and quantitative data.* If you need to measure "software quality" or "customer perception," don't just search on those terms alone—you will get mostly fluff. Instead, include terms like "table," "survey," "control group," "correlation," and "standard deviation," which would tend to appear in more substantive research. Also, terms like "university," "PhD," and "national study" tend to appear in more serious (less fluffy) research.
- *Think of Internet research in two levels: search engines and topic-specific repositories.* The problem with using powerful search engines like Google is that you might get thousands of hits, none of which are relevant. But try searching specifically within industry magazine websites or online academic journals. If I'm curious about macroeconomic or international analysis, I'll go straight to government websites like the Census, Department of Commerce, even the Central Intelligence Agency. (The CIA *World Fact Book* is my go-to place for

a variety of international statistical data.) These will give fewer but likely more relevant hits.

- *Try multiple search engines.* Even the seemingly all-powerful Google seems to miss a few items I find quickly when I use other engines. I like to use dogpile.com, bing.com, and yahoo.com to supplement searches on Google.
- *If you find marginally related research that still doesn't directly address your topic of interest, be sure to read the bibliography.* The bibliography is sometimes the best method for branching out to find more research.

THE BASIC METHODS OF OBSERVATION: IF ONE DOESN'T WORK, TRY THE NEXT

Describing in detail how you see or detect the proposed object of measurement is a useful way to begin to describe a measurement method. If you have any basis for the belief that the object even *exists,* you are observing it in some way. If someone claims customer satisfaction will increase significantly if we can only reduce call-waiting time, the person must have some reason for believing it. Have there been some complaints? Have there been downward trends in customer satisfaction as the company has grown? Measurements are almost always performed to test the truth of some idea, and those ideas don't just come from a vacuum.

If you've identified your uncertainty, identified any relevant thresholds, and computed the value of information, you've already identified something that is observable in principle. Consider the following four questions about the nature of the observation. This is a sort of cascade of empirical methods. If the first approach doesn't work, go to the next, and so on. These aren't in any particular order, but you will probably find that for some situations, it's best to start with one and then move to the others.

- *Does it leave a trail of any kind?* Just about every imaginable phenomenon leaves some evidence that it occurred. Think like a forensic investigator. Does the thing, event, or activity that you are trying to measure lead to consequences that themselves have a trail of any kind? Example: Longer waits on customer support lines cause some customers to hang up. This has to cause at least some loss of business, but how much? Did they hang up because of some unrelated reason on their end or out of frustration from waiting? People in the first group tend to call back; people in the second group tend not to. If you can identify even some of the customers who hang up and notice that they tend to purchase less, you have a clue. Now can you find any correlation between customers who hung up after long waits and a decrease in sales to that customer? (See "Example for Leaving a Trail.")

- *If the trail doesn't already exist, can you observe it directly or at least a sample of it?* Perhaps you haven't been tracking how many customers in a retail parking lot have out-of-state license plates, but you could look now. And even though staking out the parking lot full time is impractical, you can at least count license plates at some randomly selected times.

- *If it doesn't appear to leave behind a detectable trail of any kind, and direct one-time observations do not seem feasible, can you devise a way to begin to track it now?* If it hasn't been leaving a trail, you can "tag" it so it at least begins to leave a trail. One example is how Amazon.com provides free gift wrapping in order to help track which books are purchased as gifts. At one point Amazon was not tracking the number of items sold as gifts; the company added the gift-wrapping feature to be able to track it. Another example is how consumers are given coupons so retailers can see, among other things, what newspapers their customers read. Inexpensive personal sensors and apps for smart devices are available for many types of measurement about human activity.

- *If tracking the existing conditions does not suffice (with either existing or newly collected data), can the phenomenon be "forced" to occur under conditions that allow easier observation (i.e., an experiment)?* Example: If a retail store wants to measure whether a proposed returned-items policy will detrimentally affect customer satisfaction and sales, try it in some stores while holding others unchanged. Try to identify the difference.

Some Basic Methods of Observation

- Follow its trail like a clever detective. Do forensic analysis of data you already have.
- Use direct observation. Start looking, counting, and/or sampling if possible.
- If it hasn't left any trail so far, add a "tracer" to it so it *starts* leaving a trail.
- If you can't follow a trail at all, create the conditions to observe it (an experiment).

These methods apply regardless of whether this is a measurement of something that is occurring now (current sales due to customer referral) or a forecast (the expected improvement in customer referrals due to some new product feature, improvement in customer service, etc.). If it is something that describes a current state, the current state has all the information you need to measure it. If the measurement is actually a forecast, consider what you have observed already that gives you any reason to expect a change. If you can't think of anything you ever observed that causes you to have that expectation, why is your expectation justified at all?

And remember that in order to detect a trail, add a tracer/tag, or conduct an experiment, you need to observe only a few in a random sample. Remember that different elements of your decomposition may have to be measured differently. Don't worry just yet about all of the problems that each of these approaches could entail. Just identify whichever approach seems the simplest and most feasible for now.

Example for Leaving a Trail

The Value of Faster Pickup of Customer Calls: In the mid 1990s, a large European paint supplies distributor asked me how to measure the impact of network speed on sales, since the network affected how quickly inbound calls could be answered. Since the phone system kept logs of calls and hang-ups while on hold, and since the network kept a history of its utilization levels (and, therefore, response time), I recommended cross-referencing the two data sets. This showed that hang-ups increased when demand on the network increased. The company also looked at past situations where the network was slower because of other use, not increased use by customer service, as well as the sales history by day. Altogether, the company was able to isolate the difference in sales that was due just to slower network speed.

MEASURE JUST ENOUGH

Chapter 7 reviewed how to compute the value of information for a particular decision. The uncertainty, thresholds, and information value you determined say a lot about what measurement method you really need. If the information value of knowing whether your customers think your product quality has improved with a new manufacturing process (e.g., the "new" beverage formulation or the "classic" beverage formulation) is a couple of thousand dollars, you can't justify a two-month pilot market or even a major blind taste test. But if the information value is in the range of millions of dollars (which is more likely if this is the product of even a medium-size company), we should not feel daunted by a study that might cost $100,000 and lasts a few weeks. Keeping the information value in mind along with the threshold, the decision, and current uncertainty provides the purpose and context of the measurement.

Remember, the EVPI is an upper limit on what you should be willing to spend even theoretically. But the best measurement expenditure is probably far below this maximum. As a ballpark estimate, I shoot for spending approximately 10% of the EVPI on a measurement and, depending on the circumstances, sometimes even as low as 2%. I use this estimate for three reasons:

1. The EVPI is the value of perfect information. Since all empirical methods have some error, we are only shooting for a reduction in uncertainty, not perfect information. So the value of our measurement will probably be much less than the EVPI.
2. Initial measurements often change the value of continued measurement. The first few observations may be surprising, the information may be very informative, and the value of continuing the measurement may drop to zero. This means there is a value in iterative measurement. And since you always have the option of continuing a measurement if you need more precision, there is usually a manageable risk in underestimating the initial measurement effort.
3. The information value curve is usually steepest at the beginning. The first 100 samples reduce uncertainty much more than the second 100. In fact, even the first 10 samples tell you a lot more than the next 10. The initial state of uncertainty tells you a lot about how to measure it. Remember, the more uncertainty you started out with, the more the initial observations will tell you. When starting from a position of extremely high uncertainty, even methods with a lot of inherent error can give you more information than you had before.

CONSIDER THE ERROR

All measurements have error. As with all problems, the solution starts with the recognition that we have the problem—which allows us to develop strategies to compensate, at least partially. Those who tend to be easily thwarted by measurement challenges, however, often assume that the existence of *any* error means that a measurement is impossible. If that was true, virtually nothing would ever have been measured in any field of science. Fortunately, for the scientific community and for the rest of us, it's not. Enrico Fermi can rest easy.

Scientists, statisticians, economists, and most others who make empirical measurements separate measurement error into two broad types: systemic and random—although they may not use those terms explicitly. Systemic errors are those that are consistent and not just random variations from one observation to the next. For example, if the sales staff routinely overestimates next quarter's revenue by an average of 50%, that is a systemic error. The fact that it isn't always exactly 50% too optimistic, but varies, is an example of random error. Random error, by definition, can't be individually predicted but falls into some quantifiable patterns that can be computed with the laws of probability.

Systemic error and random error are related to the measurement concepts of precision and accuracy. "Precision" refers to the reproducibility and conformity of measurements, while "accuracy" refers to how close a measurement is to its "true" value. While the terms "accuracy" and "precision" (as well as "inaccuracy" and "imprecision") are used synonymously by most people, to measurement experts they are clearly different. Depending on the field, some researchers may use the terms validity and reliability to mean essentially the same as accuracy and precision (although they may not always measure them or even define them quantitatively).

A bathroom scale that is calibrated to overstate or understate weight (as some people apparently do, deliberately) could be precise but inaccurate. It is precise because if the same person stepped on the scale several times within an hour—so that the actual weight doesn't have a chance to change—the scale would give the same answer very

---

Quick Glossary of Error

Systemic error/bias: An inherent tendency of a measurement process to favor a particular outcome; a consistent bias.

Random error: An error that is not predictable for individual observations; not consistent or dependent on known variables (although such errors follow the rules of probability in large groups).

Accuracy: A characteristic of a measurement having a low systemic error—that is, not consistently over- or underestimating a value. In some fields this is used synonymously with "validity."

Precision: A characteristic of a measurement having a low random error; highly consistent results even if they are far from the true value. In some fields of research, the terms "reliability" and "consistency" will be used in the same way.

consistently. Yet it is inaccurate because every answer is always, say, eight pounds over. Now imagine a perfectly calibrated bathroom scale in the bathroom of a moving motor home. Bumps, acceleration, and hills cause the readings on the scale to move about and give different answers even when the same person steps on it twice within one minute. Still, you would find that after a number of times on the scale, the answers average out to be very close to the person's actual weight. This is an example of fairly good accuracy but low precision. Calibrated experts are similar to the latter. They may be inconsistent in their judgments, but they are not consistently overestimating or underestimating.

To put it another way, precision is low random error, regardless of the amount of systemic error. Accuracy is low systemic error, regardless of the amount of random error. Each of the types of error can be accounted for and reduced. If we know the bathroom scale gives an answer eight pounds higher than the true value, we can adjust the reading accordingly. If we get highly inconsistent readings with a well-calibrated scale, we can remove random error by taking several measurements and computing the average. Any method to reduce either of these errors is called a "control."

Random sampling, if used properly, is itself a type of control. Random effects, while individually unpredictable, follow specific predictable patterns in the aggregate. For example, I can't predict a coin flip. But I can tell you that if you flipped a coin 1,000 times, there will be 500+/−26 heads. (We'll talk about computing the error range later.) It is often much harder to compute an error range for systemic error. Systemic errors—like those from using biased judges to assess the quality of a work product or using an instrument that constantly underestimates a quantity—are *consistent* errors. They don't change randomly from one observation to the next.

If you had to choose, would you prefer the weight measurement from an uncalibrated but precise scale with an unknown error or from a calibrated scale on a moving platform with highly inconsistent readings each time you weigh yourself? I find that, in business, people often choose precision with unknown systemic error over a highly imprecise measurement with random error. For example, to determine how much time sales reps spend in meetings with clients versus other administrative tasks, they might choose a complete review of all time sheets. They would generally not conduct a random sample of sales reps on different days at different times. Time sheets have error, especially those completed for the whole week at 5 p.m. on Friday in a rush to get out the door. People underestimate time spent on some tasks, overestimate time spent on others, and are inconsistent in how they classify tasks.

Small Random Samples versus Large Nonrandom Samples

The Kinsey Sex Study: A famous debate about small random versus large nonrandom samples concerned the work of Alfred Kinsey in the 1940s and 1950s regarding sexual behavior. Kinsey's work was both controversial and popular at the time. Funded by the Rockefeller Foundation, he was able to conduct interviews of 18,000 men and women. But they were not exactly random samples. He tended to meet people by referral and tended to sample everyone in a specific group (a bowling league, a college fraternity, a book club, etc.). Kinsey apparently assumed that any error could be offset by a large enough sample. But that's not how most systemic error works—it doesn't "average out." John W. Tukey, a famous statistician who was retained by the same Rockefeller Foundation to review Kinsey's work, was quoted as saying: "A random selection of three people would have been better than a group of 300 chosen by Mr. Kinsey." In another version of this quote, he was said to prefer a random sample of 400 to Kinsey's 18,000. If the first quote is Tukey's, he may have exaggerated, but not by much. Tukey meant that the groups Kinsey sampled were often very close to homogeneous. Therefore, these groups may have counted as something closer to one random sample, statistically speaking. In the second version of the quote, Tukey is almost certainly correct: A random sample of 400 will have an easily quantifiable error, and that error may actually be much less than the systemic error of 18,000 poorly chosen samples.

If a complete review of 5,000 time sheets (say, 100 reps for 50 weekly time sheets each) tells us that sales reps spend 34% of their time in direct communication with customers, we don't know how far from the truth it might be. Still, this "exact" number seems reassuring to many managers. Now, suppose a sample of direct observations of randomly chosen sales reps at random points in time finds that sales reps were in client meetings or on client phone calls only 13 out of 100 of those instances. (We can compute this without interrupting a meeting by asking as soon as the rep is available.) As we will see in Chapter 9, in the latter case, we can statistically compute a 90% CI to be 7.5% to 18.5%. Even though the random sampling approach gives us only a range, we should prefer its findings to the census audit of time sheets if we are trying to measure total time spent. The census of time sheets gives us an exact number, but we have no way to know by how much and in which direction the time sheets err. However, if you merely want to measure the *change* in time spent, then the problems of systemic errors may not be relevant. If, unknown to me, my scale always overstates my weight by 10 pounds, and I see an increase of 8 pounds then I can still conclude my weight increased even if I'm uncertain about the amount or even the direction of the systemic error. As always, the nature of the measurement matters when interpreting error.

The error you can't count on averaging out—systemic error—is also called a "bias." The list of types of biases seems to grow with almost every year of research in decision psychology or empirical sciences in general. But there are three big biases that you need to control for: expectancy, selection, and observer biases.

A Few Types of Observation Biases

Expectancy bias: Observers and subjects sometimes, consciously or not, see what they want. We are gullible and tend to be self-deluding. Clinical trials of new drugs have to make sure that subjects don't actually know whether they have taken the real drug or a placebo. This is the previously mentioned blind test. When those who are taking the real drug are hidden from the doctors as well as the patients, this is a double-blind test. The approach I recommended for the Mitre Corporation example in Chapter 2 is an example of a blind test.

Selection bias: Even when attempting randomness in samples, we can get inadvertent nonrandomness. If we sample 500 voters for a poll and 55% say they will vote for candidate A, it is fairly likely—98.8%, to be exact—that candidate A actually has the lead in the population. There is only a 1.2% chance that a random sampling could have just by chance chosen more voters for A if A wasn't actually in the lead. But this assumes the sample was random and didn't tend to select some types of voters over others. If the sample is taken by asking passersby on a particular street corner in the financial district, you are more likely to get a particular type of voter even if you "randomly" pick which passersby to ask.

Observer bias (or the Heisenberg and Hawthorne bias): Subatomic particles and humans have something in common. The act of observing them causes them both to change behavior. In 1927, the physicist Werner Heisenberg derived a formula showing that there is a limit to how much we can know about a particle's position and velocity. When we observe particles, we have to interact with them (e.g., bounce light off them), causing their paths to change. That same year a research project was begun at the Hawthorne Plant of

(continued)

the Western Electric Company in Illinois. Initially led by Professor Elton Mayo from the Harvard Business School, the study set out to determine the effects of the physical environment and working conditions on worker productivity. Researchers altered lighting levels, humidity, work hours, and so on in an effort to determine under which conditions workers worked best. To their surprise, they found that worker productivity improved no matter how they changed the workplace. The workers were simply responding to the knowledge of being observed; or perhaps, researchers hypothesized, management taking interest in them caused a positive reaction. Although Heisenberg and Mayo were discussing very different phenomena, they have the same impact on measurement. We can no longer assume observations see the "real" world if we don't take care to compensate for how observations affect what we observe. The simplest solution is to keep observations a secret from those being observed.

CHOOSE AND DESIGN THE INSTRUMENT

After decomposing the problem, placing one or more of the decomposed parts in an observation hierarchy, aiming for "just good enough" uncertainty reduction, and accounting for the main types of error, the measurement instrument should be almost completely formed in your mind. Just answering the questions up to this point should have made some measurement methods more apparent. Let's summarize how to identify the instrument:

1. *Decompose the measurement so that it can be estimated from other measurements.* Some of these elements may be easier to measure, and sometimes the decomposition itself will have reduced uncertainty.
2. *Consider your findings from secondary research.* Look at how others measured similar issues. Even if their specific findings don't relate to your measurement problem, is there anything you can salvage from the methods they used?
3. *Place one or more of the elements from the decomposition in one or more of the methods of observation: trails left behind, direct observation, tracking with "tags," or experiments.* Think of at least three ways you detect it, and then follow its trail forensically. If you can't do that, try a direct observation. If you can't do that, tag it or make other changes to it so it *starts* leaving a trail you can follow. If you can't do that, create the event specifically to be observed (the experiment).

4. *Keep the concept of "just enough" squarely in mind.* You don't need great precision if all you need is more certainty that a productivity improvement will be over the minimum threshold needed to justify a project. Keep the information value in mind; a small value means little effort is justified and a big value means you should think bigger about the measurement method. Also, remember how much uncertainty you had to begin with. If you were originally very uncertain, how much of an observation do you really need to reduce the uncertainty?

5. *Think about the errors specific to that problem.* If it is a series of human judges evaluating the quality of work, beware of expectation bias and consider a blind. If you need a sample, make sure it is random. If your observations themselves can affect outcome, find a way to hide the observation from the subject.

Now, if you can't yet fully visualize the instrument, consider these tips, listed in no particular order. Some have been mentioned already, but all are worth reviewing.

- *Work through the consequences.* If the value you are seeking is surprisingly high, what should you see? If the value is surprisingly low, what should you see? In the example cited in Chapter 2, young Emily reasoned that if the therapeutic touch specialists could do what they claimed, they should at least be able to detect a human "aura." For a quality measurement problem, if quality is better, you probably should see fewer complaints from customers. For a sales-related software application, if a new IT system really helps salespeople sell better, why would you see sales go down for those who use it more?

- *Be iterative.* Don't try to eliminate uncertainty in one giant study. Start making a few observations, and recalculate the information value. It might have a bearing on how you continue measurement.

- *Consider multiple approaches.* If one type of observation on one of the elements in your decomposition doesn't seem feasible, focus on another. You have many options. If the first measurement method works, great. But in some cases I've measured things three different ways, after the first two were unenlightening. Are you sure you are exploring all the methods available? If you can't measure one variable in a decomposition, can you measure another?

- *What's the really simple question that makes the rest of the measurement moot?* Again, Emily didn't try to measure how well therapeutic touch worked, just whether it worked at all. In the Mitre example discussed earlier, I suggested the company determine if clients could detect *any* change in the quality of research before it tried to measure a value of the expected improvement in quality. Some questions are so basic that it is possible that their answers could make more complicated measurements irrelevant. What is the basic question you need to ask to see if you need to measure any more?

- *Just do it.* Don't let anxiety about what could go wrong with measurement keep you from just *starting* to make some organized observations. Don't assume you won't be surprised by the first few observations and considerably reduce your uncertainty.

By now you should have a pretty good idea of what you need to observe and, generally, how to observe it in order to make your measurement. Now we can talk about some specific methods of observation in two general categories: observations analyzed with "traditional" statistics and a method called "Bayesian analysis." Together, these two broad categories cover just about all empirical methods applied to physics, medicine, environmental studies, or economics. Although the traditional methods are by far the most prevalent ones, the Bayesian analysis has some distinct advantages.

Note

1. I'm using the term "about" because this is an estimation of a moving target. At the time of this writing, we have 6 to 10 decision modeling projects at various stages of development, some very complex, and not all decompositions have been counted up. But the estimates of decomposed variables probably have an error of less than +/–3.

## CHAPTER 9

Sampling Reality: How Observing Some Things Tells Us about All Things

It is the mark of an educated mind to rest satisfied with the degree of precision which the nature of the subject admits and not to seek exactness where only an approximation is possible.

—Aristotle (384 B.C.–322 B.C.)

If you want 100% certainty about the percentage of defective bricks from a kiln, you have to test all of them. Since testing the failure load of a brick requires compressing it in a press and measuring the force under which it cracks apart, this would require the destruction of every brick you make. If you want to have most of the bricks left over to use or sell, you only get to test a few bricks to learn something about all of them.

The group you want to learn about is the population—in this case, the bricks produced. A test of every single item in a group you want to learn about (e.g., testing every brick produced) is a census. Obviously, a census is impractical for bricks, since you would have no bricks left when the census is complete, but it is practical in other situations. A monthly inventory is usually a census, and the balance sheet is a census of every asset and liability. The U.S. Census tries to count every human being in the country, although in reality it falls a bit short of this.

There are a number of reasons, however, where it is impractical to test, track, weigh, or even count every item in a population. But we can still reduce uncertainty by looking at just some items from a population. Anything short of a complete census of the population is a *sample*. In effect, sampling is observing just some of the things in a population to learn something about all of the things in a population.

It might seem remarkable that looking at some things tells us anything about things we aren't looking at, but, in fact, this is most of what science does. Experiments look at only some phenomena in a universe full of phenomena. And when science discovers a "law," it says that the law applies to everything in that population, not just the few examples observed so far.

For example, the speed of light was determined with, literally, some samples of light. And no matter what measurement method was used, it had error. Therefore, scientists measured the speed of light more than once to reduce this error. Each measurement is another sample. And yet the speed of light is a universal constant that should apply to the light reflecting off this page and hitting your eyes as well as the light sampled in a lab. Even a census could be just a sample of a still larger population over time. For example, a complete inventory is just one snapshot in time, as is a balance sheet.

This point might be disconcerting to some who would like more certainty in their world, but everything we know from "experience" is just a sample. We didn't actually experience everything; we experienced some things and we extrapolated from there. That is all we get—fleeting glimpses of a mostly unobserved world from which we draw conclusions about all the stuff we didn't see. Yet people seem to feel confident in the conclusions they draw from limited samples. The reason they feel this way is because experience tells them sampling often works. (Of course, that experience, too, is based on a sample.)

For someone who needs to review the material from first-semester college statistics, there are a lot of accessible statistics books. This book doesn't try to cover all of those topics. We focus instead on the most basic and useful methods and include a bit on what standard statistics texts tend to leave out or at least deemphasize. The limitations of statistics textbooks are part of the problem for managers seeking solutions for measurement challenges. The entire industry of statistical analysis seems unconcerned with practical accessibility or the broader issue of how to measure the "immeasurable."

This chapter discusses some simple methods for drawing a lot of information from a small sample. Sampling methods are one of the reasons, as we said in Chapter 3, that you need less data than you think. But unlike the books I first learned from, we will start with some "intuition building" before we show any math, and the math presented is as limited as possible. When we do get into how to compute specific values, we emphasize quick estimates and simple tables and charts over memorizing equations. Furthermore, every example in this chapter (as well as most in this book) can be downloaded as spreadsheet examples from the supplementary website, www.howtomeasureanything.com. Make full use of that resource.

Before going further, we should cover a brief note on convention in the use of the word "sample." The size of a sample is often denoted by the letter "n" as in a sample size of "$n = 30$." The singular form sample is most often used in scientific literature to mean a single sampling procedure where n can be one or greater. It is also not uncommon to use the singular word "sample" to mean literally a single randomly selected item. In experiments, reference to a singular selected item is often called a "trial." So we can speak of "a random sample of 30" or we can use the plural "30 randomly selected samples" to mean the same thing. In both cases this refers to a single random selection procedure where $n = 30$ (i.e., 30 trials). There may be cases where the plural "samples" refers to multiple random selection procedures each with n greater than one but, when that is the case, the context should make it clear and if "samples" means multiple selected items, the word "trials" may be used, instead.

BUILDING AN INTUITION FOR RANDOM SAMPLING: THE JELLY BEAN EXAMPLE

Here is a little experiment you can try. What is your 90% confidence interval (CI) for the weight, in grams, of the average jelly bean? Remember, we need two numbers—a lower bound and an upper bound—just far apart enough that you are 90% confident that the average weight of a jelly bean, in grams, is between the bounds. Just like every other calibrated probability estimate, you have some idea, regardless of how uncertain you feel about it. A gram, by the way, weighs as much as one cubic centimeter of water (imagine a thimble full of water). Write down your range before you go any further. As explained in Chapter 5, be sure to test it with the equivalent bet and consider some pros and cons for why the range is reasonable along with other prudent calibration methods.

I took a bag of jelly beans—the type you can buy anywhere candy is sold—and began sampling them. I put several jelly beans one at a time on a digital scale. Now consider the following four questions. Answer each one before you go to the next point.

1. Suppose I told you the weight of the first jelly bean I sampled was 1.4 grams. Does that change your 90% CI? If so, what is your updated 90% CI? Write down your new range before proceeding.
2. Now I reveal that the next sample weighed 1.5 grams. Does that change your 90% CI again? If so, what is your CI now? Write down this new range.

3. Now I give you the results of the next three randomly sampled jelly bean weights, for a total of five so far: 1.4, 1.6, and 1.1. Does that change your 90% CI even further? If so, what is your 90% CI now? Again, write down this new range.

4. Finally, I give you the results of the next three randomly sampled weights of jelly beans, for a total of eight samples so far: 1.5, 0.9, 1.7. Again, does that change your 90% CI? If so, what is it now? Write down this final range.

Over the years, I've given many people this estimation problem and I get fairly consistent results. The biggest difference among the estimators was how uncertain they were about the initial estimate. I've gotten some ranges as narrow as (before sample information was revealed) 1 to 2 grams for the average jelly bean, and some were as wide as 0.1 to 100 grams, but most ranges were something like 1 to 5 grams. As the estimators were given additional information, most reduced the width of their range, especially those who started with very wide ranges. Some of those who gave a narrow range did not reduce the range at all after the first sample if the sample was within their range. But the person who gave a range like 1 to 10 grams or 0.5 to 50 grams reduced the width of their range significantly.

The true average of the population of this bag of jelly beans is close to 1.45 grams per jelly bean. Interestingly, the ranges of the estimators narrowed in on this value fairly quickly as they were given just a few additional samples. Note: The data they were given were in the order of actual samples selected from a bag of jelly beans which I weighed on a digital scale and I gave everyone this same list of values in the same order.

Exercises like this help you gain a sense—an intuition—about samples and ranges. Asking calibrated estimators for subjective estimates without applying what some would call "proper statistics" is actually very useful and even has some interesting advantages over traditional statistics, as we will soon see. Somewhat ironically, we know this works to some degree because published studies using proper statistical analysis and lots of data say so (more to come on that). For now, let's look at how most statistics texts handle small samples.

A LITTLE ABOUT LITTLE SAMPLES: A BEER BREWER'S APPROACH

There is a way to compute the 90% CI for the jelly bean problem without any reliance on calibrated estimators, using a method developed by a beer brewer. This method is widely taught in basic statistics courses and can be used for computing errors for sample sizes as small as two.

In the earliest years of the twentieth century, William Sealy Gosset, a chemist and statistician at the Guinness brewery in Dublin, had a measurement problem. Gosset needed a way to measure which types of barley produced the best beer-brewing yields. Prior to that time, a method alternatively called the "z-score" or "normal statistic" was developed to estimate a confidence interval based on random samples—as long as there were at least 30 samples. This method produces distributions in the shape of the normal distribution discussed earlier. Unfortunately, Gosset did not have the luxury of sampling a large number of batches of beer for each type of barley. But instead of assuming he couldn't measure it, he set out to derive a new type of distribution for very small sample sizes.

By 1908, he had developed a powerful new method he called the "t-statistic," and he wanted to publish it—but Guinness would not have approved. It is often reported that Guinness company had a broad prohibition against any publications by employees as a guard against the loss of trade secrets. Other sources indicate that the real motivation behind the prohibition was because Guinness simply didn't want to reveal one key competitive strategy—the fact that it was *hiring statisticians*. (By this point in the book, readers should agree that this could indeed be a competitive advantage.) Since Gosset apparently valued his job more than immediate recognition, he published his t-statistic under the name "Student." Although the true author has been long known, virtually all statistics texts still call this the "student's t-statistic."

The t-statistic is similar in shape to the normal distribution we discussed previously. For sample sizes larger than $n = 30$, the shape of the t-distribution is virtually the same as the normal distribution. But for very small samples, the shape of the distribution is much flatter and wider and the tails are thicker. The 90% CI computed with a student's t-statistic is much more uncertain than a normal distribution would indicate.

With either type of distribution, there is a relatively simple procedure (compared to much of the rest of statistics methods) for computing the 90% CI of the average of a population. Some might find the procedure to be unintuitive, and those familiar with the approach might find this to be a trivial rehash of information available in statistics texts. The first group might want to hold out for a much simpler solution (coming later in this chapter) while the second group might just skim over this material. Aiming for readers who consider themselves to be somewhere in the middle, I've opted to make my explanation as simple as possible. Suppose I want to estimate the mean of the entire population of jelly beans using the first five samples of jelly beans shown earlier. Here is how we compute a 90% CI for the estimate of the mean of the population using this small sample (of course, you can also find the example prepared in a spreadsheet in the Chapter 9 examples of www.howtomeasureanything.com):

1. Compute the sample "variance." As the name indicates, this is a way of quantifying how much samples vary from one another using the following steps—**a** through **c**. (This is a concept we'll refer to more often later.)

   a. Compute the average of the samples:

$$(1.4 + 1.4 + 1.5 + 1.6 + 1.1)/5 = 1.4$$

   b. Subtract this average from each of the samples and square the result for each sample:

$$(1.4 - 1.4)^2 = 0, (1.4 - 1.4)^2 = 0, (1.5 - 1.4)^2 = .01, \textit{etc.}$$

   c. Add all the squares and divide by 1 less than the number of samples:

$$(0 + 0 + .01 + .04 + .09)/(5 - 1) = .035$$

2. Divide the sample variance by the number of samples and take the square root of the result. In a spreadsheet we could write "= SQRT(.035/5)" to get .0837. (In statistics texts, this is called the "standard deviation of the estimate of the mean.")

3. Look up the *t*-stat in Exhibit 9.1, the simplified *t*-statistic table, next to the sample size. Next to the number 5 is the *t*-score 2.13. Note that

Exhibit 9.1 Simplified *t*-Statistic. Pick the nearest sample size (or interpolate if you prefer more precision).

Sample Size (n)	*t*-Score
2	6.31
3	2.92
4	2.35
5	2.13
6	2.02
8	1.89
12	1.80
16	1.75
28	1.70
Larger samples	(*z*-score) 1.645

for very large sample sizes, the *t*-score gets closer to the *z*-score (for the normal distribution) of 1.645.

4. Multiply the *t*-statistic by the answer from step 2: $2.13 \times .0837 = .178$. This is the sample error in grams.

5. Add the sample error to the mean to get the upper bound of a 90% CI, and subtract the same sample error from the mean to the lower bound: upper bound = $1.4 + .178 = 1.578$, lower bound = $1.4 - .178 = 1.222$.

We get a 90% CI of 1.22 to 1.58 after just a sample of five. This same procedure also gives us the answer for larger samples needed for the traditional *z*-score. The only difference is that the *z*-score we need to compute a 90% CI is always 1.645. (It doesn't change further as sample size increases.)

Whether we initially estimated something with subjective methods or a *t*-statistic or *z*-statistic, what matters is how well the approach works in reality. We might call one method more "objective," but even the subjective method has an objectively measurable performance. So, are the calibrated estimators who were given small sample data better or worse at estimating than using this simple mathematical procedure?

In the experiment with the calibrated estimators and the jelly beans, the estimators consistently gave wider ranges than what we would get if we used the *t*-statistic, but often not by much. So, based on the small sample of people I did this test with, this indicates that doing a little more math usually reduces error further than calibrated estimators alone, at least on this simple problem. After eight samples, the most conservative calibrated estimator had a range of 0.5 to 2.4 grams while the most confident estimator gave a range of 1 to 1.7 grams. After the same number of samples, the *t*-statistic gives a 90% CI of 1.21 to 1.57 grams, about the same as the five sample estimate but considerably narrower than the narrowest range among the estimators.

Even though the uncertainty reduction according to the estimators was conservative (not as narrow as it could have been), it was not entirely irrational and was still a significant reduction from the prior state of uncertainty. Perhaps the only mathematically irrational response was that some estimators refused to narrow ranges on just one or two samples, possibly because they had some preconceptions about what small samples can achieve. As we will see in Chapter 10, further studies bear out these findings. In summary, we find:

- When you have a lot of uncertainty, a few samples greatly reduce it, especially with relatively homogeneous populations.

- In some cases, calibrated estimators were able to reduce uncertainty even with only one sample—which is impossible with the traditional statistics we just discussed.
- Calibrated estimators are mostly rational yet conservative. Doing more math reduces uncertainty even further.

ARE SMALL SAMPLES REALLY "STATISTICALLY SIGNIFICANT"?

Readers may remember something about a concept called "statistical significance" from a previous undergraduate stats course. The phrase often works its way into discussions about measurement—both correctly and incorrectly. It comes up in the calculations of different legitimate measurement methods (which we will discuss more in this chapter) and it comes up in casual conversations about samples even when no specific calculation is recalled. It's such a pervasive concept in scientific measurement and what managers may remember about stats, that it's best to address the concept early. In this chapter, I discuss three types of problems in how this concept is remembered and applied:

1. The idea of "statistically significant" is often completely misremembered as some fixed minimum sample size or is invoked informally (i.e., without any calculation) as an objection to a measurement.
2. Even if the math for statistical significance is remembered and done correctly, the results are often misinterpreted.
3. Even if the math is right and interpreted correctly, the mathematically precise meaning of statistical significance is not really what a decision maker wanted to know in the first place.

There is a camp of statisticians and scientists who would prefer to avoid the concept of statistical significance entirely and remove it from all scientific method. I count myself as a sympathizer to their cause and I'll mention some thinkers from that camp at the end of this chapter (see "A Purely Philosophical Interlude #4"). Later in this chapter, we will see how statistical significance comes up in different measurement problems, including the "hypothesis testing" methods used in controlled experiments. For now, I'll just talk about one common misunderstanding and how it varies from the actual meaning of statistical significance.

I often asked my seminar audiences whether a sample of five (like the one mentioned in the Rule of Five) is "statistically significant." Most of those who took a college stats course—with varying degrees of success and many years ago—will, at first, say it is not. I then ask them what statistical significance means and rarely would anyone in the room proffer an approximate answer. At best they might remember that it has something to do with some kind of error being less than a stated "significance level." Many may simply mistakenly recall that it refers to some fixed number of required samples. Yet with only the most tenuous recall of the concept and without doing any math, they are confident in declaring whether something is statistically significant or not.

Contrary to the intuition of many, a very small sample can produce statistically significant results in its strict mathematical sense. Any college stats text will certainly have a chapter on small samples using student's *t* which, as we saw, deals with samples even smaller than five. However, whether a finding is statistically significant is not the same thing as whether your current state of uncertainty is less than it was before or what the economic value of that uncertainty reduction would be. In other words, statistical significance is not about whether the measurement was informative or economically justified. Small samples may easily fit those requirements—the requirements the decision maker cares about.

Recall the information value chart in Chapter 7. Exhibit 7.7 showed that the big payoff in information tends to be early in the information gathering process. This is the point where the Expected Cost of Information is small for an incremental reduction in uncertainty and the Expected Value of Information increases quickly. We saw that reducing uncertainty about a big risky bet can be worth a lot even, in some cases, where uncertainty is reduced only slightly. This is what matters to the decision maker.

Exhibit 9.2 shows the average relative reduction in uncertainty as sample sizes increase by showing the 90% CI getting narrower with each sample according to the student's *t*. Individual examples will, of course, depend on the data set, but if you could get the average of all the possible sampling problems you could ever come across, the average of all of them would look like this. It could have been the yields of brewed batches at Guinness, the time spent in line by customers, or the shoe sizes of Nebraskans. Regardless of the specific type of problem, a decision maker needed a narrower 90% CI for some uncertain quantity but, for some reason, only a few samples, not hundreds or thousands, can be collected. The reason could be economics, time constraints, or the shyness of Nebraskans about having their feet measured.

The graph in Exhibit 9.2 looks something like a tornado on its side. The curve on top is the upper bound of a 90% CI; the curve on the bottom is the lower bound. On the extreme left of the chart we see that the upper and lower bounds of a 90% CI tend to be far apart when the samples are small but get narrower as the number of samples increases. With real data from a specific example, such as the shoe sizes of Nebraskans, our 90% CI of the population average would look like a much more

Exhibit 9.2 How Uncertainty Changes with Sample Size

jagged funnel as we tried to narrow the CI with additional samples. It is even possible for an additional sample to sometimes increase the size of the interval from the previous data set before the next sample makes it narrower again.

However, on average, the increasing sample size will decrease the size of the interval. Exhibit 9.2 shows that after just a few samples, the 90% CI is still wide, but narrows rapidly with each new sample. Also note that while the 90% CI is much narrower at 30 samples, it wasn't much narrower than at 20 or even 10 samples. In fact, once you get to 30 samples, you have to, as a general rule, quadruple the number of samples (120) if you want the error to go down by half again. If you want only one-quarter as much error as you have at 30 samples, you need 16 times as many samples (480) to estimate the mean of the entire population.

If we think the population is somewhat homogeneous, we may need an even smaller number of samples to draw useful conclusions about the rest of the unsampled population. If we are taking a sample to test for something completely homogeneous, like the DNA in someone's blood or octane levels in gasoline, we need only one sample from a person or batch. However, if the samples vary a lot, such as the size of fish in a lake or the time spent by employees dealing with PC problems, we generally need more. Still, just not as many as many people think.

How can looking at just a few things tell us something about all things in a population? If we sample 12 people in a city to find out how often they go to the movies or whether they trust the mayor, can we learn anything about all the people we *didn't* ask? Yes, if we previously knew very little, it is possible to learn from a sample this small. And if you think about it, that's kind of amazing. Of course, whether this small sample tells us much depends in part on how we took the sample. If we just ask our friends or all the men in a local barbershop, there is good reason to believe that this group might not be representative of the total population, and it is hard to tell how far off our conclusions about the larger population might be. We need a method to ensure that we don't just systematically choose samples of a particular type.

The solution for this is genuinely random sampling from the entire population we are trying to examine. Each item in the entire population should have the same chance of being selected. If we can pick samples randomly, we still have error, but the rules of probability can tell us something about the error. We can work out the chance that we just happened to pick Democrats in a political poll of an area that, in reality, has more Republicans. As the number of people randomly sampled grows, the chance of accidentally getting a nonrepresentative group becomes smaller and smaller.

So, how many samples is enough? Do we have to survey 1,000 customers? Do we have to spot-check welds on the chassis of 50 cars? Does a drug have to be tested with more than 100 patients in a clinical trial?

I've heard many authoritative-sounding proclamations on this topic. Perhaps someone remembers that the z-stat table starts at 30 samples (a somewhat arbitrary point where the t-stat for smaller samples and z-stat roughly converge), but this particular bit of statistics trivia has nothing to do with a magic threshold of statistical significance. I've also heard 100, 600, 1,000, and other values as an amount someone has been told to use as a minimum number of required samples for a survey. In some cases, these amounts were specifically computed values to solve some problems. But I find that in all but the rarest cases, no specific calculation for some minimum sample size is offered. There is such a calculation, but its actual use is much rarer than the off-handed claims about statistically significant sample sizes.

Curiously, most of those who took the jelly bean survey also doubted whether such a small sample could be what they believed to be statistically significant. Still, they were willing to reduce the width of their ranges based on just a few samples—usually on only one sample. So apparently it's not that people don't believe that small samples can be informative. They appear to believe that statistical significance is some other standard of legitimacy they should be concerned about as decision makers. In short, the concept of statistical significance is invoked far too frequently without being based on any actual math.

Someone who really does know something about statistical significance and informative sample sizes is Barry Nussbaum, chief statistician of Statistical Support Services at the Environmental Protection Agency (EPA). I've worked with him on how to import some of my methods into statistical analysis at the EPA. He fields questions from all over the agency on how to conduct statistical analysis on different types of problems. He tells me: "When people ask for statistics support, they ask 'What's the sample size?' It is the wrong question, but it's the first one most people ask." Of course, Nussbaum needs to find out more about what they are measuring and why in order to answer that question. I couldn't agree more.

Later in this chapter, statistical significance will be discussed in a bit more detail. But, in the meantime, I hope we've established that it is not a concept to be invoked lightly as an objection to small samples. As first discussed in Chapter 7, a very small sample can probably tell you much more than you think. When your current uncertainty is great, even a small sample can produce a big reduction in uncertainty. This book is more about those things that are considered immeasurable, and in those cases, the initial uncertainty is generally great. And it is exactly in those types of problems where even a few observations can tell us a lot.

WHEN OUTLIERS MATTER MOST

A caveat should be mentioned when applying the methods discussed so far. Both the t-statistic and the normal z-statistic are types of "parametric" statistics. Parametric statistics are those that have to make some assumptions about the underlying distribution. The distribution of the population can be a variety of shapes but there are some distributions where parametric estimates of a mean will not work. And while these assumptions are usually safe to start with, they can be far off base. Even though these parametric statistics don't rely strictly on the "subjective" estimates of calibrated experts, they still start with fairly arbitrary assumptions that might be very wrong.

As Exhibit 9.2 showed, there are some populations where the estimate of the mean converges quickly. But, if we sample the income levels of individuals, the power of an earthquake, or the size of asteroids in the asteroid belt, we may find that the 90% CI for the estimate of the mean does not necessarily get narrower as sample size increases. Some samples will temporarily narrow the 90% CI, but some "outliers" are so much bigger than the rest of the population that, if they came up in the sample, they would greatly widen the CI again. As we sample, this periodic widening from extreme outliers may happen just often enough to keep the estimate of the mean from ever converging.

Exhibit 9.3 shows how some estimates of means might converge more slowly than others and methods that might apply in each situation. This exhibit shows that the easiest way to determine how quickly estimates converge is to ask: "How big are the exceptions compared to most?" In the case of samples of water from a tank in a municipal water system, the amount of contaminants in one sample will be extremely close to the amount in the next. In those cases, only one sample is required. In the case of how much time per week your coworkers spend in over-head activities not related to a particular project, outliers are unlikely to throw off the average. (There are only so many hours in the week, after all.) In those cases, parametric methods work well. In the case of earthquakes or revenue of companies, a single outlier can easily throw off the average.

Exhibit 9.3 Varying Rates of Convergence for the Estimate of the Mean

	←— Nonparametric May Be Needed —→		
	←—— Parametric Is Sufficient ——→		
	(Useful sample sizes probably smaller on the left, larger on the right)		
Convergence	Very quickly converging (Relatively homogeneous things)	Usually quickly converging (Extremes are not many times larger than the average)	Might be slowly converging (Outliers are very large compared to most)	Mean might be nonconverging (Outliers are orders of magnitude larger than most)
Examples	• Cholesterol level of your blood • Purity of a public water supply • Weight of jelly beans	• Percentage of customers who like the new product • Failure loads of bricks • Age of your customers • How much time staff spend commuting • How many movies a year people see	• Cost overruns of software projects • Downtime of a factory due to an accident	• Market value of corporations • Market fluctuations • Income levels of individuals • Casualties of wars • Size of volcanic eruptions

The types of things covered in this last column of Exhibit 9.3 are sometimes "power law" distributions. As mentioned in Chapter 6, the normal distribution is not a good fit for some phenomena, such as stock market fluctuations. But the power law is a very good fit. As odd as this might seem, populations that have power law distributions *literally have no definable mean*. Again, in such cases, sampling will eventually produce an outlier that is so different from the rest of the sample, that the estimate of the mean is greatly widened. As more sampling is done, an even more extreme outlier will appear that will widen the 90% CI again, and so on. But this kind of distribution still has characteristics that can be measured in relatively few observations. These methods are known as "nonparametric." We will show one solution to the problem of nonconverging estimates of means shortly.

THE EASIEST SAMPLE STATISTIC EVER

Nonconverging data can be a big problem for someone trying to measure. Furthermore, especially with very small samples, it is possible with the *t*-statistic to generate a 90% CI that includes an answer we know can't be right. Refer again to the small sample spreadsheet you can download from www.howtomeasureanything.com. Suppose we survey five customers about how many hours per week they spend watching reality TV shows, and enter their answers—0, 0, 1, 1, and 4 hours—into a spreadsheet. The spreadsheet will show that the lower bound of the 90% CI will be a *negative* value—which makes no sense at all. But there are solutions to both of these problems that have the added advantage of being far easier to use.

In Chapter 3, I briefly mentioned the Rule of Five. Remember, that rule states that if you randomly sample five of any population, there is a 93.75% chance that the *median* of the population is between the largest and smallest values in the sample. The median of a population is a value where exactly half of the population is below it and half above it. The *t*-statistic, however, estimates the mean of the population—the total of all the values divided by the size of the population.

But the Rule of Five is only one rule from a set of similar rules for highly simplified small-sample statistics. Like the Rule of Five, if we can come up with a method where sample values themselves can be used to directly estimate a 90% CI for the median of the population, we can quickly estimate a range without any math at all.

If we sample eight items, the largest and smallest values would make a range much wider than a 90% CI (actually, about 99.2% CI). But it turns out that if we take the second largest and smallest values, we get back to something closer to a 90% CI—about 93%. If we sample 11, the 90% CI can be approximated with the third largest and third smallest values.

Exhibit 9.4 shows similar rules for the first 11 sample sizes that can approximate a 90% CI just by counting in from the largest and smallest values by the amount shown. For example, if you can sample 18 things, the sixth largest and sixth smallest values out of the 18 samples approximated the upper and lower bounds for a 90% CI. I picked a set of sample sizes that can get close to a 90% CI with a clear preference for conservatively wider ranges when an exact 90% CI is not possible. The third column gives the confidence to show the probability that the median will be between the bounds given by the *n*th largest/smallest samples. The third column is there only to show you that the estimate is as close as possible to the true 90% CI without being too narrow. (Therefore, it is a slightly conservative estimate of the 90% CI.)

I call this the mathless 90% CI since it only requires you to count in toward the middle a certain number from the largest and smallest values in the data. There is no computing sample variance, no square roots, and no *t*-statistics tables. I computed this table based on some nonparametric methods and checked it with some Monte Carlo simulations. The derivation was a little more complicated than we can get into here (readers who are interested should not find it too difficult to derive these same results), but the result makes estimating a 90% CI from small samples

Exhibit 9.4 Mathless 90% CI for the Median of Population

| | Lower bound: ___th smallest | |
| | Upper bound: ___th largest | |
Sample Size (n)	Sample Value	Confidence
5	1st	93.75%
8	2nd	93.0%
11	3rd	93.5%
13	4th	90.8%
16	5th	92.3%
18	6th	90.4%
21	7th	92.2%
23	8th	90.7%
26	9th	92.4%
28	10th	91.3%
30	11th	90.1%

very easy. Try to commit to memory the first few sample sizes: 5, 8, 11, and 13. From those you take the first, second, third, and fourth largest and smallest, respectively, to estimate a 90% CI. Now you can quickly compute a 90% CI even by casual observations of data in your environment, without having to pull out a calculator.

There is one error I see people make about the meaning of this table. Some will look at this table and wonder why the confidence for a sample of 30 (90.1%) is lower than that for a sample of five (93.75%). Keep in mind that the interval found by taking the 11th-largest and 11th-smallest of a sample of 30 will usually be a much narrower interval found by taking the smallest and largest of a sample of five from the same population. The comparison of interval widths from this chart, on average, would look a lot like the "sideways tornado" of the t-statistic method shown in Exhibit 9.2. The mathless method requires us to use round integers (e.g., the 2nd instead of the 1.9th largest and smallest for a sample of 8). Since this can't always produce an exact 90% CI, we round to the nearest solution that gives us a CI of at least 90%.

The reason this method works as well as it does is because, in short, the "middle" of the data doesn't matter very much when computing a 90% CI of a population median or, for that matter, even a population mean. To explain this, we need just a little more exposure to parametric methods. The parametric methods include a step where we compute something called "sample variance," just as we saw with the parametric t-statistic. Remember, for each sample, we subtract the mean from the sample value and square the results. Then we add up all the squares to get the sample variance. When you perform this brief calculation, you find that almost all of the variance comes from those samples farthest from the mean. Even for larger sample sizes, the middle third of a sample typically makes up just 2% of the variance; the other 98% of the variance comes from the upper and lower thirds of the sample data. When the sample size is smaller than 12, the variance is mostly just the single largest and single smallest samples—the two extreme points.

This mathless approach generates a 90% CI just slightly wider—on average—than the t-statistic, but it avoids some of the problems of the t-statistic. In the previously mentioned survey of time spent watching reality TV shows, recall that the lower bound was a nonsensical negative 30 minutes. The upper bound would be computed to be about three hours. With the mathless table, the same set of five data points would be zero to four. The interval with the mathless table is a little wider (since the upper bound increased), but, since both bounds are actual values from the data set, we know that both are possible values of the median.

This reality TV–watching time of consumers is probably a highly skewed population. A skewed population has a lopsided distribution, and the median and mean can be different values. However, if we assumed that the population distribution is close to symmetrical, then the mean and the median are the same. In this case, the mathless table works just as well to compute a 90% CI for a mean as a 90% CI for a median.

This assumption might be a stretch in some cases, but it's actually much less of an assumption than is made in parametric statistics. As we saw earlier in this chapter, parametric methods for estimating a population mean have to assume the population distribution avoids certain specific shapes. In the case of the mathless table, we make *no* assumption at all about the distribution of the population to estimate the median.

In fact, the mathless table, since it estimates the median, *completely avoids the problem of nonconverging estimates*. The population can be distributed in all sorts of irregular ways, like the power law distribution of stock market fluctuations, the "camel-back" age distribution in the United States caused by the Baby Boomers and their children, or a uniform distribution like the spin of a roulette wheel. Both parametric methods and the mathless table work in these cases. But the mathless table also works in those cases where that might be problematic for the parametric methods, such as when the population follows a power law.

Clearly, the estimators could sometimes greatly reduce uncertainty with just a few observations, using parametric methods or nonparametric methods like the mathless table. But even though the subjective estimates have errors, the parametric methods and the mathless table have one error in common: They can consider only the values of the samples, and any prior knowledge is ignored. In other words, many of the things we consider "common sense" are excluded from these "objective" methods since they fail to consider information that calibrated estimators intuitively include.

Suppose that instead of measuring TV-watching habits, we were asking sales managers how much time they spend managing underperforming sales reps. If we sampled only five sales managers, they might give us their answers in average hours per week. Let's say they said 6, 12, 12, 7, and 1 hour per week. The *t*-statistic would compute a 90% CI of 3.2 to 12. However, that equation doesn't know that the answer of "one hour" comes from Bob, who you know has more problem sales staff members than anyone else and is probably deliberately underestimating.

The calibrated estimator, in contrast, easily handles that sort of additional information. The calibrated estimator, using simple common sense, would not have given a negative lower bound if given the same TV-watching survey information. Using a calibrated estimator might seem like an unreliable way to interpret data, since this interpretation depends on the judgment of an expert, but it is not necessarily much worse and can even avoid certain pitfalls. In the next chapter, we will see how prior knowledge like this can be applied with more mathematical precision.

A BIASED SAMPLE OF SAMPLING METHODS

How would your average executive measure the population of fish in a lake? I regularly ask this question of a room full of seminar attendees. Usually someone in the room produces the most extreme answer: drain the lake. The average executive, like the average accountant or even the average midlevel information technology (IT) manager, thinks that "measure" is synonymous with "count." So when asked to measure the population of fish, they assume they are being asked for an exact count, not just a reduction in uncertainty. With that goal in mind, they would drain the lake and, no doubt, would come up with a very organized procedure where a team picks up each dead fish, throws it in the back of a dump truck, and clicks it off on a handheld counter. Perhaps someone else counts the fish again in the truck and inspects the now-empty lake bed to "audit" the quality of the count. He or she could then report that there were exactly 22,573 fish in the lake; therefore, last year's restocking effort was successful. (Of course, they're all dead now.)

If you told marine biologists to measure the fish in the lake, they would not confuse a "count" with a "measure." Instead, the biologists might employ a method called "catch and recatch." First, they would catch and tag a sample of fish—let's say 1,000—and release them back into the lake. Then, after the tagged fish had a chance to disperse among the rest of the population, they would catch another sample of fish. Suppose they caught 1,000 fish again, and this time 50 of those 1,000 fish were tagged. This means that about 5% of the fish in the lake are tagged. Since the marine biologists know they originally tagged 1,000 fish, they conclude that the lake contains about 20,000 fish (5% of 20,000 is 1,000).

This type of sampling follows the binomial distribution, but, for large numbers like these, we can approximate it with the normal distribution. The error for this estimate can be computed using a slight variation on the previous error-estimating methods. All we have to do is change how we compute the sample variance; the rest is the same. The sample variance in this case is computed as the share within the group we are trying to measure times the share outside of the group. In other words, we take the share of tagged fish (.05) times the share of fish not tagged (.95), resulting in .0475.

Now we follow the rest of the previously defined procedure. We divide the sample variance by the number of samples and take the square root of the total: SQRT(.0475/1,000) = .007. To get our 90% CI of the share of tagged fish in the lake, we take the share we think are tagged (.05) plus or minus .007 times 1.645 (the 90% CI z-statistic) to get a range of 3.87% to 6.13% of the fish in the lake are tagged. We know we tagged 1,000, so this must mean there are a total of 1,000/.0613 = 16,303 to 1,000/.0387 = 25,865 fish in the lake. (The rounding shows slightly different answers but the exact calculation is available in the Chapter 9 example downloads.)

To some people, this might seem like a wide range. But suppose our previous level of uncertainty gave us a calibrated estimate of 2,000 to 50,000. Furthermore, suppose our objective was simply to determine if the population was increasing or dying off, and we originally stocked the lake with 5,000 fish. Anything greater than 6,000 is at least increasing population, and 10,000 or more would be healthy enough that no expensive intervention would be required. Given the initial range and the relevant threshold, this new level of uncertainty is definitely a significant improvement and an easily acceptable error. In fact, we could have sampled just a quarter of what we did in the initial catch and the recatch (250 fish each time), and we would probably still be confident the population had increased to a number greater than 6,000.

This method is a particularly powerful example of how sampling reveals something about the unseen. It has been used for estimating such things as how many people the U.S. Census missed, how many species of butterflies are still undiscovered in the Amazon, how many unauthorized intrusions have been made in an IT system, and how many prospective customers you have not yet identified. Just because you will never see all of a group doesn't mean you can't measure the size of a group.

Basically, the recatch method is merely two independent sampling methods where we compare the overlap between the two samples to estimate the size of the population. If you want to estimate the number of flaws in a building design, use two different groups of quality inspectors. Then compare how many they each caught and how many flaws were caught by both teams. The number of flaws each caught is like the number of fish caught in each of the two net castings in the previous example (1,000 each time), and the number of flaws they both found is like the number of tagged fish in the second net (50).

"Catch-recatch" in its various forms is just one of many varieties of sampling. No doubt, quite a few more powerful methods are yet to be invented. Still, knowing a little about a few important sampling methods gives you enough background to figure out how to assess observations for a wide variety of problems.

Population Proportion Sampling

The fish population example was one special variation on a very common measurement problem. Sometimes you want to estimate what proportion of a population has a particular characteristic. You might want to determine what percentage of registered voters in Virginia are Democrats. You might want to determine what percentage of customers prefer a new product feature over the old. In the case of the catch-recatch method for estimating the population of fish in a lake, we had to determine what percentage of fish in the lake were tagged. Knowing exactly how many were tagged we could then use the estimate for the percentage of tagged fish in the lake to estimate the size of the entire population.

We are trying to estimate the proportion of a population that falls in some defined set, P (uppercase), using the proportion of a sample that fell in that set, p (lowercase). For example, if we ask a sample of 100 retail customers if they have visited the store online, and 34 say yes, then $p = 34\%$. Of course, the real P could be a little different given our sampling error.

Remember, the only difference between using a sample to estimate the real population proportion, P, and estimating a mean is how we compute the variance. For a population proportion estimate, the variance is computed as $(p \times (1 - p)/n)$. In the example of customers who visited online, this would be $(.34 \times (1 - .34)/100)$, which gives us a variance of .002244. After that, everything is the same as using a z-stat. We just convert the variance to a standard deviation (by taking the square root of the variance), multiply it by our z-stat (or t-stat if the sample is less than 30), and add and subtract the result from the sample proportion, p, to get a CI. To summarize all of that in a simple calculation, we write:

For the 90% CI Upper Bound write: $= p + 1.645 \times (p \times (1 - p)/n)^{.5}$
For the 90% CI Lower Bound write: $= p - 1.645 \times (p \times (1 - p)/n)^{.5}$

This gives us a 90% CI of 26% to 42%. In this case we assumed a "normal approximation" for a population proportion. That is, under certain conditions, the distribution we just estimated is just about exactly normally distributed. The conditions required for this assumption are that $p \times n > 7$ and $(1 - p) \times n > 7$. (This standard varies a bit in different sources. I chose a common middle ground.) In other words, if our sample of 100 didn't find seven or fewer customers who visited the website or 93 or more, then this method works. But if we were trying to estimate a much smaller population proportion using a smaller sample, we might not get to use this method. For example, if we sampled only 20 customers and only four said they visited the site, then we need a different approach.

The math gets a little more complex but, fortunately, with small samples it is not hard to simply work out all the answers for every possible result for population proportions. The table in Exhibit 9.5 shows the 90% CI for several small sample sizes. If we sample 20, and only four have the characteristic we are looking for—in this case, customers who have visited the store's website—then we go to the column for 20 samples and look up the row for four "hits." We find a range of 9.9% to 38% as our 90% CI for the proportion of customers who have been to the website.

To save space, I don't show all of the ranges for hits beyond 10. But recall that as long as we have at least eight hits and eight hits less than the total sample size, we can use the normal approximation. Also, if we need to get the range for, say, 26 hits out of 30, we can invert the table by treating hits as misses and vice versa. We just get the range for four out of 30 hits, 6.6% to 27%, and subtract those values from 100% to get a range of 63% to 93.4%

The ranges in this table disguise some of the information about the actual shape of the distribution. Many of these distributions will not be very close to a normal distribution at all. Exhibit 9.6 shows what some of the distributions from the table above really look like. When the number of hits is at or near zero or at or near the total sample size, the probability distribution of the population proportion is highly skewed.

For now, you can use Exhibit 9.5 to estimate a population proportion 90% CI for small samples. If you have a sample size that is in between the samples sizes shown, you can interpolate between the columns shown to provide a rough approximation. In the next chapter, we will discuss more details about how these distributions were computed by using a very different approach. In that chapter we will also describe a spreadsheet,

					Sample Size					
	1	2	3	4	6	8	10	15	20	30
0	2.5–78	1.7–63	1.3–53	01.0–45	0.7–35	0.6–28.3	0.5–23.9	0.3–17.1	0.2–13.3	0.2–9.2
1	22.4–97.5	13.5–87	9.8–75.2	07.6–65.8	05.3–52.1	4.1–42.9	3.3–36.5	2.3–26.4	1.7–20.7	1.2–14.4
2		36.8–98.3	25–90.3	18.9–81	12.9–65.9	9.8–55	07.9–47.0	5.3–34.4	4.0–27.1	2.7–18.9
3			47–98.7	34.3–92.4	22.5–78	16.9–66	13.5–57	9.0–42	6.8–33	4.5–23
4				55–99.0	34.1–87	25.1–75	20–65	13–48	9.9–38	6.6–27
5					48–94.7	34.5–83	27–73	17.8–55	13.2–44	8.8–31
6					65–99.3	45–90	35–80	22.7–61	16.8–49	11.1–35
7						57–95.9	44–87	28–67	21–54	14–38
8						72–99.5	53–92	33–72	25–58	16–42
9							64–96.7	39–77	29–63	19–45
10							76–99.6	45–82	33–67	21–49

Number of "Hits" in Sample

Exhibit 9.5 Population Proportion 90% CI for Small Samples

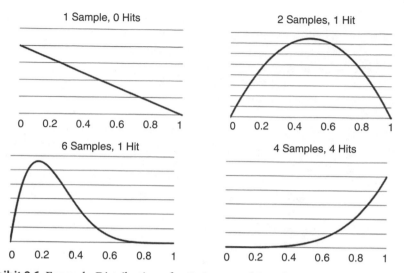

Exhibit 9.6 Example Distributions for Estimates of Population Proportion from Small Samples

available on www.howtomeasureanything.com, that can be used to compute the exact population proportion distributions for any sample size.

Spot Sampling

Spot sampling is a variation of population proportion sampling. Spot sampling consists of taking random snapshots of people, processes, or things instead of tracking them constantly throughout a period of time. For example, if you wanted to see the share of time that employees spend in a given activity, you randomly sample people through the day to see what they were doing *at that moment*. If you find that in 12 instances out of 100 random samples, people were on a conference call, you can conclude they spend about 12% of the time on conference calls (90% CI is 8% to 18%). At a particular point in time they are either doing this activity or not, and you are simply asking what share of the time this takes. This example is just big enough that we can also approximate it with a normal distribution, as we did earlier. But if you sampled just 10 employees and found that two were involved in the given activity, then we can use Exhibit 9.5 to come up with 7.9% to 47%. Again, this might seem like a wide range. But, remember, if the prior range based on a calibrated estimate was 5% to 70% and the threshold for some decision was 55%, then we have completed a valuable measurement.

How Many Cars Burn the Wrong Fuel?

A Government Agency Takes a "Just Do It" Approach to Measurement

In the 1970s, the Environmental Protection Agency knew it had a public policy problem. After 1975, automobiles were designed with catalytic converters to use unleaded gasoline. But leaded gasoline was cheaper, and drivers were inclined to continue using leaded fuel in cars with the new catalytic converters. The now-familiar narrower nozzle restrictor at the opening to the gas tank was mandated by the EPA to keep people from adding leaded gasoline to the new cars. (Leaded gasoline came out of wider nozzles that wouldn't fit in the nozzle restrictors.) But a driver could simply remove the restrictor and use leaded gasoline. Barry Nussbaum, chief statistician of Statistical Support Services at the EPA, said: "We knew people were putting leaded fuel in the new cars because when DMV [Department of Motor Vehicle] inspections were done, they looked at the restrictor to see if it was removed." Using leaded fuel in the new cars could cause air pollution to be worse, not better, defeating the purpose of the unleaded gasoline program. There was a moment of consternation at the EPA. How could it possibly measure how many people were using leaded gasoline in unleaded cars? In the "Just Do It" spirit of measurement, members of the EPA simply staked out gas stations. First, they randomly selected gas stations throughout the country. Then, armed with binoculars, EPA staff observed cars at the pump, recorded whether they took leaded or unleaded gasoline, and compared license plate numbers to a DMV list of vehicle types. This method got the EPA some bad exposure—a cartoonist for the *Atlanta Journal-Constitution* showed the EPA as Nazi-like characters arresting people who used the wrong gas, even though the EPA only observed and arrested no one. Still, Nussbaum said, "This got us into trouble with a few police departments." Of course, the police had to concede that anyone is free to observe others on and from a public street corner. But the important thing is that the EPA found an answer: About 8% of cars that should use only unleaded gas were actually using leaded gas. As difficult as the problem first sounded, the EPA recognized that if it took the obvious observation and just started sampling, it could improve on the relative uncertainty.

Serial Sampling

The serial sampling approach is generally not discussed in statistics texts. (Nor would it be here if the title of this book was *How to Measure Most Things*.) But this approach was a big help in intelligence gathering in World War II,[1] and it could be a very powerful sampling method for certain types of business problems. During World War II, spies for the Allies produced reports on enemy production of military equipment, including Germany's Mark V tanks. The reports about the Mark V were highly inconsistent, and Allied Intelligence rarely knew whom to believe. In 1943, statisticians working for the Allies developed a method for estimating production levels based on the serial numbers of captured tanks. Serial numbers were sequential and had a date embedded in them. However, looking at a single serial number did not tell them exactly where the series started. (It might not have started at "001.") Common sense tells us that the minimum tank production must be at least the difference between the highest and lowest serial numbers of captured tanks for a given month. But can we infer even more?

By treating captured tanks as a random sample of the entire population of tanks, the statisticians saw that they could compute the odds of various levels of production. Working backward, it would seem unlikely, for example, to capture by chance alone 10 tanks produced in the same month with serial numbers all within 50 increments of each other, if 1,000 tanks were produced that month. It is more likely that randomly selecting from 1,000 tanks would give us a more dispersed series of serial numbers than that. If, however, only 80 tanks were produced that month, then getting a sample of 10 tanks with that narrow range of serial numbers seems at least feasible.

Exhibit 9.7 shows how the Mark V tank production estimates from Allied Intelligence and from the statistical method compared to the actual number confirmed by postwar analysis of captured documents. Clearly, the statistical method based on the analysis of serial numbers of captured tanks is the hands-down winner in this comparison.

Exhibit 9.7 Comparison of World War II German Mark V Tank Production Estimates

Month of Production	Intelligence Estimate	Statistical Estimate	Actual (based on captured documents after the war)
June 1940	1,000	169	122
June 1941	1,550	244	271
August 1942	1,550	327	342

Source: Leo A. Goodman, "Serial Number Analysis," *Journal of the American Statistical Association* 47 (1952): 622–634.

Furthermore, an estimate with an error still considerably less than the original intelligence estimates probably could have been done with surprisingly few captured tanks. Exhibit 9.8 shows how a random sample of serial-numbered items can be used to infer the size of the entire population. Following the directions on the exhibit, consider the example of just eight "captured" items. (This could be a competitor's products, pages of a competitor's report retrieved from the garbage, etc.) The largest in the series is 100,220 and the smallest is 100,070, so step 1 gives us 150 as a result. Step 2 gives us a result of about 1.0 where the "Upper Bound" curve intersects the vertical line for our sample size of 8. In step 3 we take $(1 + 1.0) \times 150 = 300$, where the result is the upper bound. Repeating these steps for the mean and lower bound, we get a 90% CI of 156 to 300 with a mean of 195. (Note the mean is not the middle of the range—the distribution is lopsided.) Just eight captured tanks could easily have been a reasonable number to work with.

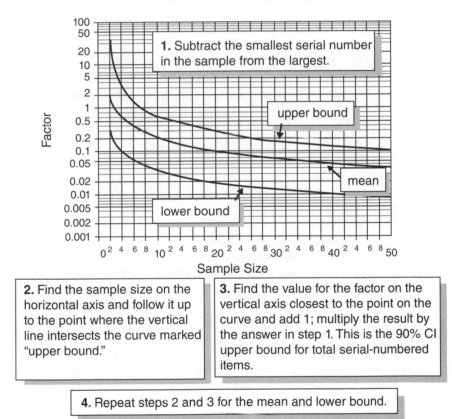

Exhibit 9.8 Serial Number Sampling

Two caveats: If several tanks are captured from the same unit, we might not be able to treat each as a separate randomly selected tank, since tanks in the same unit might be in the same series of numbers. However, that fact is usually apparent just by looking at the numbers themselves. Also, if the serial numbers are not sequential (so that each number in a range is assigned to one tank) and some numbers are skipped, this method requires some modification. Again, the distribution of numbers used should be easy to detect. For example, if only even numbers or increments of five are used, that should be obvious from the sample.

Where could this apply in business? "Serial numbers"—that is, a sequential series—show up in a variety of places in the modern world. In this way, competitors offer free intelligence of their production levels just by putting serial numbers on items any retail shopper can see. (To be random, however, this sample of items should include those from several stores.) Likewise, a few pages from a discarded report or numbers from discarded receipts tell something about the total number of pages in the report or receipts from that day. I'm not encouraging dumpster diving, but, then again, the dumpster has been used to measure a lot of interesting activities.

Measure to the Threshold

Remember, usually you want to measure something because it supports some decision. And these decisions tend to have thresholds where one action is required if a value is above it, and another is required if the value is below it. But most statistical methods aren't about asking the most relevant question: "When is X enough to warrant a different course of action?" Here I want to show you a "statistic" that directly supports the goal of not just reducing uncertainty in general but a measurement *relative* to an important decision threshold.

Suppose you needed to measure the average amount of time spent by employees in meetings that could be conducted remotely with one of the web meeting tools. This could save staff a lot of travel time and even avoid canceled or postponed meetings due to travel difficulties. To determine whether a meeting can be conducted remotely, you need to consider what is done in the meeting. If a meeting is among staff members who communicate regularly and for a relatively routine topic, you probably can conduct it remotely. You start out with your calibrated estimate that the median employee spends 3% to 15% of their time traveling to meetings that could be conducted remotely. You determine that if this percentage is actually over 7%, you should make a significant policy change toward remote meetings. The Expected Value of Perfect Information calculation shows that it is worth no more than $15,000 to study this. According to our rule of thumb for measurement costs, we might try to spend about $1,500. This means anything like a complete census of meetings is out of the question if you have thousands of employees.

Let's say you sampled 10 employees, and, after a detailed analysis of their travel time and meetings in the last few weeks, you find that only one spends less time in these activities than the 7% threshold. Given this information, what is the chance that the median time spent in such activities is actually below 7%, in which case the investment would not be justified? One "common sense" answer is 1/10, or 10%. Actually, this is another example where mere "common sense" isn't as good as a little math. The real chance is much smaller.

Exhibit 9.9 shows how to estimate the chance that the *median* of a population is on one particular side of a threshold, given that an equal or greater number of the samples in a small sample set came up on the other side.

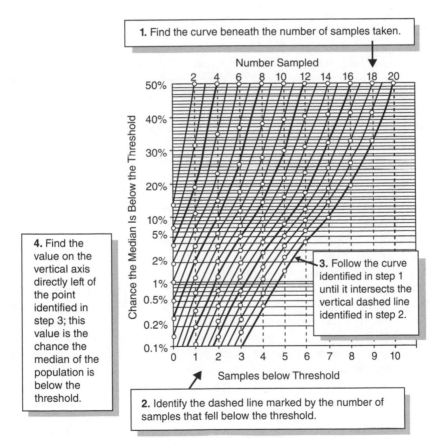

Exhibit 9.9 Threshold Probability Calculator

Try this example to practice with the calculator.

1. Look at the top of the exhibit, where it gives sample sizes, and, for the example described, find the number 10. Follow the solid curve below it.
2. Look at the bottom of the exhibit, where it lists the number of samples below the threshold, and find the number 1. Follow the dashed line above it.
3. Find the intersection of the curve and the dashed line.
4. Read the percentage to the left of the chart that corresponds with the vertical position of the intersection point. You will find it reads about 0.6%.

This small sample says there is much less than a 1% chance that the median is actually below the threshold. While this statistic seems counterintuitive, the fact is that the uncertainty about which side of a threshold the median (or even the mean) of a population sits on can be reduced very quickly by a lot. Suppose we would have sampled just four, and none of the four was below the threshold. Referring to the exhibit again, we find that there would be just under a 4% chance that the median is actually under the threshold and consequently a 96% chance that the median is above the threshold. It may seem impossible that a sample of four could provide that much certainty, but some math or a Monte Carlo simulation will confirm it.

Note that the uncertainty about the threshold can fall much faster than the uncertainty about the quantity in general. It's possible that after just a few samples you still have a fairly wide range, but, if the threshold is well outside the range, the uncertainty about the threshold can drop to virtually nothing. This is true *regardless of distribution of the population*. Because this estimate isn't thrown out of whack by extreme outliers, it doesn't matter if the distribution is a power law distribution or not.

This exhibit makes only one assumption about the measurement problem: that there was a maximum amount of uncertainty about where the median is relative to the threshold. That is, it starts with the assumption that there is no prior information about whether it is more likely that the median is really on one side of the threshold than the other. This means that we start with a 50/50 chance regarding which side of the threshold the median is really on.

If there was some prior knowledge that it was much more likely that the median was below the threshold, the exhibit won't be accurate, but it will still give us a useful result. If the chance of being below the threshold is lower than the chance of being above it, the exhibit will actually overestimate the odds that the real value is below the threshold. In our example, the range of 3% to 15% indicates that being below the threshold of 7% is less likely than being above it. The exhibit tells us that the chance of being below this threshold is 0.6%, but knowing what we do about the range, we can determine that the chance is even less than that.

If, however, our range was, say, 1% to 8%, we start with the knowledge that the true value is probably below the threshold of 7%. In that case, the exhibit underestimates the chance that the value is below the threshold. But let's consider another benchmark to help us zero in on a value. We could look at the actual midpoint of our original range and compute the threshold probability for that. With this range, we are saying that there is a 50/50 chance that the value is less than 4.5%. Of the 10 employees sampled, let's say none were below that. Our exhibit tells us that, in this situation, the chance that the true value is actually below our 7% threshold is less than 0.1%. Although this doesn't tell us exactly how unlikely it is to be below the 7% threshold, it's obvious that being much below 7% is vanishingly unlikely.

So, generally, if the samples strongly confirm prior knowledge (e.g., you get just 1 out of 10 samples below the threshold when you already knew that there is a low chance the median is below the threshold), the uncertainty drops even faster. If the samples contradict prior knowledge, it will take more samples to decrease uncertainty by the same amount. Also, remember that the exhibit gives the chance that the median—not the mean—is below or above a threshold. Of course, you can do some more math and reduce uncertainty even further. If four samples are above the threshold by a large margin, that would give a higher level of confidence than if the four samples were just barely above the threshold.

... And a Lot More

There are many more sampling methods than we can discuss in detail here. Following are just a couple more methods worth mentioning.

- "Clustered sampling" is defined as taking a random sample of groups, then conducting a census or a more concentrated sampling within the group. For example, if you want to see what share of households has satellite dishes or correctly separates plastics in recycling, it might be cost effective to randomly choose several city blocks, then conduct a complete census of everything in a block. (Zigzagging across town to individually selected households would be time consuming.) In such cases, we can't really consider the number of elements in the groups (in this case, households) to be the number of random samples. Within a block, households may be very similar, so we can't really treat the number of households as the size of the "random" sample. When households are highly uniform within a block, it might be necessary to treat the effective number of random samples as the number of blocks, not the number of households.

- In "stratified sampling," different sample methods and/or sizes are used for different groups within a population. This method may make sense when you have some groups within a population that vary widely from each other but are fairly homogeneous inside a group. If you are a fast-food restaurant and you want to sample the demographic of your customers, it might make sense to sample drive-through customers differently from walk-ins. If you run a factory and you need to measure "safety habits," you might try observing janitors and supervisors for safety procedure violations differently from welders. (Don't forget the Hawthorne effect. Try using a blind in this case.)

By now, the reader has seen a variety of basic sampling methods that should, in some combination, address a majority of measurement problems. There are two more sampling methods that require us to get into more detail: experiments and regression modeling. These two together with other sampling methods help us answer another important measurement question—how much of a change in one thing is *due* to a change in another?

EXPERIMENT

My first online buying experience was sometime in the mid-1990s. I had several texts on empirical methods in various subject areas but was looking for a book on more of a general philosophy of scientific measurement—something I could recommend to my management customers. I read all the basics (Kuhn, Popper, etc., for those readers who might be familiar with the topic), but that wasn't what I was looking for.

Then I saw a book on www.amazon.com called *How to Think Like a Scientist*.[2] The reviews were great, and it seemed like it would be something I could recommend to a typical executive. I purchased the book and within a couple of weeks it came in the mail. It wasn't what I expected. It was a children's book—recommended for ages eight and up. (At that time, Amazon did not show pictures of covers for most books, which would have made it more obvious that it was a children's book.) After receiving the book, the title seemed like a more obvious clue that it might be a children's book. I felt pretty foolish and chalked it up as another reason not to buy things on the web in the early phase of Internet retail. In a bookstore, I would not have browsed the children's section (being childless at the time). And if I saw such a book in the discount pile, the cover would have told me that it wasn't the serious "science for business" type of text I was looking for.

But then I started to flip through the pages. Although the pages were two-thirds cartoon and one-third text, it seemed to capture all the basic concepts and explain things as simply as possible. I saw how it gave a simple explanation of testing a hypothesis and making observations. I changed my mind about the purchase being a mistake. I realized I found this gem on the web precisely because I couldn't prejudge it as a children's book. And the most important message of this book is what was implied on the front cover: *Scientific method is for ages eight and up.*

The idea of performing an experiment to measure some important business quantity, unfortunately, does not come often enough to many managers. As Emily Rosa showed us, experiments can be simple affairs. As Enrico Fermi showed us, a handful of confetti used in a clever way can reveal something as incredible as the yield of an atom bomb. The idea is quite simple. As we discussed in previous chapters on the topic of selecting measurement instruments, if you need to know it, can't find where it is already measured, and can't track it in any way without overt intervention, try to create the conditions for observation with an experiment.

The word "experiment" could be broadly used to mean any phenomena deliberately created for the purpose of observation. You "experiment" when you run a security test to see if and how quickly a threat is responded to. But usually a key feature of the *controlled* experiment is that you account for possible errors. Remember from Chapter 2 how Emily Rosa set up an experiment. She suspected that existing data about therapeutic touch or even a sample of opinions from patients was probably not unbiased. So she set up an observation that allowed for a more specific and objective observation. Emily's controls consisted of a blind that concealed what she was doing from the test subjects and a random selection process.

In other situations, the control involves observing two groups of things, not just one. You watch what you are testing (the test group), and you watch something to compare it to (the control group). This is ideal in a situation where it would be hard to track an existing phenomenon or where the thing being measured has not yet happened, such as the effect of a new product formulation or the implementation of a new information technology.

You could pilot the new product or the new technology by itself. But how would you know the customers preferred the new product or if productivity really increased? Your revenue might have increased for many reasons other than the new formulation, and the productivity might change for other reasons, as well. In fact, if businesses could be affected by only one thing at a time, the whole idea of a control group would be unnecessary. We could change one factor, see how the business changed, and attribute that change entirely to that factor. Of course, in reality, we have to be able to measure even when complex systems are affected by many factors we can't even identify.

If we change a feature on a product and want to determine how much this affects customer satisfaction, we might need an experiment. Customer satisfaction and, consequently, repeat business might change for lots of reasons. But if we want to see if this new feature is cost justified, we need to measure *its* impact apart from anything else. By comparing customers who have bought products with this new feature to customers who did not, we should be better able to isolate the effects of the new feature alone.

Most of the methods you use in experiments to interpret results are the same as we already discussed—they involve one or another sort of sampling, perhaps some blinds, and so on. Perhaps the most important of these is to be able to compute the difference between a test group and a control group. If we are confident that the test group is really different from the control group, we should be able to conclude that something other than pure chance is causing these two groups to be different. Comparing these two groups is really very similar to how we previously computed the standard deviation of the estimate, but with one small change. In this case, the standard deviation we want to compute is the standard deviation of the difference between two groups. Consider the following example.

An Example Experiment

Suppose a company wanted to measure the effect of customer relationship training on the quality of customer support. The customer support employees typically take incoming calls from clients who have questions or problems with a new product. It is suspected that the main effect of a positive or negative customer support experience is not so much the future sales to that customer but the positive or negative word-of-mouth advertising the company gets as a result. As always, the company started by assessing its current uncertainty about the effects of training, identified the relevant threshold, and computed the value of information.

After considering several possible measurement instruments, managers decided that "quality of customer support" should be measured with a post-call survey of customers. The questions, they reasoned, should not just ask whether the customers were satisfied but how many friends they actually told about a positive experience with customer support. Using previously gathered marketing data, the calibrated managers determined that the new customer relationship training could improve sales by 0% to 12% but that they needed to improve it by only 2% to justify the expense of the training (i.e., 2% is the decision threshold).

They begin conducting this survey before anyone attends training, so they can get a baseline. For each employee, they sample only one customer two weeks after they called in. The key question was "Since your support call, to how many friends or family have you recommended any of our products?" The number of people the customer said they made recommendations to is recorded. Knowing some previous research about the impact of word-of-mouth advertising on sales, the marketing department has determined that one more positive report per customer on average results in a 20% increase in sales.

The training is expensive, so at first managers decide to send 30 randomly chosen customer support staffers to the training as a test group. Nevertheless, the cost of training this small group is still much less than the computed information value. The control group is the entire set of employees who did not receive training. After the test group receives training, managers continue the survey of customers, but again, they sample only one customer for each employee. For the original baseline, the test group, and the control group, the mean and variance are computed (as shown in the jelly bean example at the beginning of this chapter). Exhibit 9.10 shows the results.

The responses from customers seem to indicate that the training did help; could it just be chance? Perhaps the 30 randomly chosen staff members were already, on average, better than the average of the group, or perhaps those 30 people were, by chance, getting less problematic customers. For the test group and control group, we apply these five steps:

1. Divide the sample variance of each group by the number of samples in that group. We get .392/30 = .013 for the test group and 0.682/85 = .008 for the control group.
2. Add the results from step 1 for each group together: .013 + 008 = .021.

Exhibit 9.10 Example for a Customer Support Training Experiment

	Sample Size	Mean	Variance
Test group (received training)	30	2.433	0.392
Control group (did not receive training)	85	2.094	0.682
Original baseline (before anyone received training)	115	2.087	0.659

3. Take the square root of the result from step 2. This gives us the standard deviation of the difference between the test group and the control group. The result in this case would be 0.15.
4. Compute the difference between the means of the two groups being compared: 2.433 − 2.094 = .339.
5. Compute the chance that the difference between the test group and the control group is greater than zero—that is, that the test group really is better than the control group (and not just a fluke). Use the "normdist" formula in Excel to compute this:

$$= normdist(0, 0.339, 0.15, 1)$$

6. This Excel formula gives a result of 0.01. This shows us that there is only a 1% chance that the test group is really just as good or worse than the control group; we can be 99% certain that the test group is better than the control.

We can compare the control group to the original baseline in the same way. The difference between the control group and the original baseline is just .007. Using the same method that we just used to compare the test and the control groups, we find that there is a 48% chance that the control group is less than the baseline or a 52% chance it is higher. This tells us that the difference between these groups is negligible, and, for all practical purposes, they are no different.

We have determined with very high confidence that the training contributes to a real improvement in word of mouth advertising. Since the difference between the test and the control groups is about .4, the marketing department concludes that the improved training would account for about an 8% improvement in sales, easily justifying the cost of training the rest of the staff and ongoing training for all new staff. In retrospect, we probably could have used even fewer samples (using a student's t-distribution for samples under 30).

As we will see in the next chapter, this simplification is partly based on an assumption that the data gathered in this sample was really all the decision maker ever really knew. They had no "prior knowledge" that would override or even marginally impact the interpretation of this data. This approach is also focused more on reducing uncertainty about a decision while ignoring statistical significance.

Now, More about the Meaning of Significance

At this point, I also need to explain that the approach I just described is not exactly orthodox for scientific literature because I make no reference to computing statistical significance. The calculation I used and its interpretation are a simplification of a more typical hypothesis testing method. However, the method I just described is a valid method for a decision maker. I am using the results of an estimate of a mean to be a proxy for the uncertainty of the user—now updated with the new data.

To understand how hypothesis testing is generally discussed in business stats books and scientific literature alike, we have to spend some time discussing what question is being asked and how they answer it. When a pharmaceutical company is testing a new drug, you might think they are asking the question, "What is the probability that the drug works?" Actually, they are asking, "*Given* that what we observed was a fluke, what is the chance we would observe this difference or an even bigger difference."

The answer to the second, related but different question is referred to as the "p-value." The potential state where the observations were just a random fluke (that is, the drug didn't really work but by chance the average of the test group was better than the control group) is referred to as a "null hypothesis." If the p-value is less than some previously stated threshold—for example, .01—then they say they reject the null hypothesis. The threshold they compared the p-value to is the stated "significance level" and this procedure is called a "significance test." This is as close as they get to computing the chance that the drug works—which isn't close at all.

Significance testing is an artifact of the previously-mentioned frequentist view of probability. This definition of probability—an idealized frequency limit of a purely random, strictly repeatable process over infinite trials—is virtually impossible to apply to real-world problems like the probability of the success of a new product or effectiveness of a new drug. In order to avoid some of the messier issues with assigning probabilities to such events (i.e., assigning probabilities that we need for decisions), the statistician Ronald Fisher proposed answering a different question they *could* answer with the frequentists interpretation. The null hypothesis is a mathematically idealized idea where this particular definition of probability can be applied without much difficulty.

Terms Related to Statistical Significance

Null hypothesis—the results are a random fluke. For example, the chance there is no difference between a test group and control group other than random variation.

Alternative hypothesis—the results show some real phenomenon. For example, there really is a difference between two randomly selected

(continued)

groups where one group takes a new drug and another takes a placebo.

p-value—the chance of seeing the observed data—or something more extreme—*given* that it's just a random fluke (i.e., given that the null hypothesis is true).

Significance level—some chosen value, based only on convention and tradition in the particular field of study (such as .05), that p-value must be less than in order to reject the null hypothesis.

So, what does "statistically significant" mean?

Answer: P-value < significance level.

And that's *all* it means. It does not mean "big," "important," or even necessarily "likely to be true" (as we will see in Chapter 10, prior probabilities make all the difference. In short, it doesn't really mean "significant" the way most English speakers use the word.

The Significance of Emily Rosa's Experiment: A Counterfactual Outcome

Emily Rosa's experiment is an excellent, simple example that should help explain statistical significance. She had advice from people familiar with the methods one would see published in distinguished journals like *JAMA*, the math was exactly right, and the findings were deemed interesting enough to be published. But when Emily conducted her experiment, she didn't *really* compute the chance that the touch therapists could or couldn't detect an aura. Just like the authors of almost any published research article would have done, her advisors determined the probability that she would have seen those results if the effect she was attempting to observe (the ability to detect auras) didn't exist at all.

Recall that Emily asked the therapists to hold their hands, palms up, through holes in a screen so that they could not see their own hands. Emily, on the other side of the screen, would hold her hand over either the left or right hand of the therapist without touching it. She would then ask the therapist to determine—apparently based on Emily's own aura—which hand Emily hovered over. Her test was then to determine if the results were unlikely *assuming* the therapists were just randomly guessing which of the therapists' hands Emily's hand was hovering over.

Emily observed that the therapists guessed right 123 times out of 280. In this case, Emily happened to observe an outcome that was not only no better than random guessing but slightly unlucky even at that.

It turned out that the findings were conclusive—the therapists simply could not detect auras as they thought.

But imagine another possible outcome where, instead, the therapists happened to get 157 right instead of 123. This is as lucky as they were unlucky in Emily's actual experiment (17 more than 140 out of 280 instead of 17 less). Exhibit 9.11 shows the probability of different possible outcomes in assuming each guess had only a 50% chance of succeeding. The chance of each of these outcomes is the same as getting a given number of heads in 280 coin flips. For example, there is a .03 probability of getting exactly 132 heads in 280 coin flips or a .001 probability of getting exactly 163 heads. The probability of each of these outcomes is computed by using something called a "binomial distribution" we will discuss more in Chapter 10. For now, let's focus on how this is used to determine what is called significance.

Given that each guess has a 50% chance of being right, the chance of seeing 157 *or more* correct guesses (or heads on a coin flip) out of 280 is .024. This .024 is the p-value or the chance of seeing that result or something more extreme given that the guesses were a fluke (no better than coin flips). Emily was advised to set her "significance level" at .05 (which is close to the probability of getting 154 or more correct guesses, as

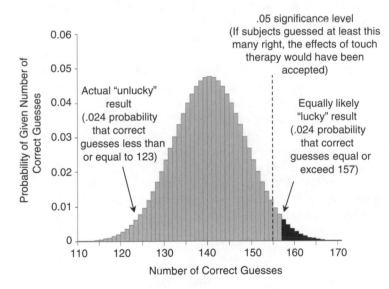

Exhibit 9.11 Probability of Correct Guesses Out of 280 Trials in Emily Rosa's Experiment assuming a 50% chance per guess of being correct

shown by the dashed line). Since .024 is less than the significance level of .05—a conventional but entirely arbitrary threshold—Emily would have had to reject that the effect was due to chance and reported that the touch therapists' skill was real.

So, this is what "statistical significance" really means. Again, it is not a statement about whether we learned anything from the observations or if the study was economically justified. Emily and her statistical advisors, following standard procedure worthy of publication in a prestigious medical journal, simply chose the conventional, arbitrary, significance level of .05 and compared it to her computed p-value.

If these were Emily's results and she accepted the hypothesis that touch therapists could detect auras, the p-value (.024) is not the chance that touch therapy doesn't work. Again, the p-value would be the chance of seeing those results or something more extreme assuming it were a random fluke (there was no real ability to detect auras). What decision makers need to know is the answer to a different question. We want to know the probability that some claim is true, what we should do given that level of uncertainty, and what the value of reducing uncertainty further would be.

So, if the hypothetical lucky result were observed instead of the actual unlucky result (luck from the point of view of the therapists, that is), how would such a finding have been used for actual decisions? If you were considering adding touch therapists to your hospital staff, would this finding be sufficient to compute the risk that it wouldn't be of any benefit? If you were an HMO trying to keep total healthcare costs low, would you consider covering touch therapy? If you were a patient would this study be sufficient for determining if you should pay for touch therapy versus paying for some other method for an affliction? No on all counts. The only use of this significance test would be to determine if it was worthy of being published in *JAMA*.

We can easily imagine practical situations where a statistically significant result would have an information value of zero. We simply imagine a situation where no result could have changed the outcome of a decision. We can also imagine situations where a result that would have failed a statistical significance test but significantly reduced our prior state of uncertainty had an information value of millions of dollars.

For a hypothesis test to be useful in a decision, we need more information than just the p-value. In the next chapter, we will show what we need to compute the odds that touch therapy works or that any proposed hypothesis is true by using *prior probabilities*. Having prior probabilities would make it clear that even if the touch therapists were a bit luckier, the probability that their method worked would still have been very low.

The downloadable Chapter 9 example spreadsheets at www .howtomeasureanything.com include the calculations for the controlled experiment and the significance test for Emily Rosa's experiment.

SEEING RELATIONSHIPS IN THE DATA: AN INTRODUCTION TO REGRESSION MODELING

One of the most common questions I get in seminars is something like, "If sales increase due to some new IT system, how do I know it went up because of the IT system?" What surprises me a bit about the frequency of this question is the fact that much of the history of scientific measurement has focused on isolating the effect of a single variable. I can only conclude that those individuals who asked the question do not understand some of the most basic concepts in scientific measurement.

Clearly, the experiment example given earlier in this chapter shows how something that has many possible causes can be traced to a particular cause by comparing a test group to a control group. But using a control and a test group is really just one way to separate out the effect of one single variable from all the noise that exists in any business. We can also consider how well one variable correlates with another.

Correlation between two sets of data is expressed as a number between +1 and −1. A correlation of 1 means the two variables move in perfect harmony: As one increases, so does the other by a perfectly predictable amount. A correlation of −1 also indicates two closely related variables, but as one increases, the other decreases in lockstep. A correlation of 0 means they have nothing to do with each other.

To get a feel for what correlated data looks like, consider the four examples of data in Exhibit 9.12. The horizontal axis could be scores on an employment test and the vertical axis could be a measure of productivity. Or the horizontal axis could be number of TV advertisements in a month and the vertical axis could be the sales for a given month. They could be anything. But it is clear that in some of the charts, the data in the two axes are more closely related, for one reason or another, in some charts than the data are in other charts.

The chart in the upper left-hand corner shows two random variables. The variables have nothing to do with each other, and there is no correlation. This is shown by the lack of a slope in the data points. The data appear flat because there is more variability in the horizontal data than in the vertical data. If the two were equally variable, the scatter would be more circular, but there would still be no slope. The chart in the lower right-hand corner shows two variables that are very closely related.

Exhibit 9.12 Examples of Correlated Data

These charts show that, before we do any math, correlations should be visually obvious if we just plot the data. If you were tracking estimated project costs versus actual project costs, and the plot comparing them looked like the graph in the lower right-hand corner, your cost estimations correlate very well with actual outcomes. If it looked like the graph in the upper left-hand corner, a person rolling dice would estimate project costs just as well. But correlation itself doesn't necessarily mean accuracy. If, in a purely hypothetical situation, you have a project manager who always underestimates actual project costs by *exactly* half, then you will still have a perfect correlation of one. The manager's estimate itself is not a close approximation to actual outcomes but it can be used to predict the outcomes perfectly (simply by multiplying by two).

If we use regression modeling with historical data, we may not need to conduct a controlled experiment. Perhaps, for example, it is difficult to tie an IT project to an increase in sales, but we might have lots of data about how something *else* affects sales, such as faster time to market of new products. If we know that faster time to market is possible by automating certain tasks, that this IT investment eliminates certain tasks, and those tasks are on the critical path in the time-to-market, we can make the connection.

A Regression Example: TV Ratings

I once analyzed the investment in a particular software project at a major cable TV network. The network was considering the automation of several administrative tasks in the production of new TV shows. One of the hoped-for benefits was an improvement in ratings points for the show, which generally results in more advertising revenue. But how could the network forecast the effect of an IT project on ratings when, as is so often the case, so many other things affect ratings?

The entire theory behind how this production automation system could improve ratings was that it would shorten certain critical-path administrative tasks. If those tasks were done faster, the network could begin promotion of the new show sooner. The network did have historical data on ratings, and, by rooting through some old production schedules, we could determine how many weeks each of these shows was promoted before airing. (We had previously computed the value of this information and determined that this minor effort was easily justified.) Exhibit 9.13 shows a plot of what these TV shows could look like on a chart showing the weeks in promotion and the ratings points for the shows. These are not the actual data from the client, but roughly the same correlation is illustrated.

Before we do any additional analysis with these data, do you at least *see* a correlation? If so, which of the charts from Exhibit 9.12 does this most resemble? Again, making such a chart is always my first step in regression analysis because usually the correlation will be obvious to the naked eye. In Excel, it's simple to make two columns of data—in this case promotion weeks and ratings points—where each pair of numbers represents one TV show. Just select the entire set of data, click on the "chart" button in Excel, choose an "XY (Scatter)" chart, follow the rest of the prompts, and you will see a chart something like the one in Exhibit 9.13.

It *looks* correlated, so exactly how correlated is it? For that, we have to get a little more technical. Instead of explaining all the theory behind

Exhibit 9.13 Promotion Period versus Ratings Points for a Cable Network

the regression modeling, I'll take our "power tool" approach and jump right into how to do it in Excel.

One simple method in Excel is to use the "=correl()" function to compute the correlation. Suppose the promotion weeks and ratings data were in the first 28 rows of columns A and B, respectively, in a spreadsheet. You would write the formula =correl(Bl:B28,Al:A28) in a cell in the spreadsheet. With our data, we get a correlation of about 0.7. Therefore, we can be fairly certain that being able to spend more time promoting a new show does help improve ratings. Now we can focus on whether and by how much we can streamline the production process and increase the amount of time we spend promoting the shows.

Another way to do this in Excel is to use the regression wizard in the Data Analysis Toolpak. (Navigating to it has changed a little between versions of Excel, so look it up in Help.) The regression wizard will prompt you to select the "Y range" and the "X range." In our example, these are the ratings points and weeks in promotion, respectively. This wizard will create a table that shows several results from the regression analysis. Exhibit 9.14 is an explanation of some of those results.

Exhibit 9.14 Selected Items from Excel's Regression Tool "Summary Output" Table

Variable Name	What It Means
Multiple R	Correlation of one or more variables to the "dependent" variable (e.g., ratings points): 0.7 in this example.
R square	Square of the multiple R. This can be interpreted as the amount of variance in the dependent (Y) variable explained by the independent (X) variable. In this example, it is the amount of variance in ratings points explained by promotion weeks.
Intercept	Where the best-fit line crosses the vertical axis. In this case, it is the estimated ratings points if promotion weeks were set to zero. This is where the best-fit line would intersect the vertical axis. This can also be produced with Excel's =intercept() function.
X variable 1	Coefficient (i.e., weight) for the dependent variable indicating how much Y changes for a given change in X. In this example, it is how much the ratings points increase for an increase of one promotion week. This can also be referred to as the "slope" of a variable and can be produced with Excel's =slope() function.

Variable Name	What It Means
P-Value	As in the experiment examples, if there really were no correlation, the probability that this correlation or higher could still be seen by chance. If you need to get published, the convention is that P-value should be below .05 or even .01, but, as discussed already, that may not be relevant. Use it as a rough indicator to the question you really need to know: Is this a real phenomenon or was it chance?

This information can be used to create a formula that would be the best approximation of the relationship between ratings and promotion time. In the formula that follows, we use Promotion Weeks to compute Estimated Ratings Points. It is conventional to refer to the computed value (in this case, Estimated Ratings Points) as the "dependent variable" and the value used to compute it (Promotion Weeks) as the "independent variable." We can use the values in the "Coefficients" column generated by Excel's Analysis Toolpak for the Intercept and X Variable 1 (Excel's label for the first independent variable—there could be many) to estimate ratings with the following formula:

Estimated Ratings = Coefficient × Promotion Weeks + Intercept

Using the values in this example gives us:

Estimated Ratings = 0.215 × Promotion Weeks + 0.877

We could also use Excel's =slope() to produce the coefficient and the =intercept() function to produce the intercept. The answers will be the same if we are looking at a single variable. If we plot the line this simple formula gives us on the chart we made, it would look like Exhibit 9.13. If we have eight promotion weeks, we can estimate that the middle of our CI for ratings points would be about 2.6. To make it even simpler, we could have ignored the intercept in this case entirely. Notice that the P-value for the intercept (well over .5) in the Summary Output indicates that this value is as much random chance as anything else. Also, since we are concerned about the effect of a *change* in promotion weeks, we really only need the slope (i.e., coefficient).

If we plot a line on the data with the estimation formula we get a "best fit" line, as shown in Exhibit 9.15. This chart shows that, while there is a correlation, there are still other factors that cause ratings not to be

Exhibit 9.15 Promotion Time versus Ratings Chart with the "Best-Fit" Regression Line Added

entirely dependent on promotion time. We use this information together with the controlled experiment to address the infamous "How do I know this if there are so many other factors?" question. It is clear that the ratings have some effect; it doesn't matter if you have quantified or can even *name* all the other factors that affect ratings.

Remember, we did all this to reduce our uncertainty about how ratings points would be improved if we implemented the proposed system. We have measured the increase in promotion weeks and then measured the relationship of promotion weeks to ratings points, in order to tell us more about the change in ratings points given a change in promotion weeks. Keep in mind that the reason that we think there is a relationship is not just because we observed it in the data. The client had other good reasons to believe that if you promote a show longer it will get better ratings.

Given that promotion weeks do affect ratings, what the client needed was a 90% CI around that best fit line in Exhibit 9.15 so that, given a change in promotion weeks, they can estimate a change in ratings. The easiest way to do this is to use the =STEYX() function in Excel. This will give us a standard deviation for the error of the Y given X (in this case, ratings points and promotion weeks, respectively). Applying this function to the data given in the spreadsheet example gives us a standard deviation of 0.543. To produce our 90% CI, we add and subtract 1.645*0.543 to the result provided by the Estimated Ratings formula (remember, a 90% CI is the mean +/– 1.645 standard deviations). In the case where we think we would save five weeks in a phase of production, given each additional week increases ratings points by about 0.215, our best estimate for an increase in ratings points is:

Slope (i.e., coefficient) × change in weeks = .215 × 5 = 1.077

90% CI = estimate +/– error = 1.077 +/– 1.645 × .543 = .18 to 1.97.

Of course, you can go to www.howtomeasureanything.com for the detailed spreadsheet to this example.

Parting Thoughts About Regression

It is important to state four additional points about regression models.

1. Perhaps the biggest misconception some managers may run into is the belief that correlation proves causation. The fact that one variable is correlated to another does not necessarily mean that one variable causes the other. If church donations and liquor sales are correlated, it is not because of some collusion between clergy and the liquor industry. It is because both are affected by how well the economy is doing. Generally, you should conclude that one thing causes another only if you have some *other* good reason besides the correlation itself to suspect a cause-and-effect relationship. In the case of the ratings points and promotion weeks, we did have such reasons.

2. The second biggest misconception about regression is that correlation isn't even *evidence* (not proof) of causation. It is not proof but it is evidence. Often those who remember just a little college stats will recall the first rule from college stats. They will blurt out "correlation doesn't mean causation" without prompting when the subject comes up. But finding no correlation makes causation unlikely, so finding a correlation leaves open that possibility. Originally, you may have had some calibrated estimate that there was a cause-effect relationship. If you show at least correlation— and you didn't know that before, causation must become more likely even if you don't prove it. In the next chapter, we will show how that works.

3. Keep in mind that these are simple linear regressions. It's possible to get even better correlations by using some other function of a variable (e.g., its square, inverse, the product of two variables, etc.) than by using the variable itself. Some readers may want to experiment with that.

4. The advantage of using Excel's regression tool over some of Excel's simpler functions, such as =correl(), is that the regression tool can do multiple regression. That is, it can simultaneously compute the coefficients for several independent variables at once. If we were so inclined, we could create a model that would correlate not only promotion time but also season, category, survey results, and several other factors to ratings. Each of these additional variables would have their own coefficient in the summary output table of the regression tool. Putting all these together, we would get a formula like this:

Estimated Ratings = Promotion Weeks Coefficient × Promotion weeks
+ Survey Approval Coefficient × Approval Rate
From Survey + . . . + Intercept

In multiple regression models, you should be careful of independent variables being correlated to each other. Ideally, independent variables should be entirely unrelated to each other. I've covered only the basics of multiple regression modeling. It is a useful tool, but proceed with caution. On this topic alone, the reader could learn much, much more. But this is enough to get you started.

Perhaps the Two Biggest Mistakes in Interpreting Correlation?

Biggest mistake: That correlation proves causation.
Second biggest mistake: That correlation isn't evidence of causation.

So far, we've covered situations where we make some assumptions about the underlying population distribution and some situations where no such assumptions are required. But there is another assumption we made in every case up to this point. Each of the measurements we discussed in this chapter, except for the subjective estimates, ignored any prior information you might have about the thing you are sampling. But this prior knowledge can make a big difference in your estimates. Now, in the next chapter, we will see how another, fundamentally different approach to measurement treats all measurements as building on prior knowledge.

Notes

1. Leo A. Goodman, "Serial Number Analysis," *Journal of the American Statistical Association* 47 (1952): 622–634.
2. Stephen P. Kramer, *How to Think Like a Scientist* (New York: HarperCollins, 1987).

Purely Philisophical Interlude #4

Who Needs "Statistical Significance"?

We already discussed that statistical significance isn't what many people casually recall and we discussed it doesn't mean what it is often thought to mean even when the math is recalled correctly. Now I'll just point out that there really is a debate among great thinkers regarding the legitimacy of statistical significance. The decision maker who avoids the issue of statistical significance entirely will have many highly respected allies. The case has even been made that science in general can do without it.

Statistical significance is the basis for almost all statistical analysis in academic research since the significance test was first developed by statistics icons like Ronald A. Fisher. It is important to remember, however, that this method was only developed in the 1930s. How did science get along without it before the 1930s? Weren't earlier experiments—like the famous confirmations of relativity, the existence of the atomic nucleus, or the effects of vaccinations—scientific? Of course they were. In fact, as soon as significance testing was proposed there were respected critics and, even though the method spread, the critics were never silenced. Here are a few of the critics:

- Paul Meehl, the previously mentioned author of *Clinical vs. Statistical Prediction*, said, "Sir Ronald has befuddled us, mesmerized us, and led us down the primrose path. I believe the almost universal reliance on merely refuting the null hypothesis is a terrible mistake, is basically unsound, poor scientific strategy, and one of the worst things that ever happened in the history of psychology."[1]
- William Edwards Deming, the great statistician who influenced statistical quality control methods more than any other individual in the twentieth century, said: "Significance or the lack of it provides no degree of belief—high, moderate, or low—about prediction of performance in the future, which is the only reason to carry out the comparison, test, or experiment in the first place."[2]
- Harold Jefferys, Ronald Fisher's long-time intellectual sparring partner in this debate, said in his book *Theory of Probability*, "What the use of [p-value] implies, therefore, is that a hypothesis that may be true may be rejected because it has not predicted observable results that have not occurred. This seems a remarkable procedure."[3]

A number of other authors to this day debate that even when done properly, statistical significance is unnecessary[4] and that its use has been a costly error in public policy.[5,6]

Having said all of this, if the reader wants his or her measurements not just to support a management decision, but to be published in a peer-reviewed scientific journal, I certainly recommend a mastery of the math of hypothesis testing. But there are at least two other reasons a decision maker should understand hypothesis testing and statistical significance. First, understanding what it means (and what it doesn't) is useful if the decision maker is going to interpret existing published academic research to inform a decision. Second, as we will see in the next chapter, part of the statistical significance calculation—the chance of seeing an observed result assuming it's a fluke—can be salvaged as a step in the direction toward what the decision maker does need.

Notes

1. P. E. Meehl, "Theoretical Risks and Tabular Asterisks: Sir Karl, Sir Ronald, and the Slow Progress of Soft Psychology," *Journal of Consulting and Clinical Psychology* 46 (1978), 817.
2. W. Edwards Deming, foreword to *Quality Improvement Through Planned Experimentation*, by Ronald Moen, Thomas Nolan, and Lloyd Provost (New York, NY: McGraw-Hill Professional, 1998).
3. H. Jeffreys, *Theory of Probability* (Oxford: Clarendon, 3rd edition: 1961; 1st edition: 1939), Section 7.2.
4. S. Armstrong, "Statistical Significance Tests Are Unnecessary Even When Properly Done," *International Journal of Forecasting* 23 (2007): 335–336.
5. D. McCloskey and S. Ziliak, *The Cult of Statistical Significance: How the Standard Error Costs Us Jobs, Justice, and Lives* (Economics, Cognition, and Society) (Ann Arbor: University of Michigan Press, 2008).
6. Stephen T. Ziliak and Deirdre N. McCloskey, "Size Matters: The Standard Error of Regressions in the American Economic Review," *Journal of Socio-Economics* 33 (August 2004): 527–546.

CHAPTER **10**

Bayes: Adding to What You Know Now

When presented new information, we have no other option than to relate it to what we already know—there is no blank space in our minds within which new information can be stored so as not to "contaminate" it with existing information.
—Clifford Konold, Scientific Reasoning Research Institute,
University of Massachusetts

In the first semester of business statistics, students learn a few methods based on a few "simplifying" assumptions. Often the assumptions don't end up simplifying very much of anything and some assumptions can turn out to be disastrously wrong. Later on in statistics, students learn about some more "advanced" methods that, to me, always seemed much more intuitive than the earlier ones.

One of the key assumptions in most introduction-to-statistics courses is that the only thing you ever knew about a population are the samples you are about to take. In fact, this is virtually never true in real-life situations.

Imagine that you are sampling several sales reps about whether an advertising campaign had anything to do with recent sales. You would like to measure the campaign's contribution to sales. One way would be simply to poll all of your sales team. But you have more information than just what they reveal. You had some knowledge prior to the poll based on historical experience with sales and advertising. You have knowledge about current seasonal effects on sales as well as the economy and measures of consumer confidence. Should this matter? Intuitively, we know this prior knowledge should count somehow. But until students get much further into their textbook, they won't (or, perhaps, will never) get to the part where they deal with prior knowledge.

A Prior-Knowledge Paradox

1. All conventional statistics assume (a) the observer had no prior information about the range of possible values for the subject of the observation, and (b) the observer *does* have prior knowledge that the distribution of the population is not one of the "inconvenient" ones.
2. The first above assumption is almost never true in the real world and the second is not true more often than we might think.

Dealing with this prior knowledge is what is called "Bayesian statistics." Early in this book we mentioned that the inventor of this approach, Thomas Bayes, was an eighteenth-century British mathematician and Presbyterian minister whose most famous contribution to statistics would not be published until after he died. Bayesian statistics deals with the issue of how we update prior knowledge with new information. With Bayesian analysis, we start with how much we know now and then consider how that knowledge is changed by new information.

A type of Bayesian analysis was the basis of some of the charts I provided in Chapter 9. For example, in the "population proportion" table, I started with the prior knowledge that, without information to the contrary, the proportion in the subgroup was uniformly distributed between 0% and 100%. Again, in the "Threshold Probability Calculator," I started with the prior knowledge that there was a 50/50 chance that the true median of the population was on either side of the threshold. In both of these cases, I took the position of maximum uncertainty. This is also called the "robust" Bayesian approach, and it minimizes the prior-knowledge assumptions including an assumption of normality. But the really useful part of Bayesian analysis is when we get to apply more prior knowledge than this.

THE BASICS AND BAYES

Bayes' theorem is simply a relationship of probabilities and "conditional" probabilities. A conditional probability is the chance of something given a particular condition. See Exhibit 10.1 for a summary of these and some other basic concepts in probability which we will need to have handy for the rest of the discussion.

Exhibit 10.1 Selected Basic Probability Concepts

I'm going to mention a few handy rules from probability theory. This is not the complete list of fundamental axioms from probability theory and it's definitely not a comprehensive list of all theorems that might be useful. But it is enough to get through this chapter.

Rule 1. How to write "Probability."

P(A) = Probability of A. P(A) has to be some value between 0 and 1, inclusive.
P(~A) = the probability of *not* A. Read the "~" sign as "no," "not," "isn't" or "won't."
If P(rain) is the probability of rain at a particular time and location, then P(~rain) is the probability it won't rain at that time and location.

Rule 2. How to write "Sometimes it depends": Conditional Probability.

P(A|B) = Conditional probability of A given B. For example:
P(Accident|Rain) is the probability of a car accident for a particular driver on a particular day given it will rain.

Rule 3. The "Something has to be true but contradictory things can't both be true" rule.

The probabilities of all mutually exclusive and collectively exhaustive events or states must add up to 1. If there are just two possible outcomes, say A or not A, then:
$$P(A) + P(\sim A) = 1.$$
For example, either it will rain or it won't. It has to be one or the other and it can't be both.

Rule 4. The probability of something is the weighted sum of its conditional probabilities.

We can extend Rule 3 to working out the probability based on all the conditions under which it could happen and the probabilities of each of those conditions.
$$P(A) = P(A|B)P(B) + P(A|\sim B)P(\sim B)$$
For example, rain has some bearing on the probability of getting in an accident in a particular car trip. The probability of a person getting in a car accident on a given trip can be:
$$P(Accident) = P(Accident|rain)P(rain) + P(accident|\sim rain)P(\sim rain)$$

Rule 5. Bayes' Theorem: How to flip a conditional probability (e.g., P(B|A) to P(A|B))

$$P(A|B) = P(A)P(B|A)/P(B)$$
Sometimes the form of this is referred to as the "general" form of Bayes by computing P(B) according to the rule stated in Rule 3 above. If we consider just two conditions for P(B) then Rule 4 allows us to substitute P(B) so that:
$$P(A|B) = P(A)P(B|A)/[P(B|A)P(A) + P(B|\sim A)P(\sim A)]$$

What follows are some examples using the simple rules we just mentioned. Some of the later examples involve some simple algebraic gymnastics. I've tried to make the examples as simple as possible but readers have an option, depending on how much detail they prefer to handle. You can work through these in detail or you can simply follow along with the Chapter 10 power tools which can be downloaded at www.howtomeasureanything.com.

For each of the problems in this subchapter, you can use the "Simple Bayesian Inversion Calculator" tool to confirm the results with or without doing the math yourself. As Exhibit 10.2 shows, to use this tool, you only need to enter the following:

1. The name of the thing you want to compute the probability of (e.g., "drug works" or "product will succeed")
2. The name of the observations that would inform the probability in question (e.g.,"positive trial" or "test market succeeds")
3. The probability that the claim in question is true (e.g., P(drug works) = 20%)
4. The probability of a particular informative observation given that the claim is true (e.g., P(positive drug trial| drug works) = 85%)
5. The probability of a particular informative observation given that the claim is false (e.g., P(positive drug trial|~drug works) = 5%)

Note that the probabilities you enter are all in the section titled "Initial Probability Matrix." This matrix looks at all the combinations of an observation being seen and combinations of whether the claim is true.

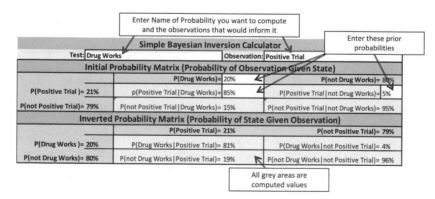

Exhibit 10.2 The Bayesian Inversion Calculator Spreadsheet*
*Downloadable from www.howtomeasureanything.com.

In this simple example, the observation is seen or not and the claim is true or not, so this makes a 2 × 2 matrix. The answers you often want are the calculations in the section titled "Inverted Probability Matrix." This is another 2 × 2 matrix but it shows combinations of the claim being true given particular observations.

This type of algebraic maneuver is called a "Bayesian inversion," and someone who begins to use Bayesian inversions in one area will soon find many other areas where it applies. It becomes a very handy calculation for the person who sees measurement problems as easily as Emily, Enrico, and Eratosthenes. Now let's work through a couple of examples.

Example: Applying Bayes to Market Tests of New Products

Suppose we were considering whether to release a new product. Based on historical experience and other information, we assign 40% to the probability that a new product will make a profit in the first year. We could write this as P(FYP) = 40%. Often a product is released in a test market first before there is a commitment to full-scale production. Of those times when a product was profitable in the first year, it was also successful in the test market 80% of the time (where by "successful" we might mean that a particular sales threshold is met). The calibrated estimator may choose to rely on this history and write the conditional probability as P(S|FYP) = 80%, meaning the "conditional" probability that a product had a successful test market (S), given (where "given" is the "|" symbol) that we knew it had a first-year profit, is 80%. Also, let's say a calibrated expert gave us the probability of a successful test where the product would eventually fail to generate a profit in the first year: P(S|~FYP) = 30%.

But we probably wouldn't be that interested in the probability that the market test *was* successful, given whether there was a first-year profit. What we really want to know is the probability of a first-year profit, depending on whether the market test was successful. That way, the market test can tell us something useful about whether to proceed with the product. This is what Bayes' theorem does. In this case, we set up Bayes' theorem with these inputs:

- P(FYP) is the probability of a first-year profit. Our calibrated expert informed partly by historical experience estimates this to be 40%.
- P(S|FYP) is the probability of a successful test market, given a product that would be widely accepted enough to be profitable the first year. This is estimated to be 80%.
- P(S|~FYP) is the probability of a successful test market, given that a product was not profitable the first year (remember, "~" means "not," "no," etc.). This is estimated to be 30%.

To follow along in the power tool, start by entering "FYP" in the cell labeled "Thing to State or Test" and "S" in "Observation." Then enter the values above for the cells referred to as P(FYP), P(S|FYP), and P(S|~FYP). Simply using Rule 4, you (or the tool) can compute that the probability of a successful test market is 50% using this information alone. This is the answer we see in the power tool in the cell referred to as P(S). Here is how it is calculated:

$$P(S) = P(S|FYP)P(FYP) + P(S|\sim FYP)P(\sim FYP)$$
$$= 80\% \times 40\% + 30\% \times 60\% = 50\%$$

Now we can compute how the results of the test market affect the probability of a first-year profit. To compute the probability of a first-year profit, given a successful test market, we set up an equation using the probabilities already given by using Bayes:

$$P(FYP|S) = P(FYP)P(S|FYP)/P(S) = 40\% \times 80\%/50\% = 64\%$$

If the test market is successful, the chance of a first-year profit is 64%. We can also work out what the chance of a first-year profit would be if the test market was not successful by changing two numbers in this calculation. The probability that a profitable product would have been successful in the test market was, as we showed, 80%. So the chance that a profitable product would have had an unsuccessful test market is 20%. We would write this as P(~S|*FYP*) = 20%. Likewise, if the probability of a successful test for all products (profitable or not) is 50%, then the overall chance of a test failure must be P(~S) = 50%. If we substitute P(~S|*FYP*) and P(~S) for P(S|*FYP*) and P(S) in the previous Bayes equation, we can compute P(FYP|~S) instead of P(FYP|S):

$$P(FYP|\sim S) = P(FYP)P(\sim S|FYP)/P(\sim S) = 40\% \times 20\%/50\% = 16\%$$

That is, the chance of a first-year profit is only 16% if the test market is judged to be a failure. If you were following along with the power tool, you should see the same answers in the cells labeled P(FYP|S) and P(FYP|~S). In summary, without the test market, we put a probability of 40% on first year profit. With the test market that probability changes to 64% if the test is successful or 16% if it is unsuccessful.

Now, you might wonder why we chose to initially estimate P(FYP), P(S|FYP), and P(S|~FYP) as opposed to some other set of variables. If you find it easier to start with estimating P(FYP|S), P(FYP|~S), and P(S), then you can certainly compute from that P(FYP) and the rest. In the tool, simply try different values for the inputs required until you get the values you expected to see in the calculated cells. The objective of a Bayesian inversion is the same as applied math in general: to give you a path from things that seem easier to quantify to something you believe to be harder to quantify.

One More Time: A Bayesian Look at Emily's Experiment

We pointed out in the previous chapter that tools like significance tests, while widely used, are not the same as a statement about the probability that an effect exists or what we need to make decisions. Clinical trials of new drugs, for example, don't usually compute the probability that a new drug works, they assume it doesn't work and then they compute the probability of the observed data occurring by chance. For an example of this, let's work through the hypothetical alternative outcome for Emily Rosa's experiment mentioned in the last chapter. This was the counterfactual outcome where the touch therapists were as lucky as they were unlucky in the actual experiment (i.e., therapists got 17 more than exactly half of the guesses right instead of 17 less). If she had gotten that outcome should we conclude that touch therapy really works?

Recall that we determined the p-value in that hypothetical alternative outcome of the experiment. The p-value in this case is the probability of getting 157 or more correct out of 280 trials, assuming that touch therapy does not work. This probability was 0.024. Let's refer to the observed outcome as the "data" and write the p-value as P(data|~TT). What we want to know is the probability that touch therapy works and we write this as P(TT|data). This probability is what we need to consider when evaluating real decisions like whether to spend money on it either as a hospital, HMO, or patient.

We could address matters of degree like how well touch therapy works or how positive or negative the data was for the claim. For now, we will keep this example very simple and look at just binary outcomes. Let's just say the data could be positive or negative and touch therapy works or it doesn't. Pulling together the probability rules we can show that in order to get to P(TT|data) we can use the following substitutions:

Substitutions in Emily's Experiment

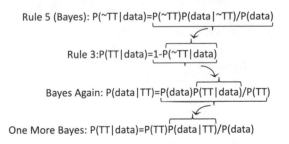

Rule 5 (Bayes): P(~TT|data)=P(~TT)P(data|~TT)/P(data)

Rule 3:P(TT|data)=1-P(~TT|data)

Bayes Again: P(data|TT)=P(data)P(TT|data)/P(TT)

One More Bayes: P(TT|data)=P(TT)P(data|TT)/P(data)

If we put all of these substitutions together into one big formula, we get to a point where we are multiplying and then dividing by P(TT). So those cancel out. We also end up multiplying and dividing the same by P(data) so we can cross out those (we still have a P(data) left in the divisor). After we get rid of these extraneous terms we simply get:

$$P(TT|data) = 1 - P(\sim TT)P(data|\sim TT)/P(data)$$

So, in order to determine the probability that it works given what we observed—that is, P(TT|data)—we have to assign prior probabilities that touch therapy doesn't work and for seeing that data. I could have gone further with the substitutions using Rule 3 on P(~TT) and Rule 4 on P(data), but you get the point. There is no way to answer P(TT|data) using the p-value (i.e., P(data|~TT)) alone. We have to assign prior probabilities regarding whether touch therapy works and the chance of seeing different data.

The decision maker assigning these prior probabilities should consider that touch therapy is not supported by any known mechanism either in physiology or physics, if not, in fact, *contradicting* what we do know about physiology and physics. There is always a chance, however, that the effect is still real and the mechanism behind it is yet undiscovered.

The decision maker should also consider that even if therapeutic touch was an illusion, patients and therapists, like most of us, could easily (and honestly) be fooled into believing it did work. The placebo effect is real and strong and has fooled many centuries of healers of all sorts. In fact, we could take it as a given that many would believe it worked regardless of evidence to the contrary.

Again, Emily's actual experimental outcome makes an extremely strong case against touch therapy. Not only were they unlucky if their guesses were no better than a coin flip, but they must have been *extremely* unlucky to guess so poorly if touch therapy actually worked. However, our counterfactual outcome shows it could have turned out differently and left open a little more room for differences of opinion. So if we had to determine P(TT|data), we have to assign priors. If the decision maker was unaware that there is no physical or physiological basis for touch therapy, then the prior might have been P(TT) = .5. In a case where a decision maker was aware of physics and physiology, it would probably be generous to give touch therapy a one in a hundred chance of working.

Let's work out the odds in a simplified situation where we consider only the "pass/fail" result of a significance test (i.e., we ignore for the moment the issue of by how much the data actually surpassed or failed the test). If our prior is that there is only a 1% chance that touch therapy works, and yet an experiment "confirms" it at a .05 significance level, what is the real answer we need—the chance touch therapy works given this hypothetically positive result to Emily's experiment? We can show the therapists needed to get at least 155 of 280 guesses right in order to pass a .05 significance test. (This requires use of the binomdist() function, to be explained shortly.)

We also have to work out P(data|TT). That is, if touch therapy really does work, what's the chance they would pass this significance test? Let's apply a relatively forgiving standard and say that if touch therapy worked, touch therapists still could only correctly detect an aura 65% of the time. If this were the case, it is virtually certain (99.97%) that they would pass a .05 significance test in 280 trials. So let's set up the problem in the Bayesian inversion calculator using "S" to refer to passing a significance test so that we write the probability that a significance test would be passed if touch therapy worked (at the stated 65% rate of correctly locating an aura) as P(S|TT) = .9997. We also write the P(TT) = .01 using the proposed prior. P(S|~TT)—the probability of finding significance given touch therapy doesn't work any better than chance—is, by definition, the significance level of .05. Entering these values into our calculation we can show:

$$P(TT|S)$$
$$= P(TT)P(S|TT)/[P(S|TT)P(TT) + P(S|\sim TT)P(\sim TT)]$$
$$= (.01)(.9997)/[(.9997)(.01) + (.05)(.99)]$$
$$= .17$$

This means that even with a "significant" result in favor of touch therapy, our prior knowledge and subsequent observations show that there is still only a 17% chance that touch therapy works. It is much more likely that passing the significance test was a random fluke if—according to your priors—it is highly unlikely the tested claim is true. If a large number of studies are done attempting to measure the relationship between personality traits and the last three digits of a person's social security number, 5% will, by definition, pass the significance test even though we know that there cannot be a relationship. If the prior P(TT) were a generous 50%, and Emily got this hypothetically positive outcome where the therapists were lucky, then P(TT|data) would be equal to 95%. However, since the *actual* outcome was as bad as it was for the therapist, P(TT|data) is very close to zero even if our prior was 50%.

We can answer another important question with the spreadsheet for the Simple Bayesian Inversion Calculator. It allows the user to enter a simple set of payoffs in a matrix to determine the value of additional information. You enter what you win if you bet on touch therapy and it works, what you lose if you bet on it and it doesn't work, and so on. If we said that a government healthcare system was considering betting on touch therapy, perhaps a billion dollars or more could be at stake. Not only do we need to consider the salaries of all therapists over several years, but the cost of treatments forgone and the benefits of this treatment over others. You can make some assumptions about the cells you would need to fill in but, in nearly all cases you would probably find that the value of even more information would be very high even if Emily would have gotten this hypothetical, but equally likely, positive outcome. In other words, instead of considering the issue settled, we would have to engage in a more serious study.

Demystifying the Urn of Mystery

If you recall the Urn of Mystery problem from Chapter 3, you probably found that the answer was counterintuitive. Nonetheless, it is an entirely correct outcome of Bayes' Theorem. It is a simple "population proportion" sampling problem based on a sample size of one assuming maximum prior uncertainty. The most uncertainty one can have in a population proportion is to assign a range of 0% to 100% on a uniform distribution—which is what we assigned prior to sampling any of the urns. We drew a single green marble and, based on that alone, we determined that there was a 75% chance that the urn was a majority green. Now let's see how we came up with an answer that so many find counterintuitive.

Again, instead of asking the question, "What's the chance that the majority of marbles in the urn are green if a randomly drawn marble is green?"; we ask a much simpler question and see how we can use Bayes to get to this first question. In the same way we addressed the market testing problem, we can ask questions like, "What's the chance that we will draw a green marble if 61% of the marbles in the urn are green?" Now that's simple. If 61% of the marbles are green, there is a 61% chance of drawing a green marble, an 85% chance if 85% are green, and so on.

Prior to the first draw, the distribution we had was uniform. Intuitively, there is a 50% chance the majority is green and a 50% chance you would draw a green marble. Since these are equal values, the terms $P(MG)$ and $P(DG)$ would cancel out in Bayes' Theorem. So in this case, it's pretty easy to see that the probability that majority are green (MG) given that you drew a green (DG) is the same as the probability of drawing green given that the majority are green, or:

$$P(MG|DG) = P(DG|MG)P(MG)/P(DG) = P(DG|MG)$$

If it is a given that the majority are green and we knew the distribution is uniform then, using Rule 4, we can see that the weighted average percentage green when we know the majority are green is 75%. So $P(DG|MG) = 75\%$. Since we also established that $P(MG|DG) = P(DG|MG)$ then it must be true that $P(MG|DG) = 75\%$.

We can even keep sampling and refine our estimate of the majority further. Exhibit 10.3 shows how the first five samples can further reduce

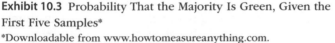

Sample (A "Hit" means Green is drawn, a "Miss" is not Green)

Exhibit 10.3 Probability That the Majority Is Green, Given the
First Five Samples*
*Downloadable from www.howtomeasureanything.com.

your uncertainty about the majority color. Remember, the Urn of Mystery
is not just a purely abstract game. It is an analogy for many measurement problems. This is an example where very few samples regarding
a population proportion can reduce uncertainty about which side of a
threshold is more likely—in this case, the threshold is a 50% population proportion. You can go to www.howtomeasureanything.com and
download Chapter 10 examples to see how this exhibit was calculated,
but later in this chapter we will get into a bit more detail about how to
answer more elaborate (and somewhat more realistic) questions like this.

USING YOUR NATURAL BAYESIAN INSTINCT

Even qualitative information can be exploited to find a way to reduce
uncertainty and to deal with messy problems that don't seem easy to
quantify mathematically. In our earlier advertising campaign example,
you may have been working with the individuals on the sales team for
a long period of time. You used their judgments in your assessment but
you have qualitative knowledge about how Bob is always too optimistic, how rational and deliberate Manuel tends to be, and how cautious
Monica usually is. Naturally, you have different degrees of respect for the
opinion of a person whom you know very well versus a younger, newer

salesperson. How does statistics take this knowledge into account? The short answer is that it doesn't, at least not in the introductory statistics courses that many people have taken.

Fortunately, there is a way to deal with this information in a way that is much simpler than any chapter in even the first semester of statistics. It is really the same as the subjective estimates in the jelly bean example where you were given a series of new observations. We will call this the instinctive Bayesian approach.

Instinctive Bayesian Approach

1. Start with your calibrated estimate.
2. Gather additional information (polling, reading other studies, etc.).
3. Update your calibrated estimate subjectively, without doing any additional math.

I call this an instinctive Bayesian approach because when people update their prior uncertainties with new information, as you did with the jelly beans, there is evidence to believe that those people update their knowledge in a way that is mostly Bayesian. In 1995, Caltech behavioral psychologists Mahmoud A. El-Gamal and David M. Grether studied how people consider prior information and new information when they assess odds.[1] They asked 257 students to guess from which of two bingo-like rolling cages balls were drawn. Each cage had balls marked either N or G, but one cage had more Ns than Gs and the other had an equal number of each. Students were told how many balls of each type were drawn after six draws.

The students' job was to determine which of the two cages the balls were drawn from. For example, if a student saw a sample of six balls where five were N and only one was G, the student might be inclined to think it was probably from the cage with more Ns than Gs. However, prior to each draw of six balls, the students were told that the cages themselves were randomly selected with a one-third, one-half, or two-thirds probability. In their answers, the students seemed to be intuitively computing the Bayesian answer with a slight tendency to overvalue the new information and undervalue the prior information. In other words, they were not quite ideally Bayesian but were more Bayesian than not.

They were not perfectly Bayesian because there was also a tendency to ignore knowledge about prior distributions when given new information. Research does show what is called a "base rate neglect."[2,3] Suppose I told you that in a roomful of criminal lawyers and pediatricians, there are 95 lawyers and five pediatricians. I randomly pick one person from the group and give you this information about him or her: The person,

Janet, loves children and science. Which is more likely: Janet is a lawyer or Janet is a pediatrician? Most people would say Janet was a pediatrician.

Even if only 10% of lawyers liked both science and children, there would still be more science- and child-loving lawyers than pediatricians in this group. Therefore, it is still more likely that Janet is a lawyer. Ignoring the prior probabilities when interpreting new information is a common error. Fortunately, some research also shows that this base rate neglect can be managed, especially where the expert is more familiar with the topic.[4] It also appears that there are at least two other defenses against this error.

1. Simply being aware of the impact the prior probability has on the problem helps. But, better yet, try to explicitly estimate each of the probabilities and conditional probabilities and attempt to find a set of values that are consistent (an example of this will be shown, shortly).
2. I also find that calibrated estimators were even better at being Bayesian. The students in the study would have been overconfident on most estimating problems if they were like most people. But a calibrated estimator should still have this basic Bayesian instinct while not being as overconfident.

I tested how close some of my clients were to being instinctively Bayesian after being calibrated. In 2006, I went back to several of my calibrated estimators in a particular government agency and asked them these five questions:

A. What is the chance a Democrat will be president four years from now?
B. What is the chance your budget will be higher four years from now, assuming a Democrat will be president?
C. What is the chance your budget will be higher four years from now, assuming a Republican will be president?
D. What is the chance your budget will be higher four years from now?
E. Imagine you could somehow see your budget four years from now. If it was higher, what then is the chance that a Democrat is the president?

Now, a person who is instinctively Bayesian would answer these questions in a way that would be consistent with Bayes' theorem. If a person said her answers to questions A through C were 55%, 60%, and 40%, then the answers to questions D and E must be 51% and 64.7%, respectively, to be consistent. The answer to D must be $A \times B + (1 - A) \times C$ because the conditional probabilities need to adhere to Rule 4.

In other words, the chance of something happening is equal to the chance of some condition times the chance of the event occurring under that condition plus the chance that condition won't occur times the chance of the event without the condition. To be properly Bayesian, a person would also have to answer A, B, D, and E such that $B = D/A \times E$.

This might not seem intuitive at first glance, but, apparently, most calibrated decision makers instinctively give answers that are surprisingly close to these relationships. Take the last example where a calibrated expert's answers to A, B, and C were 55%, 70%, and 40%. But the calibrated expert also gave 50% and 75% for questions D and E. The answers to A, B, and C logically require that the answers to D and E be 56.5% and 68.1%, not 50% and 75%. In Exhibit 10.4, we show how the subjective estimates for these questions compare to the computed Bayesian values.

Notice that a couple of the Bayesian values would have to be less than zero or greater than 100% to be consistent with the other subjective answers given. This would obviously be illogical, but, in those cases, when calibrated experts gave their subjective values, they did not realize they were logically inconsistent. However, most of the time the answers were closer to "proper Bayesian" than even the calibrated experts expected.

In practice, I use a method I call "Bayesian correction" to make subjective calibrated estimates of conditional probabilities internally consistent. This method uses Bayes rule as well as the rules 3 and 4 given earlier

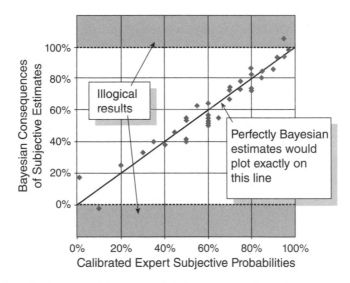

Exhibit 10.4 Calibrated Subjective Probabilities versus Bayesian

to test the consistency of subjective estimates. I show calibrated estimators what the Bayesian answers would be for some questions given their answers to other questions. They then change their answers until all their subjective calibrated probabilities are at least consistent with each other.

For example, suppose you thought there was a 30% chance you would have an accident in the factory this year that would cause a shutdown of more than an hour. If you conduct a detailed inspection of the operations, there is an 80% chance that you will pass, in which case you could reduce the chance of an accident to 10%. If you fail, you estimate a 50% chance of an accident. But notice that these are not consistent. Using Rule 4, you get 80% × 10% + 20% × 50% = 18%, not 30%. You need to change one of your estimates to get these to add up correctly. Likewise, the probability of an accident given a good inspection has to be internally consistent with the probability of passing an inspection given an accident, the probability of an accident, and the probability of passing. You can use the Simple Bayesian Inversion Calculator to assist in Bayesian corrections.

Once the issue of failing to consider prior probabilities is considered, humans seem to be mostly logical when incorporating new information into their estimates along with the old information. This fact is extremely useful because a human can consider qualitative information that does not fit in standard statistics. For example, if you were giving a forecast for how a new policy might change "public image"—measured in part by a reduction in customer complaints, increased revenue, and the like—a calibrated expert should be able to update current knowledge with "qualitative" information about how the policy worked for other companies, feedback from focus groups, and similar details. Even with sampling information, the calibrated estimator—who has a Bayesian instinct—can consider qualitative information on samples that most textbooks don't cover.

Try it yourself by considering this: Will your company's revenue be higher next year? State your calibrated probability. Now ask two or three people you consider as knowledgeable on the topic. Don't just ask them if they think revenue will be higher; ask them to explain why they believe it. Have them go into some detail. Now give another subjective probability for the chance that revenue will be higher. This new answer will, especially with the help of a Bayesian correction, be a rational reflection of the new information even though the new information was mostly qualitative.

Exhibit 10.5 shows how the calibrated expert (who is both mostly instinctively Bayesian and not over- or underconfident) compares to three other groups: the traditional non-Bayesian sampling methods such as *t*-statistics, uncalibrated estimators, and pure Bayesian estimators. This

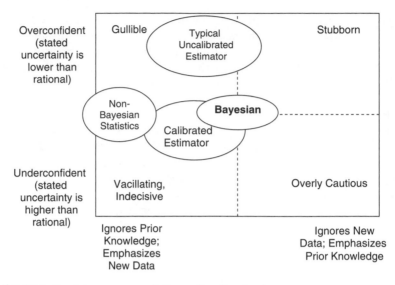

Exhibit 10.5 Confidence versus Information Emphasis

conceptual map tells you how different people and approaches stand relative to each other on their "Bayesian-ness." One axis is how confident they are relative to their actual chance of being right, and the other axis is how much they emphasize or ignore prior information.

This method might cause anxiety among those who see themselves as sticklers for "objective" measurement, but such anxiety would be unwarranted, for reasons I explain in the Purely Philosophical Interlude #5 at the end of this chapter.

For the more legitimate concerns about this method, some controls can at least partly compensate. As a method that relies on human judgment, this approach is subject to several types of previously discussed biases. Here are some controls you could use in the instinctive Bayesian approach:

- *Use impartial judges if possible.* If a department head's budget will be affected by the outcome of the study, don't rely on that person to assess new information qualitatively.
- *Use blinds when possible.* Sometimes it is possible to provide useful information to judges while keeping them in the dark about what specific problem they are assessing. If a marketing report provides transcripts from a focus group for a new product, references to the product can be deleted and judges can still determine if the reaction is positive or negative.
- *Use separation of duties.* This can be useful in conjunction with blinds. Get one set of judges to evaluate qualitative information, and

give a synopsis to another judge who may be unaware of the specific product, department, technology project, and so on. The second judge can give the final Bayesian response.

- *Precommit to Bayesian consequences.* Get judges to say in advance how certain findings would affect their judgments, and apply Bayesian correction until they are internally consistent. This way, when the actual data are available, only the Bayesian formula is used and no further references to subjective judgment are required.

HETEROGENEOUS BENCHMARKING: A "BRAND DAMAGE" APPLICATION

Anything you need to quantify can be measured in some way that is superior to not measuring it at all.

—Gilb's Law[5]

In the jelly bean sampling problem in Chapter 9, part of the uncertainty of the estimators in estimating the weight of a jelly bean was a lack of context for the measurement scale involved. One estimator said, "I'm just not sure I can picture exactly how much a gram of candy looks like." Another said, "I don't have any feel for the weights of small things."

Imagine I had told you that a business card weighs about 1 gram, a dime weighs 2.3 grams, and a large paper clip weighs 1 gram. Would that have reduced your range much? It did for some of the people I surveyed, especially those with the widest ranges. One person who had an upper bound of 20 grams immediately reduced his upper bound to 3 grams after hearing this information. Providing this information works because, as we now know, people can be instinctively Bayesian, especially calibrated estimators. They tend to update prior knowledge with new information in a fairly rational way even when the new information is qualitative or only somewhat related to the estimated quantity.

I'm calling this method of updating prior knowledge based on dissimilar but somewhat related examples the "heterogeneous benchmark" method. When people feel they have no idea what a quantity might be, just knowing a context of scale, even for unlike items, can be a huge help. If you need to estimate the size of the market for your product in a new city, it helps to know what the size of the market is in other cities. It even helps just to know the relative sizes of the economies of the different cities. This is an example of the "you have more data than you think" rule from Chapter 3. We don't need perfectly homogeneous examples to compare things to in order to reduce some uncertainty about a problem.

Getting a Sense of Scale

Heterogeneous benchmark: A method where calibrated estimators are given other quantities as benchmarks to estimate an uncertain quantity, even when those quantities seem only remotely related.
Example: Estimating the sales of a new product by knowing the sales of other products or similar products by competitors.

One intriguing example of the heterogeneous benchmark shows up in information technology (IT) security. In the Department of Veterans Affairs IT security example used in Chapters 4 through 6, I showed how we can model various security risks in a quantitative way using ranges and probabilities. But the IT security industry seems to be a bottomless pit of both curious attitudes about things that can't be measured and the number and type of "intangibles." One of these supposedly impossible measurements is the "softer costs" of certain catastrophic events.

A person who has a lot of experience with the resistance to measurement in IT security is Peter Tippett, formerly of Cybertrust. He applied his MD and PhD in biochemistry in a way that none of his classmates probably imagined: He wrote the first antivirus software. His innovation later became Norton Antivirus. Since then, Tippett has conducted major quantitative studies involving hundreds of organizations to measure the relative risks of different security threats. With these credentials, you might think that his claim that security can be measured would be accepted at face value. Yet many in the IT security industry seem to have a deeply rooted disposition against the very idea that security is measurable at all.

Tippett has a name for what he finds to be a predominant mode of thinking about the problem. He calls it the "Wouldn't it be horrible if . . ." approach. In this framework, IT security specialists imagine a particularly catastrophic event occurring. Regardless of its likelihood, it must be avoided at all costs. Tippett observes: "Since every area has a 'wouldn't it be horrible if . . .' all things need to be done. There is no sense of prioritization." He recalls a specific example, Cybertrust. "A Fortune 20 IT security manager wanted to spend $100M on 35 projects. The CIO [chief information officer] wanted to know which projects are more important. His people said nobody knows."

One particular "wouldn't it be horrible if . . ." that Tippett encounters is brand damage, a marred public image. It is possible, imagines the security expert, that something sensitive—like private medical records from a health maintenance organization or the loss of credit card data—could be breached by hackers and exploited. The security expert further imagines that the public embarrassment would so tarnish the brand name of the firm that it should be avoided, whatever the cost and however likely or unlikely it may be. Since the true cost of brand damage or the probability cannot be measured, so this "expert" insists, protection here is just as important as investments guarding against every other catastrophe—which also need to be funded without question.

But Tippett did not accept that the magnitude of the brand damage problem was completely indistinguishable from the magnitude of other problems. He devised a method that paired hypothetical examples of brand damage with real events where losses were known. He asked, for example, how much it hurts to have a company's e-mail go down for an hour, along with other benchmarks. He also asked how much more or less it hurt (e.g., "about the same," "half as much," "10 times as much," etc.).

Cybertrust already had some idea of the relative scale of the cost of these events from a larger study of 150 "forensic investigations" of loss of customer data. This study included most of the losses of customer data from MasterCard and Visa. Cybertrust surveyed chief executives as well as the general public about perceptions of brand damage. It also compared the actual losses in stock prices of companies after such events. Through these surveys and comparisons, Tippett was able to confirm that the brand damage due to customer data stolen by hackers was worse than the damage caused by misplacing some backup data.

By making several such comparisons with other benchmarks, it was possible to get an understanding of the difference in scale of the different types of catastrophes. Some amount of brand damage was worse than some things but not as bad as others. Furthermore, the relative level of loss could be taken into account along with the probability of that type of loss to compute "expected" loss.

I can't overstate the prior amount of uncertainty regarding this problem. The organizations weren't just uncertain about how bad brand damage could be. Until Tippett's study, they had no idea of the order of magnitude of the problem at all. Now they finally have at least a sense of scale of the problem and can differentiate the value of reducing different security risks.

At first, Tippett observed a high degree of skepticism in these results at one client, but he notes: "A year later one person is a bit skeptical and the rest are on board." Perhaps the holdout still insisted that no observation could have reduced his uncertainty. Again, with examples like brand damage, uncertainty is so high that almost any data informing a sense of scale is a reduction in uncertainty—therefore, a measurement.

Your organization, of course, will probably not set out to conduct a vast survey of over 100 organizations to conduct a measurement. But it is helpful to realize that such studies already exist. (Some firms sell this research.) Also, applying this method even internally can reduce uncertainty, whether your organization purchases external research or not.

Applications for Heterogeneous Benchmarks

Heterogeneous benchmarks are ideal for a simple measurement of the "soft costs" of many types of catastrophic events, especially where initial uncertainty is extremely high. Consider these examples:

- Hackers stealing customer credit card and Social Security information
- Inadvertent release of private medical data to the public
- Major product recalls
- Major industrial catastrophes at a chemical plant
- Corporate scandal

It might seem that we are focusing too much on IT security, but think about how broadly applicable this concept is. It is not just an approach for measuring brand damage from a security breach. It might be how we deal with the priority of investments meant to avoid a major product recall, corporate scandal, a catastrophic accident at a chemical plant, and the like. In fact, we can imagine how this method could apply to the positive side of these same issues. What is the value of being perceived as the "quality product" in the industry? Benchmarks are a practical way to bring some sense of scale to the problem whenever uncertainty is so high that it seems unmanageable.

If this use of benchmarks seems "too subjective," consider the objective of measurement in this case. What *is* brand damage but perception? We are not measuring some physical phenomenon but human opinions. The beginning of this measurement is understanding that something like "brand damage" is, by definition, one of public perception. And you assess public perception by, of course, asking the public. Alternatively, you can indirectly watch what the public does with its money by observing how the unfortunate event affected sales or stock price. Either way, it's been measured.

BAYESIAN INVERSION FOR RANGES: AN OVERVIEW

As mentioned earlier, many of the other charts and tables I created for this book were done with a type of Bayesian inversion. For most problems in statistics and measurement, we are asking, "What is the chance the truth is X, given what I've seen?" Again, it's actually often easier to answer the question, "If the truth was X, what was the chance of seeing what I did?" Bayesian inversion allows us to answer the first question by answering the second, easier question.

So far, in this chapter on Bayesian methods, we've only looked at situations where a claim had two possible outcomes: true or false (e.g., the product has a first-year profit, touch therapy works, etc.). And, so far, the informative observations have had only two possible outcomes (e.g., the test market fails or succeeds). We also need to measure quantities on a continuum, like the percentage of patients helped by a new procedure or the forecast of first year sales of a new product. We addressed similar problems in Chapter 9, but now we can see how to solve them while making full use of prior information.

We will consider two different kinds of measures on a continuum: a population proportion and an estimate of a population mean. The first is a bit easier than the second because, although the outcome is a range (e.g., our 90% CI is that 20% to 55% of customers do X) the observations are still binary. Recall that in a population proportion measurement, each sample is either a "hit" or "miss." The slightly more elaborate measurement to make with a Bayesian approach is where the samples themselves are also values on a continuum—for example, if we were sampling customer time in the store, the answers could be 6 minutes, 15.3 minutes, 40 minutes, and so on instead of just hit or miss. We will start with the easier one first.

Example: Percentage of Customers Kept After a Change

By sampling green and red marbles from the Urn of Mystery, we could do more than just estimate the probability of the majority being green. We can estimate a 90% CI for the population proportion of green. Knowing that the 90% CI for the proportion of green in the urn is 45% to 82% is more generally useful than just the chance green is the majority color. It is even more generally useful if we can solve this with better priors (recall that we assumed a "robust" prior for the Urn of Mystery). So let's consider a more practical business measurement problem that happens to be mathematically identical to estimating a range for the proportion of green marbles in the Urn of Mystery with priors.

Suppose we have an automotive parts store and we want to measure how many of our customers will still be around next year, given changes in the local economy and traffic patterns on nearby roads. Based on knowledge that retail in general is tightening in this area, our calibrated estimate for the 90% CI of the proportion of current customers who will still be in the area to shop at our auto parts store again in the next year is 35% to 75%. (For now, we will assume a normal distribution.) We computed that if this value is not at least 73%, we would have to postpone an expansion. We also determine that if it is lower than 50%, our only recourse would be relocation to a higher-traffic area.

Let's say we computed the value of information (using the EOL for ranges method we discussed in Chapter 7) at well over $500,000, so we definitely want to pursue a measurement. But, of course, we want to minimize the burden on customers with customer surveys. Keeping in mind that we want to measure incrementally, we see how much information we can get from sampling just 20 customers. If we sample just 20 and 14 of them said they will still be in the area to be customers a year from now, how can we change this range? (For now, we'll just assume the customer statements are a realistic reflection of actual future behavior.) Remember, typical, non-Bayesian methods can't consider prior range in the calculation.

Before we get into any details of the calculations, let's just get a visual for what the results would look like, given our initial estimate and the results of the sampling. Exhibit 10.6 shows three different distributions for estimating the percentage of our current customers who will be around in a year. These appear somewhat similar to but not exactly the same as the normal distribution first introduced in Chapter 6. As before, the "hilltops" in each of these distributions are where the outcomes are most likely and the "tails" are unlikely but still possible outcomes. The total area under each curve must add up to 100%.

Here is a little more detail on the meaning of each of the three distributions shown in Exhibit 10.6.

- The leftmost distribution is based on our initial calibrated estimate before we started taking any samples. This is our prior state of uncertainty reflected in our 90% CI of 35% to 75% for customer retention converted to a normal distribution.
- The rightmost distribution is what our uncertainty about customer retention would look like if we only had our sample results (14 out of 20 customers will be sticking around) and no prior knowledge at all. It assumes only that the percentage of customers who would be around to make a purchase in the next 12 months is somewhere between 0% and 100%. This is also called a "robust Bayesian" distribution.
- The middle distribution is the result of the Bayesian analysis that considers both the prior knowledge (our calibrated estimate of 35% to 75%) and the sample results (14 out of 20 customers surveyed said they would still be in the area).

Exhibit 10.6 Customer Retention Example
Comparison of Prior Knowledge, Sampling without Prior Knowledge, and
Sampling with Prior Knowledge (Bayesian Analysis)

Notice that the Bayesian result (in the middle) appears to be sort of an average of the two other distributions: the distribution based on prior knowledge only and the distribution based on the sampling results only. But it is more than that. It is also *narrower than either of the other distributions.* This is an important feature of this method. Prior knowledge based on calibrated estimates and the results of random sampling tell you a little more (sometimes a lot more) than either piece of information alone.

To see how the middle distribution is calculated, consider that simpler type of question we always try to start with: If X were the case, what is the chance of this observation? So, we ask: If 90% of all customers would say they plan to be around to shop again at the automotive parts store, what is the expected number of customers out of 20 who would say the same? Simple: 90% of 20, or 18. If it was 80%, we would expect to get 16. Of course, we know that, by chance alone, a random sample of 20 could get us 15 or maybe even 20 customers who would say they will shop here again. So we need to know not just the expected outcome but the chance of each of these specific results.

We use a special distribution, mentioned earlier and just briefly, called the "binomial distribution" to help with this. Recall that the binomial distribution allows us to compute the chance of a certain number of "hits," given a certain number of "trials," and given the probability of a single hit in one trial. This same concept applied to estimating the odds of different guesses by touch therapists in Emily Rosa's experiment and computing the mathless table.

For example, if you were flipping a coin, you could call getting heads a hit, the number of flips would be the trials, and the chance of a hit is 50%. Suppose, for example, we wanted to know the chance of getting exactly four heads out of 10 flips if the chance of getting heads is 50%. Instead of explaining the entire formula and the theory behind the field of combinatorics, I'm going to skip straight to the Excel formula. In Excel, we simply write:

$= binomdist$ (*number of hits, number of trials, probability of a hit*, 0)

With the numbers in our coin-flipping example, we write = binomdist (4,10,.5,0), and Excel returns the value of 20.5%. The zero at the end tells Excel that we want only the chance of that particular result. Using a "1" will produce the cumulative probability (i.e., the chance that the stated number of hits *or less* will occur). This result means that there is a 20.5% chance that 10 coin flips will produce exactly four heads.

In our automotive parts chain example, a customer who says, "Yes, I will shop here again in the next 12 months" is a hit, and the sample size is the number of trials. (We can ask anonymously by asking customers to check their response on a card they then insert in a box, so that customers don't feel pressured to answer yes.) Using the binomial distribution, a manager can work out the chance of a specific result, such as the chance that 14 out of a random sample of 20 customers will say they will shop here again, if, in reality, 90% of the total population of customers would shop here again. Again, in Excel, we write = binomdist(14,20,.9,0), which gives us just under a 1% chance that we would have gotten exactly 14 hits out of 20 randomly sampled customers if, in fact, 90% of the entire population of customers would have said they would shop here again. For the chance it would be something *up to and including* 14 hits out of 20, we write = binomdist (14,20,.9,1) to get 1.1%. Either way, we see that 14 hits would be fairly unlikely if there really was a 90% chance of each of 20 samples being a hit.

Now, suppose we apply a discrete approximation method like the one we first discussed in Chapter 7. Dividing the range of possible population proportions into many increments, we computed this chance for a population where 1% would plan to return the next year, then 2%, 3%, and so on for every possible 1%-wide increment from 1% to 99%. (There are situations where increments much smaller than 1% could be useful, but we will keep it simple for now.) Setting up some tables in an Excel spreadsheet, we can compute the chance of a specific result, given each of the hypothetical population proportions. In each little increment, we get the probability of getting exactly 14 out of 20 customers saying "yes" to our repeat-shopping question, given a specific population proportion. For each increment, we conduct a calculation with Bayes' theorem. We can put it all together like this:

$$P(Prop = X | Hits = 14 \ of \ 20) = (Prop = X)$$

$$\times P(Hits = 14 \ of \ 20 | Prop = X)/P(Hits = 14 \ of \ 20)$$

where:

P(*Prop* = X|*Hits* = 14 *of* 20) is the probability of a given population proportion X, given that 14 *of* 20 random samples were hits.

P(*Prop*=X) is the probability that a particular proportion of the population will shop here again (e.g., X = 90% of the population of customers really would say they will shop here again).

P(*Hits* = 14 *of* 20|*Prop* = X) is the probability of 14 hits out of a random sample of 20, given a particular population proportion is equal to X.

P(*Hits* = 14 *of* 20) is the probability that we would get 14 hits out of 20, given all the possible underlying populating proportions in our initial range.

We know how to compute P(*Hits* = 14 *of* 20|*Prop* = 90%) in Excel: = binomdist(14,20,.9,0). Now we have to figure out how to compute P(*Prop* = X) and P(*Hits* = 14 *of* 20). We can work out the probability of each 1% increment by going back to the = normdist() function (previously mentioned in Chapters 7 and 9) in Excel and using the calibrated estimate. For instance, to get the probability that between 78% and 79% of our customers are repeat customers (or at least say they are on a survey), we can write the Excel formula:

= *normdist*(.79, .55, .122, 1) − *normdist*(.78, .55, .122, 1)

The .55 is the mean of our original calibrated range of 35% to 75%. The .122 is the standard deviation (remember there are 3.29 standard deviations in a 90% CI): (75% − 35%)/3.29. The normdist formula gives us the difference between the probability of getting less than 79% and the probability of getting less than 78%, resulting in a value of 0.5%. We repeat this for each 1% increment in our range so we can compute the probability the population proportion is X (i.e., P(*Prop* = X) for every remotely likely value of X in our range).

Computing the value of P(*Hits* = 14 *of* 20), given all possible population proportions, builds on everything we've done so far. To compute P(Y) when we know P(Y|X) and P(X) for every value of X, we add up the product of P(Y|X) × P(X) for every value of X. Since we know how to compute P(*Hits* = 14 *of* 20|*Prop* = X) and P(*Prop* = X) for any value of X, we just multiply these two values for each X and add them all up to get P(Hits = 14 of 20) = 8.09%.

Now, for each 1% increment, we compute the P(Prop = X), P(Hits = 14 of 20|Prop = X), and P(Prop = X|Hits = 14 of 20). P(Hits = 14 of 20) is 8.09% for all the increments in the range.

If we cumulatively add the chance of each increment being the population proportion, we find that the values add up to about 5% by the time we get to a population proportion of 48% and cumulative value increases to 95% by the time we get to 75%. This means our new 90% CI is about 48% to 75%. This is the result shown as the middle probability distribution in Exhibit 10.6. This result is narrower than either the original calibrated estimate or the sample data alone. Again, the detailed table showing all of these calculations is available at www.howtomeasureanything.com.

Now let's look at the impact this Bayesian analysis had on our decision. We previously determined that if customer retention was less than 73%, we should defer some planned expansions, and that if it was less than 50%, we should pull up stakes and move to a better area. With only our initial estimate that 35% to 75% of customers will be here in a year, we would be fairly sure we should defer expansion. And since there is a 34% chance that customer retention could be below the 50% threshold, we might have to move. With the sample data alone, we are fairly sure we are not below the 50% threshold but not so sure we are below the 73% threshold. Only with the Bayesian analysis using both the original estimate and the sample data are we fairly confident that we are below the 73% threshold yet above the 50% threshold. We should not move but we should defer planned expansion investments. (See Exhibit 10.7.)

We still have uncertainty about the desired course of action but much less than we would without Bayesian analysis. If we still had a significant information value, we might decide to sample a few more customers and repeat the Bayesian analysis. With each new sampling, our range would be even narrower and the effect of our original calibrated estimate would diminish as the new sample data becomes more extensive. If we were to sample, say, over 200 customers, we would find that our initial estimate changed the result very little. Bayesian analysis matters most when we can gather only a few samples to adjust an initial estimate.

Exhibit 10.7 Summary of Results of the Three Distributions versus Thresholds

Source of Distribution	Confidence in Deferred Expansion (Retention <73%)	Confidence in Changing Location (Retention <50%)
Based on initial calibrated estimate (35% to 75%)	93%	34%
Based on sample alone (14 of 20 surveyed will stay)	69%	4.3%
Bayesian analysis using both initial estimate and sample data	91%	6.5%

We could also have used the population proportion chart used in Chapter 4 (although we would be looking up the range for customers who *didn't* say they would shop again, since the subgroup sizes are all less than 50% of the sample size). But we couldn't take into account this stated initial range. The chart in Chapter 9 was, by the way, also derived with a Bayesian inversion, except I started with the widest possible uncertainty that any population proportion can possibly have. Like the Urn of Mystery example, I assumed a uniform distribution of 0 to 100% for a population proportion. Using a Bayesian inversion with this wide initial range (in fact, the maximum possible uncertainty for a population proportion with the absolute minimum prior knowledge) is the robust Bayesian approach used to generate the rightmost distribution in Exhibit 10.6.

Unlike the original Urn of Mystery using uniform distribution of 0% to 100% as a prior, in this customer retention example we had the prior knowledge that results near 0% or near 100% were unlikely. The Bayesian range takes this prior knowledge into account. As the number of samples increase, however, the effect of the initial range diminishes. After getting to 60 samples or more, the answer will begin to get closer to what the parametric population proportion method from Chapter 9 would produce.

If you can master this type of analysis, you can take it further and see how to analyze problems where the initial distribution was some other kind of shape instead of normal. For example, the distribution could be uniform, or it could be normal truncated, so that it is not implied that more than 100% of the customers could be repeat shoppers. (The upper tail of a normal 90% CI gives a small chance of that being the case.) Again, see the supplementary website for examples of both of these distributions.

Bayes for Estimates of Means

Now, consider that instead of estimating a population proportion, we wanted to estimate how much time a customer spends in a store on average. When we sample customers we don't get "yes" or "no" answers like we did in the previous example. We will get some number of minutes per visit. We could still use tools from Chapter 9, like the Student's *t* or mathless table, but, recall that those don't consider any prior knowledge of the data other than assuming the absolute minimum amount of knowledge. To consider prior knowledge for a measurement where the samples have a range of values, we have to get a bit more detailed. Fortunately, it is just an extrapolation on the Bayesian population proportion method we just described.

Imagine that in the Urn of Mystery you didn't just have green and red marbles. Imagine instead that each marble had a number printed on it.

Each marble could represent a sample from a population representing how much a person spends on movies per year, the days someone stuck to a diet or anything else you might have sampled with methods from Chapter 9. There are lots of ways these values could be distributed within the Urn and we're not sure which applies. It could be a completely uniform distribution of values from 0 to 1,000. It could be normally distributed with a mean of 650 and with 90% being within +/−100 of that mean. It could be something skewed to the left or right.

If we knew exactly which of these distributions the population followed then, of course, we would know exact parameters like the mean of the population, the median, what percentage of the population was under 250, and so on. The challenge in estimating these parameters based on a given sample set—for example, 24, 44, 28, 33, and 51—is that they could have come from several possible population distributions. Such a sample could have come from a population with a mean of 45 and a standard deviation of 20, or a population with a mean of 30 and a standard deviation of 15, or even a population with a uniform distribution between 20 and 70.

But this same sample also makes other distributions extremely unlikely or even impossible. This sample can't come from a population with a mean of 385 and a standard deviation of 15 or a uniform distribution of 3 to 17. Even the first sample would have eliminated those distributions. Nor is a population with a uniform distribution of 0 to 1,000 likely to produce such a sample set since they are all so close to each other compared to that range.

We will answer this problem in a way similar to how we answered the population proportion problem. Only this time, a "hit" is when a sample falls in a specific interval on a wide range. Perhaps I divide my range of possible values up into 100 increments of 10. Then a hit for the increment 140–150 is when a chosen sample falls in that range. The other 99 increments would count this as a miss.

For a given population distribution, I would be able to work out the probability that a sample would fall in that increment. That's part of what we need. We also need the probability that a particular distribution is the actual population distribution. I probably already have some priors about the possible distributions. Perhaps I could start with the prior that the values in the population—whatever it is—are normally distributed. Perhaps I know that samples within the population routinely vary by a factor or two or three or perhaps I know (as in the jelly bean example) that they are relative homogeneous.

This could be an astronomical task, assigning priors to all possible distributions. But we can make it much simpler just by accepting a lower level of resolution. In this example, I've defined just four increments.

Exhibit 10.8 Example Prior Distribution of Ranges (Low Resolution)

They could represent increments of 250 units each to make up the range of 0 to 1,000 (0 to 250, 251 to 500, etc.) or any other reasonable set of increments you choose. Then I defined just four possible distributions. Again, if this level of resolution is too low for you, we can always divide the population into 100 increments and 100 possible distributions or even more. But the same principles will apply. Exhibit 10.8 shows these four increments and their probabilities according to four possible types of distributions.

Let's suppose I start with a prior probability of 10%, 20%, 40%, and 30%, to distributions A, B, C, and D, respectively. Then we start drawing one sample at a time. I won't go into as much detail here as I did with some previous examples, but it's still the same concept and you can see the Chapter 10 downloads at www.howtomeasureanything.com.

With each individual item sampled—starting even with the first one— we slightly reduce our uncertainty about which distribution we are drawing from. The chart in Exhibit 10.9 shows how the probability of each distribution changes with each sample. At first, all of the distributions are

Exhibit 10.9 Chance of Each Population Distribution Based on Example of Sampling

still potential candidates. After just 10, two of the possible distributions become virtually impossible (A and C). In this hypothetical example, after a sample of n = 20 or so, it's clear that we've been drawing from distribution B. Of course, this represents one particular simulation of samples. Since these are random samples, we could have had some different results and zeroing in on the right distribution could have happened faster or slower—but the right distribution will emerge eventually.

Since we are computing the probability of a particular population distribution, we could also update our estimate of the mean, median, standard deviation, or any other population parameter we like. If we make a much higher-resolution Bayesian range calculation sheet—with far more distributions and far more increments per distribution—we can still use other strategies to keep it simple. Instead of assigning a probability to each distribution manually as we did here, we could, for example, assume both the distributions and our uncertainties about them are normal distributions. We can then assign probabilities to a set of distributions using a range of means and a range of standard deviations. I might define a set of all of the normal distributions with a mean of 50 to 150, using increments of 10 and standard deviations of 10 to 30, using increments of 5. This would be 77 individual distributions (counting the first and last values in each set of increments). I could then say that my 90% CI for the means is 70 to 130 and that my 90% CI for standard deviations is 10 to 25. Now (using a much bigger spreadsheet to handle all these possibilities), we can start a Bayesian sampling of ranges which, as before, starts to reduce uncertainty even on the first sample.

A technique like this could be applied to virtually any other measurement problem you like. Bayesian methods can be used for controlled experiments and regression models. They can be used in catch-recatch, spot sampling, clustered sampling, or any other sampling method you like. If you have a tolerance for generating lots of combinations of fine-resolution problems in a big spreadsheet (or don't mind learning R), there is no limit to the application of Bayesian methods. Readers may like to challenge themselves to produce such tools without additional guidance but, if additional guidance is needed, check www.howtomeasureanything.com for an additional example.

THE LESSONS OF BAYES

Although it may seem cumbersome at first, Bayes' theorem is one of the most powerful measurement tools at our disposal. It is the way it reframes the measurement question that makes it so useful. Given a particular observation, it may seem more obvious to frame a measurement by asking the question, "What can I conclude from this observation?" or, in probabilistic terms, "What is the probability X is true, given my observation?" But Bayes showed us that we could, instead, start with the question, "What is the probability of this observation if X were true?" The second form of the question is useful because the answer is often more straightforward and it leads to the answer to the first question. It also forces us to think about the probability of different observations given a particular hypothesis and what that means for interpreting an observation.

Taken to its logical conclusion, this tool offers a rebuttal to a list of common objections to the possibility of a measurement. Skeptics of a measurement often claim that something is immeasurable because they can imagine all sorts of potential errors in a measurement (whether or not they even attempted the measurement yet). Or, if not errors, they imagine potentially ambiguous, inconclusive results or the possibility of missing observations. They would then assume that because errors or inconclusive results are possible, the proposed observation has no bearing on the measurement.

Bayes does not let the measurement skeptic off the hook that easily. These objections are simply a misunderstanding of the methods of measurement—one of the three categories of misunderstandings (mentioned in Chapter 3) that led some to believe there are such things as "immeasurable." When we apply Bayes in detail, we find that the conditions that would make an observation meaningless are not so easy to achieve as long as the observation—or even the lack of it—has *something* to do with the thing being measured.

To get a better understanding of these problems, let's consider four common claims which, while seemingly very different, all boil down to the same misunderstandings about conditional probabilities and Bayes. These statements have been made by experts and layman at many levels which go unchallenged and which are fundamentally statements about conditional probabilities. Politicians, armchair statisticians, and even professional scientists have uttered them.

Myth 1: Absence of Evidence

"Absence of evidence is not evidence of absence" has been said before but perhaps the most famous use of the phrase was when then-Secretary of Defense Donald Rumsfeld was making the case for military action in Iraq in 2002.[6] Remember that the main case presented to the public for invading Iraq was the threat of weapons of mass destruction (WMD). Conclusive evidence had not been found after multiple inspections and various intelligence leads were assessed. Of course, finding actual WMD would be conclusive evidence that Iraq possessed WMD. However, the phrase "Absence of evidence is not evidence of absence" assumes that not finding WMD after several inspections would have no bearing on the previously assessed risk.

Note that I'm not just making a judgment based on 20/20 hindsight with this particular decision in history. Of course, the inspections were problematic and there was evidence that Saddam Hussein had used chemical weapons previously on his own countrymen. So it is not irrational to consider it possible that Hussein had WMD. I'm asking the more general question: Is it really ever true that the absence of evidence is not evidence of absence?

Certainly, absence of evidence is not *proof* of absence, but that's not what this famous phrase states. What we care about is uncertainty reduction for decisions and if something can reduce our uncertainty, it suffices as evidence. What we want to do is determine whether the probability of absence is any different at all if we haven't found evidence.

First, I propose considering only the most conclusive evidence: that WMD are actually found. Absence of evidence would seem to mean the absence of *any* evidence, including finding actual WMD. Now, let's take as a given that if inspections had found actual WMD, then that would be conclusive proof that Iraq possessed WMD. Also, if WMD were not there, then it would be impossible to find WMD. Let's write out this issue using the language of probability. It should be obvious that:

P(Find|Absent) = 0 and P(Absent|Find) = 0

Likewise, P(~Find|Absent) = 1 and P(~Absent|Find) = 1

What we want to know is the probability of absence given a lack of finding WMD after a few inspections and whether that is different than the probability of absence without even having conducted the WMD inspections at all. Given Bayes, we can write the probability of absence of WMD given a lack of finding any WMD as:

P(Absent|Find) = P(Absent)P(~Find|Absent)/P(~Find)

Since we've established that P(~Find|Absent) = 1 then we can show

P(Absent|~Find) = P(Absent)/P(~Find)

Clearly, if we already knew that the probability of not finding WMD after inspections is 1, then we can substitute P(~Find) with a 1 in the equation above and get P(Absent|~Find) = P(Absent). Otherwise, it should then be obvious that if P(~Find) < 1, then in order to get this equation to work out it needs to be the case that:

P(Absent|~Find) > P(Absent)

We can also get to the same conclusion by a different approach. Just by using Rule 4, we can write that:

$$P(Absent) = P(Absent|Find)P(Find) + P(Absent|\sim Find)P(\sim Find)$$

Here, we are stating the initial probability of absence is a weighted average of the conditional probabilities given that we find WMD and given that we don't find WMD. If finding WMD makes the probability of absence zero, then not finding them would have to be a conditional probability higher than P(Absent) in order for the equation to work out right. Remember, we've already established that P(Absent|Find) = 0. This reduces the equation above:

$$P(Absent) = P(Absent|\sim Find)P(\sim Find)$$

As long as we didn't already know we wouldn't find WMD (i.e., P(~Find) = 1), then the probability of absence changed when we didn't find WMD. This is the same equation that led us to P(Absent|~Find)>P(Absent) earlier. So, contrary to the secretary's statement, absence of evidence *is* evidence of absence (of course, just not proof of absence).

Myth 2: Correlation Is Not Evidence of Causation

Another common claim we can investigate is "Correlation is not evidence of causation." I already mentioned in Chapter 9 that "Correlation is not proof of causation" is a perfectly valid point but that claiming correlation does not constitute even evidence is a fallacy. Sometimes it is said in published scientific journals but, even then, without being challenged. In one case I found, it was boldly asserted in the article's title itself—"Confusion over Antibiotic Resistance: Ecological Correlation Is Not Evidence of Causation"—and published in a respected journal.[7] Even when the claim is made so predominantly in the article, no reviewers challenged this claim (or at least not vociferously enough to keep it from being published with that language).

So let's investigate this a bit further using the same tools we just applied to our previous common, unchallenged, misconception. We can certainly agree that correlation alone does not necessarily prove causation. But it should be obvious that if there is no correlation, then there can't be causation. Also, if there is causation, there must be correlation. In other words:

$$P(Cause|\sim Corr) = 0 \text{ and } P(Corr|Cause) = 1$$

In fact, one of these statements can prove the other. Based on our Rule 3 from probability rules, we can also say:

$$P(\sim Corr|Cause) = 1 - P(Corr|Cause)$$

Using Bayes we can say:

P(Cause|Corr) = P(Cause) P(Corr|Cause)/P(Corr)

Since we've established that P(Corr|Cause) = 1, then:

P(Cause|Corr) = P(Cause)/P(Corr)

As we showed with the claim about absence of evidence, as long as P(Corr) isn't 1, then:

P(Cause|Corr) > P(Cause)

So, correlation does at least increase the probability of causation. Another common and unchallenged statement turns out to be false.

Myth 3: Ambiguous Results Tell Us Nothing

It is sometimes said of a medical test or some study that one result would confirm some claim but the alternative result tells us nothing. The earliest example I could find of this in scientific literature was a reference to using microscopes in the diagnosis of tuberculosis: "A positive result with a microscope is evidence of the disease . . . but a negative result is not evidence either way." This is simply the "Absence of evidence is not evidence of absence" claim in another form.

From the previous two proofs, the reader should see a pattern in how I'm addressing these claims. Even when observations are seemingly ambiguous or incomplete, it can be informative. For any claim X, a conclusive observation would make X certainly true—in other words P(X|Conclusive) = 1. If there is a possible conclusive result, then the inconclusive result must at least change the probability. Rule 4 tells us that:

P(X) = P(X|Conclusive)P(Conclusive) +
       P(X|Inconclusive)P(Inconclusive)

As we already saw in the previous examples, if we substitute P(X|Conclusive) with a value of "1," then we end up with P(X) > P(X|Inconclusive) in order for Rule 4 to add up correctly. Don't get me wrong: I'm not referring to situations where we fail to find supporting evidence as a result of *not even looking* for evidence. In that case, P(X) should remain unchanged. But if looking for evidence could have either of just those two results—supporting or simply "not supporting"—then either result changes the probability of X.

Having said that, it is possible to set up situations where the lack of a conclusive result doesn't change. We could, for example, have three possible outcomes—confirming (positive), ambiguous, disconfirming (negative)—and where the probability of the confirming and disconfirming results are exactly equal to each other. But these special cases seem hard to find in the real world.

Myth 4: "This *Alone* Tells Me Nothing"

I sometimes hear professionals say, "This alone tells me nothing . . . I have to know many other things before I can make a judgment." I've heard this in reference to assessing the success of movies, evaluating operational risks, or predicting the success of new products. Again, this is probably just another form of the same misconceptions already mentioned. If something helps a judgment when considered among many other variables, then it probably tells you something even in isolation.

Suppose you needed to assess the probability that a new product will sell more than $10 million in the first year of sales, you determine that in order to make an informed decision, you need to know what product line it is in, how it will be marketed, what its price will be, and the general growth for demand in the industry. You are then told that only information about the product line will be available at the time you need to make the assessment. The price isn't set yet, nor is the marketing strategy and certainly we can't know exactly how to predict broader economic trends. You might say that based on the product line alone, you can't assess a probability.

Actually, you can always assess a base rate probability even if all you knew were that this was a product to be proposed in your firm. Imagine a set of potential products and one is selected at random without being revealed to you. Apply the equivalent bet from Chapter 5 and you will determine a probability of $10 million in sales in the first year based on no other information than it is one of the proposed products.

Now consider that the probability you assigned must have been a weighted average of different product lines. Each of those product lines could be considered along with all the combinations of other variables one would like to include. But if knowing the product line matters at all, there must be at least some combinations of all the variables where, if only the product line were different, the estimate of probability would be different. Think of all of the possible combinations of price, marketing strategy, and growth in market demand. With each combination of these other three variables, think about what your judgment would be with each possible product line. Some of them must be different when the product line is changed. If not, the product line is information in *neither* the aggregate with all the other variables nor in isolation. If some cases do exist where product line changes the probability, then the product line must tell you something in isolation.

Think of it like this: If you knew nothing of my health other than that I smoked, would you assign a different 90% CI to my lifespan than if you only knew that I didn't smoke? I can see someone saying, "Yes, but there are so many other factors that affect your life span." True enough. But which version of me would you bet money on living longer?

Notes

1. David M. Grether and Mahmoud A. El-Gamal, "Are People Bayesian?: Uncovering Behavioral Strategies," *Social Science Working Paper 919*, California Institute of Technology (1995).
2. Maya Bar-Hillel, "The Base-Rate Fallacy in Probability Judgments," *Acta Psychologica* 44 (1980): 211–233.
3. D. Lyon and P. Slovic, "Dominance of Accuracy Information and Neglect of Base Rates in Probability Estimation," *Acta Psychologica* 40 (1976): 287–298.
4. A. K. Barbey and S. A. Sloman, "Base-Rate Respect: From Ecological Rationality to Dual Processes," *Behavioral and Brain Sciences* 30 (2007): 241–297.
5. T. DeMarco, *Peopleware: Productive Projects and Teams,* 2nd ed. (New York: Dorset House Publishing Company, February 1, 1999).
6. U.S. Department of Defense. *DoD News Briefing—Secretary Rumsfeld and General Myers* (Washington, DC: Federal News Service, 2002).
7. Louis A. Cox and Randall S. Singer, "Confusion over Antibiotic Resistance: Ecological Correlation Is Not Evidence of Causation," *Foodborne Pathogens and Disease* 9, no. 8 (2012): 776.

A Purely Philosophical Interlude #5

Are Priors a Problem?

The main objection some will have to the use of prior probabilities is that it is subjective. There are multiple problems with that objection.

First, the alternative methods that manage to avoid subjective prior probabilities still do not avoid subjectivity. The significance level discussed in the previous chapter was invented in an attempt to avoid issues like subjective priors. But, as we saw, a significance level is just another subjective and entirely arbitrary choice. It simply substitutes one type of subjectivity for another.

Second, as we saw, priors are the only way to get to the question we really need to answer. We want to know P(Claim | Observations). Every attempt to avoid any priors always forces us to end up answering a different question like P(Observations | ~Claim).

Third, the assumption of total ignorance prior to any observation is not only just another subjective position, it is almost certainly false. In other words, in order to avoid making statements they don't feel are objective, the skeptics of subjective priors inevitably end up choosing the one position that can't usually be true.

Finally, as we saw in Chapter 5, even the performance of subjective estimators can be objectively measured. In total, our 900-plus different subjects, each taking multiple calibration exercises with 10 to 20 questions each, have provided us with well over 100,000 total data points for measuring the performance of subjective estimates. Philip Tetlock (first mentioned in Chapter 3) tracked 82,000 subjective estimates of real-world events. Each of these is more data than the typical phase III drug trial that any major pharmaceutical company is required to employ. The research of Grether and El-Gamal, Armstrong and MacGregor, Brunswik, Dawes, and others mentioned in this book show how subjective estimates can be objectively tested and even improved. Given all of this data, the performance of the human expert as an "instrument" is much better understood than it was at the beginning of the twentieth century when some statisticians were attempting to create methods to avoid using the human expert as an instrument.

Note that there is no rule in statistics that specifically excludes particular instruments based on whether they are mechanical, electronic, or even biological and intelligent. All measurement instruments have measurable errors including random errors, systemic errors, and even occasional outliers. The difference in these errors among different types of instruments is merely a matter of degree. Consider that conventional statistical methods avoiding subjective priors are applied in the social sciences and they are actually measuring issues related to the subjective opinions of human subjects. Apparently, even to the skeptics of priors, subjectivity is a valid subject of "objective" study.

Sometimes the objections are not so much about whether subjective priors may be used, but whether there is a *scientific consensus* on the topic. Note that consensus is an entirely invented requirement that, like the imagined "requirement" that instruments cannot be sentient biological entities, appears nowhere in the mathematics of statistics. Furthermore, if there is no consensus, artificial requirements like significance levels only brush that problem under the rug. Decision makers may choose to use consensus if they have it but consensus isn't required. If a decision maker believes that one strategy has a higher probability of success with the same payoff as another strategy, then it would be irrational for that decision maker to prefer the second strategy. However, if collective opinions are sought, there is always a way to determine an aggregate probability even if there is not a consensus. In Chapter 13, we discuss how a tool known as "prediction markets" does just that and how they add even more data points to the measure of humans as a measurement instrument.

## PART IV

Beyond the Basics

## CHAPTER 11

Preference and Attitudes: The Softer Side of Measurement

The brand damage example in Chapter 10 is one instance of a large set of subjective valuation problems. The term "subjective valuation" can be considered redundant because, when it comes to value, what does "objective" really mean? Is the value of a pound of gold "objective" just because that is the market value? Not really. The market value itself is the result of a large number of people making subjective valuations.

It's not uncommon for managers to feel that concepts such as "quality," "image," or "value" are immeasurable. In some cases, this is because they can't find what they feel to be "objective" estimates of these quantities. But that is simply a mistake of expectations. All quality assessment problems—public image, brand value, and the like—are about human preferences. In that sense, human preferences are the only source of measurement. If that means such a measurement is subjective, then that is simply the nature of the measurement. It's not a physical feature of any object. It is only how humans make choices about that thing. Once we accept this class of measurements as measurements of human choices alone, then our only question is how to observe these choices.

OBSERVING OPINIONS, VALUES, AND THE PURSUIT OF HAPPINESS

Broadly, there are two ways to observe preferences: what people say and what people do. *Stated* preferences are those that individuals will say they prefer. *Revealed* preferences are those that individuals display by their actual behaviors. Either type of preference can significantly reduce uncertainty, but revealed preferences are usually, as you might expect, more revealing.

Measuring preferences, attitudes, and values are part of the field of psychometrics. This field also includes the measure of personality, aptitudes, knowledge, and anything else a psychologist might want to measure about a person. Among a psychometrician's measurement tools are questionnaires used to survey these features of people.

If we use a questionnaire to ask people what they think, believe, or prefer, then we are making an observation where the statistical analysis is no different from how we analyze "objective" physical features of the universe (which are just as likely to fool us as humans; the controls are just different). We simply sample a group of people and ask them some specific questions. The form of these questions falls in one of a few major categories. Psychometricians use an even more detailed and finely differentiated set of categories, but four types are good enough for beginners:

1. *The Likert scale.* Respondents are asked to choose where they fall on a range of possible feelings about a thing, generally in the form of "strongly dislike," "dislike," "strongly like," "strongly disagree," and "strongly agree."
2. *Multiple choice.* Respondents are asked to pick from mutually exclusive sets, such as "Republican, Democrat, Independent, other."
3. *Rank order.* Respondents are asked to rank order several items. Example: "Rank the following eight activities from least preferred (1) to most preferred (8)."
4. *Open ended.* Respondents are asked to simply write out a response in any way they like. Example: "Was there anything you were dissatisfied with about our customer service?"

Psychometricians often refer to the questionnaire itself as an instrument. The words "survey" or "poll" may sometimes be used to mean a set of questionnaires given as a random sample as part of a measurement. It is also not uncommon to use the word survey to refer to a questionnaire—as in "please take this survey/poll." A person who participates in a survey by answering a questionnaire is called a respondent. A poll or survey may be further qualified as an opinion poll or opinion survey to differentiate them from surveys that ask questions about objective personal data, such as income.

Questionnaires are designed to minimize or control for a class of biases called "response bias," a problem unique to this type of measurement instrument. Response bias occurs when a questionnaire, intentionally or not, affects respondents' answers in a way that does not reflect their true attitudes. If the bias is done deliberately, the survey designer is angling for a specific response (e.g., "Do you oppose the criminal negligence of

Governor . . . ?"), but questionnaires can be biased unintentionally. Here are five simple strategies for avoiding response bias:

1. *Keep the question precise and short.* Wordy questions are more likely to confuse.
2. *Avoid loaded terms.* A "loaded term" is a word with a positive or negative connotation, which the survey designer may not even be aware of, that affects answers. Asking people if they support the "liberal" policies of a particular politician is an example of a question with a loaded term. (It's also a good example of a highly imprecise question if it mentions no specific policies.)
3. *Avoid leading questions.* A "leading question" is worded in such a way that it tells the respondent which particular answer is expected. Example: "Should the underpaid, overworked sanitation workers of Cleveland get pay raises?" Sometimes leading questions are not deliberate. Like loaded terms, the easiest safeguard against unintended leading questions is having a second or third person look the questions over. The use of intentional leading questions leads me to wonder why anyone is even taking the survey. If they know what answer they want, what "uncertainty reduction" are they expecting from a survey?
4. *Avoid compound questions.* Example: "Do you prefer the seat, steering wheel, and controls of car A or car B?" The respondent doesn't know which question to answer. Break the question into multiple questions.
5. *Reverse questions to avoid response set bias.* A "response set bias" is the tendency of respondents to answer questions (i.e., scales) in a particular direction regardless of content. If you have a series of scales that ask for responses ranging from 1 to 5, make sure 5 is not always the "positive" response (or vice versa). You want to encourage respondents to read and respond to each question and not fall into a pattern of just checking every box in one column.

Of course, directly asking respondents what they prefer, choose, desire, and feel is not the only way to learn about those things. We can also infer a great deal about preferences from observing what people do. In fact, this is generally considered to be a much more reliable measure of people's real opinions and values than just asking them.

If people say they would prefer to spend $20 on charity for orphans instead of the movies but, in reality, they've been to the movies many times in the past year without giving to an orphanage once, then they've revealed a preference different from the one they've stated. Two good indicators of revealed preferences are things people tend to value a lot:

time and money. If you look at how they spend their time and how they spend their money, you can infer quite a lot about their real preferences.

Now, it seems like we've deviated from measuring true "quantities" when survey respondents say they "strongly agree" with statements like "Christmas decorations go up too early in retail stores." But the concepts we've introduced in earlier chapters haven't changed. You have a decision you have to make and if you knew this quantity, you would have less chance of making the wrong decisions. You have a current state of uncertainty about this variable (e.g., the percentage of shoppers who think Christmas decorations go up too early is 50% to 90%), and you have a point where it begins to change the decision (if more than 70% of shoppers strongly agree that decorations go up too early, the mall should curtail plans to put them up even earlier). Based on that information, you compute the value of additional information and you devise a sampling method or some other measurement appropriate to that question at that information value.

There are some very important cautionary points about the use of these methods. For one, the scale itself frames the question in a way that can have a huge effect on the answers. This is called "partition dependence." For example, suppose a survey of firefighters asked how long it would take to put out a fire at various facilities. Suppose that we gave 50 firefighters Questionnaire I and another 50 Questionnaire II. (See Exhibit 11.1.)

Of course, we would expect that the choices for B and C would change with the new scale. But should the scale in Survey II make any difference to how often choice A is used? Choice A is identical between the two questionnaires, yet we would find the frequency of A being chosen would be lower in Survey II than Survey I.[1] In this example, you could avoid partition dependence just by calibrating them and ask for an estimate of the actual quantity. If that was not practical, you might need to use more than one survey to minimize that effect.

Note that methods using scales like this can be legitimate for measuring public opinion but in other cases they are simply half-baked decision

Exhibit 11.1 Partition Dependence Example: How Much Time Will It Take to Put Out a Fire at Building X?

Questionnaire I	Questionnaire II
A: Less than 1 hour	A: Less than 1 hour
B: 1 to 4 hours	B: 1 to 2 hours
C: More than 4 hours	C: 2 to 4 hours
	D: 4 to 8 hours
	E: More than 8 hours

analysis methods. If you want to know something about what the public is thinking, then opinion polls using scale responses can be a useful way to get a stated preference. If, however, you are using a series of scales like this to decide how to spend your budget on big acquisitions, there are a number of other problematic issues (more on this in the next chapter). Yes, we have departed from the type of unit-of-measure–oriented quantities we've focused on up to this point. Whenever we assessed exactly why we cared about a quantity, we generally were able to identify pretty clear units, not Likert scales. But we do have another step we can introduce. We can correlate opinion survey results to other quantities that are unambiguous and much more useful. If you want to measure customer satisfaction, isn't it because you want to stay in business by keeping repeat customers and getting word-of-mouth advertising?

Actually, you can correlate subjective responses to objective measures, and such analysis is done routinely. Some have even applied it to measuring happiness. (See the "Measuring Happiness" inset.) If you can correlate two things to each other, and then if you can correlate one of them to money, you can express both of them in terms of money. And if that seems too difficult, you can even ask them directly, "What are you willing to pay?"

Measuring Happiness

Andrew Oswald, professor of economics at the University of Warwick, produced a method for measuring the value of happiness.[2] He didn't exactly ask people directly how much they were willing to pay for happiness. Instead, he asked them how happy they are according to a Likert scale and then asked them to state their income and a number of other life events, such as recent family deaths, marriages, children born, and so on.

This allowed Oswald to see the change in happiness that would be due to specific life events. He saw how a recent family death decreased happiness or how a promotion increased it. Furthermore, since he was also correlating the effect of income on happiness, he could compute equivalent-income happiness for other life events. He found that a lasting marriage, for example, makes a person just as happy as earning another $100,000 per year. (Since my wife and I just had our 17-year anniversary, I'm about as happy as I would be if I had earned an extra $1.7 million in that same 17-year period without being married. Of course, this is an average, and individuals would vary a lot. So I tell my wife it's probably a low estimate for me, and we can continue to have a happy marriage.)

A WILLINGNESS TO PAY: MEASURING VALUE VIA TRADE-OFFS

To reiterate, *valuation*, by its nature, is a subjective assessment. Even the market value of a stock or real estate is just the result of some subjective judgments of market participants. If people compute the net equity of a company to get an "objective" measure of its value, they have to add up things like the market value of real estate holdings (how much they think someone else would be willing to pay for it), the value of a brand (at best, how much more consumers are willing to pay for a product with said brand), the value of used equipment (again, how much someone else would pay for it), and the like. No matter how "objective" they believe their calculation is, the fundamental unit of measure they deal in—the dollar—is a measure of value.

This is why one way to value most things is to ask people how much they are willing to pay for it or, better yet, to determine how much they *have been* paying for it by looking at past behaviors. The willingness to pay (WTP) method is usually conducted as a random sample survey where people are asked how much they would pay for certain things— usually things that can't be valued in any other way. The method has been used to value avoiding the loss of an endangered species, improvements in public health and the environment, among others.

In 1988, I had my first consulting project as a new employee with Coopers & Lybrand. We were evaluating the printing operations of a financial company to determine whether the company should outsource more printing to a large local printer. The board of directors of the company felt there was an "innate value" on working with businesses in the local community. Plus, the president of the local printer had friends on the board. He asked, "I'm not in the financial services business, why are you in the printing business?" and he was lobbying to get more of the printing outsourced to his firm.

A few skeptics on the board engaged Coopers & Lybrand to evaluate the business sense of this. I was the junior analyst who did all the numbers on this project. I found that not only did it make no business sense to outsource more printing but that, instead, the company should in-source more of it. The company was large enough that it could compete well for skilled printing professionals, it could keep all of its equipment at a high usage rate, and it could negotiate good deals with suppliers. The company already had a highly skilled staff who knew quite a lot about the printing business.

Whether printing should be part of the "core business" of such a company could be argued either way, but the cost-benefit analysis was clearly in favor of keeping what the company did in house and doing even more. There was no doubt the company would have paid more to have this large volume of printing done externally, even after taking into account all employee benefits, equipment maintenance, office space, and everything else. The proposed outsourcing would have cost this company several million dollars per year more than it spent to get the same service and product. Some argued that the company might even get lower-quality service by outsourcing since the large printing staff within the finance company doesn't have any other customer priorities to worry about. The net present value of the proposed outsourcing would have been a worse-than-*negative* $15 million over five years.

So the choice came down to this: Did the company value this printer's friendship and its sense of community support of small businesses by more or less than $15 million? As the junior analyst, I didn't see my role as one of telling the board members how much they should value it; I simply honestly reported the cost of their decision, whatever they chose. If they valued this community friendship (in this particular limited case, anyway) more than $15 million, the financial loss would have been acceptable. If they valued it less, the financial loss would have been unacceptable. In the end, they decided that the gain in this particular friendship and this specific type of "community support" wasn't worth *that* much. They didn't outsource more and even decided to outsource less.

At the time, I referred to this as a type of "art buying" problem. You might think it would be impossible to value a "priceless" piece of art, but if I at least make sure you know the price the artist is asking, you can decide whether the value exceeds the price for yourself. If someone said something Picasso created was "priceless" but nobody could be enticed to spend $10 million for it, then clearly its value is less than that. We didn't attempt to value the friendship exactly, we just made sure the company knew how much it would be paying for it; and then it could make the choice.

A modification of WTP is the Value of a Statistical Life (VSL) method. With the VSL, people are not directly asked how much they value life but rather how much they are willing to pay for incremental reduction in the risk of *their own* death. People routinely make decisions where they, in effect, make a choice between money and a slight reduction in the chance of an early death. You could have spent more on a slightly safer car. Let's say it amounts to an extra $5,000 for a 20% reduction in dying from an automobile collision, which has only, say, a 0.5% chance of causing your death anyway (given how much you drive, where you drive, your driving habits, etc.), resulting in an overall reduction of mortal risk of one-tenth of 1%. If you opted against that choice, you were saying the equivalent of "I prefer keeping $5,000 to a 0.1% lower chance of premature death." In that case, you were valuing your VSL at something less than $5,000/.001, or $5 million (because you declined the expenditure). You could also have spent $1,000 on your deductible for a medical scan that has a 1% chance of picking up a fatal condition that, if detected early, can be prevented. In that case, you opted to take it, implying your VSL was at least

$1,000/.01, or $100,000. We can continue to look at your purchasing decisions for or against a variety of other safety-related products or services and infer how much you value a given reduction of life-threatening risk and, by extrapolation, how much you value your life.

There are some problems with this approach. First, people are pretty bad at assessing their own risk on all sorts of issues, so their choices might not be all that enlightening. Dr. James Hammitt and the Harvard Center for Risk Analysis observed:

> *People are notoriously poor at understanding probabilities, especially the small ones that are relevant to health choices. In a general-population survey, only about 60% of respondents correctly answered the question "Which is a larger chance, 5 in 100,000 or 1 in 10,000?" This "innumeracy" can confound people's thinking about their preferences.*[3]

If people are really that mathematically illiterate, it would be fair to be skeptical about valuations gathered from public surveys. Undeterred by the limited mathematical capacity of some people, Hammitt simply adjusts for it. Respondents who answer questions like these correctly are assessed separately from those who didn't understand these basic concepts of probability and risk.

Second, in addition to the mathematical illiteracy of at least some respondents, those of us who measure such things as the value of life and health have to face a misplaced sense of righteous indignation. Some studies have shown that about 25% of people in environmental value surveys refused to answer on the grounds that "the environment has an absolute right to be protected" regardless of cost.[4] The net effect, of course, is that those very individuals who would probably bring up the average WTP for the environment are abstaining and making the valuation smaller than it otherwise would be.

As first discussed in Chapter 3, these indignations at measurement have no legitimate ethical foundation or, at the very least, reveal a fundamental hypocrisy. Those same individuals have a choice right now to forgo any luxury, no matter how minor, to give charitable donations on behalf of protecting the environment. Right now, they could quit their jobs and work full time as volunteers for Greenpeace. And yet they do not. Their behaviors often don't coincide with their claim of incensed morality at the very idea of the question. Some are equally resistant to the idea of placing a monetary value on a human life, but, again, they don't give up every luxury to donate to charities related to public health.

There may be explanations for this disconnect between their claim that certain things are beyond monetary valuation while making personal choices that appear to put a higher value on personal luxuries, even minor ones. As Hammitt's study (and many others) has shown, a surprisingly large share of the population is so mathematically illiterate that resistance to valuing a human life may be part of a fear of numbers in general. Perhaps for these people, a show of righteous indignation is part of a defense mechanism. Perhaps they feel their "innumeracy" doesn't matter as much if quantification itself is unimportant, or even offensive, especially on issues like these.

Measuring the values related to human happiness, health, and life is a particularly touchy topic. An Internet search of the phrase "being reduced to a number" will produce hundreds or thousands of hits, most of which are an objection to some form of measurement applied in any way to a human being. Modeling the world mathematically is as uniquely a human trait as language or art, but you would rarely find anyone complaining of being "reduced to a poem" or "reduced to a painting."

Granted, these values are highly uncertain and are represented by extremely wide ranges. Yet, surprisingly, the initial wide ranges on these highly contested values are good enough for many purposes. I've done several risk/return analyses of federal government projects where one component of the benefit of the proposed investment was decreased public health risk. In every one, we simply used wide ranges gathered from a variety of VSL or WTP studies. After computing the value of information, rarely did that range, as wide as it was, turn out to be what required further measurement.

For those who would get anxious at the idea of using any monetary value at all for such things, they should think of the alternative: Ignoring the factor effectively treats the value as zero in a business case, which causes an irrational undervaluation of (and lack of sufficient priority for) the effort the business case was trying to argue for. With only one exception in the many cases I worked on did the value of information even guide us to measuring such variables any further. In most cases the real uncertainty was, surprisingly, *not* the value of public safety or welfare. The initial ranges (as wide as they were) turned out to be sufficient, and measurement focused on other uncertain variables.

By the way, the range many government agencies used, based on a variety of VSL and WTP studies, was (at the time I was involved in analysis using these numbers) $2 million to $20 million to avoid one premature death randomly chosen from the population. If you think that's too low, look at how you spend your own money on your own safety. Also look at how you choose to spend money on some luxury in your life—no matter how modest—instead of giving more to AIDS or cancer research. If you really thought each and every human life was worth far, far more than that range, you would already be acting differently. When we examine our own behaviors closely, it's easy to see that only a hypocrite says "Life is priceless."

PUTTING IT ALL ON THE LINE: QUANTIFYING RISK TOLERANCE

One common area where internal trade-offs have to be made to evaluate
something is the tolerance for risk. No one can compute for you how
much risk you or your firm should tolerate, but you can measure it. Like
the VSL approach, it is simply a matter of examining a list of trade-offs—
real or hypothetical—between more reward or lower risk.

For managing financial portfolios, some portfolio managers do exactly
that. In 1990, the Nobel Prize in Economics was given to Harry Markowitz
for Modern Portfolio Theory (MPT). First developed by Markowitz in the
1950s, the theory has since become the basis for most portfolio optimization methods.

Along with other authors, I have criticized some of the assumptions
of MPT (e.g., modeling stock market volatility with normal distributions).
But there are still many useful components. Perhaps the simplest component of MPT is a chart that shows how much risk investors are willing to
accept for a given return. If they are given an investment with a higher
potential return, investors are usually willing to accept a little more risk.
If they are given an investment with much more certainty, they are willing to accept a lower return. This is expressed as a curve on a chart
where risk and return are just barely acceptable. Exhibit 11.2 shows what
someone's investment boundary might look like.

This is a little different from the chart Markowitz used. His risk axis
was really historical volatility of the return on a particular stock (capital
gains or losses as well as dividends). But investments like information

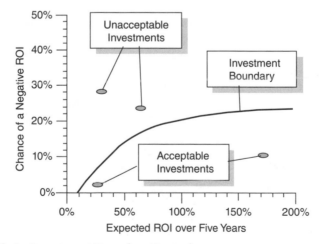

Exhibit 11.2 An Investment Boundary Example

technology (IT) projects or new product development don't typically have "historical volatility." They do, however, share another characteristic of risk that is more fundamental than Markowitz's measure: They have a chance of a loss.

You can quickly construct your own investment boundary or one for your firm. Imagine a large investment for your portfolio. What would a "large"—but not uncommon—investment be: $1 million? $100 million? Whatever it is, pick a size and state it explicitly for the rest of this example.

Now imagine you computed, using a Monte Carlo simulation, the return from thousands of scenarios. The average of all the possible returns is an annual return on investment (ROI) of 50% for five years. But there is enough uncertainty about the ROI that there is a chance it actually will be negative—let's say a 10% chance of a negative ROI. Would you accept this investment? If so, let's raise the risk to 20%; if not, lower it to 5%. Would you accept it now? Repeat the previous step, raising or lowering the risk, until the return and risk are just barely acceptable. This point is on your investment boundary. Now increase the ROI to 100%. What would the risk have to be to make it just barely acceptable? That would be another point on your investment boundary. Finally, suppose you could make an investment that had no chance of a negative return. How low of an average ROI are you willing to accept if there were no chance of a negative return?

Each of these three points is a point on your investment boundary. If you need to, you can fill in the boundary curve with a few more points at higher or lower ROIs. But sooner or later the curve that connects these points will become obvious to you.

In addition to the difference in the risk axis, it's worth mentioning a few additional caveats for those sticklers for MPT. You have to have a different investment boundary for investments of different sizes. Markowitz originally meant the investment curve to be for the entire portfolio, not for individual fixed investments. But I just make three curves—one for a small investment, another for an average-size investment, and one for the largest investment I'm likely to assess—and the interpolation is fairly obvious. (I wrote a simple spreadsheet that interpolates the curve for me, but you can get just as close by visualizing it.)

I often use this simple tool to evaluate each investment independently for a number of reasons. Opportunities for new projects can come at any time in the year while several other projects are in progress. There is rarely an opportunity to "optimize" the entire portfolio as if we could opt in or out of any project at any point.

In 1997 and 1998, I wrote articles in *InformationWeek* and *CIO Magazine* on the investment boundary approach I've been using in the

Applied Information Economics method.[5] I've taken many executives through this exercise, and I've collected dozens of investment boundaries for many different types of organizations. In each case, the investment boundary took between 40 and 90 minutes to create from scratch, regardless of whether there was one decision maker in the room or 20 members of an investment steering committee.

Of all the people who ever participated in those sessions—all policy makers for their organization—not one failed to catch on quickly to the point of the exercise. I also noticed that even when the participants were a steering committee consisting of over a dozen people, the exercise was thoroughly consensus building. Whatever their disagreements were about which project should be of higher priority, they seemed to reach agreement quickly on just how risk averse their organization really was.

Research shows other potential benefits for documenting risk preferences in some quantitative way. As we shall see in Chapter 12, our "preferences" are not as innate as we think. They are influenced by many factors that we would like to think have no bearing on them. For example, one interesting experiment showed that people who were playing a type of betting game were more likely to choose riskier bets if they were shown a fleeting image of a smiling face.[6] As the next chapter shows, our preferences evolve during decision making and we even forget that we didn't used to have those preferences.

Perhaps the most important impact of identifying these boundaries is that working with executives to document the firm's investment boundary seems to make all the executives more accepting of quantitative risk analysis in general. Just as the calibration training seemed to dissipate many imagined problems with using probabilistic analysis, the exercise of quantifying risk aversion this way seemed to dissipate concerns about quantitative risk analysis in executive decision making. The executives felt a sense of ownership in the process, and, when they see a proposed investment plotted against their previously stated boundary, they recognize the meaning and relevance of the finding.

The impact this has on decisions is that risk-adjusted ROI requirements are considerably higher than the typical "hurdle rates"—required minimum ROIs—sometimes used by IT decision makers and chief financial officers. (Hurdle rates are often in the range of 15% to 30%.) This effect increases rapidly as the sizes of proposed projects increase. The typical IT decision maker in the average development environment should require a return *of well over 100%* for the largest projects in the IT portfolio. The risk of cancellation, the uncertainties of benefits, and the risk of interference with operations all contribute to the risk and, therefore, the required return for IT projects. These findings have many consequences for IT decision makers, and I present some of them here.

It is not too bold a statement to say that a software development project is one of the riskiest investments a business makes. For example, the chance of a large software project being canceled increases with project duration. In the 1990s, those projects that exceeded two years of elapsed calendar time in development had a default rate that exceeded the worst rated junk bonds (something over 25%).

Yet most companies that use ROI analysis do not account for this risk. The typical hurdle rates are not adjusted for differences in the risk of IT projects, even though risk should be a huge factor in the decision. If the decision makers looked at the software development investment from a risk/return point of view, they would probably make some very different decisions from those that would be made with fixed hurdle rates.

QUANTIFYING SUBJECTIVE TRADE-OFFS: DEALING WITH MULTIPLE CONFLICTING PREFERENCES

The investment boundary is just one example of the "utility curves" business managers learn about in first-semester economics. Unfortunately, most managers probably thought such classes were purely theoretical discussions with no practical application. But these curves are a perfect tool for defining how much of one thing a manager is willing to trade for another thing. A variety of other types of curves allows decision makers to explicitly define acceptable trade-offs.

"Performance" and "quality" are examples where such explicitly defined trade-offs are useful in the measurement of preferences and value. Terms like "performance" and "quality" are often used with such ambiguity that it is virtually impossible to tell anything more than that more "performance" or "quality" is good, less is bad. As we've seen before, there is no reason for this ambiguity to persist; these terms can be clarified just as easily as any other "intangible."

When clients say they need help measuring performance, I always ask, "What do you mean by 'performance'?" Generally, they provide a list of separate observations they associate with performance, such as "This person gets things done on time" or "She gets lots of positive accolades from our clients." They may also mention factors such as a low error rate in work or a productivity-related measure, such as "error-free modules completed per month." In other words, they don't really have a problem with how to observe performance at all. As one client put it: "I know what to look for, but how do I total all these things?

Does someone who gets work done on time with fewer errors get a higher performance rating than someone who gets more positive feedback from clients?"

This is not really a problem with measurement, then, but a problem of documenting subjective trade-offs. It is a problem of how to tally up lots of different observations into a total "index" of some kind. This is where we can use utility curves to make such tallies consistent. Using them, we can show how we want to make trade-offs similar to these:

- Is a programmer who gets 99% of assignments done on time and 95% error free better than one who gets only 92% done on time but with a 99% error-free rate?
- Is total product quality higher if the defect rate is 15% lower but customer returns are 10% higher?
- Is "strategic alignment" higher if the profit went up by 10% but the "total quality index" went down by 5%?

For each of these examples, we can imagine a chart that shows these trade-offs similar to how we charted trade-off preferences for risk and return. Each point on the same curve is considered equally valuable to every other point on that curve. In the investment boundary example, each point on the curve has the identical value of zero. That is, the risk is just barely acceptable given the return, and the decision maker would be indifferent to the options of acceptance versus rejection of the proposed investment.

We could define multiple other utility curves on the same chart for investments of greater value than zero, each with a constant utility. Sometimes economists refer to utility curves as "iso-utility" curves, meaning "constant or fixed utility." Because a person would be indifferent to any two points on the same utility curve, it is also accepted convention in economics to refer to a utility curve as an indifference curve. In the same way that the elevation lines on a relief map show points of equal altitude, a utility curve is made of points that are all considered to be equally valuable.

Exhibit 11.3 shows a chart with multiple utility curves. It is a hypothetical example of how management might value trade-offs between quality of work and punctuality. This could be used to clarify the requirements for job performance for a programmer, engineer, copy editor, and so on. It is easy to see that if workers A and B had the same amount of on-time work, but A had a higher error-free work rate, A would be considered preferable. The curve clarifies preferences when the choice is not that clear—such as when worker A has better work quality but B has better punctuality.

The curves are drawn by management such that any two points on the same curve are considered equally valuable. For example, management

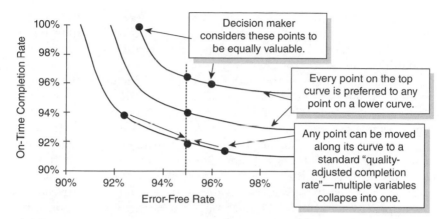

Exhibit 11.3 Hypothetical "Utility Curves"

drew the top curve in a way that indicates it considers a worker who has 96% error-free work and a 96% on-time completion rate to be equal to one who has 93% error-free work and a 100% on-time completion rate. Keep in mind that this is just the hypothetical valuation of some particular manager, not a fixed, standard trade-off. Your preferences would probably be at least a little different.

A series of similar curves was drawn where any point on one curve is considered preferable to any point on a curve below it. Although only a few curves need to be drawn for reference, there are really an infinite number of curves between each of those shown. Management simply draws enough curves to interpolate as necessary.

The utility curve between any two things (e.g., quality and timeliness or risk and return) provides for an interesting way to simplify how we express the value of any point on the chart. Since every point can be moved along its curve without changing its value, all points can be considered equivalent to a position on a single standardized line. In this case, we standardize quality and express the relative value of any point on the chart in terms of quality-adjusted, on-time rate. We collapsed two variables into one by answering the question "A worker with error-free rate X and on-time completion Y is just as good as a 95% error-free rate and _____ on-time completion rate."

The same is routinely done with risk and return. Using a series of risk/return curves, we can take the risk and return of any investment and express it simply as risk-adjusted return. This method of collapsing two different factors can be done no matter how many attributes there are. If, for example, I created utility curves for factor X versus Y and then I create utility curves for Y versus Z, anyone should be able to infer my utility curve for X versus Z. In this manner, several different factors affecting such topics as job performance, evaluating new office locations, choosing a new product line, or anything else can be collapsed into a single standardized measure.

Furthermore, if any of the trade-offs I defined include a trade-off for money, I can monetize the entire set of factors. In the case of evaluating different investments with different risks (e.g., the chance of a negative return, worst-case return, etc.) and different measures of return (e.g., seven-year internal rate of return, first-year return, etc.), it is sometimes useful to collapse all these different considerations into a certain monetary equivalent (CME). The CME of an investment is the fixed and certain dollar amount that the investor considers just as good as the investment.

Suppose, for example, I had to buy you out as a partner in a real estate development firm. I give you the option of buying a vacant lot in the Chicago suburbs for $200,000 to do with as you please or I give you $100,000 cash right now. If you were truly indifferent between these choices, you consider the CME of the vacant lot investment to be $100,000. If you thought buying the lot at that price was a fantastically good deal, your CME for the investment might be, say, $300,000. This means you would consider the option of making this investment—with all its uncertainties and risks—to be just as good as being given $300,000 cash in-hand. You might have defined trade-offs for dozens of variables to come to this conclusion, but the result couldn't be simpler. No matter how complicated the variables and their trade-offs, you will always prefer a $300,000 CME to $100,000 cash.

This is exactly how I've helped many clients prioritize investments where there are a variety of risks and ways of looking at the return. We collapse all the variables into one CME by defining trade-offs between each of the variables and a certain monetary value of some kind. This is a very powerful tool in general for deciding whether 12 different parameters describing quality, for example, could be combined into one monetary quality value. Even though your choices may be subjective, you still can be entirely quantitative about the trade-offs.

Next we'll turn to situations where the trade-offs aren't necessarily just subjective values of decision makers.

KEEPING THE BIG PICTURE IN MIND: PROFIT MAXIMIZATION VERSUS PURELY SUBJECTIVE TRADE-OFFS

Very often, such trade-offs between different factors do not have to be purely subjective. Sometimes it makes more sense to reduce them to a profit or shareholder value maximization problem. A clever analyst should be able to decompose the issues like Fermi and set up a statistically valid spreadsheet model that shows how error rates, punctuality, and the like affect profit. These solutions all boil down to an argument that there is only one important preference—such as profit—and that the importance of factors like productivity and quality are entirely related to how they affect profit. If this is the case, there is no need to make subjective trade-offs between things like performance and customer satisfaction, quality and quantity, or brand image and revenue.

This is really what all business cases should be about. The cases use several variables of costs and benefits to compute some ultimate measure like net present value or return on investment. There is still a subjective choice, but it's a simpler and more fundamental choice—it's the choice of what the ultimate goal to strive for should really be. If you can get agreement on what the ultimate goal should be, the trade-offs between different indicators of performance (or, for that matter, quality, value, effectiveness, etc.) might not be subjective at all. For example, the fact that a $1 million cost reduction in one area is just as preferable as a $1 million reduction in another is not really a subjective trade-off, because they both affect profit identically. Here are three more examples of how people in some very different industries defined some form of "performance" as a quantifiable contribution to some ultimate goal.

1. Tom Bakewell of St. Louis, Missouri, is a management consultant who specializes in measuring performance in colleges and universities. In this environment, Bakewell notes, "People have said for decades that you can't measure performance." Bakewell argues that the financial health of the institution—or, at least, the avoidance of financial ruin—is the ultimate measure struggling colleges should stay focused on. He computes a type of financial ratio for each program, department, or professor; compares them to other institutions; and ranks them in this manner. Some would argue that this calculation misses the subtle "qualitative" performance issues of a professor's performance, but Bakewell sees his measurement philosophy as a matter of necessity: "When I get called in, they've played all the games and the place is in a financial crisis. They explain why they can't change. They've cut everywhere but their main cost, which is labor." This pragmatic view is inevitably enlightening. Bakewell observes: "Generally, they usually know who isn't productive, but sometimes they are surprised."

2. Paul Strassmann, the guru of chief information officers, computes a "return on management" by dividing "management value added" by the salaries, bonuses, and benefits of management.[7] He computes management value added by subtracting from revenue the costs of

purchases, taxes, money, and a few other items he believes to be outside of what management controls. Strassmann argues that management value added ends up as a number (expressed in dollars per year) that management policy directly affects. Even if you take issue with precisely what Strassman subtracts to get management value added from revenue, the philosophy is sound: The value of management must show up in the financial performance of the firm.

3. Billy Bean, the manager of the Oakland A's baseball team, decided to throw out traditional measures of performance for baseball players. The most important offensive measure of a player was simply the chance of not getting an out. Likewise, defensive measures were a sort of "out production." Each of these contributed to the ultimate measure, which was the contribution a player made to the chance of the team winning a game relative to his salary. At a team level, this converts into a simple cost per win. By 2002, the Oakland A's were spending only $500,000 per win, while some teams were spending over $3 million per win.[8]

In each of these cases, the decision makers probably had to change their thinking about what performance really means. The methods proposed by Bakewell, Strassmann, and Bean probably met resistance from those who want performance to be a more qualitative measure. Detractors would insist that some methods are too simple and leave out too many important factors. But what does performance mean if not a quantifiable contribution to the ultimate goals of the organization? How can performance be high if value contributed relative to cost is low? As we've seen many times already, clarification of what is being measured turns out to be key. So, whatever you really mean by "performance" (or, for that matter, productivity, quality, etc.), any thorough clarification of its real meaning might guide you to something more like these three examples.

Notes

1. K. E. See, C. R. Fox, and Y. Rottenstreich, "Between Ignorance and Truth: Partition Dependence and Learning in Judgment under Uncertainty," *Journal of Experimental Psychology: Learning, Memory and Cognition* 32 (2006): 1385–1402.

2. Andrew Oswald, "Happiness and Economic Performance," *Economic Journal* 107 (1997): 1815–1831.

3. James Hammitt, "Valuing Health: Quality-Adjusted Life Years or Willingness to Pay?" *Risk in Perspective*, Harvard Center for Risk Analysis, March 2003; J. K. Hammitt and J. D. Graham, "Willingness to Pay for Health Protection: Inadequate Sensitivity to Probability?" *Journal of Risk and Uncertainty* 18, no. 1 (1999): 33–62.

4. Douglas Hubbard, "Risk vs. Return," *Information Week*, June 30, 1997.
5. Douglas Hubbard, "Hurdling Risk," *CIO*, June 15, 1998.
6. "Cheery Traders May Encourage Risk Taking," *New Scientist*, April 7, 2009.
7. Paul A. Strassmann, *The Business Value of Computers: An Executive Guide* (New Canaan, CT: Information Economics Press, 1990).
8. Michael Lewis, *MoneyBall* (New York: W. W. Norton & Company, 2003).

CHAPTER 12

The Ultimate Measurement Instrument: Human Judges

The human mind does have some remarkable advantages over the typical mechanical measurement instrument. It has a unique ability to assess complex and ambiguous situations where other measurement instruments would be useless. Tasks such as recognizing one face or voice in a crowd pose great challenges for software developers (although progress has been made) but are trivial for a five-year-old. And we are a very long way from developing an artificial intelligence that can write a critical review of a movie or business plan. In fact, the human mind is a great tool for genuinely objective measurement. Or, rather, it would be if it wasn't for a daunting list of common human biases and fallacies.

It's no revelation that the human mind is not a purely rational calculating machine. It is a complex system that seems to comprehend and adapt to its environment with an array of simplifying rules. Nearly all of these rules prefer simplicity over rationality, and many even contradict each other. Those that are not quite rational but perhaps not a bad rule of thumb are called "heuristics." Those that utterly fly in the face of reason are called "fallacies."

If we have any hope of using the human mind as a measurement instrument, we need to find a way to exploit its strengths while adjusting for its errors. In the same way that calibration of probabilities can offset the human tendency for overconfidence, there are methods that can offset other types of human judgment errors and biases. These methods work particularly well on any estimation problem where humans are required to make a large number of judgments on similar issues. Examples include estimating costs of new construction projects, the market potential for new products, and employee evaluations. It might be very difficult to consider all the qualitative factors in these measurements without using human judgment, but humans need a little help.

HOMO ABSURDUS: THE WEIRD REASONS BEHIND OUR DECISIONS

The types of biases mentioned in Chapter 8 are just one broad category of measurement errors. They deal with errors in observations in an attempt to do a random sample or controlled experiment. But if we are trying to measure a thing by asking a human expert to estimate it, we have to deal with another category of problems: cognitive biases. We already discussed one such example regarding the issue of statistical overconfidence, but there are more. Some of the more striking biases in human judgment follow.

- *Anchoring.* Anchoring is a cognitive bias that was discussed in Chapter 5 on calibration, but it's worth going into a little further. It turns out that simply thinking of one number affects the value of a subsequent estimate *even on a completely unrelated issue.* In one experiment, the previously mentioned research team of Amos Tversky and 2002 Economics Nobel Prize winner Daniel Kahneman asked subjects about the percentage of member nations in the United Nations that were African. One group of subjects was asked whether it was more than 10%, and a second group was asked whether it was more than 65%. Both groups were told that the percentage in the "Is it more than . . . ?" question was randomly generated. (In fact, it was not.) Then each group was asked to estimate how much it thought the percentage was. The group that was first asked if it was more than 10% gave an average answer of 25%. The group that was asked if it was more than 65% gave an average answer of 45%. Even though the subjects believed that the percentage in the previous question was randomly selected, the percentage affected their answers. In a later experiment, Kahneman showed that the number subjects anchor on didn't even have to be related to the same topic. He asked subjects to write down the last four digits of their Social Security number and to estimate the number of physicians in New York City. Remarkably, Kahneman found a correlation of 0.4 between the subjects' estimate of the number of physicians and the last four digits of their Social Security number. Although this is a modest correlation, it is much higher than can be attributed to pure chance.
- *Halo/horns effect.* If people first see one attribute that predisposes them to favor or disfavor one alternative, they are more likely to interpret additional subsequent information in a way that supports their conclusion, regardless of what the additional information is. For example, if you initially have a positive impression of a person, you are likely to interpret additional information about that person in a positive light (the halo effect). Likewise, an initially negative

impression has the opposite effect (the horns effect). This effect occurs even when the initially perceived positive or negative attribute should be unrelated to subsequent evaluations. An experiment conducted by Robert Kaplan of San Diego State University shows how physical attractiveness causes graders to give essay writers better evaluations on their essays.[1] Subjects were asked to grade an essay written by a student. A photograph of the student was provided with the essay. The grade given for the essay correlated strongly with a subjective attractiveness scale evaluated by other judges. What is interesting is that all the subjects received the exact same essay, and the photograph attached to it was randomly assigned.

- *Bandwagon bias.* If you need something measured, can you just ask a group of people in a room what they think instead of asking them each separately? Additional errors seem to be introduced with that approach. In 1951, a psychologist named Solomon Asch[2] told a group of test subjects (students) that he was giving them an eye exam. (See Exhibit 12.1.) When asked which line was closest in length to the test line, 99% correctly chose C. But Asch also ran tests where several students in the room were each asked, in turn, to pick the line closest in length. What the test subjects didn't know is that the first few students were part of the experiment and were secretly instructed to choose A, after which the real test subject would pick an answer. When there was one other person in the room who picked the wrong answer, the next person was only 97% likely to choose the right answer. When there were two or three persons choosing the wrong answer before the test subject answered, only 87% and 67%, respectively, chose the right answer. When there was a group reward offered if everyone in the group got it right (adding pressure to conform), *only 53%* of subjects gave the right answer.
- *Emerging preferences.* Once people begin to prefer one alternative, they will actually change their preferences about additional information

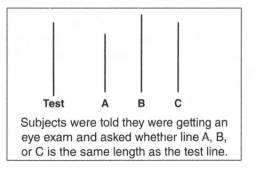

Subjects were told they were getting an eye exam and asked whether line A, B, or C is the same length as the test line.

Exhibit 12.1 Asch Conformity Experiment

in a way that supports the earlier decision. This sounds similar to the halo/horns effect, but it involves not just interpreting new data—it is *actually changing one's preferences* midcourse in the analysis of a decision in a way that supports a forming opinion. For example, if managers prefer project A over project B and, after they made this choice, you then tell them that project A is less risky but much longer than project B, they are more likely to tell you that they always preferred less risk to faster completion times. But if you told them that B is the less risky and longer option, they are more likely to respond that they always preferred faster completion and realization of benefits to a lower risk. This holds true *even if people didn't originally support that decision* and are tricked into believing they did. A version of this is called "choice blindness."[3] As part of an experiment, grocery store customers were asked to taste two jams and state which they preferred. Then as the subjects were distracted with questions from another researcher, the two jars and their labels were switched. The subjects were asked again to taste the jam that they believed was the one they previously preferred. Fully 75% could not detect the switch at all and yet went into great detail explaining why they preferred that jam over the other.

Fortunately, there is something we can do about every one of these irrational effects on the human ability to estimate. Jay Edward Russo at Cornell, a leading researcher in cognitive bias, is developing some solutions. To alleviate the effect of emerging preferences, for example, Russo proposes a simple form of a blind. He has experts explicitly rank the order of preferences before they begin evaluation of individual alternatives. This prevents them from later claiming "I always preferred this feature to that feature" to support their initial decision.

These biases aside, we rely on human experts because, for certain unstructured problems, it is assumed that a human expert is the only possible solution. Consider the problem of selecting movie projects from a set of proposals. I was once involved in creating a statistical model for predicting which kinds of movie projects would likely be box office successes. The people who are paid to review movie projects are typically ex-producers, and they have a hard time imagining how an equation could outperform their judgment. In one particular conversation, I remember a script reviewer talking about the need for his "holistic" analysis of the entire movie project based on his creative judgment and years of experience. In his words, the work was "too complex for a mathematical model."

But when I looked at the past expert predictions of box office success and actual box office receipts, I found *no correlation*. In other words, if I had developed a random number generator that produced the same distribution of numbers as historical box office results, I could have predicted outcomes just as well as the experts. But some historical data had strong correlations. It turns out, for example, that how much the distributor is willing to spend promoting the movie has a modest correlation with box office results. Using a few more variables, we created a model that had a significant correlation with actual box office results. This was a huge improvement over the previous track record of the experts.

Unfortunately, unfounded belief in the "expert" is not limited to just the movie industry. It exists in a wide range of industries for a variety of problems where it is assumed that the expert is the best tool available. How, after all, can all that knowledge be bested by an algorithm? In fact, the idea that messy problems are always best solved by human experts has been debunked for several decades.

In the 1950s, Paul Meehl, the American psychologist mentioned earlier in this book, proposed the (still) heretical notion that expert-based clinical judgments about psychiatric patients might not be as good as simple statistical models. A true skeptic, he collected scores of studies showing such things as historical regression analysis, based on medical records, produced diagnoses and prognoses that matched or beat the judgment of doctors and psychoanalysts. As a developer of the test known as the Minnesota Multiphasic Personality Inventory, Meehl was able to show that his personality tests were better than experts at predicting several behaviors regarding neurological disorders, juvenile delinquency, and addictive behaviors.

In 1954, he stunned the psychiatric profession with his monumental, classic book, *Clinical versus Statistical Prediction*. By then he could cite over 90 studies that challenged the assumed authority of experts. Researchers like Robyn Dawes (1936–2010) of the University of Michigan were inspired to build on this body of research, and every new study that was generated only confirmed Meehl's findings, even as they expanded the scope to include experts outside of clinical diagnosis.[4] The library of studies they compiled included these findings:

- In predicting college freshman GPAs, a simple linear model of high school rank and aptitude tests outperformed experienced admissions staff.
- In predicting the recidivism of criminals, criminal records and prison records outperformed criminologists.
- The academic performance of medical school students was better predicted with simple models based on past academic performance than with interviews with professors.
- In a World War II study of predictions of how well Navy recruits would perform in boot camp, models based on high school records

and aptitude tests outperformed expert interviewers. Even when the interviewers were given the same data, the predictions of performance were best when the expert opinions were ignored.

Confidence in experts is due, in part, to what Dawes called "the illusion of learning." They feel as if their judgments *must* be getting better with time. Dawes believes that this is due, in part, to inaccurate interpretations of probabilistic feedback. Very few experts actually measure their performance over time, and they tend to summarize their memories with anecdotes. They are right sometimes and wrong sometimes, but the anecdotes they remember tend to be more flattering to them. This is also a cause of the previously mentioned overconfidence and why most managers—at least on the first try—tend to perform poorly on calibration tests.

The illusion of learning extends to the analytical methods experts might use. They may feel better about the decisions they make after analyzing a problem, even though that analysis method may not improve the decisions at all. The following studies show that it is possible to use extensive qualitative analysis or even methods called "best practices" without improving outcomes—even though confidence in decisions may increase.

- A study of experts in horse racing found that as they were given more data about horses, their confidence in their prediction about the outcomes of races improved. Those who were given some data performed better than those who were given none. But as the amount of data they were given increased, actual performance began to level off and even degrade. However, their confidence in their predictions continued to go up even after the information load was making the predictions worse.[5]
- Another study shows that, up to a point, seeking input from others about a decision may improve decisions, but beyond that point the decisions actually get slightly worse as the expert collaborates with more people. Yet, again, the confidence in the decision continues to increase even after the decisions have not improved.[6]
- In 1990, one research study showed that as people gathered more information about stock portfolios they became more confident in their portfolio decisions—but their portfolios actually performed worse than those using less information. It appeared that people consistently overreacted to news about the market.[7]
- A 1999 study measured the ability of subjects to detect lies in controlled tests. Some subjects received training in lie detection and some did not. The trained subjects were more confident in judgments

about detecting lies even though they were *worse* than untrained subjects at detecting lies.[8]

The fact that at least some processes apparently increase an expert's confidence without improving (or, in fact, degrading) judgment should give managers pause about adopting any "formal" or "structured" decision analysis method. Research clearly shows that there is room to question many traditional applications of the human expert. And, in addition, we find that experts are overconfident and will increase their confidence with more analysis even when it shows no measurable improvement.

As with the previously discussed experimental and sampling biases, the first level of protection is acknowledging the problem. Imagine how the effects listed here can change expert estimates on project costs, sales, productivity benefits, and the like. Then think of methods such as blinds, control groups given different information, and so on that would offset these effects. Experts may feel as if their estimate could not be affected by these biases, but, then again, they would not be aware of it, anyway. We each might like to think we are less intellectually malleable and have a better "expert track record" than the subjects in these studies. But I find the most gullible people are the ones who insist they are impervious to these effects.

GETTING ORGANIZED: A PERFORMANCE EVALUATION EXAMPLE

You might think that the head of the Information and Decision Sciences Department at the University of Illinois at Chicago (UIC) would come up with a fairly elaborate quantitative method for just about everything. But when Dr. Arkalgud Ramaprasad needed to measure faculty productivity, his approach was much more basic than you might suspect. "Previously they had the 'stack of paper' approach," says Dr. Ram (as he prefers to be called). "The advisory committee would sit around a table covered with files on the faculty and discuss their performance." In no particular order, they would discuss the publications, grants awarded, proposals written, professional awards, and the like of each faculty member and rate them on a scale of 1 to 5. Based on this unstructured approach, they were making important determinations on such things as faculty pay raises.

Dr. Ram felt the error being introduced into the evaluation process was, at this point, mostly one of inconsistently presented data. Almost any improvement in simply organizing and presenting the data in an orderly format would be a benefit. To improve on this situation, he simply organized all the relevant data on faculty performance and presented it in a large matrix. Each row is a faculty member, and each column is a particular category of professional accomplishments (awards, publications, etc.).

Dr. Ram does not attempt to formalize the analysis of these data any further, and he uses an arbitrary five point scale. Evaluations are based on a consensus of the advisory committee, and this approach simply ensures they are looking at the same data. It seemed too simple. When I suggested that the columns of data could at least be part of some validated index or scoring scheme, he replied, "When data is presented this way, they see the difference between them and other faculty instead of focusing on the arbitrary codification. There is a discussion about what the points should be, but there is no discussion about the data." Because previously they were looking at different data, there would have been more error in the evaluations.

This is another useful example of a very productive perspective regarding measurement. Some would (and, no doubt, do) shoot down any attempt to measure faculty productivity because the new method would introduce new errors and would not handle a variety of exceptions. Or, at least, that's what they would claim. (It is just as likely that the concerns voiced by faculty were entirely about how some would fare poorly if their performance was measured.) But Dr. Ram believes that whatever the flaws of the new measurement method might be, it is still superior to how faculty was being measured before. His method may indeed be a reduction in uncertainty and therefore a measurement. As Stevens's taxonomy (Chapter 3) allows, Dr. Ram may be able to say, with some confidence, that person A has better performance than person B. Given the nature of the decisions this evaluation supports (who gets a promotion or raise), that is all that is needed.

My objection to this approach is that it probably would not be difficult to use a more analytical technique and improve the evaluation process even further. Dr. Ram has not addressed any of the cognitive biases we discussed; he has only corrected for the potential noise and error of considering inconsistent data on each faculty member.

Furthermore, we don't really know if this is an improvement since the performance of the method is not measured. How do we know, after all, that this process doesn't simply cause the "illusion of learning" mentioned by Dawes? There is plenty of evidence to suggest that such methods like Dr. Ram's might not be as effective as they are perceived to be. We saw examples earlier that showed that even when experts were provided with "structured data," they performed more poorly than simple statistical models. For this reason, I consider the step of "getting organized" to be a necessary precursor to the rest of the methods we can consider, but not a solution by itself.

SURPRISINGLY SIMPLE LINEAR MODELS

Another approach exists that is not the most theoretically sound or even the most effective solution, but it is simple. If you have to make estimates for a list of similar items, some kind of weighted score is one way to go. If you are trying to estimate the relative "business opportunity" of, say, a list of real estate investments, you could identify a few major factors you consider important, evaluate these factors for each investment, and combine them somehow into an aggregate score. You might identify factors such as location desirability, cost, market growth for that type of real estate, liens, and so on. You might then weight each factor by multiplying it times some number and adding them all up to get a total value.

While I used to categorically dismiss the value of weighted scores as something no better than astrology, subsequent research has convinced me that they may offer some benefit after all. (And any fair researcher should always be able to say that sufficient empirical evidence would change their mind.) Unfortunately, the methods that seem to have some benefits are not usually the ones businesses typically employ.

According to the decision science researcher and author Jay Edward Russo, the efficacy of weighted scores "depends on what you are doing now. People usually have so far to go that even simple methods are a big improvement." Indeed, even the simplest weighted scores might improve on human decision making—once certain errors introduced by the score itself are accounted for.

Robyn Dawes wrote a paper in 1979 titled "The Robust Beauty of Improper Linear Models."[9] Remarkably, he claims: "The weights on these models often don't matter. What you have to know is what to measure, then add." The problems Dawes, Meehl, and other researchers were finding with experts were in the area of unstructured evaluation tasks, such as clinical diagnosis and college admissions. The simple linear model apparently provides enough structure to, in many cases, outperform the human expert.

There are just two clarifications worth making about their claims. First, Dr. Ram's experience with faculty evaluation is consistent with what Russo and Dawes seem to be saying. The previous methods were so riddled with error that organization itself seemed to be a benefit in measurement.

Furthermore, when Dawes is talking about a score, he is actually talking about a normalized z-score (first mentioned in Chapter 9), not an arbitrary ordinal scale. He takes the values for one attribute among all of the evaluated options and creates a normalized distribution for it so that the average is zero and each value is converted to a number of standard deviations above or below the mean (e.g., –1.7, +.5, etc.). He might, for example, take all the publication rankings from Dr. Ram's faculty rating table and go through these five steps:

1. For each attribute column in a table of evaluated options, evaluate them on some ordinal or cardinal scale. Note: Cardinal scales with real units (e.g., cost in dollars, duration in months) are preferred when available for the type of problem being considered.
2. Compute the mean for all of the values in each column.
3. Use the Excel population standard deviation formula =stdevp() to compute a standard deviation for each column.
4. For each value in a column, compute the z-score as $z = (value - mean)/standard\ deviation$.
5. This will result in a score with a mean of 0, a lower bound as low as -2 or -3, and an upper bound as high as $+2$ or $+3$.

One reason Dawes' z-score might avoid the problems of other weighted scoring methods is that it takes care of inadvertent weighting. In a scheme where the score is not converted to z-score, you may happen to use a wider range of values for one attribute than another, effectively changing the weight in a decision. For example, suppose the real estate investments are evaluated on each factor on an arbitrary scale of 1 to 10. But one criterion, location desirability, varies a lot, and you tend to give out scores ranging from 3s to 9s, while on the criterion of market growth, you tend to give very consistent scores of 4s or 5s. The net effect is that even if you think market growth is more important, you end up weighting location higher simply because of arbitrary differences in the size of "units" between different variables. Dawes's method of converting data to a z-score handles this problem.

Although this simple method doesn't directly address any of the cognitive biases we listed, the research by Dawes and Russo seems to indicate that this particular version of weighted scores might benefit decision making, if only a little. Just thinking about the problem this way seems to cause at least a slight uncertainty reduction and improvement in the decisions. However, for big and risky decisions, where the value of information is very high, we can and should get much more sophisticated than merely getting organized and using a weighted score.

HOW TO STANDARDIZE ANY EVALUATION: RASCH MODELS

As I surveyed the wide landscape of statistical methods for this book, I made a point of looking outside of areas I've dealt with before. One of the areas that was new to me was the set of methods used in educational testing, which included some almost unheard of in other fields of measurement. It was in this field where I found a book with the inclusive-sounding title *Objective Measurement*.[10] The title might lead you to believe such a book would be a comprehensive treatment of the issues of measurement that might be interesting to any astronomer, chemical engineer, or economist. However, this *five-volume work* is only about human performance and education testing.

It's as if you saw an old map titled "Map of the World" that was really a map of a single, remote Pacific island, made by people unaware that they were on just one part of a larger planet. One expert in the educational testing field told me about something he called "invariant comparison"—a feature of measurement he considered so basic that it was simply "measurement fundamentals, statistics 101 stuff." Another said, "It is the backbone of what physicists do." All but one of the several physicists and statisticians I asked later about it said they haven't even heard of it, at least not using that terminology. Apparently, what those in the educational measurement field consider "fundamental" to everyone is just fundamental to themselves. (To be fair, I'm sure some will think the same of a book claiming it teaches how to measure anything.)

Still, there is actually something very interesting to be learned from the educational testing area. The experts in this field deal with all the issues of judging the performance of humans—a large category of measurement problems where businesses can find many examples they label "immeasurable." The concept of invariant comparison deals with a key problem central to many human performance tests, such as the IQ test. "Invariant comparison" is a principle that says if one measurement instrument says A is more than B, then another measurement instrument should give the same answer. The comparison of A and B, in other words, does not vary with the type of measurement instrument used. This might seem so obvious to a physicist that it hardly seems worth mentioning. You would think that if one weight scale says A weighs more than B, another instrument should give the same answer regardless of whether the first instrument is a spring scale and the second is a balance or digital scale. Yet this is exactly what could happen with an IQ test or any other test of human performance. It is possible for one IQ test, having different questions, to give a very different result from another type of IQ test. Therefore, it is possible for Bob to score higher than Sherry on one test and lower on another.

Another version of this problem arises when different human judges have to evaluate a large number of individuals, as in the earlier "unstructured interview" examples provided by Meehl and Dawes. Perhaps there are too many individuals for each judge to evaluate, so the individuals are divided up among the judges, and each person may get a different set of judges. Perhaps one judge evaluates only one aspect of a subject while evaluating different aspects of another person, or different people have to be evaluated on problems with different levels of difficulty.

For example, suppose you wanted to evaluate the proficiency of project managers based on their performance when assigned to various projects. If you have a large number of project managers, you probably have to have several judges, each assigned to a single project manager. The judges, in fact, might be the project managers' immediate superiors (as others are not familiar with the project). The assigned projects, also, probably vary greatly in difficulty. But now suppose all project managers, regardless of their project or whom they reported to, had to compete for the same limited pool of promotions or bonuses. Those assigned to a "hard grader" or a difficult project would be at a disadvantage that had nothing to do with their performance. The comparison of different project managers would not be invariant (i.e., independent) of who judged them or the projects they were judged on. In fact, the overriding determinant of their relative standing among project managers may be related entirely to factors they did not control.

In 1961, a statistician named Georg Rasch developed a solution to this problem.[11] He proposed a method for predicting the chance that a subject would correctly answer a true/false question based on (1) the percentage of other subjects in the population who answered that particular item correctly and (2) the percentage of other questions that the subject answered correctly. Even if test subjects were taking different tests, the performance on a test by a subject who never took it could be predicted with a computable error.

First, Rasch computed the chance that a randomly selected person from the population of test subjects would answer a question correctly. This is simply the percentage of people who answered correctly from those who were given the opportunity to answer the question. This is called the "item difficulty." Rasch then computed the log-odds for that probability. "Log-odds" are simply the natural logarithm of the ratio of the chance of getting the answer right to the chance of getting it wrong. If the item difficulty was 65%, that meant that 35% of people got the answer right and 65% got it wrong. The ratio of getting it right to getting it wrong is .538, and the natural log of this is –0.619. If you like, you can write the Excel formula as:

$$= \ln(P(A) / (1 - P(A))$$

where $P(A)$ is the chance of answering the item correctly.

Rasch then did the same with the chance of that person getting any question right. Since this particular person was getting 82% of the answers right, the subject's log-odds would be ln(.82/.18), or 1.52. Finally, Rasch added these two log-odds together, giving 0.9. To convert this back to a probability, you can write a formula in Excel as:

$$= 1/(1/\exp(.9) + 1)$$

The calculation produces a value of 71%. This means that this subject has a 71% chance of answering that question correctly, given the difficulty of the question and the subject's performance on other questions. Over a large number of questions and/or a large number of test subjects, we would find that when the subject/item chance of being correct is 70%, about 70% of those people got that item correct. Likewise for 90%, 80%, and so on. In a way, Rasch models are just another form of calibration of probabilities.

Mary Lunz of Measurement Research Associates, Inc. in Chicago applied Rasch models to an important public health issue for the American Society of Clinical Pathology. The society's previous pathologist certification process had a large amount of error, which needed to be reduced. Each candidate is assigned one or more cases, and one or more judges evaluate each of their case responses. It is not practical to have each judge evaluate every case, nor can cases be guaranteed to be of equal difficulty.

Previously, the best predictor of who was given certification was simply the judge and the cases the candidates were *randomly* assigned to, not, as we might hope, the proficiency of the candidate. In other words, lenient examiners were very likely to pass incompetent candidates. Lunz computed standard Rasch scores for each judge, case, and candidate for each skill category. Using this approach, it was possible to predict whether a candidate would have passed with an average judge with an average case even if the candidate had a lenient judge and an easy case (or a hard judge and a hard case). Now variance due to judges or case difficulty can be completely removed from consideration in the certification process. None too soon for the general public, I'm sure.

Given what we have covered about Bayesian methods, I might consider using that. Conditional probabilities based on case and judge difficulty could be considered. Note that Rasch and Bayes can give different answers so there is a choice to be made between them. Bayes is more mathematically well-founded and I would use it exclusively only if Rasch lacked empirical evidence of working. But since Rasch has evidence of working and since it seems easy to apply in certain problems, it should be considered a solution if the Bayesian model gets too complex.

Measuring Reading with Rasch

A fascinating application of Rasch statistics is measuring the difficulty of reading text. Jack Stenner, PhD, is president and founder of Meta-Metrics, Inc., and used Rasch models to develop the Lexile Frame-work for assessing reading and writing difficulty and proficiency. This framework integrates the measurement of tests, texts, and students, making universal comparisons in common languages possible in these areas for the first time. With a staff of 65, MetaMetrics has done more in this area than perhaps any other institution, public or private, including:

- All major reading tests report measures in Lexiles. About 20 million U.S. students have reading ability measures in Lexiles.
- The reading difficulty of over 200,000 books and tens of millions of magazine articles is measured in Lexiles.
- The reading curricula of several textbook publishers are structured in Lexiles.
- State and local education institutions are adopting Lexiles rapidly.

A text of 100 Lexiles is first grade, while 1,700-Lexile text is found in Supreme Court decisions, scientific journals, and the like. Meta-Metrics can predict that a 600-Lexile reader will have an average 75% comprehension of a 600-Lexile text. (This book is 1,240 Lexiles.)

REMOVING HUMAN INCONSISTENCY: THE LENS MODEL

In the 1950s, a decision psychology researcher named Egon Brunswik wanted to measure expert decisions statistically.[12] Most of his colleagues were Freudians interested in the hidden decision-making process that experts went through. Brunswik was more interested in describing the decisions they actually made. He said of decision psychologists: "We should be less like geologists and more like cartographers." In other words, they should simply map what can be observed externally and should not be concerned with what he considered hidden internal processes.

With this end in mind, Brunswik began to run experiments where experts would make an estimate of something (say, the admission of a graduate school applicant or the status of a cancerous tumor) based on some data provided to the expert. Brunswik would then take a large number of these expert assessments and find a best-fit regression model. (This is done easily now using the regression tool in Excel, as shown in

Chapter 9.) The result would be a formula with a set of implicit weights used by the decision maker, consciously or unconsciously, to determine what the estimate should be.

Amazingly, he also found that the formula, while simply based on expert judgments and no objective historical data, was better than the expert at making these judgments. In other words, the formula *based only on analysis of expert judgments* would predict better than the expert in such problems as who would do well in graduate school or which tumor was malignant. This became known as the Lens Model.

The Lens Model has been applied in a wide variety of situations including medical prognosis, aircraft identification by naval radar operators, and the chance of business failure based on financial ratios. In each case, the model was just as good as human experts, and in most cases, it was a significant improvement. (See Exhibit 12.2.) My firm has now applied it to forecasts related to military logistics, cybersecurity, estimating movie box office receipts, prioritizing R&D projects, and even in prioritizing agricultural projects in the developing world.

The Lens Model does this by removing the error of judge inconsistency from the evaluations. The evaluations of experts usually vary even in identical situations. As discussed at the beginning of this chapter, human experts can be influenced by a variety of irrelevant factors yet still maintain the illusion of learning and expertise. The linear model of the expert's evaluation, however, gives perfectly consistent valuations.

Fortunately for experts, this seems to indicate that they know *something*. In fact, experts are usually those who identified what factors to

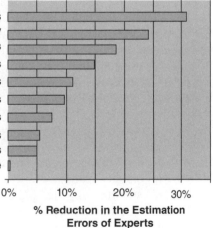

Exhibit 12.2 Effect of Lens Model on Improving Various Types of Estimates

include in the statistical models in the first place. Meehl's findings about the ineffectiveness of experts don't necessarily mean that the experts don't really know anything. But when they are asked to apply their knowledge, they can do so only with a great deal of inconsistency. Furthermore, since the Lens Model is a mathematical expression based on known data inputs, it can be automated and applied to much larger data sets that would be entirely impractical for human judges to assess one by one.

The seven-step process is simple enough. I've modified it somewhat from Brunswik's original approach to account for some other methods (e.g., calibration of probabilities) we've learned about since Brunswik first developed this approach. (See Exhibit 12.3.)

1. Identify the experts who will participate.
2. If they will be assessing a probability or range, calibrate them.
3. Ask them to identify a list of factors relevant to the particular item they will be estimating (e.g., the duration of a software project affects the risk of failure or the income of a loan applicant affects the chance he will repay), but try to keep it down to 10 or fewer factors.
4. Generate a set of scenarios using a combination of values for each of the factors just identified—they can be based on real examples or purely hypothetical. Make 30 to 50 scenarios for each of the judges you are surveying.
5. Ask the experts to provide the relevant estimate for each scenario described.
6. Perform a regression analysis as described in Chapter 9. The independent "X" variables are those given to the judges for consideration. The dependent "Y" variable is the estimate the judge was asked to produce.
7. For each of the columns of data in your scenarios, there will be a coefficient displayed in the output table created by Excel. Pair up each variable with its coefficient, multiply the coefficient by its data item, and then add up all these products for each of the coefficient/variable pairs—just as the section on multiregression analysis in Chapter 9 shows. This is the quantity you are trying to estimate.

This process will produce a table with a series of weights for each of the variables in our model. Since the model has no inconsistency whatsoever, we know that at least some error has been reduced.

We can quickly estimate how much less uncertainty we have with this model by estimating the inconsistency of judges. We can estimate inconsistency by using some duplicate scenarios unknown to the judges. In other words, the seventh scenario in the list may be identical to the twenty-ninth scenario in the list. After looking at a couple of dozen

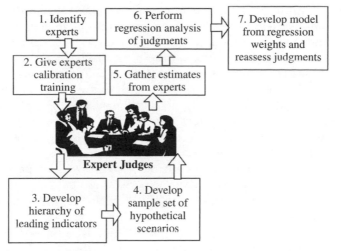

Exhibit 12.3 Lens Model Process

scenarios, experts will forget that they already answered the same situation and often will give a slightly different answer. Thoughtful experts are fairly consistent in their evaluation of scenarios. Still, inconsistency accounts for 10% to 20% of the error in most expert estimates. This error is completely removed by the Lens Method.

Robyn Dawes, the proponent of simple, nonoptimized linear models, agrees that Brunswik's method shows a significant improvement over unaided human judgment but argues that it might not be due to the "optimization" of weights from regression. In published research of four examples, Dawes showed that the Lens Model is only a slight improvement on what he has called "improper" models, where weights are not derived from regression but are all equal or, remarkably, *randomly* assigned.[13]

Dawes concluded that this is the case because, perhaps, the value of experts is simply in identifying factors and deciding whether each factor is "good" or "bad" (affecting whether they would be positive or negative weights), and that the exact magnitude of the weights do not have to be optimized with regression. Dawes's examples may not be representative of Lens Models applied to estimating problems in business,[14] but his findings are still useful, for two reasons.

1. Dawes's own data do show some advantage for optimal linear models over improper models, even if it is only slight.
2. His findings give even further support to the conclusion that some consistent model—with or without optimized weights—is better than human judgment alone.

Still, I find the effort to create optimal models, especially for really big decisions, is easily justified by even a slight improvement over simpler models. And we can often do better than even "optimal" linear models. The regression models I use for business tend to have a few conditional rules, such as "The duration of a project is a differentiating factor only if it is more than a year—all projects less than a year are equally risky." In that sense, the models are not strictly linear, but they get much better correlations than purely linear Lens Models. All of the studies Dawes refers to in his original paper are strictly linear and generally achieve lower correlations than I get with nonlinear models.

I find these conditional rules from two sources: experts' explicit statements and the patterns in their responses. For example, if an expert evaluating the chance that the scope of a software project will be significantly expanded tells me that she doesn't make any distinction among projects less than 12 months long, I won't just use the original "project duration" as a variable. Instead, I might change the variable so that any value less than 12 months is a 1, 13 months is a 2, 14 a 3, and so on. Or, even if the expert didn't tell me that, it might be apparent by looking at her judgments. Suppose we plotted the expert's judgments on "chance of change in requirements" (something significant, say, more than a 25% increase in effort) as a function of "project duration in months," and we saw the chart shown in Exhibit 12.4.

If you see something other than a straight line in these data, you are not alone. A project that takes longer than one year introduces a different set of factors. Perhaps some of the variables matter to the expert more or less depending on the length of the project. A Lens Model that allows for

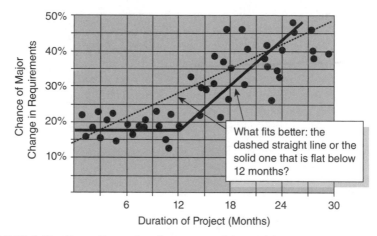

Exhibit 12.4 Nonlinear Example of a Lens Model Variable

such nonlinear conditions not only fits the expert's opinions better; more important, it can fit actual project outcomes better.

I also sometimes find that a variable is a better fit if I use even more elaborate rules. Perhaps the correlation with a variable is best with its logarithm, with its inverse, or by making it part of a product of other variables. Experimentation is encouraged. I generally try several versions of nonlinear variables on the same data, and I usually find one version that stands out as a clear winner. But otherwise, I try to keep the models to relatively few variables and I try to avoid the sin of "overfitting" the model to the data. So don't just invent nonlinear models that fit better. A nonlinear rule should make sense within the context of the problem (e.g., a project that takes twice as long is more than twice as complex, etc.).

It turns out that you can use weighted decision models at many different levels of complexity. If you feel confident in experimenting with nonlinear methods, that's your best shot. If you can't do that but can handle linear regression, do that. If you don't feel comfortable using regression at all, stick with Dawes's equally weighted z-scores. Each method is an improvement on the simpler method, and all improve on unaided experts.

PANACEA OR PLACEBO?: QUESTIONABLE METHODS OF MEASUREMENT

The Big Measurement "Don't"

Above all else, don't use a method that adds more error to the initial estimate.

Some readers might think that, so far, my approach has been to lower the bar for what counts as measurement so much that this change in standards alone makes everything "measurable." I've stated, after all, that in order to count as a measurement, any reduction in uncertainty would suffice. The existence of all sorts of errors in an observation is not an obstacle to measurement as long as the uncertainty is less than it was before.

Even methods that analyze what would normally be thought of as "subjective" still count as measurement (e.g., Rasch and Lens models) if there is overwhelming evidence that such methods really do result in more accurate estimates. But even under these apparently relaxed constraints, I do not count certain methods as proper measurements. At this point, it is time to offer a few caveats and to judiciously apply some brakes as we speed off into several new measurement methods.

The "uncertainty reduction" definition of measurement we have been using definitely makes measurement more feasible on just about everything (since we don't have to worry now about exactitudes). However, that definition is also a hard constraint. If a method doesn't actually result in reduced uncertainty or, worse yet, *adds* uncertainty to a quantity, then it does not suffice as a measurement and has absolutely no economic value to a decision maker. Applying some skepticism in the spirit of Emily Rosa, Paul Meehl, and Robyn Dawes, we should discuss two common measurement methods: the typical cost-benefit analysis and the subjective weighted score.

As I began writing this book, I put out a general solicitation to a large number of my contacts for measurement solutions I could use as case studies. I said I was looking for "interesting examples of difficult or impossible-sounding measurement problems which had clever solutions and, preferably, surprising results that had changed a major decision." There was no shortage of ideas, and I conducted many more phone interviews for case studies than what I eventually included in this book. I did notice, however, that many analysts, consultants, and businesspeople seemed to equate "measure" with "business case." They didn't provide examples of resourceful uses of observations to reduce uncertainty about an unknown quantity. Instead, they were explaining how they made a business-case justification for a pet project.

To be fair, I believe the cost-benefit analysis (CBA) certainly does count as the type of decomposition mentioned in Chapter 8, and it may, by itself, reduce uncertainty without further measurement. Just as Fermi did with his questions, a business case breaks the problem down and, without technically being a measurement based on new observations, reveals something about what you already knew. I also pointed out that in the cases I've assessed in the past couple of decades, decomposition alone was sufficient to reduce uncertainty in only 25% of the high-information-value variables. In most cases where an effort was justified to reduce uncertainty, some empirical observation still was necessary.

In contrast, the examples of measurements so many businesses seem to produce are *only* the decomposition types (i.e., the business case) without any attempt at empirical methods. Every variable was simply the initial estimate—either from a single expert or agreed to by "committee"—and was always a point value with no range to express any uncertainty about the variable. No survey, experiment, or even methods to improve subjective judgments were ever applied or even considered. The same people who enthusiastically submitted a business case as an example of measurement could not, no matter how much I pressed them, think of a single quantity in their CBA that was arrived at after some kind of real-world observation like a survey or experiment.

A very different behavior occurs when the task is to generate exact values for a business case, especially one where the estimator has a stake in the outcome, as opposed to a calibrated estimator providing an initial 90% confidence interval (CI). Sitting in a room, one or more people working on the business case will play a game with each estimate. Forced to choose exact values, no matter how uncertain or arbitrary, the estimators ask: "How much should this value be to be agreeable to others and still be sufficient to prove my (predetermined) point?" It is almost as if the terms "consensus" and "fact" are used as synonyms. The previously discussed Asch experiment on the bandwagon bias is only one problem with this approach.

A different and disturbing trend in management decision making is to develop a type of weighted score where the score and the weight are both subjective scales with arbitrary point values, not z-scores like those Dawes used. Like the simple linear models discussed previously, these methods might ask a project portfolio manager to rate a proposed project in categories such as "strategic alignment," "organizational risk," and so on.

Most of these methods have between 4 and 12 categories of evaluation, but some have over 100. The proposed project is typically given a score of, say, 1 to 5 in each of these categories. The scores in each category are then multiplied by a weighting factor—perhaps also a scale of 1 to 5—which is meant to account for the relative importance of each of the scores categorized. The weighting factors are usually standardized for a given company so that all projects are evaluated by comparable criteria. The adjusted scores are then totaled to give an overall score for the proposed project.

Scores are methods of attempting to express relative worth, preference, and so on, without employing a real unit of measure. Although scoring is fairly called one type of ordinal measurement system we discussed in Chapter 3, I've always considered an arbitrary score to be a sort of measurement wannabe. The problems with this method are one of the key criticisms I make about popular risk assessment methods in my second book *The Failure of Risk Management: Why It's Broken and How to Fix It*. The popular scoring method introduces additional errors for six reasons (these are the reasons I still have reservations about Dr. Ram's faculty evaluation method).

1. Scoring methods tend to ignore problems of partition dependence mentioned in Chapter 11. Arbitrary choices about where to draw the line between different ordinal values—or even the number of ordinal values given—can have a very large effect on responses.
2. Scores are often used for situations where proper quantitative measures are feasible and would be much more enlightening

(e.g., converting a perfectly good return on investment (ROI) to a score or computing risk as a score instead of treating it like an actuary or financial analyst would).

3. Researchers have shown that such ambiguous labels used by such scoring methods don't help the decision maker at all and actually add an error of their own. One issue is that verbal labels or five-point scales are interpreted very differently by those who assess risks and may come to "agreement" without realizing that they have very different conceptions about the underlying risk. This creates what one researcher refers to as "the illusion of communication."[15]

4. Scores can be revealing if they are part of a survey of a large group (e.g., customer satisfaction surveys), but they are much less enlightening when individuals use them to "evaluate" options, strategies, investments, and the like. People are rarely surprised in some way by a set of scores they applied themselves.

5. Scores are merely ordinal, but many users add error when they treat these ordinal scores as a real quantity. As previously explained, a higher ordinal score means "more" but doesn't say how much more. Multiplying and adding ordinal scores to other ordinal scores has consequences users are often not fully aware of. Therefore, the method is likely to have unintended consequences.[16]

6. Ordinal scales add a kind of extreme rounding error called "range compression."[17] When applied to risk analysis, the riskiest item in the "medium" risk category actually can be many times riskier than the least risky item in the same category. Many users of these methods tend to cluster their responses in a way that makes, for example, a five-point scale behave more like a two-point scale—effectively reducing the "resolution" of the method even further and lumping together risks that are, in fact, orders of magnitude different.

It's worth getting a little deeper into how this scoring is different from the z-scores Robyn Dawes used and the weights generated from the Lens Model. Dawes's "improper" linear models and Brunswik's optimized Lens Models use more objective inputs, such as project duration in months for an IT project or grade point average for a graduate-school applicant. None of the inputs was an arbitrary scale of 1 to 5 set by the experts. Also, the weights Dawes and Brunswik used were ratios—not ordinal scales—and Brunswik's were empirically determined. The psychology of how people use such scales is more complicated than it looks. When experts select weights on a scale of 1 to 5, it's not necessarily clear that they interpret a 4 to mean twice as important as a 2. The five-point (or seven-point or whatever) scale adds additional error to the process because of these ambiguities.

The only positive observation we can make about arbitrarily weighted point-scale systems is that apparently managers often have the sense to ignore the results. I found that decision makers were overriding the results from weighted-scoring models so often that there was apparently no evidence that the scores even *changed decisions,* much less improved decisions. This is strange since, in many cases, the managers spent quite a lot of time and effort developing and applying their scoring method.

One of these methods is sometimes used in IT and is misleadingly referred to as "Information Economics."[18] It is represented as objective, structured, and formal, but, in fact, the method is not based on any kind of accepted economic model and cannot truly be called economics at all. Upon closer examination, the name turns out to be entirely a misnomer. The method is more accurately called "subjective and unadjusted weighted scores for IT."

The total score this method produces for a proposed IT system has no meaning in financial terms. The definitions of the different scores in a category and the weight of a category are not tied to any scientific approach, either theoretical or empirical. The method is actually nothing more than another entirely subjective evaluation process without the error-correcting methods of Rasch and Lens models. Many users of IT weighted scores claim they see a benefit, but there is no demonstrated measurable value to this process.

The Information Economics method adds new errors in another way. It takes a useful and financially meaningful quantity, such as an ROI, and converts it to a score. The conversion goes like this: An ROI of 0 or less is a score of 0, 1% to 299% is a score of 1, 300% to 499% is a 2, and so on. In other words, a modest ROI of 5% gets the same score as an ROI of 200%. In more quantitative portfolio prioritization methods, such a difference would put a huge distance between the priorities of two projects. The user of this approach began with a meaningful and significant differentiation between two projects; now they are both a "1" in the ROI category. This analysis has the net effect of "destroying" information.

A report by IT management author Barbara McNurlin agrees with this assessment. McNurlin analyzed 25 different benefit estimation techniques, including various weighted-scoring methods.[19] She characterizes those methods, none of which she considers as based in theory, as "useless."

Paul Gray, a book reviewer for the *Journal of Information Systems Management,* may have summed it up best. In his review of a book titled *Information Economics: Linking Business Performance to Information Technology,* one of the definitive books about the Information Economics method, Gray wrote: "Don't be put off by the word 'economics' in the title: the only textbook economics discussed is in an appendix on cost curves."[20] Meant as an accolade, Gray's words also sum up the key weakness of the approach: This version of information economics contains no actual economics.

Another popular version of arbitrary weighted scores is called the "Analytic Hierarchy Process" (AHP).[21] AHP is different from other weighted scores in two ways. First, it is based on a series of pairwise comparisons instead of directly scored attributes. That is, the experts are asked if one attribute is "strongly more important," "slightly more important," and so on over another attribute, and different choices are compared within the same attribute in the same manner. For example, subjects would be asked if they preferred the "strategic benefits" of new product A over new product B. They would then be asked if they preferred the "development risk" of A over B. They would also be asked if "strategic benefit" was more important than "development risk." They would continue comparing every possible choice within each attribute, then every attribute to each other. Pair-wise comparisons avoid the issue of developing arbitrary scoring scales, which could be an advantage to this method. However, strangely enough, AHP still converts the data on the comparisons to an arbitrary score.

The second difference between AHP and other arbitrary weighted-scoring methods is that a "consistency coefficient" is computed. This coefficient is a method for determining how internally consistent the answers are. For example, if you prefer strategic benefit to low development risk and prefer low development risk to exploiting existing distribution channels, you should not prefer exploiting existing distribution channels to strategic benefit. If this sort of circularly inconsistent result happens a lot, the consistency calculation will have a low value. A perfectly consistent set of answers earns a consistency value of 1.

The consistency calculation is based on a method from matrix algebra called "Eigenvalues," used to solve a variety of mathematical problems. Because AHP utilizes this method, it is often called "theoretically sound" or "mathematically proven." If the criteria for theoretical soundness were simply, at some point in a procedure, using a mathematical tool (even one as powerful as Eigenvalues), proving a new theory or procedure would be much easier than it actually is. Someone could find a way to use Eigenvalues in astrology or differential equations in palm readings. In neither case will the method become more valid merely because a mathematical method that is proven in another context has been applied.

The fact is that AHP is simply another weighted-scoring method that has the one noise-reducing method (the consistency coefficient) for recognizing inconsistent answers. But that hardly makes the outputs "proven," as is often claimed. The problem is that comparing attributes like strategic alignment and development risk is usually meaningless.

If I asked you whether you prefer a new car or money, you should ask me, first, what kind of car and how much money I'm talking about. If the car was a 15-year-old subcompact and the money was $1 million, you would obviously give a different answer than if the car was a new Rolls-Royce and the money was $100. Yet I've witnessed that when groups of people engage in this process with an AHP tool, no one stops to ask "How much development risk versus how much manufacturing costs are we talking about?" Amazingly, they simply answer as if the comparison were clearly defined. Doing this introduces the danger that one person simply imagines a completely different trade-off than someone else. It merely adds another unnecessary level of noise.

There has been considerable debate about even the theoretical validity of AHP, much less whether it actually improves decisions. One of the first problems discovered was something called "rank reversal."[22] Suppose you used AHP to rank alternatives A, B, and C in that order, A being the most preferred. Suppose then that you delete C; should it change the rank of A and B so that A is second best and B is best? As nonsensical as that is, AHP can result in exactly that. (A modification to AHP called the "Ideal Process Mode" resolves this problem. What I find curious is that before the problem was resolved, the original position among AHP proponents was that rank reversal actually made sense and needed no "resolving.")

Other problems continue to surface. One issue is a violation of what is called the "independent criterion" requirement in preferences. If we add another criterion to an already-ranked list of choices, and that criterion is identical for every choice, the ranks should not change. Suppose you are evaluating where to hold the company picnic and you ranked the options with AHP. Then someone decides that you should have included "distance from the office" as a criterion, but all the choices have exactly the same distance. It makes no sense that an additional criterion for which all options are rated the same should change the ranks, and yet it can.[23] In my second book, *The Failure of Risk Management,* I quote several decision analysis researchers who, because of these problems, insist AHP is not a credible tool. (I mention AHP in that book because so many use AHP to assess risks instead of proper probabilistic methods.)

But even the theoretical flaws should not themselves be an obstacle. So what if there are theoretical flaws? None of the theoretical papers on the topic attempts to compute how common such problems would be in actual practice. (None of them attempts any kind of empirical study that would seem to be required for this evaluation.) There is, however, one "showstopper" criterion for whether cost-benefit analyses or various weighted scores could count as a measurement: *The result has to be an improvement on your previous state of knowledge.*

Regardless of the method used, it must be shown that actual forecasts and decisions are improved over time. Although hundreds, perhaps thousands, of case studies have been written for tools like AHP, there is still no evidence of significant, measurable improvements to decisions over a long run compared to a control group. (Most case studies simply describe the process in some particular applications, don't bother to measure performance, and are purely anecdotal.)

Calibration training, the Rasch model, and Monte Carlo modeling have ample, published, and measurable evidence of improving decisions. Even a small fraction of the kind of empirical research cited by Meehl and Dawes would suffice to show that such methods are measurably improving decisions. The kind of data collected for the Lens Model, as shown in Exhibit 12.2, would be convincing evidence for the efficacy of AHP and simpler, popular weighted-scoring methods. If popular scoring methods could show evidence like this, I promise I would be an instant convert and dedicated proponent.

But even though AHP has been widely used since the 1980s, as recently as 2008, there are still calls for the testing of its validity empirically by the academic community.[24] The few studies that have been done do not appear actually to measure against objectively observable outcomes of success; rather, they measure only how well the output agrees with the *original* subjective preferences of the users.[25] Another study attempted only to measure whether AHP is useful in predicting the subjective forecasts of others, not whether it matched objective outcomes about the forecasted item. (Even for that task, researchers could conclude only that it sometimes worked a little and sometimes didn't.[26])

But even without evidence for or against the entire method, there are several known measurable problems with key *components* of softer scoring methods and AHP. None addresses the previously mentioned problems unique to ordinal scales, such as range compression, partition dependence, or the illusion of communication. (A kind of partition dependence has been specifically tested for AHP; it has been observed that the arbitrary choice of scales makes a major change in results.[27]) Nor do the softer scoring methods attempt to address the typical human biases discussed in the previous chapters. Most of us are systematically overconfident and tend to underestimate uncertainty and risks unless we avail ourselves of the training that can offset such effects. (See Chapter 5.) And there is no reason to believe that any of these methods somehow avoid the previously described issues of anchoring, the bandwagon effect, the halo/horns effect, and choice blindness. (See Chapter 11.)

We should not be surprised, however, that these methods have such passionate proponents. As discussed earlier in the chapter, we know that decision makers will experience an increase in confidence in their decisions even when the analysis or information-gathering methods are found to be ineffectual. This is part of what Dawes called the "illusion of learning."

All of these same effects probably were present in the confident touch therapists measured by Emily Rosa in Chapter 2. The therapists had never bothered to measure their performance in any placebo-controlled manner. Emily's simple experiment showed that their belief that they could do this task was an illusion. Managers might think that example doesn't apply to them. After all, it is not as if they believe in supernatural auras. But why do they think they are any different? Have they been measuring their decision-making performance? If not, they need to consider the possibility that they are no different from the "experts" measured by Meehl, Dawes, and Emily Rosa. As mentioned earlier in this chapter, it turns out that there is a kind of placebo effect in analysis. Decision makers can become more confident in their decisions for no other reason than the appearance of structure and formality. This is why we should—just as in clinical drug trials—consider that any perceived benefit may be an illusion.

COMPARING THE METHODS

Once we adjust for certain known problems, human judgment is not a bad measurement instrument after all. If you have a large number of similar, recurring decisions, Rasch and Lens models can definitely reduce uncertainty by removing certain types of errors from human judgment. Even Dawes's simple z-score seems to be a slight improvement on human judgment.

As a benchmark for comparison, we will use the objective linear model based purely on historical data. Unlike the other methods discussed in this chapter, historical models do not depend on human judgment in any way and, consequently, typically perform much better, as Meehl conclusively showed. Usually we'd prefer to use this sort of method, but in many cases where we need to quantify "immeasurables," these detailed, objective, historical data are harder to come by. Hence the need for the other methods, such as Lens, Rasch, and so on.

In Chapter 9, we discussed how to perform regression analysis to isolate and measure the effects of multiple variables. If we have lots of historical data on a particular recurring problem, complete documentation on each of the factors, and the factors are based on objective measures (not subjective scales), *and* we have recorded the actual results, we can create an objective linear model.

While the Lens Model correlates input variables to expert estimates, the objective model correlates input variables to actual historical results.

On each of the Lens Model studies mentioned in Exhibit 12.2, a regression model also was completed on historical data. The study shown about cancer patient life expectancy, for example, involved giving the doctors medical chart data on cancer patients and then building a Lens Model on their estimates for life expectancy. The study also kept track of *actual* life expectancy by continuing to track the patients. While the Lens Model of the physicians' prognoses had just 2% less error than human judges, the objective model had fully 12% less error. For all the studies listed in Exhibit 12.2, the Lens Model had on average 5% less error than an unaided human estimator of a measurement while objective linear models had on average 30% less error than the human experts.

Of course, even objective linear models are not the ultimate answer to improving on unaided human judgment. More elaborate decomposition of the problem, as we discussed in previous chapters, usually can reduce uncertainty even further. If we were to arrange these methods on a spectrum ranging from unaided and unorganized human intuition to the objective linear model, it would look something like Exhibit 12.5.

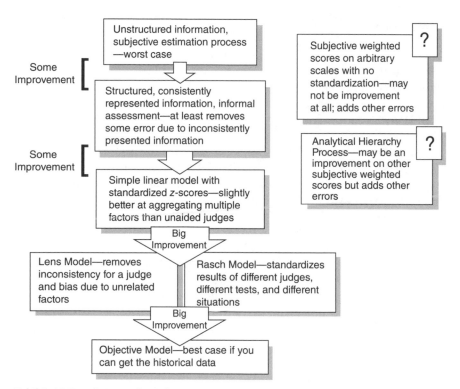

Exhibit 12.5 Relative Value of Estimation Methods for Groups of Similar Problems

If historical data is available, that is probably an improvement on unaided human judgment. But the other methods that simply correct for certain errors in human judgment without the use of historical data also have value. Methods such as Rasch and Lens models are empirically proven to help remove some startling errors from human judgment and make it possible to turn the human expert into a very flexible, calibrated, and powerful instrument of measurement.

EXAMPLE: A SCIENTIST MEASURES THE PERFORMANCE OF A DECISION MODEL

Clearly, there is a need to measure experts and methods meant to improve expert judgment. If that seems daunting, take heart. Here is one example of how a scientifically-minded manager (in fact, a real scientist) measured the results of a proposed forecasting method. Life Technologies, Inc. is a global life sciences company that produces laboratory equipment and materials. The firm has 10,000 employees in 180 countries. That means just about any kind of laboratory researcher having anything to do with life or health research including genetics or clinical trials for new drugs would know and use their products.

The scientists at Life Technologies have lots of ideas for products and someone has to make choices about which to pursue. They need to decide among a myriad of products like sophisticated new genetic analysis devices or kits for detecting various diseases. A key consideration in this decision is the revenue that could be generated within the first two years of launch. Of course, forecasting revenue for new technologies— especially in a field where technologies are not new for long—is a challenge. And estimating project costs in R&D is not simple either. R&D projects are, by their nature, uncertain in duration and even in whether anything will ever come of it before someone has to cancel the initiative.

Like many firms, Life Technologies relied primarily on the opinions of their best experts to estimate the revenue for new products. The VP of R&D in Molecular & Protein Biology, Paul Predki, realized that these estimates could be improved. "We discovered that we had a tendency to be overly optimistic in our forecasts" said Predki. In 2011, he asked me to help develop a decision model for new product assessment.

The solution we developed was an interesting combination of multiple methods I've already discussed. As always, we start by clearly defining the decision—a product approval based on a two-year revenue forecast, project cost estimates, production costs, and so on. We calibrated the experts he would normally rely on for new product revenue forecasts and then built a Monte Carlo model for a "pilot" product they wanted to evaluate. Some estimates, like project costs, cost of manufacturing, and pricing came directly from their calibrated experts.

The critical revenue forecasts, on the other hand, were based on the Lens modeling method discussed previously. Several of their experts were asked to estimate first- and second-year revenue for over 50 hypothetical new products. Each product was described with a set of parameters the experts felt would inform their estimates. Some parameters were related to marketing strategy, some were related to describing the target market; some were related to details of the product itself, and so on. After the estimates were collected, we used a regression modeling method to approximate expert estimates based on the data they were given. This model was then used to generate the revenue estimate used in the Monte Carlo simulation.

As you might expect of a scientist like Predki (a PhD in biochemistry), he tested the new model using statistical methods he would use in any published research. He applied the Lens model to 16 products which were not used in the original study and for which he had revenue data. He then compared the Lens model estimates to the estimates for those products originally provided by experts. Predki notes "The most surprising result was that even our 'simple' forecasting algorithm consistently outperformed human experts." For both years combined, the correlation of the expert judgments to actual outcomes was significantly improved and the new model eliminated a systemic overestimation of revenues.

In all, there was a *76% reduction* in the error of forecasting revenues compared to the human experts. *That* is how a scientist shows a decision analysis method is working.

Notes

1. Robert Kaplan, "Is Beauty Talent? Sex Interaction in the Attractiveness Halo Effect," paper presented at the *Annual Meeting of the Western Psychological Association*, Los Angeles, California, April 8–11, 1976.
2. S. E. Asch, "Effects of Group Pressure upon the Modification and Distortion of Judgment," in H. Guetzkow, ed., *Groups, Leadership and Men* (Pittsburgh: Carnegie Press, 1951).
3. Peter Johansson, Lars Hall, Sverker Sikström, and A. Olsson, "Failure to Detect Mismatches between Intention and Outcome in a Simple Decision Task," *Science* 310, no. 5745 (2005): 116–119.
4. R. Dawes, *House of Cards: Psychology and Psychotherapy Built on Myth* (New York: Simon & Schuster, 1996).
5. C. Tsai, J. Klayman, and R. Hastie, "Effects of Amount of Information on Judgment Accuracy and Confidence," *Organizational Behavior and Human Decision Processes* 107, no. 2 (2008): 97–105.

6. C. Heath and R. Gonzalez, "Interaction with Others Increases Decision Confidence but Not Decision Quality: Evidence against Information Collection Views of Interactive Decision Making," *Organizational Behavior and Human Decision Processes* 61, no. 3 (1995): 305–326.

7. P. Andreassen, "Judgmental Extrapolation and Market Overreaction: On the Use and Disuse of News," *Journal of Behavioral Decision Making* 3, no. 3 (July/September 1990): 153–174.

8. S. Kassin and C. Fong, "I'm Innocent!: Effects of Training on Judgments of Truth and Deception in the Interrogation Room," *Law and Human Behavior* 23 (1999): 499–516.

9. Robyn M. Dawes, "The Robust Beauty of Improper Linear Models in Decision Making," *American Psychologist* 34 (1979): 571–582.

10. M. Wilson and G. Engelhard (eds.), *Objective Measurement* 5 (Elsevier Science, January 15, 1999).

11. G. Rasch, "On General Laws and the Meaning of Measurement in Psychology," *Proceedings of the Fourth Berkeley Symposium on Mathematical Statistics and Probability* (Berkeley: University of California Press, 1980), 321–334.

12. Egon Brunswik, "Representative Design and Probabilistic Theory in a Functional Psychology," *Psychological Review* 62 (1955): 193–217.

13. Robyn M. Dawes and Bernard Corrigan, "Linear Models in Decision Making," *Psychological Bulletin* 81, no. 2 (1974): 93–106.

14. In at least one of the four examples, the "experts" were students. In two of the remaining examples, the experts were predicting the opinions of other experts (clinical psychologists predicting diagnoses by other clinicians and faculty predicting the evaluations given by the admissions committee). Also, most of the experts I model appear to be at least slightly better at predicting outcomes than the experts Dawes's research discusses.

15. D. V. Budescu, S. Broomell, and H. Por, "Improving Communication of Uncertainty in the Reports of the Intergovernmental Panel on Climate Change," *Psychological Science* 20, no. 3 (2009): 299–308.

16. L. A. Cox Jr., "What's Wrong with Risk Matrices?" *Risk Analysis* 28, no. 2 (2008): 497–512.

17. Ibid.

18. M. Parker, R. Benson, and H. E. Trainor, *Information Economics: Linking Business Performance to Information Technology* (Englewood Cliffs, NJ: Prentice-Hall, 1988).

19. Barbara McNurlin, *Uncovering the Information Technology Payoff* (Rockville, MD: United Communications Group, 1992).

20. Paul Gray, book review of *Information Economics: Linking Business Performance to Information Technology, Journal of Information Systems Management* (Fall 1989).

21. A survey of literature shows that "analytical" is also used in the name instead of "analytic," even in peer-reviewed journal articles, but most proponents seem to use "analytic." T. Saaty, *The Analytic Hierarchy Process: Planning, Priority Setting, Resource Allocation* (New York: McGraw-Hill, 1980).

22. A. Stam and A. Silva, "Stochastic Judgments in the AHP: The Measurement of Rank Reversal Probabilities," *Decision Sciences Journal* 28, no. 3 (Summer 1997).

23. Joaquín Pérez, José Jimeno, and Ethel Mokotoff, "Another Potential Short-coming of AHP," *TOP: An Official Journal of the Spanish Society of Statistics and Operations Research* 14, no. 1 (June 2006).
24. Robert T. Clemen, "Improving and Measuring the Effectiveness of Decision Analysis: Linking Decision Analysis and Behavioral Decision Research," *Decision Modeling and Behavior in Complex and Uncertain Environments* 21 (2008): 3–31.
25. P. Schoemaker and C. Waidi, "An Experimental Comparison of Different Approaches to Determining Weights in Additive Utility Models," *Management Science* 28, no. 2 (February 1982).
26. M. Williams, A. Dennis, A. Stam, and J. Aronson, "The Impact of DSS Use and Information Load on Errors and Decision Quality," *European Journal of Operational Research* 176, no. 1 (January 2007): 468–481.
27. Mari Pöyhönen and Raimo P. Hämäläinen, "On the Convergence of Multi Attribute Weighting Methods," *European Journal of Operational Research* 129, no. 3 (March 2001): 569–585.

## CHAPTER 13

New Measurement Instruments for Management

I wonder what minds like Eratosthenes, Enrico, and Emily might have been able to measure if they only had used some of the measurement instruments mentioned in this book. No doubt, a lot. But, unfortunately, these instruments are not nearly as widely utilized as they could be, and big, risky decisions have probably suffered because of it.

Again, when I talk about measurement instruments, I'm not just talking about tabletop devices used in some scientific observation. I'm talking about things you are already aware of but may not have considered as types of measurement instruments. This includes technologies like new personal wireless devices and even the entire Internet.

THE TWENTY-FIRST-CENTURY TRACKER: KEEPING TABS WITH TECHNOLOGY

One of the methods of observation we discussed was using instrumentation to track a phenomenon that, up until that point, was not being tracked. By inserting something into the phenomenon itself, you make it easier to observe. To measure the motion of the upper atmosphere, my father, as an employee of the National Weather Service, would release balloons into the wind carrying a radio transponder and basic meteorological measurement devices. In the fish population example we discussed, the much simpler tag is introduced into the population so that its size could be measured with the catch and recatch method. If something is difficult to observe as it is, there are multiple ways to insert tags, probes, or tracers into the process.

It's not just what the instruments do but their cost that creates so many possibilities. The simple radio frequency ID (RFID), for example, has revolutionized the measurement of certain activities in business but could be used on so much more. The RFID is a small strip of material that reflects a radio signal and sends a unique identifier along in the reflected signal. RFIDs currently are produced for just 10 to 20 cents each and are used mostly for inventory tracking.

When I asked the renowned physicist and author Freeman Dyson what he thought to be the most important, most clever, and most inspiring measurement, he responded without hesitation, "GPS [Global Positioning System] is the most spectacular example. It has changed everything." Actually, I was expecting a different kind of response, perhaps something from his days in operations research for the Royal Air Force during World War II, but GPS made sense as both a truly revolutionary measurement instrument as well as a measurement in its own right. GPS is economically available for just about anyone and comes with a variety of software support tools and services. Yet many people may not think of GPS when they think of a new measurement instrument for business, partly because GPS is already so ubiquitous. But when a mind like Dyson's believes it's the most spectacular example of a measurement, we should listen.

Most vehicle-based industries benefit from the measurement capabilities GPS technology provides. One firm that is helping transportation companies to fully exploit GPS is GPS Insight, based in Scottsdale, Arizona. The company provides vehicle-mounted GPS units on a wireless network that can be accessed through the company's website. Tracking over 50,000 commercial and government vehicles, GPS Insight provides not only current locations but flexible reports. It overlays the locations of the vehicles against maps and data accessible with Google Earth. As anyone familiar with Google Earth knows, it takes satellite photos of Earth and patches them together in software with information about roads, businesses, and countless other custom Geographic Information System data layers. People can download Google Earth for free and see satellite images of their neighborhood or anywhere else.

The images on Google Earth are not real time and sometimes are over two years old; however, the road and other data are usually more current. The image of my neighborhood used to show a construction project that had been completed over two years earlier. And some areas are not as well covered as others. In many locations you can easily make out cars, but in my tiny boyhood hometown of Yale, South Dakota, the resolution is so low that you can barely see any of the roads in the picture. Still, the coverage, resolution, and timeliness of the images has been improving and, no doubt, will improve over time.

Third-party high-quality aerial photographs are available on the Internet, however, and GPS Insight typically provides them for customers by adding them to Google Earth as an overlay. The cost is trivial, ranging between $1 and $10 per square mile.

A clever person could use each of these tools as a measurement instrument in its own right. But by combining GPS, wireless networks, Internet access, and Google Earth, GPS Insight is able to produce detailed reports of vehicle locations, driver activities, and driving habits that were not previously practical to track. These reports succinctly show trip times, stop times, and their averages and variances, which help to determine where to drill down. By drilling down, exact locations, times, and activity can be determined, such as a two-hour stop at a building at 43rd and Central. By turning on "bars and restaurants" in Google Earth, even the exact restaurant can be determined.

Other types of reports quantify who is speeding, how long various vehicles are used throughout the day versus payroll hours, when vehicles are used outside of normal business hours, whether the prescribed route is taken, and how many miles and hours are spent driving in each state for simplified fuel tax reporting purposes. Because this tool reduces uncertainty on many quantities in an economical fashion, it qualifies as a very useful measurement instrument.

Developments in mobile devices have made even more types of tracking widely available and, in turn, the availability of these measurements will transform whole areas of research. There is a phenomenon sometimes referred to as the "Quantified Self" movement. This is part of a revolution in cheap and relatively accurate personal measurement devices, many of which are related to personal health. Using products like Fitbit or Bodymedia, a person can track his or her level of activity throughout the day. I've used these tools in an ongoing experiment for tracking my own activity levels and health and the trends are already revealing. Some people are taking it further and working on personal mobile devices for detecting disease.[1-3]

Using devices to track our locations and activities objectively may also have a profound impact on social science research. The social sciences research about social activities and time with friends, for example, have relied heavily on self-reported surveys. Yet self-reported surveys have turned out to be highly inconsistent with what objective location tracking data says. We spend very different amounts of time with very different people than what we would typically remember to put on a survey.[4,5]

Generally, long-term health studies with thousands of subjects are expensive and the data is not widely available. A study like the Framingham Heart Study, with about 12,000 subjects, is about as large as long-term health studies ever get.[6] This study has been the basis for research regarding heart health for decades. Now, what new medical research will become possible when millions (or even billions) of people not just from one location but from all over the world begin to routinely track and share health information?

If Eratosthenes could measure the circumference of Earth by looking at shadows, I wonder what sorts of economic, political, and behavioral phenomena he could measure with web-based GPS. If Enrico Fermi could measure the yield of an atom bomb with a handful of confetti, I wonder what he could have done with a handful of RFID chips. If Emily could debunk therapeutic touch with a simple experiment with a cardboard screen, I wonder what she can measure now with a slightly bigger budget and a few new tools.

In short, we have no shortage of data. I spend much time earlier in this book explaining how a few observations are informative when uncertainty is high and you are betting a lot of money. But we should also remember another point made in Chapter 3: You have more data than you think. Or perhaps you are aware that you have a lot of data but were unaware of what could be derived from it. Building on traditional databases and more advanced analysis tools, the field of "predictive analytics" is finding ways to fully leverage the vast amounts of data we have. Eric Siegel, author of *Predictive Analytics: The Power to Predict Who Will Click, Buy, Lie, or Die* describes both existing and emerging analytical tools for fully exploiting massive data.[7] Leveraging this data will become more important as we begin to exploit the largest source of data in the world—the Internet itself.

MEASURING THE WORLD: THE INTERNET AS AN INSTRUMENT

The Internet has made measurable what was previously immeasurable: The distribution of health information in a population, tracking (in real time) health information trends over time, and identifying gaps between information supply and demand.
        —Gunther Eysenbach, MD, developer of Infodemiology

In 2006, Dr. Gunther Eysenbach of the University of Toronto showed how search patterns on Google could be used to anticipate flu outbreaks. He developed a tool that collected and interpreted search terms from Google users in different geographic locations. Eysenbach correlated the searches for terms like "flu symptoms" with actual flu outbreaks that were later confirmed and showed that he could predict the flu outbreaks a *full week earlier* than the health authorities could using traditional hospital reporting methods.[8] Subsequent research saw similar results. He called this approach to the study of outbreaks "Infodemiology" and published this and supporting findings in a relatively new medical journal called the *Journal of Medical Internet Research*.[9] Yes, there is such a journal, and more are sure to come.

In the 1980s, the author William Gibson wrote several works in a genre of science fiction that he can take large credit for creating. He coined the term "cyberspace" as a future version of the Internet where users did not just use a keyboard and mouse but, instead, "jacked in" with a probe inserted directly into the brain and entered a virtual reality. Some of the characters specialized in flying around a type of data landscape looking for patterns, trying to identify such things as market inefficiencies that might allow them to turn a quick buck.

As science fiction writers often are, Gibson was unrealistic in some respects. While it sounds like fun, I personally see limited research value in flying over data landscapes in cyberspace. I think I get more useful data faster by using good Google, Excel, and perhaps a data analysis tool like Tableau on a monitor together with some flat-screen graphs. But the idea of Gibson's cyberspace being not just a repository of data but a kind of real-time pulse of everything that goes on in the whole planet is not far from reality. We really do have an instantly accessible vast landscape of data. Even without flying over it in virtual reality, we can see patterns that can affect important decisions.

There is nothing novel in touting the wondrous possibilities of the Internet—nothing could be more cliché. But a particular use seems to be underexploited. The Internet itself may be the most important new instrument of measurement most of us will see in our lifetimes. It is simple enough to use the Internet with some search engines to dig up research on something you are trying to measure. But there are several other implications for the Internet as a measurement instrument, and it is quickly becoming one of the key answers to the question of how to measure anything.

My third book, *Pulse: The New Science of Harnessing Internet Buzz to Track Threats and Opportunities*, is entirely dedicated to this topic.[10] In *Pulse* I describe six ways that people leave their digital footprints on the web.

1. What we search for—What we search for on Google can be revealed through Google Trends (www.google.com/trends) and can be used to forecast unemployment, retail sales, travel, and much more.[11–13]
2. Who we "friend"—Our social networks revealed on Facebook and LinkedIn have been used to measure several social trends.[14] The field of computational social science uses this information to research how depression,[15] sleep disorders,[16] health,[17] and other behaviors can be a function of those we associate with.[18–20]

3. What we say—Blogs and Twitter have been used to estimate changes in consumer confidence, presidential approval ratings, and even how much money movies will make.[21,22]
4. Where we go—When we voluntarily reveal our location to apps, the information can be used to estimate changes in the economy since we tend to visit different locations when money is tight. The accelerometers in your smart phone also help track *how* you move. This is helpful because we tend to move differently when we are sick and this information can be used to detect outbreaks early.[23]
5. What we buy—eBay and Amazon both provide quite a lot of publicly available data about sales of individual items. Amazon provides sales ranks that show how well some items sell compared to others and eBay actually shows the results of every individual auction. Shifts in what we buy say a lot about the economy and trends in general preferences. Analysis of Craigslist activity has been used to forecast unemployment and foreclosures.[24]
6. What we play—While games don't yet make as much information publicly available and ready for analysis as other sources, it is something that has a lot of potential. We do know that mood affects choices of strategies in games and if we could ever capture that data. It could be a huge new source of sociological data.[25]

Almost all of this data is publicly accessible. All of this data can be cross referenced even further. Anything currently estimated using expensive survey methods can be researched in different ways by any Internet-literate college student.

There is quite a lot of information on the Internet, and it changes fast. You need an efficient way of gathering what you need. Internet "screen-scrapers" are a way to gather all this information on a regular basis without hiring a 24/7 staff of interns to do it. Todd Wilson, president and founder of www.screen-scraper.com, says, "There are certain sites that change every three or four seconds. Our tool is very good at watching changes over time on the web." You could use a screen-scraper to track used-market versions of your product on www.ebay.com, correlate your store's sales in different cities to the local weather, or even check the number of hits on your firm's name on various search engines hour by hour. (If you simply want to be alerted to new entries and aren't concerned with building a database, try signing up for Google Alerts.)

A preferred source for this data is to get it directly from the service provider instead of using a screen-scraper. Amazon and Facebook would rather you didn't use screen-scrapers because they can bog down a site's performance if used by too many people. To discourage this, the service providers make Application Program Interfaces (APIs) available to developers. This gives developers direct access to large amounts of data in a way that the service provider can control and in a way that limits the burden on the service providers' infrastructure.

Developers have used APIs to develop several useful "mashups" and other data sources. Data may be pulled from multiple sources and presented in a way that provides new insight. A common angle with mashups now is to plot information about business, real estate, traffic, and so on against a map site like MapQuest or Google Earth. I use www.metricjunkie.com to track the ranks of my books on Amazon. In *Pulse*, I also showed how using Amazon book ranks can be used to estimate changes in consumer debt levels by tracking the ranks of books about bankruptcy and getting out of debt.

I've found a mashup of Google Earth and real estate data on www.housingmaps.com that allows you to see recently sold home prices on a map. Another mashup on www.socaltech.com shows a map that plots locations of businesses that recently received venture capital. At first glance, you might think these sites are just for looking to buy a house or find a job with a new company. But how about research for a construction business or forecasting business growth in a new industry? We are limited only by our resourcefulness.

You can imagine almost limitless combinations of analysis Facebook and/or YouTube use to measure cultural trends or public opinion. eBay gives us tons of free data about the behavior of sellers and buyers and what is being bought and sold, and several powerful analytical tools exist to summarize all the data on the site. Comments and reviews of individual products on the sites of Sears, Walmart, Target, and Overstock.com are a source of free information from consumers if we are clever enough to exploit them. The mind reels with possibilities.

Or, instead of mining the web for information with screen-scapers and mashups, you could use the web to facilitate direct surveys of clients, employees, and others. Key Survey is one such web-based survey firm (www.keysurvey.com). These firms offer a variety of statistical analysis capabilities; some have an "intelligent" or adaptive survey approach where the survey dynamically asks different questions depending on how respondents answer earlier questions. Although these capabilities can be very valuable, many clients of web-based survey services find that the cost reduction alone is reason enough to use these methods of measurement.

Consider these statistics. It used to cost *Farm Journal,* a client of Key Survey, an average of $4 to $5 per respondent for a 40- to 50-question survey of farmers. Now, using Key Survey, it costs *Farm Journal* 25 cents per survey, and it is able to survey half a million people.

National Leisure Group

Another client of Key Survey is National Leisure Group (NLG), a major leisure cruise line that generates about $700 million in annual revenue.

Julianna Hale is the director of human resources (HR) and internal communications for the National Leisure Group. She originally brought the Key Survey tool in for HR use, specifically employee satisfaction, performance coach assessments, and training evaluations, but later saw its potential for measuring customer satisfaction. She says, "When you are in the travel industry, every penny is hard to come by. It's a very small profit margin." Given these constraints, it was still important to measure how positive NLG's image was with customers. "We had a lot of great closers [salespeople] but low repeat rates," Hale explains. "So we created a customer experience department and started measuring customer satisfaction. It took us a while to buy into the measurement. It was a big battle."

Every six to eight months, Key Survey put together a customer survey across departments. Being sensitive to the use of customers' time, the company had to do it efficiently. Hale recounts: "There were several iterations of the customer survey but everyone eventually signed off on it." A "postbooking" survey was sent in an automated e-mail right after a reservation was made, and another was sent in a "welcome home" e-mail after the customer returned from the cruise. Hale says: "We just wanted to see what kind of results we would get. We were getting a 4% to 5% response rate initially, but with the welcome-home e-mail we were getting an 11.5% response rate." By survey standards, that is very high. In a clever use of a simple control, NLG compares responses to questions like "Will you refer us to a friend?" before and after customers take the trip to see if scores are higher after the vacation.

When they found that clients weren't as happy after the trip, NLG decided to launch a whole new program with the sales team. Hale says, "We had to retrain the sales team to sell in a different way and get the customer to the right vacation." Simply discovering the problem was a measurement success. Now the company needs to measure the effect of the new program.

PREDICTION MARKETS: A DYNAMIC AGGREGATION OF OPINIONS

The Internet has also made possible a new, dynamic way to make measurements by aggregating opinions with a mechanism similar to what the stock market uses. After the financial crisis of 2008, some readers might not think it makes sense to call these mechanisms "efficient" (even though that particular crisis wasn't really so much about instability in the stock market itself). However, there are places where methods like these work. When an economist talks about the stock market being efficient, he or she means that it is very hard to beat the market consistently. For any given stock at any given point in time, its price is just about as likely to move up as move down in the very short term. If this was not true, then market participants would bid up or sell off the stock accordingly until that "equilibrium" (if such a thing exists in the market) was achieved.

This process of aggregating opinions is better at forecasting than almost any of the individual participants in the market are. Far better than an opinion poll, participants have an incentive not only to consider the questions carefully but even, especially when a lot of money is involved, to expend their own resources to get new information to analyze about the investment. People who place bids irrationally tend to run out of money faster and get out of the market. Irrational people also tend to be "random noise" that cancels out in a large market since irrational people are just as likely to overvalue a stock as undervalue it (although our "herd instinct" can magnify irrationality in markets). And because of the incentive for participation, news about the value of the company is quickly reflected in its stock price.

This is exactly the type of mechanism the new "prediction markets" are trying to summon. Although they've been researched at least as far back as the early 1990s, they were introduced to a much wider audience in 2004 by the popular book *The Wisdom of the Crowds* by James Surowiecki.[26] Several software tools and public websites have created "markets" for such things as who will win the Oscar for Best Actress or who will be the Republican nominee for president. Exhibit 13.1 shows some examples of various prediction market tools.

Participants in this market buy or sell shares of "claims" about a particular prediction, let's say, who will be the Republican nominee for U.S. president. The claim usually states that one share is worth a given amount if it turns out to be true, often $1. You can bet for the claim by buying a "Yes" share and against it by buying a "No" share. That is, you make money if the claim comes true if you own a "Yes" share, and you make money if the claim turns out to be false if you buy a "No" share. A "retired" share is one that has already been judged true or false and the rewards have been paid.

If you are holding 100 "Yes" shares that a particular person becomes the nominee and, in fact, that person becomes the nominee, you would win $100. But when you first bought those shares, it was far from certain that the claim would turn out to be true. You might have paid only five cents

Exhibit 13.1 Summary of Available Prediction Markets

Consensus Point www .consensuspoint.com	A service for businesses that want to set up prediction markets for internal use. Developed by some of the same people who created Foresight Exchange, the business has a lot of flexibility in how to set up and create reward systems for good forecasters, including monetary incentives.
Foresight Exchange www.ideosphere .com	A free website available to the public and one of the earliest experiments on the concept of prediction markets. All bets are "play money." Claims are proposed by the public and reviewed by volunteers. It is an active market with a large number of players, and a good way to get introduced to prediction markets.
NewsFutures www .newsfutures.com	A direct competitor for Consensus Point, it offers businesses services to set up prediction markets.

each for the claims when you bought them a few months prior to the candidate's announcement; the cost may have gone up when the candidacy was announced, down a bit when another popular candidate made an announcement to run, and generally went up each time another candidate dropped out. You can make money by holding the shares to the end or by selling at any point you think the market is overpricing the claim.

But the claims examined in prediction markets don't have to be political victories, Oscars, or who wins *Dancing with the Stars*. They can be any forecast you are trying to measure, including whether two competitors will merge, the sales of a new product, the outcome of some critical litigation, or even whether the company will still be in business. Exhibit 13.2 shows the price on Foresight Exchange's website, www .ideosphere.com, for the retired claim "Apple Computer dies by 2005." This claim would have paid $1 for each "Yes" share a player owned if Apple ceased to exist as a viable corporate entity by January 1, 2005. The exact meaning of the claim—how it is judged if Apple is bought or merged into another firm, restructured in bankruptcy, and so on—is spelled out in a detailed description and judge's notes written by the person who will be judging whether the claim is true or false.

As we know now, Apple did not go out of business, and anyone who owned "Yes" shares would find they were worth nothing. But people who bet against the claim by buying "No" shares would have made $1 per share owned. Like stock prices, the price at various times reflects news available in the market. (The chart shows some key events

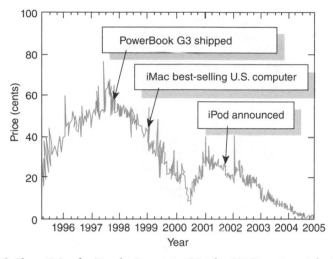

Exhibit 13.2 Share Price for "Apple Computer Dies by 2005" on Foresight Exchange

in Apple history before the claim retired.) Unlike stock prices, however, the price of a "Yes" share is immediately convertible to the chance the company would go out of business. In January 1999, the price of the "Yes" shares was about 30 cents, meaning that the market was saying that there was a 30% chance that Apple computer would no longer be in business by January 1, 2005. By 2004, the price of "Yes" shares dropped below five cents per share as it was becoming more obvious that Apple would still be in business at the beginning of the next year.

What is interesting about prediction markets is how well the prices seem to match the probability of the claim coming true. When large numbers of retired claims are examined, we can see how well prediction markets work. Just like calibrated experts, we determine if a calculated probability is a good one by looking at a large number of old predictions historically and seeing what actually happened. If a method for producing a probability is a good one, then when it tells us each of a set of events is 80% likely, about 80% should actually be correct. Likewise, of all the claims that sell at 40 cents, about 40% should eventually become true. Exhibit 13.3 shows how well this test holds up for News Futures, Foresight Exchange, and a now-defunct prediction market TradeSports.

The chart shows prices for TradeSports and NewsFutures on the same set of 208 National Football League (NFL) games collected in research published in *Electronic Markets*.[27] I overlaid on these data my findings from analysis of 353 Foresight Exchange claims collected from all Foresight Exchange data (not just NFL games), limited to only those claims that had a significant number of transactions.

Exhibit 13.3 Performance of Prediction Markets: Price versus Reality

This is an empirical validation of Bruno de Finetti's "operational definition" of risk. Recall from Chapter 5 that he literally equated the price of a contract and probability. We can see that as the price increases, so does the probability that the event will come true. TradeSports, a real-money gambling site, is a well-calibrated fit (i.e., the probability of an event is very close to its price). NewsFutures fits just as well even though players use play money, not real money. (The best players are allowed to use their "money" to bid on prizes like iPods.)

Foresight Exchange is very different from the other two sites. The exchange uses only play money and does not offer players the chance to buy a prize. Players simply get a $50 allowance of play money every week. There is nothing to spend the money on but claim shares, and there is no reward but bragging rights for the best forecasters. This may be why almost everything in this market is overpriced (i.e., prices are higher than the probability of the event coming true would justify). Another reason might be related to the fact that the claims in Foresight Exchange are submitted by the general public. Most of the claims in this exchange are long shots—many of them fairly bizarre; only 23% of all claims ever come true. It is interesting, though, how *consistent* the overpricing is. It is so consistent that we could simply apply an adjustment factor to the market price to convert it to a probability that is just about as good as Trade Sports or News Futures.

Some companies, such as General Electric (GE) and Dow Chemical, are beginning to examine prediction markets as useful tools for measuring the chance of specific future events. GE, for example, used these markets to measure the probability that different innovations proposed by employees would be marketable. One useful way to apply prediction markets for a measurement is to bet on the threshold. If a new product is a good investment only if the first-year revenue is $25 million, the company can set up a claim, "Product X will generate more than $25 million revenue in the first 12 months after going to market."

There are some important differences between prediction markets and stock markets we need to keep in mind. The items bought and sold in the stock market are highly interrelated. Moves in some stocks affect many other stocks. However, bets on who will win in a reality TV show contest are probably not related at all to who will win the next presidential election. There appears to be no such thing as a "market bubble" or "market panic" in a set of unrelated bets. Furthermore, we should still keep in mind what we are comparing things to. We are comparing prediction markets to unaided human experts. There is no doubt that prediction markets are vast improvements over unaided human experts. Remember the definition of measurement from Chapter 3. Measurement does not mean 100% right 100% of the time.

Prediction markets are definitely powerful new tools for measuring things that might seem impossible to measure. Proponents of prediction markets are almost evangelical in their zeal, believing these tools are the end-all and be-all of measuring virtually anything. I've heard some proponents state that to create a business case, you simply create a claim for every single variable in the business case and open it up to the market. After Surowiecki's book came out, the fervor only increased.

With that in mind, some cautions are in order. Prediction markets are not magic. They are just a way to aggregate the knowledge of a group of people and, especially if real money is used, to provide people with incentives to do research on their trades. Other methods we discussed also work well and may be preferable, depending on your needs. Exhibit 13.4 summarizes the judgment-improving methods we have discussed so far.

Exhibit 13.4 Comparison of Other Subjective Assessment Methods to Prediction Markets

Calibration Training	Best when lots of quick, low-cost estimates are needed. Requires only one expert to work, and an answer is immediate. Should be the first estimating method in most cases—more elaborate methods can be used if the information value justifies it.
Lens Model	Used when there are a large number of repeated estimates of the same type (e.g., assessment of investments in a big portfolio) and when the same type of data can be gathered on each. Once created, the Lens Model generates instant answers for this class of problems regardless of the availability of the original expert(s). The model can be created using only hypothetical scenarios.

(continued)

Exhibit 13.4 (*Continued*)

Rasch Model	Used to standardize different estimates or assessments from different experts or tests on different problems. Unlike the Lens Model, it requires a large set of real evaluations (not hypothetical). All are taken into consideration for standardization.
Prediction Market	Best for forecasts, especially where it is useful to track changes in probabilities over time. It requires at least two market players for even the first transaction to occur. It is not ideal if you need fast answers for a large number of quantities, homogeneous or not. If the number of claims exceeds the number of transactions in a market, many claims will have no estimate.

A Lesson Learned: The DARPA "Terrorism Market" Affair

In 2001, the Defense Advanced Research Projects Agency (DARPA) Information Awareness Office (IAO) decided to research the possibility of using prediction markets in policy analysis, based on studies that showed such markets outpredict individual experts on a variety of topics. This experiment would blow up into a public controversy.

In 2002, demonstration markets were created to predict the spread of SARS (severe acute respiratory syndrome) and security threat levels. These markets were planned to be run only within government agencies, but concerns that there would not be enough traders and legal problems with conditional transfers of money between agencies led to trading being opened to the general public.

One report showed a mocked-up screen with possible miscellaneous predictions, such as the assassination of Yasser Arafat and a missile attack from North Korea. The example did not go unnoticed. On July 28, 2003, U.S. Senators Ron Wyden (D-Ore.) and Byron Dorgan (D-N.D.) wrote 'to the director of the IAO, John Poindexter: "The example that you provide in your report would let participants gamble on the question, 'Will terrorists attack Israel with bioweapons in the next year?' Surely, such a threat should be met with intelligence gathering of the highest quality—not by putting the question to individuals betting on an Internet website, spending taxpayer dollars to create terrorism betting parlors is as wasteful as it is repugnant." A media firestorm ensued.

Within two days, the program was canceled and Poindexter resigned. Robin Hanson of George Mason University, a team member and widely recognized as the conceptual leader of prediction markets, stated: "No one from Congress asked us if the accusations were correct, or if the more offending aspects could be cut from the project. DARPA said nothing."

The senators framed the issue as a moral one and assumed that the program would not be effective. They also implied that the program would somehow displace other intelligence-gathering methods, when, of course, intelligence agencies have always used multiple methods in concert. If their indignation was based on the idea that terrorists could get rich by exploiting this market, again, their indignation was misplaced. Their position ignored the fact that market participants could have won only trivial amounts, since there was a $100 limit on any trade. Hanson summarized the entire affair: "They had to take a position on a project they knew little about. As a million-dollar project in a trillion-dollar budget, it was an easy target." The net effect of the moral and political posturing was that a very cost-effective tool that may have been a significant improvement on intelligence analysis was taken away.

Notes

1. A. E. Cetin, A. F. Coskun, B. C. Galarreta, M. Huang, D. Herman, A. Ozcan, and H. Altug, "Handheld High-Throughput Plasmonic Biosensor using Computational On-Chip Imaging," *Light: Science & Applications (Nature Publishing Group)* (2013).
2. A. F. Coskun, R. Nagi, K. Sadeghi, S. Phillips, and A. Ozcan, "Albumin Testing in Urine Using a Smart-Phone," *Lab on a Chip.* doi:10.1039/C3LC50785H (2013).
3. A. Ozcan, "Cost-Effective and Compact Microscopic Analysis and Diagnosis on a Cell Phone" presented at the World Reconstruction Conference, Geneva, May 11, 2011.
4. H. R. Bernard and P. D. Killworth, "Informant Accuracy in Social Network Data II," *Human Communications Research* 4 (1977): 3–18.
5. H. R. Bernard, P. D. Killworth, D. Kronenfeld, and L. Sailer, "The Problem of Informant Accuracy: The Validity of Retrospective Data," *Annual Review of Anthropology* 13 (1985): 495–517.
6. James H. Fowler and Nicholas A. Christakis, "Dynamic Spread of Happiness in a Large Social Network: Longitudinal Analysis Over 20 years in the Framingham Heart Study," *British Medical Journal 337*, no. a2338 (2008): 1–9.
7. E. Siegel, T. Davenport *Predictive Analytics: The Power to Predict Who Will Click, Buy, Lie, or Die* (Hoboken, NJ: John Wiley & Sons, 2013).
8. G. Eysenbach, "Infodemiology: Tracking Flu-Related Searches on the Web for Syndromic Surveillance," *AMIA Annual Symposium Proceedings* (2006): 244–248.

9. G. Eysenbach, "Infodemiology and Infoveillance: Framework for an Emerging Set of Public Health Informatics Methods to Analyze Search, Communication and Publication Behavior on the Internet," *Journal of Medical Internet Research* (2009).

10. Douglas Hubbard, *Pulse: The New Science of Harnessing Internet Buzz to Track Threats and Opportunities* (Hoboken, NJ: John Wiley & Sons, 2011).

11. M. Ettredge, J. Gerdes, and G. Karuga, "Using Web-Based Search Data to Predict Macroeconomic Statics," *Journal Commun ACM* 48 (2005): 87–92.

12. F. D'Amuri, "Predicting Unemployment in Short Samples with Internet Job Search Query Data," *Bank of Italy Economic Research Department,* October 2009.

13. F. D'Amuri and J. Marcucci, "'Google It!' Forecasting the U.S. Unemployment Rate with a Google Job Search Index," Bank of Italy Economic Research Department, November 2009.

14. J. H. Fowler and N. A. Christakis, "Cooperative Behavior Cascades in Human Social Networks," *PNAS: Proceedings of the National Academy of Sciences* 107, no. 9 (March 2010): 5334–5338.

15. J. N. Rosenquist, J. H. Fowler, and N. A. Christakis, "Social Network Determinants of Depression," *Molecular Psychiatry* 16, no. 3 (2010): 273–281. doi:10.1038/mp.2010.13.

16. S. C. Mednick, N. A. Christakis, and J. H. Fowler, "The Spread of Sleep Loss Influences Drug Use in Adolescent Social Networks," *PLoS One* 5, no. 3 (2010): e9775.

17. N. A. Christakis and J. H. Fowler, "Social Network Sensors for Early Detection of Contagious Outbreaks," *PloS One* 5, no. 9 (2010): e12948. doi:10.1371/journal.pone.0012948.

18. John T. Cacioppo, James H. Fowler, and Nicholas A. Christakis, "Alone in the Crowd: The Structure and Spread of Loneliness in a Large Social Network," (December 1, 2008) http://ssrn.com/abstract=1319108.

19. A. L. Hill, D. G. Rand, M. A. Nowak, and N. A. Christakis, "Infectious Disease Modeling of Social Contagion in Networks," *PLoS Computational Biology* 6, no. 11 (2010): e1000968. doi:10.1371/journal.pcbi.1000968.

20. J. N. Rosenquist, J. Murabito, J. H. Fowler, and N. A. Christakis, "The Spread of Alcohol Consumption Behavior in a Large Social Network," *Ann Intern Med* 152, no. 7 (2010): 426–433.

21. B. O'Connor, R. Balasubramanyan, B. Routledge, and N. Smith, "From Tweets to Polls: Linking Text Sentiment to Public Opinion Time Series," Proceedings of the International AAAI Conference on Weblogs and Social Media, Washington, DC (May 2010).

22. G. Mishne and N. Glance, "Predicting Movie Sales From Blogger Sentiment," Association for the Advancement of Artificial Intelligence (AAAI) 2006 Spring Symposium on Computational Approaches to Analysing Weblogs.

23. A. Madan, M. Cebrian, D. Lazer, and A. Pentland, "Social Sensing for Epidemiological Behavior Change," *UbiComp, 10* (September 26–29, 2010).

24. Z. Aljarboua, "Craigslist & The Economy: Predicting Unemployment and Foreclosure Trends from Online Classified Advertisements," submitted for

publication in *Proceedings of the International Conference on Business, Economics, Finance and Management Sciences*, Paris, France, 2010.

25. Jane McGonigal, quoted in Samantha Murphy, "Saving the World, One Hit Point at a Time," *New Scientist*, May 25, 2010.

26. James Surowiecki, *The Wisdom of Crowds* (New York: Anchor Books, 2005).

27. Emile Servan-Schreiber, Justin Wolfers, David M. Pennock, and Brian Galebach, "Prediction Markets: Does Money Matter?" *Electronic Markets* 14, no. 3 (September 2004).

CHAPTER 14

A Universal Measurement Method: Applied Information Economics

In 1984, the consulting firm the Diebold Group assembled the chief executive officers (CEOs) and chief financial officers (CFOs) of 10 major companies in a room at the prestigious Chicago Club to give presentations to their peers in 30 of Chicago's biggest firms. The companies, including IBM, Mobil Oil, AT&T, and Citibank, gave presentations on the process they used when making big investment decisions. The presentations were consistent and simple: If an investment was considered strategic, it received funding. No attempt at computing a return on investment (ROI) was made, much less any attempt at quantifying risk. This came as a surprise to some of the 30 Chicago companies represented in the room.

Ray Epich, a venerable sage of information technology (IT) wisdom, was present in the room. Ray graduated with the first-ever class of the Massachusetts Institute of Technology Sloan School of Business. He was a consultant at the Diebold Group and at my former employer, Riverpoint. In addition to being a very entertaining storyteller (he has regaled many with several entertaining stories of Alfred P. Sloan and John Diebold), Ray, like Paul Meehl and Emily Rosa, had a knack for being skeptical of common claims of experts. Ray didn't believe the CEOs could make good decisions based only on how "strategic" they thought the investment seemed to be.

Ray had plenty of counterexamples for the "success rate" of this decision-making approach. "Mead Paper tried to put sap in the paper and blew $100 million" was one example he related. He also mentioned a conversation with Bob Pritzker, of The Marmon Group, the third richest family in the world at the time. "I asked him how he did capital budgeting. He said my guys call me on the phone and I say 'yes or no.' He said he couldn't afford guys to do the ROI." Since then, perhaps a new appreciation at The Marmon Group for doing a few simple calculations may have combined with some healthy skepticism about executive gut feelings. Perhaps not.

Such was the world I entered when I first began as a management consultant with Coopers & Lybrand in 1988. I was working on several interesting quantitative problems, and even if they didn't start out as quantitative problems, I tended to define them in that way. That was and is just my world outlook. Through no deliberate career planning of my own, however, I was getting assigned more often as an analyst in large software development projects and, eventually, as a project manager.

Around this time, I first noticed that the quantitative methods routinely used in some parts of business and government were rare or even unheard of in other parts, especially IT management. Things I saw measured in one part of business were frequently dismissed as immeasurable in IT. This is when I decided that someone needed to develop a method for introducing proven quantitative methods to IT.

By 1994, I was employed by DHS & Associates (now Riverpoint) in Rosemont, Illinois. The management at DHS & Associates also saw the need for more quantitative solutions in IT, and the company culture afforded consultants a lot of leeway in developing new ideas. The same year, I began to assemble the method I called Applied Information Economics (AIE). Although I developed it for IT, it turned out to address fundamental measurement challenges in all fields. Since then, I've had the opportunity to apply AIE to a large number of other problems, including research and development portfolios, insurance, engineering projects, market forecasts, military logistics, environmental policy, and even the entertainment industry.

BRINGING THE PIECES TOGETHER

In the beginning of this book, we discussed a general framework for any measurement problem. I'll reiterate that five-step framework and then explain how the steps are used in practice in two real-life projects.

1. Define the decision and the variables that matter to it (see Chapter 4).
2. Model the current state of uncertainty about those variables (see Chapters 5 and 6).
3. Compute the value of additional measurements (see Chapter 7).
4. Measure the high-value uncertainties in a way that is economically justified (see Chapters 8 through 13).

5. Make a risk/return decision after the economically justified amount of uncertainty is reduced. (See the risk/return decision described in Chapters 6 and 11.) Return to step 1 for the next decision.

Because they were to be used in practical organizational settings, I had to put these steps together in a specific procedure that I could teach to others. After the first few projects, the five steps I just outlined tended to be regrouped into a set of distinct phases. I found that for the decision definition and the modeling of the current state of uncertainty, a series of workshops was the best data-gathering approach. I called this "Phase 1," and it included one workshop just for the calibration training of the experts.

After the workshops, the next phase started when I computed the value of additional information and could identify what needed to be measured and how. This calculation and most of the empirical methods didn't require as much input from those I met with in the workshops. The value of information was a straightforward calculation (which I could do quickly with the macros that I wrote). Likewise, the empirical measures were random samples, surveys, or controlled experiments, and usually I needed only limited guidance about information sources for them. Each time I completed an empirical measurement of some kind, I would update the model, run the information value calculations again, and see if further measurements were still needed.

The final phase came after we concluded that there was no economic value for additional measurements. Since we tended to find very few items with a significant information value (see Chapter 7), and since there tended to be a high value for small, incremental measurements (again, Chapter 7), the termination of empirical measures tended to happen soon even for variables that were very uncertain at first. In the final phase, we could simply present the results and show how the final analysis compared to the defined risk/return boundary of the decision makers. We see a summary of how these phases map to the original steps in Exhibit 14.1.

To this I added a "Phase 0" to capture all of those up-front planning, scheduling, and preparation tasks that come up early in any project. I show more details for each of these steps next.

- **Phase 0: Project Preparation**
  - *Initial research. Interviews, secondary research, and prior reports are studied so the AIE analyst can get up to speed on the nature of the problem.*
  - *Expert identification. Four or five experts who provide estimates is typical, but I've included as many as 20 (not recommended).*
  - *Workshop planning. Four to six half-day workshops are scheduled with the identified experts.*

Phase 1

Workshops for decision definition, calibration training, and initial calibrated estimates

Define the decision and identify relevant variables. Set up the "business case" for the decision, using these variables.

Model the current state of uncertainty. Use calibrated 90% confidence intervals and probabilities in a Monte Carlo simulation.

Calibration Training

Phase 2

Starts with first information value calculation, then empirical measurements, and subsequent modifications to the model

Compute the value of additional information. Use methods from Chapter 7 to determine what to measure and how much effort to spend on measuring it.

No — Is there a value to more information?

Yes

Measure where the information value is high. Reduce uncertainty using any of the methods mentioned in Chapters 8 through 13.

Phase 3

Determining optimum decisions; findings and recommendations

Optimize decision. Use the quantified risk/return boundary of the decision makers (Chapters 6 and 11) to determine which decision is preferred.

(Return to Phase 1 for the follow-on decisions.)

Exhibit 14.1 Summary of the AIE Process: The Universal Measurement Approach

- **Phase 1: Decision Modeling**
  - *Decision problem definition. In the first workshop, the experts identify what specific problem they are trying to analyze. For example, are they deciding whether to proceed with a particular investment, or is the dilemma just about how to modify the investment? If the decision is an investment, project, commitment, or other initiative, we need to have a meeting with decision makers to develop an investment boundary for the organization.*
  - *Decision model detail. By the second workshop, using an Excel spreadsheet, we list all of the factors that matter in the decision being analyzed and show how they add up. If it is a decision to approve a particular major project, we need to list all of the benefits and costs, add them into a cash flow, and compute an ROI (as in any simple business case).*
  - *Initial calibrated estimates. In the remaining workshops, we calibrate the experts and fill in the values for the variables in the*

decision model. These values are not fixed points (unless values are known exactly). They are the calibrated expert estimates. All quantities are expressed as 90% confidence interval (CI) or other probability distributions.

- **Phase 2: Optimal Measurements**
  - ○ *Value of information analysis (VIA). At this point, we run a VIA on every variable in the model. This tells us the information values and thresholds for every uncertain variable in the decision. A macro I wrote for Excel does this very quickly and accurately, but the methods discussed earlier in the book are a good estimate.*
  - ○ *Preliminary measurement method designs. From the VIA, we realize that most of the variables have sufficient certainty and require no further measurement beyond the initial calibrated estimate. Usually only a couple of variables have a high information value (and often they are somewhat of a surprise). Based on this information, we choose measurement methods that, while being significantly less than the Expected Value of Perfect Information (EVPI), should reduce uncertainty. The VIA also shows us the threshold of the measurement—that is, where it begins to make a difference to the decision. The measurement method is focused on reducing uncertainty about that relevant threshold.*
  - ○ *Measurements methods. Often starting with some form of decomposition, the measurement methods then target some newly decomposed variable for, random sampling, subjective-Bayesian, controlled experiments, Lens Models (and so on) or some combination thereof are all possible measurement methods used to reduce the uncertainty on the variables identified in the previous step.*
  - ○ *Updated decision model. We use the findings from the measurements to change the values in the decision model. Decomposed variables are shown explicitly in their decision model (e.g., an uncertain cost component may be decomposed into smaller components, and each of its 90% CIs is shown).*
  - ○ *Final value of information analysis. VIAs and measurements (the previous four steps) may go through more than one iteration. As long as the VIA shows a significant information value that is much greater than the cost of a measurement, measurement will continue. Usually, however, one or two iterations is all that is needed before the VIA indicates that no further measurements are economically justified.*
- **Phase 3: Decision Optimization and the Final Recommendation**
  - ○ *Completed risk/return analysis. A final Monte Carlo simulation shows the probabilities of possible outcomes. If the decision is about some major investment, project, commitment, or other ini-*

tiative (it's usually one of them), compare the risk and return to the investment boundary for the organization.

○ *Identified metrics procedures. There are often residual VIAs (variables with some information value that were not practical or economical to measure completely but would become obvious later on). Often these are variables about project progress or external factors about the business or economy. These are values that need to be tracked because knowing them can cause midcourse corrections. Procedures need to be put in place to measure them continually.*

○ *Decision optimization. The real decision is rarely a simple "yes/no" approval process. Even if it were, there are multiple ways to improve a decision. Now that a detailed model of risk and return has been developed, risk mitigation strategies can be devised and the investment can be modified to increase return by using what-if analysis.*

○ *Final report and presentation. The final report includes an overview of the decision model, VIA results, the measurements used, the position on the investment boundary, and any proposed ongoing metrics or analysis for the future, follow-on decisions.*

This seems like a lot to digest, but it is really just the culmination of everything covered in the book so far. Now let's turn to a couple of examples in areas that many of the participants in my study presumed to be partly or entirely immeasurable.

CASE: THE VALUE OF THE SYSTEM THAT MONITORS YOUR DRINKING WATER

The Safe Drinking Waters Information System (SDWIS) at the Environmental Protection Agency (EPA) is the central system for tracking drinking water safety in the United States and ensuring quick response to health hazards. When the branch chief for the SDWIS program, Jeff Bryan, needed more money, he had to make a convincing business case. His concern, however, was that the benefits for SDWIS were ultimately about public health, which he didn't know how to quantify economically.

Mark Day, deputy chief information officer and chief technology officer for the Office of Environmental Information, suggested that Bryan conduct an AIE analysis to measure the value. Day, who had spearheaded most of the AIE projects at the EPA to date, even said his office would split the cost.

Phase 0

In Phase 0, the planning phase, we identified 12 persons who would represent the expertise of the EPA on SDWIS and its value. We scheduled five half-day workshops to take place within a three-week period. Jeff Bryan was considered a "core team" person—one we would rely on to identify other experts and to be available for other questions.

Phase 1

In the very first workshop (when the decision is defined), it became apparent that EPA managers were really not analyzing SDWIS as a whole, even though that had been my initial assumption. The system had been in place for years, and terminating it or replacing it was not seriously considered. The real dilemma was simply about the justification of three specific improvements to SDWIS: reengineering an exception tracking system, web-enabling the application for access by states, and modernizing the database. These three initiatives required initial commitments of about $1 million, $2 million, and $500,000, respectively, plus ongoing maintenance. We had to answer which of these improvements was really justified and, of those that were justified, the best priority.

The spreadsheet had to show three separate business cases, one for each of the proposed system modifications, each with its own benefits. The problem was how to compare the cost to health benefits. The Office of Management and Budget already required the EPA to produce economic arguments for any proposed environmental policy. The EPA had to compute costs of compliance and benefits to the public for each policy it wanted to enforce. Several such studies showed the economic impact of different types of the most common drinking water contamination. The EPA often resorted to a willingness-to-pay (WTP) argument, but sometimes it used only workdays lost in calculating the cost of contamination.

By focusing on how SDWIS is supposed to help public health in the next two workshops, we were able to define a spreadsheet model that tied in the SDWIS modifications to an economic valuation of health benefits. The model had a total of 99 separate variables identified, structured as shown in Exhibit 14.2.

Each of the boxes in the exhibit represents a handful of variables in the spreadsheet business case. For example, for web-enabled access for states, we were estimating how much time is spent in certain activities, how much those activities would be reduced, and the impact on how much sooner violations of water safety regulations could be corrected.

In the last two workshops of Phase 1, we took all the experts through calibration training and asked for initial estimates of every variable in the

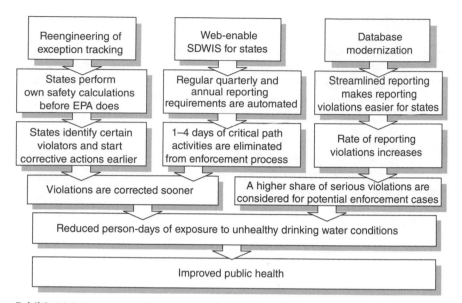

Exhibit 14.2 Overview of the Spreadsheet Model for the Benefits of
SDWIS Modification

model. The results from the calibration training showed that the experts
were very well calibrated (i.e., 90% of real answers were within the stated
90% CI). Every variable in the model had some level of uncertainty, and
some of the variables had very wide ranges. For example, one of the
proposed benefits included an expected increase in the reporting rate of
violations—not all water contamination gets reported. The increase was
highly uncertain, so experts put a 90% CI of 5% to 55% on the reporting
rate increase.

The spreadsheet computed a return on investment for each of the
three modifications to SDWIS. At this point, we had a detailed model that
showed the experts' current state of uncertainty.

Phase 2

In Phase 2, we ran a VIA. Even though the ranges in all the variables
expressed a lot of uncertainty, only one variable merited measurement:
the average health effects of new safe drinking water policies. The entire
purpose of SDWIS was to track contaminations better and to make corrections more quickly and efficiently. While the upper bound of potential
health benefits for a single policy was on the order of $1 billion per year,
there was also a chance the benefits could be lower than the cost of
compliance for the policy. In other words, the economic benefits of these

policies were so uncertain that the calibrated experts actually allowed for the possibility that the net benefits were negative.

If there is no net value to enforcing water regulations (i.e., value of the health impacts minus the cost of compliance), there is no benefit in enforcing the regulations better and faster. All of the uncertainties about state adoption rates of the technology, efficiency improvements, improved reporting rates, and the like turned out to have an information value of zero. All we had to do was reduce our uncertainty about the net economic benefits of drinking water policies. But the potential health benefits (i.e., the upper bounds) were very large compared to the small cost of the SDWIS upgrades. This put the threshold for the economic benefit measurement just barely above zero. In other words, what we really had to reduce uncertainty about was whether the net economic benefits of the drinking water policies were positive at all. We set out to reduce our uncertainty about that and that alone.

Since many of the previous water policy economic analyses varied somewhat in the methods they used, we decided to start with a simple instinctive-Bayesian approach based on a more detailed review of all the economic analysis done to date.

The reason calibrated experts included the possibility of a negative net benefit for water policies was that, out of several economic analyses, one showed a negative economic impact for one particular water policy. On further review, it turns out that this particular economic analysis looked only at extremely conservative economic impacts of water contamination—basically, just workdays lost and the economic impact of the loss. However, most people would agree that being sick is worse than just losing a couple of days of wages. The other economic analyses included WTP values for avoiding illness in addition to lost wages. Every analysis that included WTP values for avoiding illness had, as a worst case, a slightly positive net benefit.

As a result, we created a more detailed breakdown of the individual benefits of each water policy. Then we showed a calibrated 90% CI for what the real benefits of the least beneficial policy would be if it included all the same benefits as all the other policies. It became obvious that there was virtually no chance that the net economic impact of water policies would be negative. We updated the model to show this information. The next VIA showed that no further measurement was required to justify any of the SDWIS modifications.

Phase 3

In Phase 3, we ran a final Monte Carlo simulation on each of the three investments. With the reduced uncertainty about the economic benefits of the water policies, each one turned out to be a highly desirable investment. There was, however, a way to improve on the previously planned implementation schedule. The improved exception reporting had a very high potential return (the average ratio of benefits to costs was about three to one), but there was enough uncertainty that there was still a 12% chance of a negative return. The other two modifications had less than a 1% chance of a negative return. We plotted these three investments on the investment boundary (Chapter 11) we had already documented for the EPA. All three were acceptable, but not equally so. The reengineering of exception reporting had the highest risk and lowest return of the three.

The need for some ongoing metrics was also identified. Adoption rates by state users and how quickly the new system could be implemented were two of the more uncertain items. Therefore, they had "residual" VIAs (i.e., they still had some value to measurement, but it was low). We recommended that the EPA should accelerate the other two investments and defer the reengineering of exception reporting. The adoption rates experienced in the other two investments would be considered before beginning development for the exception reporting, in case they were low enough to cancel development (unlikely, but possible).

Epilogue

Mark Day got what he came to expect from an AIE analysis. He said, "Translating software to environmental and health impacts was amazing. The fact that software modules could be traced through a chain of events to some benefit to the public was assumed but never quantified. I think people were frankly stunned anyone could make that connection." He also notes the impact that quantitative analysis has on the decision process. "The result I found striking was the level of agreement of people with disparate views of what should be done. From my view, where consensus is difficult to achieve, the agreement was striking." To Day, the benefit of the VIA was another important part of the process. "Until then, nobody understood the concept of the value of the information and what to look for. They had to try to measure everything, couldn't afford it, and so opted for nothing. The number of variables quickly overwhelmed the ability to measure because they don't know what really matters," said Day.

Unlike Day, Jeff Bryan had no exposure to the AIE process before this project. He said, "I was the guy kicking and screaming coming into this AIE analysis. I didn't want to pull people away from what they were doing to do a study like this. But it turned out to be valuable." He was also initially skeptical about calibration, "but after going through the process, and seeing people respond to estimates, I could see the value of calibration." To Bryan, perhaps the most useful step was simply visualizing the connection between an information system and the goals of the program. "The chart [Exhibit 14.2] showed how SDWIS connected to public health and how to compute the benefits. I didn't think that just defining the problem quantitatively would result in something that eloquent. I wasn't getting my point across, and the AIE approach communicated the benefits much better. I can't tell you how many times I used the chart." Finally, and most important, Bryan followed through. "We followed every last recommendation—including the content and timing of recommendations."

I have presented this example for two reasons:

1. It is an example of how an intangible like public health is quantified for an IT project. I've seen many IT projects dismiss much more easily measured benefits as "immeasurable" and exclude them from the ROI calculation.
2. This example is about what *didn't have* to be measured. Only 1 variable out of 99 turned out to require uncertainty reduction. The initial calibrated estimates were sufficient for the other 98.

As usual, the measurements that would have been considered without doing the VIA probably would have been some of the much lower-value measurements, such as costs and productivity improvement, and the bigger uncertainties, such as public health, would be ignored.

CASE: FORECASTING FUEL FOR THE MARINE CORPS

In the fall of 2004, I was asked to apply AIE on a very different type of problem from what I was used to in business and government. A highly regarded consulting firm was the contractor on a project with the Office of Naval Research and the U.S. Marine Corps (USMC) to examine ways logistics planners could better forecast fuel requirements for the battlefield. For operations in Iraq, the USMC used hundreds of thousands of gallons of fuel per day just for ground units alone. (Aviation used about three times as much.) Running out of fuel was an unacceptable scenario for operational success and for the safety of the Marines on the ground.

For planning and logistics purposes, however, logistics managers had to start making preparations 60 days in advance in order to have sufficient fuel in place when needed. Unfortunately, it is impossible to predict precisely what the battlefield requirements will be that far out. Because uncertainty was so high and the risk of running out was unacceptable, the natural reaction is to plan on delivering three or four times as much fuel as best estimates say would be needed.

Chief Warrant Officer 5 (CWO5) Terry Kunneman, a 27-year USMC veteran, oversaw policy and procedures for bulk fuel planning at Headquarters Marine Corps. "We knew we were working off of older and less reliable consumption factors. In OIF [Operation Iraqi Freedom], we found that all of the traditional systems we had were not working well. It was garbage in, garbage out," said CWO5 Kunneman. Luis Torres, the head of the fuel study at the Office of Naval Research, saw the same problems. Torres notes, "This was all part of an overall directive to reduce the consumption of fuel. The problem was brought up to us that the method we were using had inherent errors in the estimating process."

The amount of additional fuel needed for a safety margin was an enormous logistics burden. Fuel depots dotted the landscape. Daily convoys pushed the fuel from one depot to the next depot farther inland. The depots and, especially, the convoys were security risks; Marines had to put themselves in harm's way to protect the fuel.

If the USMC could reduce its uncertainty about fuel requirements, it would not have to have so much fuel on hand and it still would not increase the chance of running out. At the time, the USMC used a fairly simple forecasting model: It counted up all the equipment of different types in the deployed units, then subtracted equipment that was missing due to maintenance, transfer, combat losses, and the like. Then it identified which units would be in "assault" mode and which would be in an "administrative/defensive" mode for approximate periods of time during the next 60 days. Generally, if a unit is in the assault mode, it is moving around more and burning more fuel. Each piece of equipment has a different average consumption measured in gallons per hour and also hours of operation per day. The hours of operation usually increased when the equipment was in a unit that was in assault mode. For each unit, the USMC computed a total daily fuel consumption based on the unit's equipment and whether it is in the assault mode. Then it added up all the unit fuel consumptions for each day for 60 days.

The accuracy and precision of this approach was not very high. Fuel estimates could easily be off by a factor of two or more (hence the large safety margins). Even though I had never before dealt with forecasting supplies for the battlefield, I approached the problem the same way I did any other big measurement problem: using AIE.

Phase 0

In Phase 0, I reviewed several previously conducted studies on armed forces' fuel requirements. None offered any specific statistical forecasting methods in detail. At best, they talked about potential methods, and only at a high level. Still, they gave me a good background for the nature of the problem. We identified several logistics experts who could participate in the workshops, including CWO5 Kunneman and Luis Torres. Six half-day workshops were scheduled to occur within a three-week period.

Phase 1

The first workshop in Phase 1 was set on defining the forecasting problem. Only then was it clear that the USMC wanted to focus on the total fuel use of ground forces only and for a 60-day period for a single Marine Expeditionary Force (MEF), a force consisting of tens of thousands of Marines. Using the existing fuel forecasting tables we studied in Phase 0, I constructed a series of "where does all the fuel go?" charts. The charts gave everyone on the team (but especially us analysts who didn't work with this every day) a sense of orders of magnitude about fuel use. It was clear that most of the fuel does not go into tanks or even armored vehicles in general. True, the M-1 Abrams gets a mere third of a mile per gallon, but there are only 58 tanks in an MEF. In contrast, there are over 1,000 trucks and over 1,300 of the now-famous HMMWVs, or Humvees. Even during combat, trucks were burning eight times as much fuel as the tanks.

Further discussion about what this equipment is actually doing when it burns fuel caused us to make three different types of models. The biggest part of the model was the convoy model. The vast majority of trucks and Humvees burned most of their fuel as part of a convoy on specific convoy routes. They traveled in round-trip convoys an average of twice a day. Another part of the model was the "combat model." The armored fighting vehicles, such as the M-1 tank and the Light Armored Vehicles (LAVs), spent less time on convoy routes and tended to burn fuel more as a function of specific combat operations. Finally, all the generators, pumps, and administrative vehicles tended to burn fuel at both a more consistent and much lower rate. For this group, we just used the existing simple hourly consumption rate model.

In one of the workshops, the experts were calibrated. All showed a finely tuned ability to put odds on unknowns. They estimated ranges for all the quantities that were previously given only point values. For example, where the seven-ton truck was previously assumed to burn exactly 9.9 gallons per hour, they substituted a 90% CI of 7.8 to 12 gallons per hour. For vehicles typically running in convoys, we had to include ranges for the distance of the typical convoy route and how much route conditions might change fuel consumption. For armored vehicles used in combat operations, we had to estimate a range for the percentage of time they spent in the assault over a 60-day period.

These added up to just 52 basic variables describing how much fuel was burned in a 60-day period. Almost all were expressed as 90% CIs. In a way, this was not unlike any business case analysis I had done. But instead of adding up the variables into a cash flow or return on investment, we simply had a total fuel consumption number for the period. A Monte Carlo simulation based on these ranges gave a distribution of possible results that was very similar to the error and distribution of real-life fuel consumption figures.

Phase 2

In Phase 2, we computed the VIA using Excel macros. (In this case, the information value chart in Exhibit 14.3 of this book would have worked, too.) Since the decision was not expressed in monetary gains or losses, the VIA produced results that meant, in effect, change in error of gallons forecast per day. The biggest information values then were details about convoy routes, including distances and road conditions. The second highest information value was how combat operations affected fuel consumption on combat vehicles. We designed methods to measure both.

To reduce uncertainty about fuel use in combat operations, we opted for a Lens Model based on estimates of field logistics officers from the First Marine Division. These were mostly battalion staff officers and some unit commanders, all with combat experience in OIF. They identified several factors that they felt would change their estimate of fuel use by combat vehicles, including chance of enemy contact (as reported in the operations plan), familiarity with the area, whether terrain was urban or desert, and the like. I gave them each calibration training, then created a list of 40 hypothetical combat scenarios for each officer and gave them data on each of these parameters. For each of these scenarios, they provided a 90% CI for fuel use for the type of vehicle they commanded (tanks, LAVs, etc.). After compiling all of their answers, I ran regression models in Excel to come up with a fuel use formula for each vehicle type.

For the road condition variables in the convoy model, we decided we needed to conduct a series of road experiments in Twenty-Nine Palms, California. The other contractors on the project procured Global Positioning System (GPS) equipment and fuel flow meters that would be attached to the trucks' fuel lines. Prior to this study, no one on the team knew anything about fuel flow meters. I just told these consultants: "Somebody does stuff like this all the time. Let's get resourceful and find out who does this and how." In short order, they found a supplier of digital fuel flow meters on Google, and we were briefed on how to use them. They also figured out how to dump the data to a spreadsheet and synchronize the GPS and fuel flow data sources. Including travel time, it took three people a couple of weeks to do both the road tests and the Lens Model, including the setup and development of the Excel system.

The GPS units and fuel flow meters were hooked up to three trucks of two different types. Initially there was some concern that larger samples were needed, but, taking the incremental measurement principle to heart, we thought we would first see just how much variance we would measure in these trucks—two of which were identical models, anyway. The GPS units and fuel flow meters recorded location and consumption data several times each second. This information was continuously captured in an onboard laptop computer while the vehicle was driven. We drove the trucks in a variety of conditions, including paved roads, cross-country, different altitudes (parts of the base varied in altitude significantly), level roads, hilly roads, highway speeds, and so on. By the time we were done, we had 500,000 rows of fuel consumption data for a variety of conditions.

We ran this data through a huge regression model. There were far more rows than Excel 2003 could handle, but it was much more detail than we really needed. We consolidated the data into six-second increments and ran different regressions for different tests.

By the time we were done with both measurements, we saw several surprising findings. The single biggest cause of variation in fuel forecast was simply how much of the convoy routes were paved or unpaved, followed by other simple features of the convoy route. Furthermore, most of these data (other than temperature) are always known well in advance, since the modern battlefield is thoroughly mapped by satellites and unmanned surveillance aircraft. Therefore, uncertainty about road conditions is a completely avoidable error. Exhibit 14.3 summarizes the forecast errors due to other specific variables.

Exhibit 14.3 Summary of Average Effects of Changing Supply Route Variables for a Marine Expeditionary Force (MEF)

Change	Change in Gallons/Day
Gravel versus Paved	10,303
+5-mph average speed	4,685
+10-meter climb	6,422
+100-meter average altitude	751
+10-degree temperature	1,075
+10 miles of route	8,320
Additional stop on the route	1,980

The combat vehicle model was no less of a revelation for the team. The single best predictor of fuel use by combat vehicles was not chance of enemy contact but simply whether the unit had ever been in that area before. When uncertain of their environment, tank commanders leave their fuel-hungry turbine engines running continuously. They have to keep hydraulics pressurized just to be able to turn the turret of the tank, and they want to avoid the risk—however small—of not being able to start the engine in a pinch. Other combat vehicles besides tanks tend to use a little more fuel by taking longer but more familiar routes or even, sometimes, by getting lost.

The familiarity with the area was, like the route-related measurements, always a factor planners would know in advance. They knew whether a unit had been in an area before. Taking this into account reduced the daily fuel consumption error about 3,000 gallons per day. Putting the chance of enemy contact into the model reduced error by only 2,400 gallons per day—less than all but three of the supply route–related factors. In fact, it is barely more than the effect that one additional stop on the convoy route would account for.

Phase 3

In Phase 3, we developed a spreadsheet tool for the logistics planners that took all these new factors into account. On average, it would reduce the error of their previous forecasting method by about half. According to the USMC's own cost-of-fuel data (it costs a lot more to deliver fuel in the battlefield than to your local gas station), this would save at least $50 million per year per MEF. There were two MEFs in Iraq at the time the first edition of this book was written.

Epilogue

This study fundamentally changed how the USMC thought about fuel forecasts. Even the most experienced planners in USMC logistics said they were surprised at the results. CWO5 Kunneman said, "What surprised me was the convoy model that showed most fuel was burned on logistics routes. The study even uncovered that tank operators would not turn tanks off if they didn't think they could get replacement starters. That's something that a logistician in 100 years probably wouldn't have thought of." The more "abstract" benefits of an everything-is-measurable philosophy seemed obvious to CWO5 Kunneman. "You are paying money for fuel. If they tell me it's hard data to get, I say I bet it's not. How much are you paying for being wrong in your forecast?" Torres agreed. "The biggest surprise was that we can save so much fuel. We freed up vehicles because we didn't have to move as much fuel. For a logistics person, that's critical. Now vehicles that moved fuel can move ammunition."

Like the SDWIS case, this is an example of what we didn't have to measure as much as what we did measure. There were many other variables that might otherwise have been examined in much more detail, but we were able to avoid them completely. This is also an example of how much one can do with a hands-on, just-do-it approach to measurement. The bright computer programming consultants on the team, who told me they never change the oil in their own cars themselves, pulled up their sleeves and got greasy under a truck to attach the fuel flow meters and GPS systems. In the end, the fuel consumption measurements turned out to be easy because, in part, we never doubted that it was possible if the team was just resourceful enough. This is a sharp contrast to a previous study done by the Office of Naval Research that was more like typical management consulting: heavy on high-minded concepts and visions, no measurements and no new information.

The final lesson here for measurement skeptics is what such measurement efforts mean for the safety and security of people. We didn't need to explicitly compute the value of the security and safety of Marines for this project (although we could have done so with WTP or other methods), but less fuel being moved means fewer convoys, which put Marines in danger of roadside bomb and ambushes. I like to think I could have saved someone's life with the right measurements. I'm glad fear and ignorance of measurements didn't get in the way of that.

CASE: MEASURING THE VALUE OF ACORD STANDARDS

Perhaps one of the more abstract items I've been asked to measure was the value of standards—not just for one organization but for an entire industry. In the insurance industry, parties have to routinely speak to each other and share data among themselves as well as to state and federal agencies. If they all handled data differently, there would be a substantial additional cost just in routine communications.

Standards like these don't just evolve accidentally. They are specifically designed by industry associations. The client in this case was the not-for-profit industry association ACORD (Association for Cooperative Operations Research and Development). With hundreds of member organizations including insurance companies, brokers, agencies, financial services, and industry solution providers, ACORD facilitates the development of open data standards in the insurance and related industries. Since the value of standards tends to increase as they are more widely adopted, ACORD is also an active advocate for these standards in the industry.

The president of ACORD, Greg Maciag, approached me to find out how he could help its members demonstrate the value of ACORD standards. Greg Maciag, his staff, and the ACORD members intuitively recognized that using the same standards across an industry had value, but they needed to measure it.

Phase 0

Unlike most of our projects, this initiative would involve several independent organizations—each a volunteer among ACORD members representing some major insurance company. In Phase 0, we recruited several participating insurance and reinsurance companies. Each organization sent one member to represent them in the series of AIE modeling workshops.

Phase 1

In the spring of 2012, HDR conducted several half-day workshops both onsite and remotely (via WebEx) with the industry representatives. As always the first objective was to define the specific decisions that would be informed by measuring the value of standards. In the first workshop, the participating insurance companies decided to model the decision from the point of view of a project manager trying to make the case for adopting standards for a given implementation.

The heavy lifting in applying standards is done in ongoing software implementation projects done within insurance companies and other organizations. These are software projects, not necessarily related to standards, which are routinely required to add new features to some major existing application (e.g., a new report, e-signatures, etc.) or to comply with new federal regulations. Implementation projects may occur several times a year in each of several business processes within each insurance company. Industry-wide, there are easily thousands of such implementations per year.

These implementations are a matter of keeping up with changing business requirements and would be done even if ACORD standards were not used. In some cases, an ACORD standard has not yet been adopted but is being proposed for the first time. Sometimes even within member organizations there is a debate about whether to utilize ACORD standards in some particular implementation project. As usual in software, the initial costs are more apparent and the long-term benefits seem abstract and difficult to measure—which means the latter are often entirely ignored. The challenge to ACORD and its advocates among its members is to measure the benefits so that decisions about whether to implement standards were fully informed.

Several potential benefits of standards were identified. Many of them were related to reducing the friction for communication between industry participants. But most were related to simply making use of work already done by others such as the data models for customer data, various transactions, and more. The benefits included:

- Lower cost per transaction—A transaction could be monetary or something nonmonetary with an external organization which is facilitated in some way by using common standards.
- Lower error rates in a process—Some mistakes in data entry are due to switching between different data formats. Standards eliminate this source of errors.
- Reusability of code—The more widely used standards are within an organization, the more likely it will be that new implementations can build on existing code.
- Faster implementations—Using already-developed standards saves time in data and process design for new systems. This accelerates the business benefits of the proposed system.
- Improved business intelligence—Certain reports can be designed and implemented faster when unique, nonstandard approaches don't have to be developed. Decisions based on these reports are then made faster and more accurately. This is similar to other information value calculations.

Each of these benefits was decomposed into multiple variables which each required an estimate. A total of 45 individual variables were identified. Each participating member was then asked to identify some real-world implementation where standards were being considered. We were actually modeling five different implementation decisions for five different insurance companies. Each of these decisions would have its own set of estimates.

The participating subject matter experts all attended calibration training and performed exceptionally well. As always, most of the variables they needed to estimate were extremely uncertain but, with their skill at calibration, they were able to express their uncertainty appropriately using probabilities and wide ranges including the possibility of not having a benefit at all. For example, for those members skeptical of benefits in business intelligence, they didn't just provide a wide range for the reduction in decision errors. They also placed a binary probability on whether a business intelligence benefit would be experienced at all— sometimes as low as 5%.

Phase 2

We ran a Value of Information Analysis on each standards implementation project separately. The results varied from project to project, of course, but there were some consistent findings. The information values for individual cases were never more than $40,000 for a particular variable. But since these were representative of implementation projects which are done several times a year, several business processes from individual cases were then extrapolated to an approximate information value for the industry. Exhibit 14.4 shows the results of the expected value of perfect information (EVPI) calculations across the entire insurance industry (a conservatively estimated lower bound of a 90% CI is shown).

This made a lot of sense to the participating insurance company members. The additional development cost of adding standards to an implementation project was typically in the range of a few hundred thousand dollars. But they directly impacted business processes or lines of business that sometimes generated hundreds of millions in revenue and costing a lower but similar magnitude. If a feature could slightly increase efficiency of effectiveness of such a process and if standards could accelerate that benefit by months or even just a couple of weeks, the impact would be many times the size of the implementation effort itself.

In the same manner, the largest cost of a standards implementation was not the labor of developers but the delay in the implementation of the first project in which standards were used. After that, it is hoped that the acceleration of benefits in future implementations more than makes up for the delay of business benefits in the first implementation.

As a result of the VIA, we conducted a survey of ACORD members to reduce uncertainty about the effects of standards on implementation project delivery times. While frequency of reports made with ACORD standards was also a relatively high information value, it was felt that this quantity could easily be known exactly for a given implementation

Exhibit 14.4 The Information Value Results Extrapolated to the Entire Insurance Industry

Variable	Estimated Industrywide EVPI
Reduction in duration due to ACORD standards	> $4MM
Additional duration due in first ACORD standards project	> $1.5MM
Increase in costs of first ACORD standards project	> $100K
Frequency of reports made easier with ACORD standards	> $400K
All other variables (41 in total)	> $700K

project if the estimators were given more time to query existing data. The uncertainty about effects on implementation project duration, however, was not only universally uncertain across all case studies—it was also something that many members thought would be difficult to get more data on.

A total of 149 survey responses were collected using a combination of written surveys, web-based surveys, and real-time automated response surveys conducted at a major annual ACORD conference. The survey determined: (1) who had relatively complete records of implementation project durations both before and after the adoption of standards, and (2) an estimate of the impact on the implementation schedule.

We handled the estimates differently for organizations that said they had complete records of past project durations. Those that were less complete were compared for consistency with those that had more complete data. A simple comparison of the means of the two groups (as explained in experiments in Chapter 9) showed that those who didn't keep detailed records gave answers that were at least consistent with those who did keep records. One member provided a set of actual data and this was consistent with other subjectively recalled responses. The average response was a time savings of 23%, with half saying they saved 50% or more.

Phase 3

The deliverable for this project was more like the U.S. Marine Corps and less like the EPA SDWIS. Instead of making a recommendation on a single investment, our objective was to develop a reusable tool that ACORD members could use to estimate the value of implementing standards in a proposed implementation. We created a "fill-in-the-blank" decision model with a built-in Monte Carlo in Excel. Project managers could just provide their own estimates on several parameters in each of the value-areas. We called this the Value of Integration (VOI) tool.

The previous survey was not literally used as the one estimate to be used on all individual cases. The previous survey provided a benchmark that the user could either use as a default, to base another estimate on, or to ignore entirely. All other estimates were based on calibrated estimates of users or on empirical sources suggested for each variable.

Using an automated version of the tools mentioned in Chapters 6 and 7, we estimated the risk of a proposed use of standards and suggestions for what to measure further. A project manager could then present to his or her leadership a case for adopting standards. Given these are executives in the insurance industry, they should have no problem accepting a probabilistic analysis of benefits, costs, and risks.

Epilogue

Using the small sample estimation methods from the few cases we analyzed and extrapolating that to the entire industry, we estimated that ACORD standards had a value of well over $1 billion a year to the industry. Over the life of ACORD, the benefits were surely in the range of several billion dollars. This is a key figure ACORD needed. Greg Maciag observed, "I was not surprised that industry standards save the industry billions of dollars, but it was good to be able to say so with authority. That was a great accomplishment. But HDR went further because large industry numbers are not easily internalized by company executives. They are more interested in how savings can be realized by their own firms."

The process itself was also useful to the ACORD members. Maciag added that "the AIE process was a real eye-opener. It not only provided us with tools to measure observable outcomes, it also provided a means to look more introspectively at how people make observations and calculations." The calibrated estimates, followed by empirical measurements to create probabilistic models seemed to resonate particularly well with people in this industry. To Maciag, "It proved to be a great life skill about how to reduce uncertainty and better manage risk. It all comes down to looking at the information right in front of your face, but doing so correctly and having the tools to see it."

At the time of this writing, the VOI is being rolled out to more ACORD members.

IDEAS FOR GETTING STARTED: A FEW FINAL EXAMPLES

In this book, we covered several examples of measurement including performance, security, risk, market forecasts, the value of information, and the basic ideas behind valuing health and happiness. I introduced some concepts behind basic empirical measurements, including random sampling, experiments, and regression analysis.

This information might seem overwhelming. But, as with almost everything else in business or life, it's often just a matter of getting started on a few examples, working through a problem, and seeing the results. Here I'm going to introduce some possible measurement problems that we have not already discussed. I'm going just deep enough into each of these to get you going down the right path in thinking through the measurement problem.

For each of these problems, the standard measurement steps still apply, even though I might not mention each step in detail. I suggest a possible clarification for each one, but you will still need to think through your initial uncertainty, the value of information, decomposition, and selecting a measurement instrument. However, I provide enough information to start you off on that path.

Quality

I was once asked by an executive, who said she was a member of a professional quality association, how to measure quality. She added that there is a recurring debate about how to measure quality in the group's monthly meetings. I thought this was odd because the person who is sometimes called the "Father of Quality," W. Edwards Deming, treated quality as a quantity. She seemed familiar with Deming, but she did not know that he was a statistician. He preached that if you don't have a measurement program, you don't have a quality program. To Deming, quality was the consistency with which expectations were met. The lack of meeting defined expectations is a defect. Measuring quality in a manufacturing process was, to Deming, a matter of measuring the frequency of different types of defects and measuring variances from the expected norm.

I consider Deming's view of quality fundamentally necessary to the concept of quality measurement, but perhaps not sufficient by itself. With all due respect to Deming, I think a complete definition of quality would have to include more than this. A very cheaply made product may perfectly fit the expectations of the manufacturer and yet be perceived as low quality by consumers. And if customers don't think the product has quality, why should the producer think it does? Any complete description of quality would have to include a survey of customers.

It might also be helpful to remember the distinction between stated and revealed preferences. In a survey, customers state their preferences. When they are making (or not making) purchases, they reveal their preferences. The ultimate expression of quality is the premium customers are willing to pay for a product. This "premium revenue" can also be compared to advertising dollars spent since—generally—products perceived as high quality have people willing to pay a premium even without the additional advertising that would otherwise be required. Perhaps quality products get more repeat business and more word-of-mouth advertising. Everything mentioned so far lends itself at least to a random survey method and, for the clever analyst, some type of "implied price premium" based on the purchasing behaviors of customers.

Value of a Process, Department, or Function

A question like "What is the value of _____?" is about as loaded as a measurement question gets. Usually, the perceived difficulty in measuring value is really the lack of a clear definition of why it is being measured. I sometimes hear chief information officers (CIOs) ask how to measure the value of information technology. I ask, "Why, are you considering getting rid of it?" All valuation problems in business or government are about a comparison of alternatives. If you were to attempt to compute the value of IT for a company, you would presumably have to compare it against the costs and benefits of not having IT. So unless you really are considering doing without IT (or whatever you want to know the value of), the question is irrelevant.

Perhaps, however, the CIO really needs to know whether the value of IT has improved since she took charge. In that case, she should focus on computing the net benefits of specific decisions and initiatives made since she started. This question could also be looked at as the type of performance-as-financial-impacts measurement discussed in previous chapters. If a CIO is asking for the value of IT because she wants to argue against outsourcing her entire department, she is not really asking about the value of IT itself, just the value of keeping it in house versus outsourcing it.

No value question will ever be asked that doesn't ultimately imply alternatives. If you have the right alternatives defined and the true decision defined, the value question will be much more obvious.

Innovation

Just like anything else, innovation, if it is real, is observable in some way. Like some other measurement problems, the challenge here is probably more of an issue of defining what decision is being supported. What would you do differently based on possible findings from a measurement of innovation? If you can identify at least some real decision—perhaps evaluating teams or research and development (R&D) efforts for bonuses or termination—read on. Otherwise, there is no business purpose in measuring it.

If you can identify at least one decision this measurement actually could affect, I propose using one of three possible methods. First, there is always the method of leaving it a purely subjective but controlled evaluation. Use independent human judges with Rasch models and controls to adjust for judge biases. Controls would include a blind where the identities of teams or persons are kept from the judges while the judges consider just creative output (e.g., advertisements, logos, research papers, architectural plans, or whatever else the creative teams develop). This might be useful if you are trying to evaluate the quality of research in R&D based on a portfolio of ideas being generated. The Mitre example in Chapter 2 might provide some insight.

Another method might be based on other indicators of innovation that are available when the work has to be published, such as patents or research papers. The field of bibliometrics (the study and measurement of texts, e.g., research papers) uses methods like counting and cross-referencing citations. If a person writes something truly groundbreaking, the work tends to be referenced frequently by other researchers. In this case, counting the number of citations a researcher gets is probably more revealing than just counting the number of papers he or she has written. The same method can be used where patents are produced, since patent applications have to refer to similar existing patents to discuss similarities and differences. An area of research called "scientometrics" attempts to measure scientific productivity.[1] Although it usually compares entire companies or countries, you might check it out.

Since the beginning of the twenty-first century, several software tools have emerged that claim to measure innovation. On closer inspection, these tools are mostly made of the soft scoring methods debunked in Chapter 12. I often find that those who were interested in these tools couldn't even really define the first most important step in the measurement process: What is the decision you hope to resolve with this measurement? What would they do differently if they found out their "innovation" was higher or lower than expected? Chapter 12 alone provides enough information to put you on guard against any feel-good methods that show no empirical evidence of improving decisions.

A final method worth considering is similar to the performance-as-financials approach discussed in Chapter 13. As the Madison Avenue guru David Ogilvy said, "If it doesn't sell, it isn't creative." Things might seem creative but not actually be creative in a way that is relevant to the business. If the objective was to innovate a solution to a business problem, what was the business (i.e., ultimately financial) impact? How about measuring researchers the way Tom Bakewell measured the performance of academics or the way Billy Bean measured the performance of baseball players (Chapter 12)?

Information Availability

I've modeled information availability at least four different times, and every model ends up with the same variables. Improved availability of information means you spend less time looking for it and you lose it less often.

When information is lost, either you do without it or you attempt to re-create it. Looking for a document or attempting to re-create it is simply measured in terms of the cost of effort in these undesirable and avoidable tasks. If the only option is to do without it, there is a cost of making less informed decisions that are more frequently wrong. To get started, the average duration of document searching, the frequency of document re-creation, and the frequency of going without (per year) are quantities calibrated estimators can put ranges on.

Flexibility

The term "flexibility" itself is so broad and ambiguous it could mean quite a lot of things. Here I'll just focus on how three specific clients defined and measured it. Since they gave such different answers, it will be useful to go into a little detail. In clarifying what "flexibility" meant, these three clients came up with:

> **Example 1.** Percent reduction in average response time to unexpected network availability problems (e.g., more quickly fixing virus attacks or unexpected growth of demand on the network)
>
> **Example 2.** Percent reduction in average development time for new products
>
> **Example 3.** The ability to add new software packages if needed (The previous IT system had several custom systems that did not integrate with Oracle-based applications.)

All three were related to some proposed IT investment, either infrastructure or software development. As usual, we had to compute the monetary value of each of these for each year in a cash flow so that we could compute a net present value and rate of return for the investment:

> **Example 1.** Monetary value for each year of a five-year ROI
> (current downtime hours per year)
> × (average cost of one hour of downtime)
> × (reduction in downtime from new system)
>
> **Example 2.** Monetary value for each year of a seven-year ROI
> (new product developments per year)
> × (percent of new products that go to market)
> × (current product development time in months)
> × (additional gross profit of new product introduced one month earlier) + (cost of development))
> × reduction in time spent
>
> **Example 3.** Monetary value for each year of a five-year net present value (NPV)
> (number of new applications per year)
> × (NPV of additional average lifetime maintenance for custom applications compared to standardized package)
> + (additional near-term cost of custom development compared to standardized package)

Since these were each large, uncertain decisions, EVPIs were in the hundreds of thousands to millions of dollars. But, as often happens, in each of these cases the most important measurement was not what the client might normally have chosen. We applied the methods that follow for these measurement problems.

> **Example 1.** We developed a post-downtime survey for 30 people after each of five downtime events. The client was able to determine whether people were affected at all by a downtime and, if so, how much time they actually were unproductive.
>
> **Example 2.** We decomposed product development time into nine specific activities, used calibrated estimators to estimate time spent in each activity as a percentage of the whole, and used calibrated estimators who were given information about additional studies to estimate the reduction in each activity.
>
> **Example 3.** We identified specific applications that would be considered in the next couple of years and computed the development and maintenance cost of each relative to an equivalent custom package.

In each example, the measurements cost less than $20,000; the figure ranged from 0.5% to 1% of the computed EVPI. In each case, the initial uncertainty was reduced by 40% or more. Additional VIA showed no value to additional measurements. After the measurement, Examples 1 and 3 had clear cases for proceeding with the investment. Example 2 was still very risky and was justified only after a significant reduction in scope and costs as part of a pilot deployment.

Flexibility with Options Theory

In 1997, the Nobel Prize in Economics went to Robert C. Merton and Myron Scholes for developing Options Theory and, specifically, the Black-Scholes formula for valuing financial options. (The Nobel Prize is given only to living persons; another contributor, Fischer Black, had died before the prize was awarded.) A call option in finance gives its owner the right, but not the obligation, to purchase some other financial instrument (stock, commodity, etc.) at a future point at a given price. Likewise, a put option gives the owner the right to sell it at a given price. If, for example, you have a call option to buy a share of stock at a price of $100 one month from now and, by then, the stock is trading at $130, you can make some money by exercising the option to buy it at $100 and turn it over immediately for a $30 profit. The problem is that you don't know how much the stock will be selling for in one month and whether your option will be of any value. Until the Black-Scholes formula was derived, it was not at all clear how to price such an option.

This theory got more popular buzz in the business press than most economic theories do, and it became fashionable to apply Options Theory not just to the pricing of put or call options but to how internal business decisions are made.

This became known as "real" Options Theory, and many managers attempted to formulate a large number of business decisions as a type of options valuation problem. Although this method might make sense in some situations, it was overused. Not every benefit of a new technology, for example, can necessarily be expressed as a type of option valuation problem. In reality, most "real options" don't even boil down to an application of Black-Scholes but rather a more traditional application of decision theory.

If, for example, you run a Monte Carlo simulation for a new IT software platform, and that platform gives you the option to make changes if future conditions make such changes beneficial, the simulation will show that, on average, there is a value to having the option compared to not having the option. This does not involve the Black-Scholes formula, but it is actually what most real option problems are about. Using the same formula that is used to price stock options might be appropriate, but only if you can literally translate the meaning of every variable in Black-Scholes to your problem. Inputs to Black-Scholes formulas include exercise price, strike price, and the price volatility of the stock. If it's not apparent what these items really mean in a given business decision, then Black-Scholes is probably not the solution. (The supplementary website, www.howtomeasureanything.com, has examples of options valuations with and without Black-Scholes.)

It is now known that Black-Scholes has some faulty assumptions that have contributed to many financial disasters. (Some think the downfall of the inventors' company, Long-Term Capital Management, was early evidence of these faulty assumptions, but the firm's collapse had more to do with how it was leveraged, which is not addressed in Options Theory.) As I mentioned earlier with Modern Portfolio Theory, Options Theory also assumes market volatility is normally distributed. In my book, *The Failure of Risk Management*, I show that the assumption of a normally distributed market volatility can underestimate probabilities that are off by *several orders of magnitude* when it comes to the rarer extreme of events.[2]

SUMMARIZING THE PHILOSOPHY

If you think you are dealing with something "impossible" to measure, keep in mind the examples from SDWIS and the USMC. Meeting such a measurement challenge is really pretty simple when you think about it.

- If it's really that important, it's something you can define. If it's something you think exists at all, it's something you've already observed somehow.
- If it's something important and something uncertain, you have a cost of being wrong and a chance of being wrong.
- You can quantify your current uncertainty with calibrated estimates.
- You can compute the value of additional information by knowing the "threshold" of the measurement where it begins to make a difference compared to your existing uncertainty.
- Once you know what it is worth to measure something, you can put the measurement effort in context and decide on the effort it should take.
- Knowing just a few methods for random sampling, controlled experiments, Bayesian methods or even merely improving on the judgments of experts can lead to a significant reduction in uncertainty.

In retrospect, I wonder if Eratosthenes, Enrico, and Emily would have been deterred by any of the "impossible" measurement problems we have considered. From their actions, it seems clear to me that they at least intuitively grasped almost every major point this book makes about measurement. Perhaps quantifying current uncertainty and computing the value of information itself and how it affects methods would have been new to them. Even though our measurement mentors could not have known some of the methods we discussed, I suspect they still would have found a way to make observations that would have reduced uncertainty.

I hope, if nothing else, that the examples of Eratosthenes, Enrico, and Emily and the practical cases described make you a little more skeptical about claims that something critical to your business cannot be measured.

Notes

1. Paul Stoneman, ed., *Handbook of the Economics of Innovation and Technological Change* (Malden, MA: Basil Blackwell, 1995).
2. D. Hubbard, *The Failure of Risk Management: Why It's Broken and How to Fix It* (Hoboken, NJ: John Wiley & Sons, 2009), 181–187.

Calibration Tests
(and Their Answers)

ANSWERS TO CALIBRATION QUESTIONS IN CHAPTER 5:

#	Question	Answer
1	In 1938 a British steam locomotive set a new speed record by going how fast (mph)?	126
2	In what year did Sir Isaac Newton publish the universal laws of gravitation?	1685
3	How many inches long is a typical business card?	3.5
4	The Internet (then called "Arpanet") was established as a military communications system in what year?	1969
5	In what year was William Shakespeare born?	1564
6	What is the air distance between New York and Los Angeles in miles?	2,451
7	What percentage of a square could be covered by a circle of the same width?	78.5%
8	How old was Charlie Chaplin when he died?	88
9	How many pounds did the first edition of this book weigh?	1.23
10	The TV show *Gilligan's Island* first aired on what date?	September 26, 1964
	Statement	**Answer**
1	The ancient Romans were conquered by the ancient Greeks.	FALSE
2	There is no species of three-humped camels.	TRUE
3	A gallon of oil weighs less than a gallon of water.	TRUE
4	Mars is always farther away from Earth than Venus.	FALSE
5	The Boston Red Sox won the first World Series.	TRUE
6	Napoleon was born on the island of Corsica.	TRUE
7	"M" is one of the three most commonly used letters.	FALSE
8	In 2002 the price of the average new desktop computer purchased was under $1,500.	TRUE
9	Lyndon B. Johnson was a governor before becoming vice president.	FALSE
10	A kilogram is more than a pound.	TRUE

There are more calibration tests on the following pages.

ADDITIONAL CALIBRATION TESTS

Calibration Survey for Ranges: A

#	Question	Lower Bound (95% chance value is higher)	Upper Bound (95% chance value is lower)
1	How many feet tall is the Hoover Dam?		
2	How many inches long is a 20-dollar bill?		
3	What percentage of aluminum is recycled in the United States?		
4	When was Elvis Presley born?		
5	What percentage of the atmosphere is oxygen by weight?		
6	What is the latitude of New Orleans? Hint: Latitude is 0 degrees at the equator and 90 at the North Pole.		
7	In 1913, the U.S. military owned how many airplanes?		
8	The first European printing press was invented in what year?		
9	What percentage of all electricity consumed in U.S. households was used by kitchen appliances in 2001?		
10	How many miles tall is Mount Everest?		
11	How long is Iraq's border with Iran in kilometers?		
12	How many miles long is the Nile?		
13	In what year was Harvard founded?		
14	What is the wingspan (in feet) of a Boeing 747 jumbo jet?		
15	How many soldiers were in a Roman legion?		
16	What is the average temperature of the abyssal zone (where the oceans are more than 6,500 feet deep) in degrees F?		
17	How many feet long is the Space Shuttle Orbiter (excluding the external tank)?		
18	In what year did Jules Verne publish *20,000 Leagues Under the Sea*?		
19	How wide is the goal in field hockey (feet)?		
20	The Roman Coliseum held how many spectators?		

Answers are on page 390.

Answers for Calibration Survey for Ranges: A

#	*Answers*
1	726
2	6-3/16ths (6.1875)
3	65%
4	1935
5	21%
6	30
7	25
8	1450
9	26.7%
10	5.5
11	1458
12	4,160
13	1636
14	196
15	6,000
16	39°F
17	122
18	1870
19	12
20	50,000

Calibration Survey for Ranges: B

#	Question	Lower Bound (95% chance value is higher)	Upper Bound (95% chance value is lower)
1	The first probe to land on Mars, Viking 1, landed there in what year?		
2	How old was the youngest person to fly into space?		
3	How many meters tall is the Willis (formerly Sears) Tower?		
4	What was the maximum altitude of the Breitling Orbiter 3, the first balloon to circumnavigate the globe, in miles?		
5	On average, what percentage of the total software development project effort is spent in design?		
6	How many people were permanently evacuated after the Chernobyl nuclear power plant accident?		
7	How many feet long were the largest airships?		
8	How many miles is the flying distance from San Francisco to Honolulu?		
9	The fastest bird, the peregrine falcon, can fly at a speed of how many miles per hour in a dive?		
10	In what year was the double helix structure of DNA discovered?		
11	How many yards *wide* is a football field?		
12	What was the percentage growth in Internet hosts from 1996 to 1997?		
13	How many calories are in 8 ounces of orange juice?		
14	How fast would you have to travel at sea level to break the sound barrier (mph)?		
15	How many years was Nelson Mandela in prison?		
16	What is the average daily calorie intake in developed countries?		
17	In 1994, how many nations were members of the United Nations?		
18	The Audubon Society was formed in the United States in what year?		
19	How many feet high is the world's highest waterfall (Angel Falls, Venezuela)?		
20	How deep beneath the sea was the *Titanic* found (miles)?		

Answers are on page 392.

Still not calibrated? Get more calibration tests at www.howtomeasureanything.com.

Answers to Calibration Survey for Ranges: B

#	Answers
1	1976
2	26
3	443
4	6.9
5	20%
6	135,000
7	803
8	2,394
9	200
10	1953
11	53.3
12	70%
13	120
14	760
15	27
16	3,300
17	185
18	1905
19	3,212
20	2.5 miles

Calibration Survey for Binary: A

	Statement	*Answer True/ False*	*Confidence that you are correct (circle one)*
1	The Lincoln Highway was the first paved road in the United States, and it ran from Chicago to San Francisco.		50% 60% 70% 80% 90% 100%
2	Iron is denser than gold.		50% 60% 70% 80% 90% 100%
3	More American homes have microwaves than telephones.		50% 60% 70% 80% 90% 100%
4	"Doric" is an architectural term for a shape of a roof.		50% 60% 70% 80% 90% 100%
5	The World Tourism Organization predicts that Europe will still be the most popular tourist destination in 2020.		50% 60% 70% 80% 90% 100%
6	Germany was the second country to develop atomic weapons.		50% 60% 70% 80% 90% 100%
7	A hockey puck will fit in a golf hole.		50% 60% 70% 80% 90% 100%
8	The Sioux were one of the "Plains" Native American tribes.		50% 60% 70% 80% 90% 100%
9	To a physicist, "plasma" is a type of rock.		50% 60% 70% 80% 90% 100%
10	The Hundred Years' War was actually over a century long.		50% 60% 70% 80% 90% 100%
11	Most of the fresh water on Earth is in the polar ice caps.		50% 60% 70% 80% 90% 100%
12	The Academy Awards (Oscars) began over a century ago.		50% 60% 70% 80% 90% 100%
13	There are fewer than 200 billionaires in the world.		50% 60% 70% 80% 90% 100%
14	In Excel, a "^" means "take to the power of."		50% 60% 70% 80% 90% 100%
15	The average annual salary of airline captains is over $150,000.		50% 60% 70% 80% 90% 100%
16	By 1997, Bill Gates was worth more than $10 billion.		50% 60% 70% 80% 90% 100%
17	Cannons were used in European warfare by the eleventh century.		50% 60% 70% 80% 90% 100%
18	Anchorage is the capital of Alaska.		50% 60% 70% 80% 90% 100%
19	Washington, Jefferson, Lincoln, and Grant are the four presidents whose heads are sculpted into Mount Rushmore.		50% 60% 70% 80% 90% 100%
20	John Wiley & Sons is not the largest book publisher.		50% 60% 70% 80% 90% 100%

Answers are on page 394.

Answers for Calibration Survey for Binary: A

#	*Answers*
1	FALSE
2	FALSE
3	FALSE
4	FALSE
5	TRUE
6	FALSE
7	TRUE
8	TRUE
9	FALSE
10	TRUE
11	TRUE
12	FALSE
13	FALSE
14	TRUE
15	FALSE
16	TRUE
17	FALSE
18	FALSE
19	FALSE
20	TRUE

Calibration Survey for Binary: B

	Statement	*Answer True/ False*	*Confidence that you are correct (circle one)*
1	Jupiter's "Great Red Spot" is larger than Earth.		50% 60% 70% 80% 90% 100%
2	The Brooklyn Dodgers' name was an abbreviation for "trolley car dodgers."		50% 60% 70% 80% 90% 100%
3	"Hypersonic" is faster than "subsonic."		50% 60% 70% 80% 90% 100%
4	A "polygon" is three dimensional and a polyhedron is two dimensional.		50% 60% 70% 80% 90% 100%
5	A 1-watt electric motor produces 1 horsepower.		50% 60% 70% 80% 90% 100%
6	Chicago is more populous than Boston.		50% 60% 70% 80% 90% 100%
7	In 2005, Walmart sales dropped below $100 billion.		50% 60% 70% 80% 90% 100%
8	Post-it Notes were invented by 3M.		50% 60% 70% 80% 90% 100%
9	Alfred Nobel, whose fortune endows the Nobel Peace Prize, made his fortune in oil and explosives.		50% 60% 70% 80% 90% 100%
10	A BTU is a measure of heat.		50% 60% 70% 80% 90% 100%
11	The winner of the first Indianapolis 500 clocked an average speed of under 100 mph.		50% 60% 70% 80% 90% 100%
12	Microsoft has more employees than IBM.		50% 60% 70% 80% 90% 100%
13	Romania borders Hungary.		50% 60% 70% 80% 90% 100%
14	Idaho is larger (area) than Iraq.		50% 60% 70% 80% 90% 100%
15	Casablanca is on the African continent.		50% 60% 70% 80% 90% 100%
16	The first man-made plastic was invented in the nineteenth century.		50% 60% 70% 80% 90% 100%
17	A chamois is an alpine animal.		50% 60% 70% 80% 90% 100%
18	The base of a pyramid is in the shape of a square.		50% 60% 70% 80% 90% 100%
19	Stonehenge is located on the main British island.		50% 60% 70% 80% 90% 100%
20	Computer processors double in power every three months or less.		50% 60% 70% 80% 90% 100%

Answers are on page 396.

Still not calibrated? Get more calibration tests at www.howtomeasureanything.com.

Answers to Calibration Survey for Binary: B

#	Answers
1	TRUE
2	TRUE
3	TRUE
4	FALSE
5	FALSE
6	TRUE
7	FALSE
8	TRUE
9	TRUE
10	TRUE
11	TRUE
12	FALSE
13	TRUE
14	FALSE
15	TRUE
16	TRUE
17	TRUE
18	TRUE
19	TRUE
20	FALSE

Index